Authoring Authorware

A Practical Guide

John C. Shepherd, Ph.D.
Duquesne University

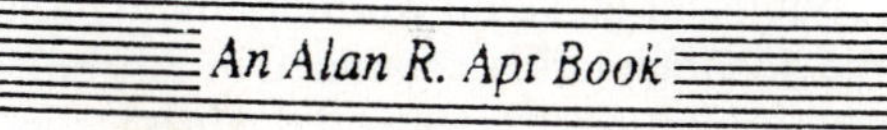

Prentice Hall, Upper Saddle River, New Jersey 07458

Library of Congress Cataloging in Publication Data

Shepherd, John C.
    Authoring Authorware: a practical approach/ John C. Shepherd
        p.   cm.
    Includes bibliographical references and index.
    ISBN 0-13-660226-6
    1.   Multimedia systems. 2. Macromedia Authorware. I. Title.
  QA76.575.S55   1998
  006.7'869—dc21   98-32340
                                       CIP

Acquisitions editor: Toni Holm/Alan Apt
Editorial and production supervision: Sharyn Vitrano
Editor-in-chief: Marcia Horton
Managing editor: Bayani DeLeon
Director of production and manufacturing: David W. Riccardi
Manufacturing buyer: Julia Meehan
Art director: Jayne Conte
Cover designer: Bruce Kenselaar

©1998 by Prentice-Hall, Inc.
Simon & Schuster/A Viacom Company
Upper Saddle River, New Jersey 07458

For my guys and gals: Barb, Chris, Megan, Mickey...and, of course, Eiger, without whose help I would have been done six weeks earlier.

Printed in the United States of America
10 9 8 7 6 5 4 3

ISBN 0-13-660226-6

Prentice-Hall U.K. Limited, *London*
Prentice-Hall of Australia Pty. Limited, *Sydney*
Prentice-Hall Canada Inc., *Toronto*
Prentice-Hall Hispanoamericana, S.A., *Mexico*
Prentice-Hall of India Private Limited, *New Delhi*
Prentice-Hall of Japan, Inc., *Tokyo*
Simon & Schuster Asia Pte. Ltd., *Singapore*
Editora Prentice-Hall do Brasil, Ltda., *Rio de Janeiro*

Preface

Courses in instructional design often include theory and hands-on instruction using a Computer Based Training package, such as Macromedia's Authorware. While preparing to teach such a course, the author noted that while there were several textbooks covering instructional design theory, there didn't appear to be any that adequately covered Authorware. One could find reference books or technical treatments of Authorware functions, but there did not appear to be a text suitable as a teaching tool. As a result, as the author taught the course, a set of notes was developed, which students could use both as a tutorial and as a reference. This text is the culmination of that effort.

KEY FEATURES

There are texts that serve as tutorials and those that serve as references. Students complain that tutorials are great but don't go far enough. They learn what is in the tutorials but can't use the textbook as a comprehensive reference to determine how to perform tasks that aren't covered as part of a tutorial.

When a reference-type text is used, students complained they couldn't use the text to do anything because it contains no step-by-step examples on how to do anything.

With this text, we tried to provide both paradigms. Specifically, the text includes several key features.

Detailed Discussion of Key Features

Each topic is described in detail, usually with an accompanying algorithm, or set of steps that describes how to implement that topic in Authorware. Instead of simply describing what a feature is, you will be able to use that feature by following the steps provided.

Hand-on Lab Sessions with Solutions Included

After a topic is described, and an algorithm provided, you will be directed to use it to create a small Authorware project. It's only through application of a concept that long-term learning is realized.

In most cases, the student-directed projects have been included on the accompanying CD-ROM. This way, you can preview what you are going to do, then follow the steps need to accomplish it. In case you get lost, you can refer to the CD-ROM to immediately see where you went wrong.

End-of-Chapter Exercises

Each chapter contains several problems that use concepts developed in that chapter. As the text proceeds, the problems get more difficult as they utilize concepts previously learned. This way repetition increases long-term retention.

Multimedia Topic Discussions

Because Authorware has significant multimedia capabilities, it is important that the student understand the consequence of choosing various kinds of multimedia, and the impact that choice has on the resulting project. For example, Authorware supports several different sound formats, each with differing characteristics and consequences. Rather than simply stating these options, the text defines and refines them. For example, the student will be able to state the reason for using 16-bit sample sizes, and 44KHz sample rates.

Continuing Case

A digital video case at the end of most chapters reinforces concepts from those chapters. The case isn't meant to be complete, but rather a mechanism for you to practice what you hopefully learned in the chapters.

CD-ROM

The CD-ROM contains materials for each chapter. Included for each chapter are:

- Images and clip art
- Sounds
- Solutions for chapter lab sessions

Authoring for the World Wide Web

The last chapter covers an important topic: How to author for the Internet or that organization's intranet. Shockwave, Afterburner, WWW server and browser requirements are discussed.

Advanced Coverage

The text includes coverage of Open Database Connectivity (ODBC) and ActiveX. ODBC is a standard way for applications, such as Authorware, to interact with databases. Perhaps you have heard of Oracle, Sybase, and Microsoft's Access. These are all database management systems that you can access from Authorware. You could store student progress, passwords, or even test questions is such a database.

ActiveX is a Microsoft product where small applets, called ***controls***, are created once, and then used by many different applications, including Authorware. You could create an ActiveX control, and use it both on a World Wide Web page, and in an Authorware piece.

CONTENTS AT A GLANCE

Getting Started

Authorware is a powerful language for developing interactive multimedia titles, or *pieces*. This introduction looks at interactivity, multimedia and then at the capabilities and features of Authorware.

INTERACTIVE MULTIMEDIA

Macromedia's Authorware is a software development tool for creating interactive, multimedia applications. Authorware can accommodate most of the media types we think of when describing the term *multimedia*. Text, graphics, sound, animations, and digital video can all be integrated to create an application that stimulates and involves the user. Working closely with the computer operating system, Authorware coordinates interfacing with hardware, memory, and resource and file management. These are all areas that until recently caused the development of multimedia applications to be the territory of seasoned specialists.

Authorware is capable of creating exciting interactive projects. Common interactive components that are easy to create in Authorware are buttons, pull-down menus, hot spots, hot objects, and hot text. These are all elements of a project, or *piece* as it is usually called in Authorware, which, after user or mouse interactions, trigger events to occur. As an example, imagine a photograph of a group of sports equipment. Such a photograph might be taken inside a sporting goods store. If the items in the picture were hot spots, clicking on a golf ball, for example, could display the prices and types of golf balls sold by the store.

Multimedia Authoring

When working in Authorware, we commonly use the term *authoring* instead of programming. The term authoring signifies that software development is being done at a level above the bits and bytes coding, or programming level. Authorware provides the environment that interfaces with the bits and bytes level programming while letting the author work at a more user-friendly level.

Development Steps

Multimedia development is a complex process. It usually requires a team of people with diverse skills and a lot of coordination to take a project from conception to completion. The main phases of the development process are design, scripting, asset acquisition and development, construction, testing, and delivery.

During the design phase, first the project objectives and the content to be delivered are defined. Then the appropriate treatment, flow, navigation, and functionality are determined. With all these components defined, a detailed production script can be produced that describes all media elements required to be seen, heard, or with which to interact. The script also contains instructions that the author needs to properly assemble the project. After preparing the script, the media elements or *assets* are created. Some will be in the format of still graphics or animation sequences; others will be audio and video files. Armed with the script and this variety of assets, it is the author's responsibility to integrate the pieces into one unit. The integrated application is then tested, refined, and delivered.

USES

Authorware is used for a variety of purposes, among them ***Computer-based training*** (CBT), interactive presentations, simulations, games and many others. The next section explores its primary use: Computer-Based Training.

Computer-Based Training

Authorware is primarily designed to facilitate the creation of computer based training programs, however, its rich capabilities enable it to be used for many other computer applications. Computer-based training is the utilization of the computer and allied technologies to provide training or education. CBT courses are designed using a structured approach called instructional design. The instructional design process determines what the driving objectives of the application are and then develops the best approach to achieve them. There are two core components of CBT*: computer managed instruction* (CMI) and ***computer aided instruction*** (CAI).

Authorware's development environment is extremely well suited for building training applications because it provides continual monitoring of many elements necessary for effective training. With no additional programming, it can track the progress of users and assess their score after they finish a piece. It is easy to apply time limits for testing or task completion or to limit the number of tries or wrong answers before "help" or "feedback" is provided. CMI refers to the management of course materials of the types we just described: testing, judging answers, tracking the percentage of right answers, determining time spent on the training application, handling exit and restart, and so forth. Authorware does all of this and more.

The CAI is the actual training application content. Typical content models include tutorials, drill, practice, and simulations. Through its multimedia-rich capabilities, Authorware can provide these models with a more robust environment, one where it has been shown that the use of more than one medium enhances learning and retention. To be of maximum benefit, such environments must be interactive, and Authorware easily provides the developer with this ability.

Other Computer Applications

Authorware can produce many other types of computer applications as well. These often take the form of corporate communication applications, sales and marketing applications, and even interactive games. Again, its ease of use and inherent ability to create interactive multimedia applications make it appropriate for a variety of developmental uses.

FEATURES

Authorware is an icon-based language, with a scripting language which, when needed, provides most of the functionality of conventional, command-based languages. Once the piece is complete, it can be run on both Macintosh and Windows computers, and distributed on CD-ROM, the World Wide Web (WWW), or run conventionally from a local disk drive or over a network.

Graphic Icon-Based Programming

Macromedia designed Authorware to reduce the difficulty of use for nonprogrammers. This was accomplished by designing icon building blocks, each with very distinct functionality. Trainers, teachers, and other nontechnical people can develop projects in Authorware. Instead of writing complex code, the author uses Authorware's icons to organize project flow, control, user interaction, and the presentation of all media. When the icons cannot do what is required, the author can use Authorware's scripting language.

Powerful Scripting Language

The Authorware icons are made even more flexible with the use of a scripting language. This is an area of project development where actual programming skills are useful. Carefully scripted code can control variables, project flow, and interactive behavior as well as interface with other applications and the operating system.

Cross Platform Capabilities

Authorware is optimized for today's powerful desktop computers. The Windows version takes full advantage of both Windows 95® and Windows NT® (32-bit operating systems). Similarly, the Macintosh® version is Power PC native, so performance on the Macintosh is optimized for the most recent versions of that product line. You can create a multimedia title on a Macintosh and run it on a Windows machine, or vice versa. To do this, however, you'll need to create a run-time version of your Authorware piece for each platform. You might author a project on a Macintosh, open, convert, and package the piece to run on the Windows computer. Of course, the reverse can also be done.

Distribution Flexibility

After a project is created Authorware provides several distribution options. Windows and Macintosh applications can be created in both 16 and 32-bit optimized versions. The developed code can also be optimized for delivery over the Internet, or an organization's intranet. Yet another option is a hybrid distribution approach, where some content resides on CD-ROM, with other content being delivered from World Wide Web (WWW) servers, local hard drives and file servers.

The process of creating an application from a project file is called ***packaging***. A packaged application is created so that an end user can run it without having access to the Authorware environment.

BOOK NOTATION

Your Turn When you see this symbol, it means it's time for you to work with Authorware. To ensure you don't miss anything, check the box ❑ you see before each step once you have completed it.

Contents

Chapter 2 Managing Text and Graphics   **25**

Chapter 7 Calculating and Branching 217

Chapter 9 Advanced Navigation 299

Chapter 10 Multimedia 313

Authorware Fundamentals

*M*acromedia's Authorware is a software development tool for creating interactive multimedia applications. It is primarily designed to facilitate the creation of computer-based training programs. However, its rich capabilities enable it to be used for many other computer applications. Combining an icon-based approach to programming, a highly integrated interface, and a powerful scripting language, Authorware provides a complete solution for creating and distributing robust software applications. This chapter looks at these features and capabilities and introduces you to the graphical Authorware environment.

At the conclusion of this chapter, you will be able to:

- Explain the components that make up the Authorware interface.
- Navigate within the Authorware interface.
- Explain the options when starting a new Authorware piece.
- Open, run, and package an Authorware piece.

INTERFACE COMPONENTS

We begin our exploration of Authorware by first studying the components of the Authorware interface. The Authorware interface follows many of the standard Microsoft Windows conventions and functionality. The Windows Control Bar, Menu Bar and Tool Bar are all examples of this. Some unique characteristics of these will be discussed below.

The Windows Control Bar

The Windows Control Bar features standard Windows functionality. That is, it gives you the ability to control the author menus, minimize, maximize and close the Authorware interface window. To view the Control Bar, click on the Authorware icon that appears next to the word "Authorware".

The Menu Bar

The Menu Bar offers a series of drop-down menus filled with the features that give the multimedia developer control and Authorware its power and flexibility. Many of these menus have standard functionality. The ones specific to Authorware will be covered in detail throughout this book in the most appropriate chapters.

The Toolbar

The Toolbar features shortcut buttons that make doing common tasks in Authorware easier and faster. As Table 1.1 shows, the tool bar contains many familiar, and a few unfamiliar icons.

You should recognize the icons for opening files, copy, paste, cut, and the text editing icons, including bolding, italicizing, and underlining. The icons that are new include the Control Panel, the run icon, functions, and variables.

Table 1.1. The Authorware Toolbar

Icon	Description
New	Creates a new Authorware file. In Windows, the extension will be .A4W. A good rule to follow is to save the piece immediately and assign a meaningful name.
Open	Opens an existing file.
Save All	Saves all open files —the Authorware piece plus libraries.
Import	Import text and graphics, sound, and movies directly into display or interaction icons.
Undo	Removes the effects of the last operation or command.
Cut	Removes the selected object and places it on the Clipboard.
Copy	Makes a copy of the selected object on the Clipboard.
Paste	Pastes the object stored on the Clipboard at the insertion point.
Find	Displays the Find/Replace dialog box.
[Default Style] ▼ Styles boxes	Changes the font characteristics to predetermined settings called *Styles*.
Bold	Changes the selected text to the bold font style.
Italic	Changes the selected text to the italic font style.
Underline	Underlines the selected text.
Restart	Run the piece from the beginning of the flowline
Control Panel	Displays the Authorware Control Panel.
Functions	Displays the Functions dialog box so you can choose a built-in function.
Variables	Displays the Variables dialog box.
Help	Activates Authorware help facility.

Increasing the Viewing Area

Sometimes every pixel of the viewing window is needed while authoring. You can remove the toolbar from the interface by deselecting Toolbar from the View menu (Ctrl+Shift+T). This option toggles the Toolbar on and off.

WINDOW TYPES

The unique components of the Authorware interface look simple at first glance, but their powerful capabilities are soon discovered. There are two types of windows: ***Design Windows***, which contain ***flowlines,*** and ***Presentation windows***, where images can be imported, objects can be drawn and text can be entered. Using the ***toolbox***, a collection of text and draw tools, you can easily modify the Presentation window contents. Ancillary windows, called ***palettes***, may also be opened. For example, along the left side of the screen will be the icon palette. Other palettes can be optionally displayed.

The Design Window

Figure 1.1 shows the design window. It is where the "programming" is done and may be called the flowline. Technically, the flowline is within the Design window, but we'll usually refer to them both as the flowline.

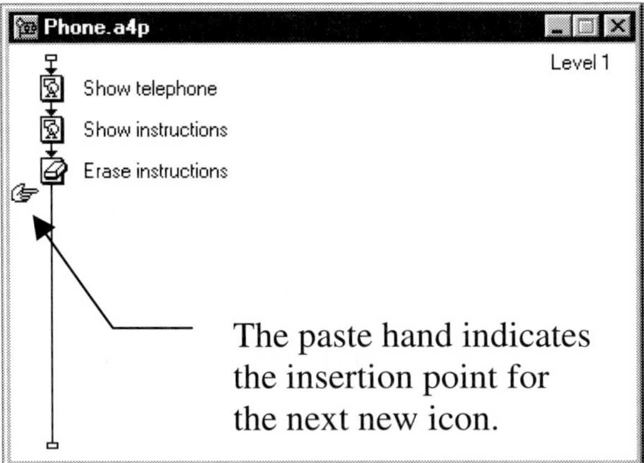

Figure 1.1. The Authorware Design Window with Some Icons on the Flowline.

The Flowline

The flowline in Authorware provides an area in which to arrange icons to create a project, or piece. Here, they form a sort of "road map" that is followed when a user executes a project. Icons are dragged from the tool palette, which appears to the left of the design window, to the flowline. The icons are placed on the flowline at the spot indicated by the *paste hand*. (See Figure 1.1) The physical length of the flowline is bounded by the size of its design window — It never is displayed with scroll bars. To add to a flowline that is at its maximum length, group icons into *map icons.* These combine one or more icons into an aggregate called a *map*.

The icons are executed sequentially beginning with the first icon and ending with the last. Linearity can be altered if Authorware encounters an interaction, decision, or framework icon. Pieces that run without interactivity are called *linear pieces*.

The Tool Palette

The Authorware Tool Palette provides all the building blocks for creating projects. They control what the user sees and hears. They determine how they interact with a project and how they are managed while interacting with the application.

Each icon represents a different type of content. For example, a display icon is used to present text and graphics, while a movie icon can show these Windows digital movie types: QuickTime for Windows (MOV), Microsoft Audio Video Interleaved (AVI) files, Director movies (DIR, DXR), Autodesk FLC, FLI and CEL animation files, BMP movies, and MPEG movies. Figure 1.2 shows the Tool Palette.

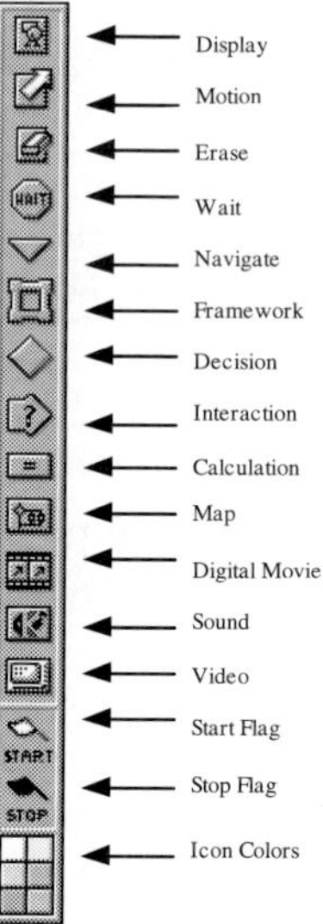

Figure 1.2. The Authorware Tool Palette.

Table 1.2 provides a description of each Tool Palette icon. Refer to it when you want to know what a particular icon can do.

Table 1.2. The Icons in the Authorware Tool Palette

Icon	Purpose
Display	Used to show graphics and text.
Motion	Moves graphics, text, or digital video along paths you define and at speeds you specify.
Erase	Deletes an icon's contents. A single erase icon can delete content from several previous icons.
Wait	Holds the program flow until a mouse is clicked, a key pressed or a specified unit of time elapses.
Navigate	Specifies where to jump to in a hypertext/hypermedia interaction. It is used with the framework icon
Framework	Controls project navigation, flow, and organization.
Decision	Specifies branching based on program-defined specification or conditions.
Interaction	Creates displays and controls event interactions that respond to the user input. These may take the form of hot spots, hot objects, or buttons.
Calculation	Provides a mechanism for Authorware scripting. Calculation icons can be standalone or integrated into other icon types.
Map	A grouping of icons. Each map can be opened to show its own flowline.
Movie	Displays and controls digital movies - Director, QuickTime, MPEG, Video for Windows, FLI, FLC, PICs files.
Sound	Plays and controls digital audio - WAV, PCM or AIFF file.
Video	Controls Laser Disk players.
Start/Stop flags	Instead of always running a piece from beginning to end, these flags can be placed along a flowline to mark temporary start and stop points.
Colors	Icons can be color-coded. For example, you might use yellow to designate icons under construction, or different colors for different development personnel or teams.

The Presentation Window

In the ***Presentation window*** (see Figure 1.3), the project can be viewed as the user will eventually see it. It provides a visual work area where graphic and text objects are assembled. The Presentation window is a 640 X 480-pixel window (the default size), where your piece is displayed. This size can be changed, but the default size is the most commonly supported one for both Macintosh and Windows computers. Many of the icons have an effect on the Presentation window, because this is where you, the author, place graphical, and text content. While the author of the piece utilizes both the design and the Presentation windows, users see only the Presentation window. The size of the Presentation window can also be changed using the scripting language.

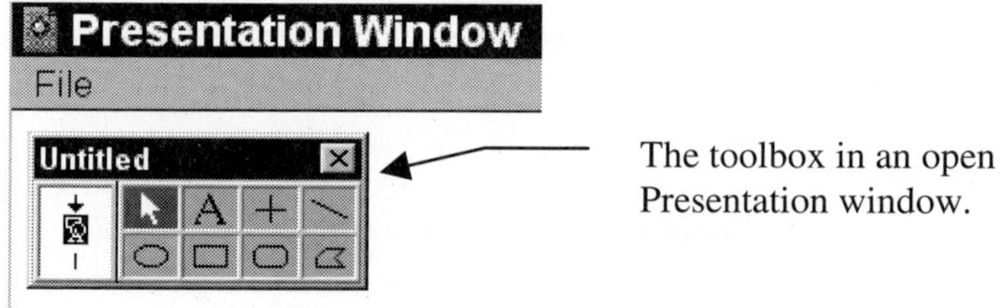

The toolbox in an open Presentation window.

Figure 1.3. The Presentation Window. The Presentation window is empty and the toolbox is visible.

When an empty display icon is encountered, or an existing icon edited, Authorware opens the Presentation window and the ***toolbox*** palette. We discuss the toolbox palette later in this chapter.

Switching Between Windows

To switch between the two main windows, under the <u>W</u>indow menu, choose <u>D</u>isplay or <u>P</u>resentation. Successive keying of the hot-key (Ctrl+1) toggles between the two windows.

Your Turn
❏ Drag a display icon to the flowline.
❏ Notice its name is "Untitled. "
❏ Double-click the "Untitled display icon.
❏ Click on the "A" you see in the toolbox. This represents the text tool.

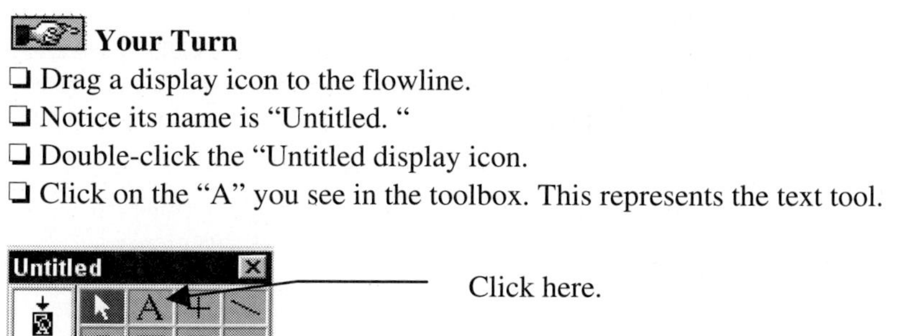

Click here.

❑ Type your name.

❑ Experiment with the <u>W</u>indow menu and the "hot-keys" to switch between the Presentation window and the Design window.

❑ To execute/run your piece choose <u>C</u>ontrol><u>R</u>estart. Alternatively, you can open the Control Panel, then push the Run button, or you can push the Restart icon .

THE CONTROL PANEL

The Control Panel is used mainly as a debugging tool. It can also be used to stop, pause, restart, or trace your piece. We first examine the icons associated with the Control Panel.

To activate the control panel, click on the control panel button on the toolbar. You will then see the Control Panel window shown in Figure 1.4.

Figure 1.4. The Control Panel Window.

The buttons, from left to right, are: Restart, Reset, Stop, Pause, Play, and Show-Hide Trace.

Restart

Pushing this button will run your piece from the beginning.

Reset

Push the reset button to make Authorware start your piece from the beginning. It will also clear the trace window, if it was open. If a start flag was found on the flowline, the Reset button will be replaced with a Reset From Flag button.

Stop

Push the Stop button to stop the piece.

Pause

The Pause button functions like a stop flag. Pushing the Pause button will temporarily stop the piece until the Play button is pushed.

Play

This button runs the piece from the start flag or from wherever the Pause button was pushed.

Show-Hide Trace

Pushing this button will expand or contract the Control Panel window to show or hide additional trace functionality.

The Expanded Control Panel

If you push the Show-Hide Trace button, the Control Panel will expand like that shown in Figure 1.5.

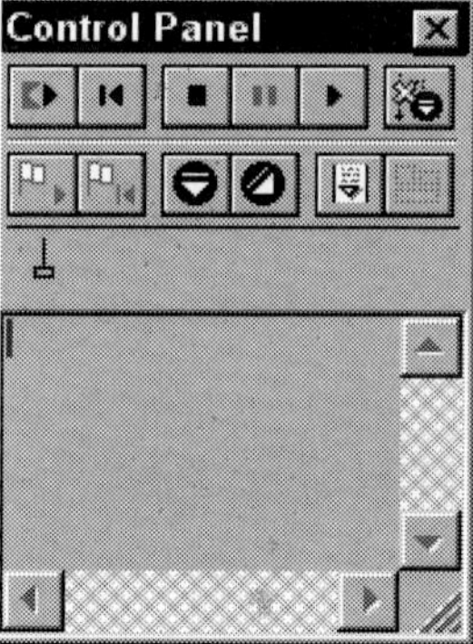

Figure 1.5. The Expanded Control Panel.

The new buttons, from left to right, are: Restart from Flag/Restart, Reset from Flag, Step Over, Step Into, Trace On/Trace Off, and Show Invisible Items.

Restart from Flag/ Restart

This button starts the tracing process by running your piece from the start flag. If there is no start flag, the Restart from Flag button is replaced with the Restart button.

Reset from Flag/Reset

If there is a start flag on the flowline, this button resets the trace, then runs from the start flag. As we have seen before, if there is no start flag, the button is replaced with a Reset button.

Step Over/ Step Into

Use the Step Over button to make Authorware enter the next icon. If it's a branching icon, then Authorware executes each icon in order without pausing. If the icon was a map, the Control Panel only shows the map icon, not the underlying detail. Use the Step Into button to see more detail about a given icon.

The Step Into button function is similar: It also enters the next icon, but if a map is encountered, each component of that icon is also executed and results shown in the Control Panel window. In effect, use Step Over to get close to a problem's solution, use Step Into to delve more deeply into a problem.

Trace On/Off

Use this button to turn on or off the display of trace information.

Show Invisible Items

Many Authorware items are not normally visible—Target areas, for example. Push the Show Invisible Items button to show or hide such items.

Control Panel Content

While the Control Panel is open, and the piece running, as each icon is encountered, the following information is displayed:

- The icon's level.
- The type of icon.
- The icon's title.

This serves as a visual reference, indicating which icon is being executed at any point in time and is indispensable as a debugging tool.

SETTING UP A NEW PROJECT

To begin a new project, choose File>New>File, and then choose Modify> File> Properties. The dialog box that appears (File Properties) is shown in Figure 1.6. Its properties affect the entire piece. Note that there are two tabs: Playback and Interaction. We begin our discussion with the Playback options first.

The Playback Tab

The options found here mainly affect the Presentation window: Deleting the Menu bar, altering the title one sees in the Presentation window and so on.

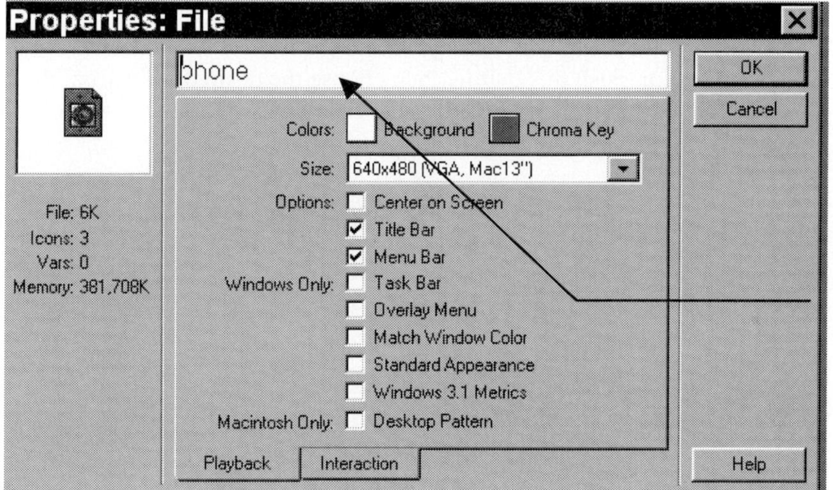

The title area.

Figure 1.6.   The Properties File Dialog Box. These settings affect the entire piece.

This dialog box provides information about the current piece, and is used to establish global settings that affect the entire presentation. Items such as the wait button label (Push the Interaction tab to see it), Presentation window options and restart/return options can be set here.

In the File Properties dialog box, the File label shows the size of the current project and the number of icons and variables it contains. The Memory label shows how much memory is available to the application during authoring.

Title

You can enter a title in the area at the top. The value you assign to the Title field will be used in the title bar of the packaged version. The default title is the actual file name. If this field value is changed, it does not alter the actual file name. Suppose you save your project file as "MYWORK.a4p". This will be the title of your piece. Changing the Title field to "MYTITLE" would not change the actual physical file name.

Authorware pieces are assigned a .a4p extension. This convention is used for both Macintosh and Windows versions.

Colors

The Background button in the Colors section is used to select the color canvas for the background. Objects are placed over this background as the project is developed. If you are providing your own background image, then you won't need to be concerned with this option. We have provided several backgrounds on your CD-ROM in the Backgrounds folder. Instead of using a plain background, you might want to consider a template, or panel. You can see several panels and background in the Templates folder on your CD-ROM.

If you don't use an image as a background, and you don't change the Background color option, your piece will have a white background, because that is the default color. To change the background color, push this button, then choose the desired color from the palette (see Figure 1.7). Chroma Key is only used with video overlay cards and won't be discussed here.

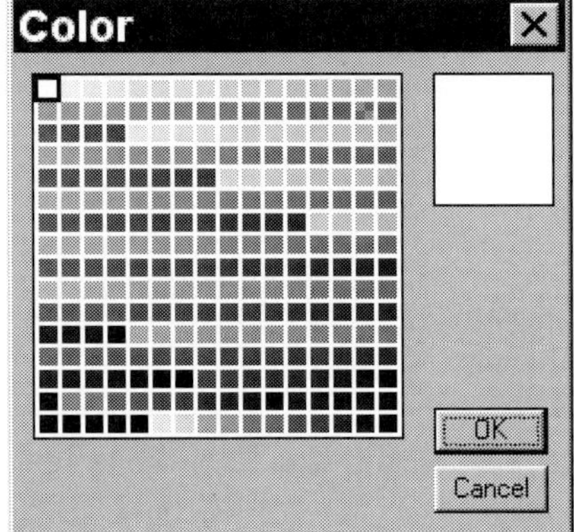

Figure 1.7. The Color Palette. To view it push the Colors Background button in Figure 1.6.

Size

As you might think, the size variable controls the physical dimension of the Presentation window. Select a size equal to the smallest display on which your piece may run. There are nine sizing options, as shown in Figure 1.8.

Each of the first eight choices define preset resolutions (in *pixels* - picture elements). The Use Full Screen option says to make the presentation fill the screen, regardless of size.

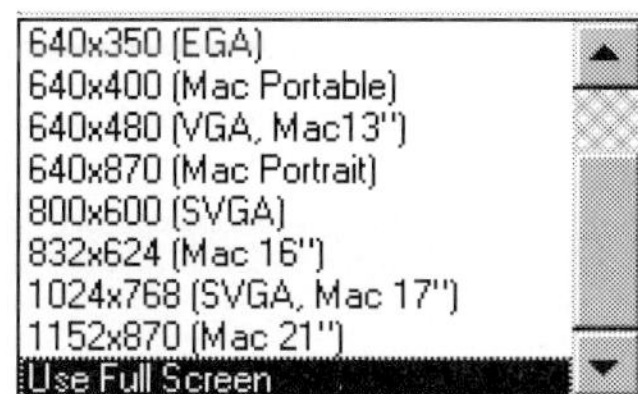

Figure 1.8. The Nine Size Options.

Options

Figure 1.9 reproduces the Options section from Figure 1.6.

Figure 1.9. The Options Section of the File Properties Dialog Box.

Options within this section define various characteristics of the Presentation window. Largely, this section allows your application to take on more or fewer characteristics common to the operating system on which your piece will run. The reasons for changing many of these parameters are both physical and functional.

Center on Screen Choosing the Center on Screen option forces the Presentation window to always be centered, regardless of the playback monitor's size.

Title Bar The Title bar option you see in Figure 1.9 turns the title bar on or off when the Presentation window is larger than the selected screen size. If the window is smaller than the screen, the title bar is always displayed.

Task Bar At the bottom of Windows 95 screens is the task bar. It shows active and minimized applications as icons plus a caption. When your Authorware project is the same size or larger than the display screen, the task bar overwrites your Authorware screen. The default setting eliminates the task bar in situations like this. If you want the user's task bar to always be visible, check this option.

Menu Bar Many applications benefit from the functionality of a menu bar because users are accustomed to this interface type. While the Presentation window is open, there is, by default, a menu bar with a single File Quit menu item, as shown in Figure 1.10.

Figure 1.10. The Presentation Window. There is a single menu bar command: File.

You can add to this menu bar as long as you don't remove the checkmark. If you do turn this feature off, the user cannot quit the piece unless you provide a quit button, or the user strikes Ctrl+Q. This feature can also be manipulated dynamically during application execution using the `ShowMenuBar` variable to show or hide the menu bar. *Variables* are objects that contain single values that can be changed as the need arises. We typically include variables in calculation icons.

Overlay Menu If the Overlay Menu option is selected, it makes Authorware show the menu bar overlapping the Presentation window. If deselected, the menu bar appears above the Presentation window. Figure 1.11 shows the results with and without the feature being active.

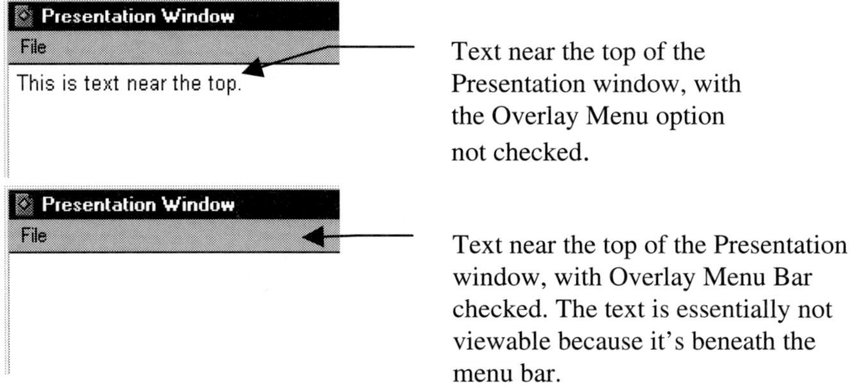

Text near the top of the Presentation window, with the Overlay Menu option not checked.

Text near the top of the Presentation window, with Overlay Menu Bar checked. The text is essentially not viewable because it's beneath the menu bar.

Figure 1.11. Use of the Overlay Menu Bar Option.

Match Window Color With Windows 95, users can control the look of their desktop: button colors, title bar colors, and so on through the Window's 95 Display icon in the Control Panel applet. Figure 1.12 shows how this is accomplished.

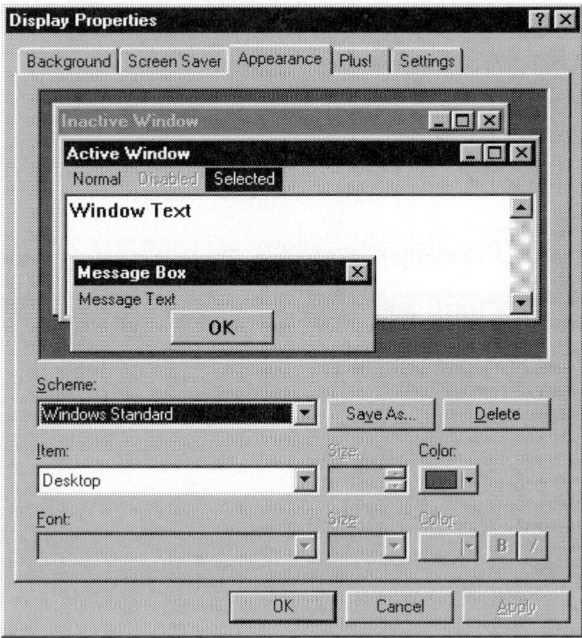

Figure 1.12. Changing Desktop Properties under Windows 95.

If the Match Window Color option is checked, it will force your Authorware windows to match the user's choice for the background color. While it makes your project look like the user's other Windows 95/98 applications, the color choice made by the user may clash with your graphics.

Standard Appearance If you select this option, the Authorware buttons, and other 3D objects will take on the appearance established by the user, not by your project. As just mentioned, the color of items such as buttons can also set by the user through the Display icon in the Control Panel in Windows 95.

Windows 3.1 Metrics Windows 95/98 properties for menu bars, title bars and borders are different than those of Windows 3.X. This means what looks good on Windows 95/98 might not look so good on Windows 3.1 computers. Checking this option ensures uniformity between the two platforms (Windows 3.X and Windows 95/98).

Your Turn
❑ Create a new piece.
❑ Open the File Properties dialog box.
❑ Choose VGA as the size.
❑ Set the Background color to a pale yellow.

❏ Enter "My Presentation" in the Title area.
❏ Click OK to close the dialog box.
❏ Choose File Save and save your work as MYWORK.

The Interaction Tab

Pushing this tab opens a new dialog box, shown in Figure 1.13.

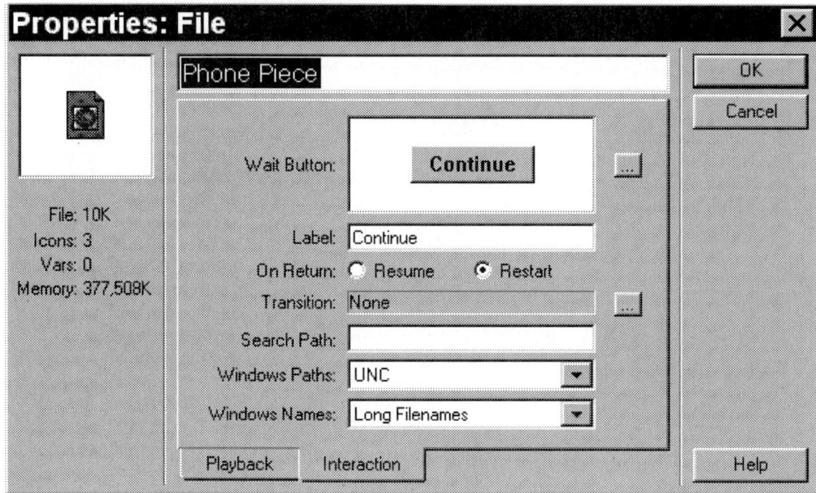

Figure 1.13. The Interaction Tab for the Properties:File Dialog box. Use these options
to specify values for interactive components of your Authorware piece.

Wait Button

These options enable you to alter the way the Wait button displays. Wait buttons are automatically created when a wait icon is used and at various other times. The default label is
"Continue". Entering the substitute label in the Label field can change this. Push the ▣ button to open the Buttons window, shown as Figure 1.14.

Figure 1.14. The Buttons Dialog Box. Chapter 5 will demonstrate how to use the button editor to create new buttons or alter existing ones.

Push the Add or Edit buttons to activate the Button Editor, where you can choose another button or even create your own. We'll discuss the button editor in Chapter 5.

Label

Enter a substitute label for the Continue button. For example, you might enter "Press Me". Now, whenever a Wait button is referenced, its label will read "Press Me". Figure 1.15 shows the default Wait button and another Wait button with the "Press Me" caption. Only one caption can be associated with the Wait button, this means you couldn't use Wait as the caption early in your piece, then switch to Press Me later.

Figure 1.15. The Default Wait Button and a Wait button with a New Caption.

On Return

These options specify how to handle situations where a user quits, then resumes the application at a later time. Use the Resume option to restart exactly where the user left off. Multiple users can be tracked. User information is stored in a .REC file in the A4W_DATA folder. This is found within the Windows folder on Windows platforms. The default name contains the first eight letters of the piece's name plus the .REC extension. When multiple users run a piece, we typically create a folder for each of those users. The Restart option is the default. When it is chosen, the piece always plays from the beginning.

Transition

Transitions refer to the special effects the user will see when he or she returns to the piece. Figure 1.16 shows the Return Transition dialog box.

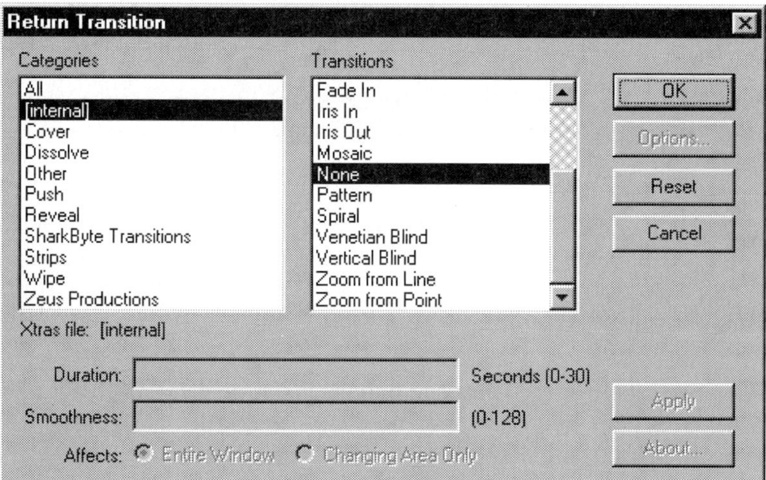

Figure 1.16. The Return Transition Dialog Box. Use it to apply special effects to objects and icons.

There are two categories of transition: Internal (called Effects in earlier versions of Authorware) and Director Transitions, called Xtras. The latter group comes from Macromedia's companion authoring environment, Director®. As you can see from Figure 1.16, there are many Xtras transitions you can select among. With either Xtras or internal transitions, you can vary the duration (between zero and 30 seconds), control the smoothness, and choose whether to apply the transition to the entire presentation or just a portion of the window.

Search Path

Authorware looks for content in the following sequence:

- The directory where the file was located when you first loaded it. (After a piece is packaged or the file is moved, Authorware will no longer find the file unless you specify the file's new location.)
- The directory where the piece is located.
- The directory that contains Authorware or RUNA4W, whichever is currently running.
- The Windows directory.
- The Windows System directory.

To specify additional locations, use the Search Path field. In this field of the Properties File dialog box, you can enter paths to external files necessary to run an application. This field is needed because in many circumstances breaking up an application into smaller pieces enables it to be updated more easily, be better organized or run more efficiently. On Windows computers, you might use values like this: C:\A3W\VIDEO; C:\GRAPHICS; D:\AUDIO. Note the semicolons and lack of spaces.

Windows Paths

The drop-down menu for Windows Paths has two options: DOS and UNC. Historically, Windows-based computers used drive letters as part of their path: C:\A4W\MOVIES, for example. Some networks use a different approach, known as the ***universal naming convention*** (UNC). Under UNC a path contains a server name plus the hierarchical path to the desired file. On a Windows NT server named MMTSERVER, the above path would be denoted as: \\MMTSERVER\A4W\MOVIES.

Windows Names

On Windows 95/98 and Windows NT systems, you can choose between DOS (8.3) and long file names in the drop-down menu for Windows Names in the Properties: File dialog box. Be careful though: If your users run Windows 3.X, long file names are not supported and your project won't run properly, if at all.

OTHER GLOBAL SETTINGS

Under the Modify menu, select the File choice. Note that besides Properties, you also see Font Mapping and Palette. We'll discuss these options next.

Font Mapping

The Modify>File>Font Mapping menu choice is used when porting pieces between Macintosh and Windows platforms. The Font Mapping dialog box shown in Figure 1.17 appears when the Font Mapping option is selected.

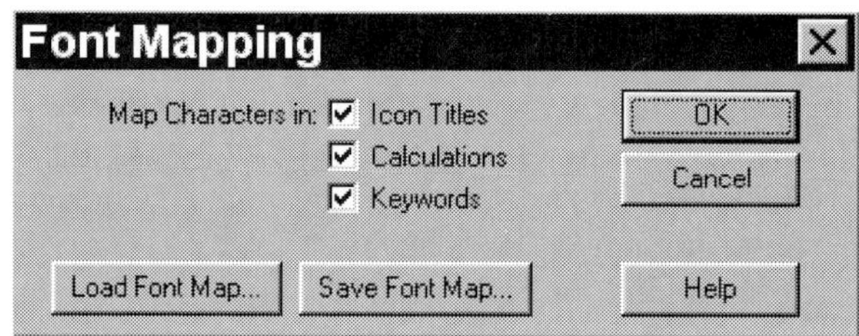

Figure 1.17. The Font Mapping Dialog Box. This is used when porting between Macintosh and Windows versions of Authorware.

Font mapping between Macintosh and Windows is a time-consuming, often frustrating, undertaking. You will find that even if the same font exists on both platforms, it might not look the same or even be the same size. This can result in pieces where the vertical dimension of text on buttons is larger than the buttons themselves (the text is truncated). Another potential problem is a single word that was designated as "hot text" on the original platform, is, after conversion, no longer hot, or that multiple words, or even the wrong words, are "hot". If you anticipate playback on both platforms, you should regularly test your piece several times on both platforms during the development phase.

Unlike the other parameters we have examined, this one is best utilized after the piece is complete. If font mapping is used when the piece is first being built, there won't be any fonts to map! Fonts only become available after they are selected using the text tool.

Font information is kept in a text (ASCII) file named **Fontmap.txt**. Its default location is the same folder as Authorware 4. Figure 1.18 shows a portion of the default **Fontmap.txt** file.

```
; From Mac to Windows 3.1
;Mac:"Helvetica" => Win:"Arial" 10=>6 12=>8 14=>9 18=>11 24=>16 36=>23 48=>32
; From Mac to Windows NT 4.0
;Mac:"Helvetica" => Win:"Arial" 10=>7 12=>8 14=>9 18=>12 24=>16 36=>28 48=>32
; From Windows 3.5.1 or NT4 to Mac
;Win:"Arial" => Mac:"Helvetica" 10=>13 12=>16 14=>18 18=>23 24=>31 36=>47
; Common mappings on Macintosh
Mac:"Chicago"        => Win:"Mac Chicago" 12=>10 14=>12 18=>14 24=>18 36=>24
Mac:"Courier"        => Win:"Courier New"
Mac:"Geneva"         => Win:"System" 12=>10 14=>12 18=>14 24=>18 36=>24
Mac:"New York"       => Win:"MS Serif"
Mac:"Symbol"         => Win:"Symbol"  Map None
Mac:"Times"          => Win:"Times New Roman" 12=>10 14=>12 18=>14 24=>18
Win:"Courier"        => Mac:"Courier"
Win:"Courier New"    => Mac:"Courier"
```

Figure 1.18 . A Portion of the Default **Fontmap.txt** File.

The file specifies both platform and size conversion information. For example, the last two lines say when a Windows-developed Authorware specifies Courier New or Courier, and that piece is running on a Macintosh computer, substitute the Macintosh Courier font. The general pattern the file follows is as follows:

```
Originating Platform:Font Name=>New Platform:=>Font
Name[old size => NewSize].
```

In the first section of Figure 1.18, you can see how to map Helvetica between a Macintosh and a Windows 3.1 configuration. (It's to be converted to Arial). In addition, a 10-point character on the Macintosh is to be converted to a 6-point character on the Windows 3.1 version.

Although we didn't show it, there is also a section that maps ASCII characters between the two platforms. For example, ASCII codes above 128 on a Windows platform generally display graphic symbols, such as might be used to construct a box (We need four corner symbols, and a horizontal and a vertical line). Specifying the ASCII value on one platform and the corresponding ASCII value on the other does the mapping. When there is no need for ASCII mapping, the clause Map None is used. You can see this on the line for the Symbol font.

The Font map is loaded automatically when you start a new piece or open an existing one. The Font Mapping dialog box in Figure 1.17 is used when you have used a text editor to modify the **Fontmap.txt** file, or want to replace it with a new one. To replace the default **Fopntmap.txt** with a new one:

1. Push the Load Font Map button.

2. When the Load Font Mapping dialog box opens (see Figure 1.19), select the file you want as your new font mapping file, then push the OK Button.

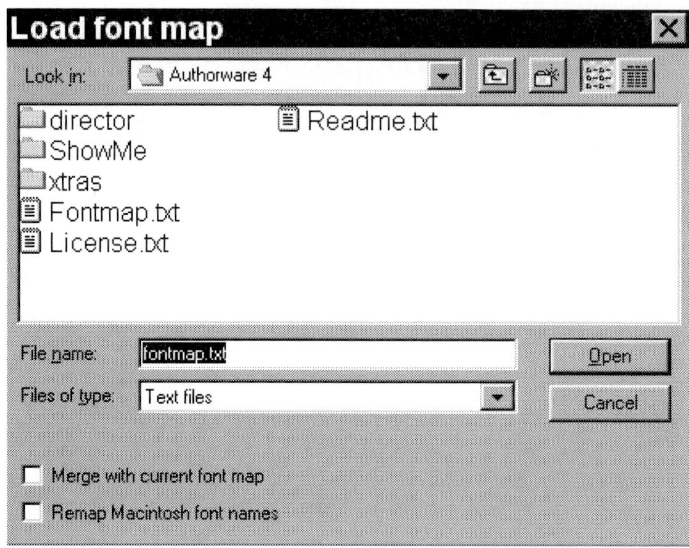

Figure 1.19. The Load Font Dialog Box. To view it, push the Load Font Map button on the Font Mapping dialog box (see Figure 1.17).

The new font map will load, effectively overwriting the existing one. The options at the bottom of Figure 1.19 enable you to merge the new map file with the existing one —the original font map is not replaced, and the other option forces Authorware to update all fonts in the piece with the new ones you saved in the **Fontmap.txt** file. One final comment: You can edit the **Fontmap.txt** using any word processor, but be sure to save the text as text, not in the word processor's native format.

Color Palette

To view the current palette, select the Modify>File>Palette menu item. Clicking on this option in the Properties: File dialog box lets you use choose an alternate palette to use. Figure 1.20 shows the Palette dialog box.

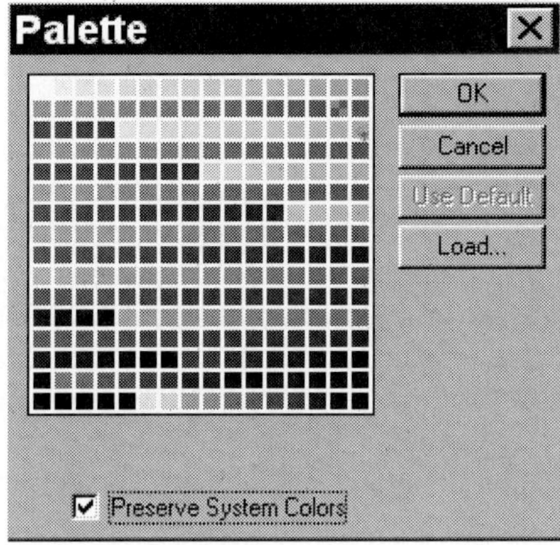

Figure 1.20. The Palette Dialog Box. Use it to load new palettes or customize existing ones.

The default Windows palette matches that of the Macintosh, except for the first and last set of 10 colors, which the Windows version uses for the system colors.

Palette Window

The Use Default button changes the palette back to the original Windows 256-color palette. Custom palettes can be imported with the Load button. After clicking on this button, supply the path and file name for the custom palette to use. Checking Preserve System Colors forces Authorware to make all Windows components (title bars, scroll bars, and so on) maintain their system colors.

Your Turn

We are going to start a continuing project. In this chapter, we'll create the piece by specifying the desirable file properties.

❏ Start a new piece.

❏ Specify these options: Select a resolution of 640 X 480; center the presentation; show both a menu bar and a title bar; specify a Windows 95 Wait button-style; choose Arial Black as the button font; choose UNC paths; and long windows name.

❏ Save your piece as **DigVid1**.

SUMMARY

Authorware is a cross-platform, interactive, multimedia-authoring package. Best-suited for computer based training (CBT), Authorware can also be used to create interactive multimedia presentations, kiosks or World Wide Web pages. Rather than burden the developer with a cumbersome programming language, Authorware projects can be constructed almost entirely without programming efforts. Icons are dragged to a flowline, opened and their content specified. The project is run an icon at a time, a concept known as linear execution. When this isn't suitable, interaction, navigation, and framework icons can enable sophisticated interactions, such as hypermedia, hypertext, button pushing, and hot spots.

When a project is begun, its global settings must be determined. Using the <u>M</u>odify> <u>F</u>ile><u>P</u>roperties menu choice, the project can be customized to change the default background, alter the default title that appears in the title bar area, specify where to search for external files, specify the size of the Presentation window, select the type of path and file naming convention, and assign many other properties of the project. Once the global settings are specified, content is added.

We will look at text and graphical content in Chapter 2.

STUDY EXERCISES

1.1. Assume you are authoring on an Intel® machine but want to run the project on Macintoshes as well. Show the options you'd choose to minimize cross-platform differences.

1.2. Contrast the purposes of the two window types.

1.3. Differentiate between the toolbar and the tool palette. What are the purposes of each? Which is used to "program"?

Managing Text and Graphics

*I*n chapter 1, we saw how to use the flowline together with the icon palette to present multimedia content. This chapter looks specifically at managing the graphic and text elements of a project. We will show this can be done through the use of the display, erase, and wait icons.

Most of the graphics and text content is added to Authorware through the use of display icons. Each display icon can contain one or more graphic objects. Object types include text, lines, simple, and complex shapes. When encountered on the flowline, the display icon presents its objects in the Presentation window. Authorware provides features that allow easy manipulation of alignment and display characteristics of display icon objects. Display icons can accommodate content from other applications; that is, text and graphics can be imported when the capabilities above Authorware's limitations are desired.

Once presented, content can be removed using the erase icon. The erase icon is usually used to remove the contents of display icons, but can also be used to remove all other icon types. There are times when you want to delay the display or erase of an object. The wait icon is used when this is desired. As the chapter winds down, you will be introduced to the map icon, which groups many icons into one.

Another feature of Authorware is the *library*. Libraries are designed to make authoring more efficient both in how work is done and in how information is stored. Libraries also provide a way to organize and share content when several authors are working on a project concurrently.

At the conclusion of this chapter, you will be able to:

- Manage external media.
- Use the toolbox to create graphics objects.
- Manipulate all aspects of toolbox objects.
- Import text and graphics.
- Use the erase icon to remove other icons.
- Use a wait icon to control project flow.
- Create a library and use it to store display icons.

GRAPHIC IMAGES

It may be helpful here to discuss the types of graphic images. The information stored in a graphic file is generally structured in one of two formats, *bitmap* or *vector-based*. Any image displayed on a computer monitor is created by thousands of tiny dots called picture elements (*pixels*). Bitmap graphics retain the information of every pixel needed to display an image. In general, bitmaps are static. They are created to fill specific dimensions of display space with a specific number of colors. In order to edit or change a bitmap graphic, a *paint* software program is needed to literally reassign different colors to pixels.

Vector-based graphics are comprised of one or more geometric objects that are colored and arranged to create the overall image. Each object is defined mathematically. These objects each retain their unique identities. This allows each component object to be selected and manipulated within the software program it was created in. Although it has the ability to manipulate and display both image formats, Authorware can only create vector-based images. This creation is done using display icons.

Supported File Formats

Authorware supports the importing of many graphics formats. On the Windows platform, the following graphics file formats are supported:

- BMP (bitmap)

- DIB (device independent bit map)
- RLE (run length encoded)
- WMF (Windows metafile)
- PIC (Macintosh Picture file)
- GIF (Graphics Interchange Format)
- PNG (Portable Networks Graphics)
- TGA (Targa)
- JPG (Joint Photographic Experts Group)
- LRG (Macromedia xRes files)
- PSD (Photoshop)
- TIF (Tagged Image File Format)
- EPS (Encapsulated PostScript)

Authorware's Presentation window and accompanying toolbox are not intended to replace paint and vector-based packages such as Macromedia's xRes and Freehand, nor Adobe's Illustrator and Photoshop. In most cases it's preferable that you develop your graphics in one of those packages, save your work in one of the above formats, and then import into your Authorware piece. We'll show how to import graphics in this chapter.

Cross-Platform Issues

A gratifying fact is that images imported into one development platform, play back on the other. For example, a BMP image you import to your Windows application will display when the product runs on the Macintosh, even though the Macintosh development package doesn't support BMP files.

COMMON ICON CHARACTERISTICS

In general, all the icons in the tool palette behave similarly: They are all designed to be dragged to the flowline from the palette and then customized by the author. Upon placement on the flowline they are given the label "Untitled". To help organize the project icons, each should be renamed with a descriptive label. Icon labels should make sense when read down the flowline. There will be many examples of this in the following chapters.

Icons can gain their content in one of two ways. The first is by double-clicking on the icon on the flowline. The second way is by prompting the author for input when an empty icon is encountered. While running a project, the flow will stop at an empty icon and present the appropriate prompt for the author's input.

Previous versions of Authorware generally embedded assets into the Authorware piece. If you imported a graphic or created it with the Authorware toolbox, that graphic became part of the Authorware piece. New with Authorware 4 is the ability to link to external media, rather than embed it. The next section discusses this important concept.

EXTERNAL MEDIA

Prior versions of Authorware stored most media as part of the Authorware file. Authorware 4 allows you to separate the external media from the Authorware portion. For example, you might distribute the Authorware portion over the Internet, but have graphics, sound, and digital video on a local CD-ROM. This is a significant improvement over earlier releases and makes intranet, Internet and other forms of distributed content possible.

Using External Media

To use external media:

- Store the image, sound, or digital media in its final location.
- Add a display icon to the flowline
- Link an icon to the external media by checking the "Link to File" option in the Import dialog box shown in Figure 2.1.

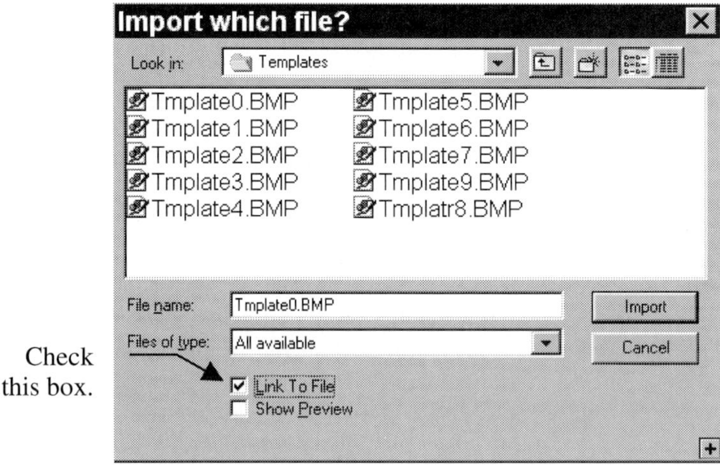

Figure 2.1. Linking Instead of Embedding Assets. Check the Link to File box.

Managing External Media

To manage the external media, use the External Media Browser. Open it by selecting External Media Browser from the Window menu (Ctrl+Shift+X). Figure 2.2 shows the External Media Browser dialog box.

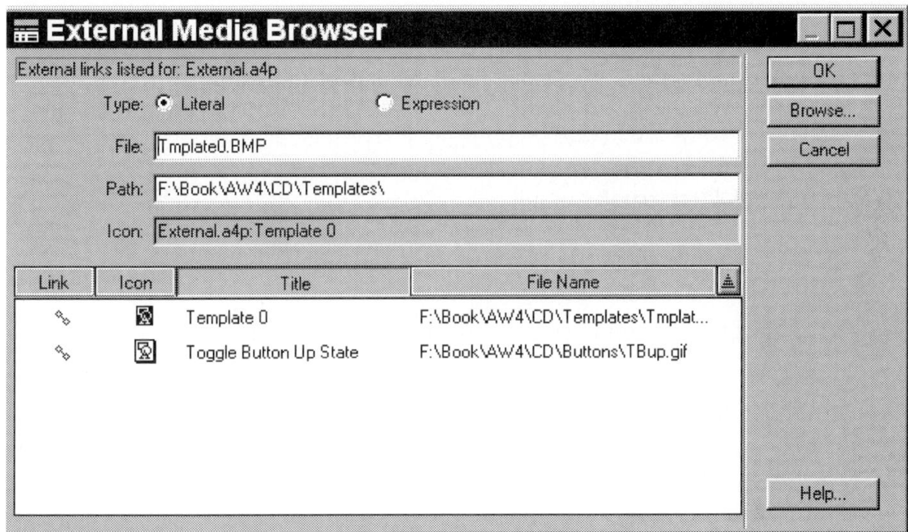

Figure 2.2. The External Media Browser. Use it to manage links to external media.

You use the External Media Browser to help keep track of your external files that are used in your Authorware piece. You can even create variables whose values point to the content. For example, you could create a variable called ButtonState. Then assign one of two values to ButtonState: `ButtonUp.GIF` and `ButtonDown.GIF`. One points to a file that contains a graphic of the button in its up state, while the other value would point to a file containing a graphic of the button it its down state.

To see this dialog box, you must first select an icon that contains an external link. If a given icon contains multiple links to external media, there will be multiple files names associated with that icon name.

 **Your Turn**

❏ Open and run the **External.a4p** file in the Chapter2 folder on your CD-ROM.

❏ Use the Window>External Media Browser menu choice, or use Ctrl+Shift+X to open the External Media Browser window, shown in Figure 2.2.

It didn't run properly, did it! You need to adjust the link values of the two images so they point to your CD-ROM. The general syntax will be as follows:

```
DriveLetter:\FolderName\FileName.BMP
```

For example, if your CD-ROM drive is D: the **Tmplate0.bmp** link should read:

```
D:\Templates\Tmplate0.bmp
```

Once the External Media Browser is open, use it to:

- Switch between a hard-coded path (literal) and an expression (variable).
- Use the Browse button to select a new file to link to the icon.

Editing Linked Content

Let's see how to edit a link to an external file.

- First, select the icon and then open the External Media Browser.
- Next, enter the new file name and/or the new path into the File text box, or use the Browse command to select it.
- Push the OK button.

Your Turn
❏ If the **External.a4p** file isn't open, open it at this time.
❏ Open the External Media Browser.
❏ Select the Template0 display icon in the External Media Browser.
❏ Push the Browse button and point Authorware to the **Tmplate0.bmp** file on your CD-ROM.
❏ Make the Toggle Button Up Sate display icon point to the **TBUp.gif** file on you CD-ROM.
❏ Restart the piece. It should now run.

If you are successful, Authorware updates some internal information is stores about display, interaction, sound or movie icons. For example, if you update a link to a graphic and then open the Image Properties dialog box (Select the image, then choose <u>M</u>odify>I<u>m</u>age Properties). The (new) name or (new) location will display in the File text area. See Figure 2.3 for an example. Also note in Figure 2.3 that the Storage value is set to External, indicating the media have been separated from the Authorware portion.

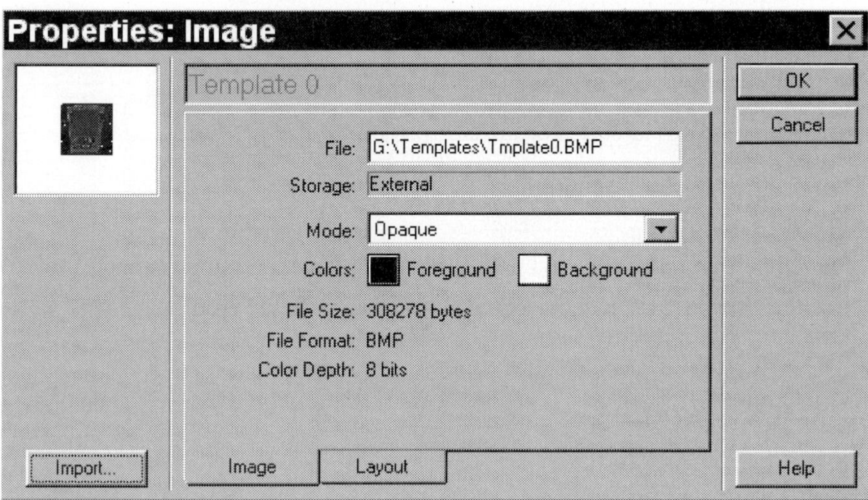

Figure 2.3. The Image Properties Dialog Box. The File and Storage fields indicate the
location of the external media and the fact that it is not embedded, but instead linked to an external file. Notice the location is now the G: drive

Using Variables

You can use a variable to point to the file, instead of hard-coding it. Suppose you have a
variable named `Template`. Using a calculation icon, you might set its value to
`F:\Book \AW4\CD\Templates\Tmplate0.BMP`.

Alternatively, set it to another value depending on a condition or expression. This allows maximum flexibility when creating a piece. Using variables makes it much easier to
port to other platforms or configurations.

Figure 2.4 shows how to set up the External Media Browser to use a variable named
`Template`. We first checked the Expression radio button, then entered `Template` as the
Expression value.

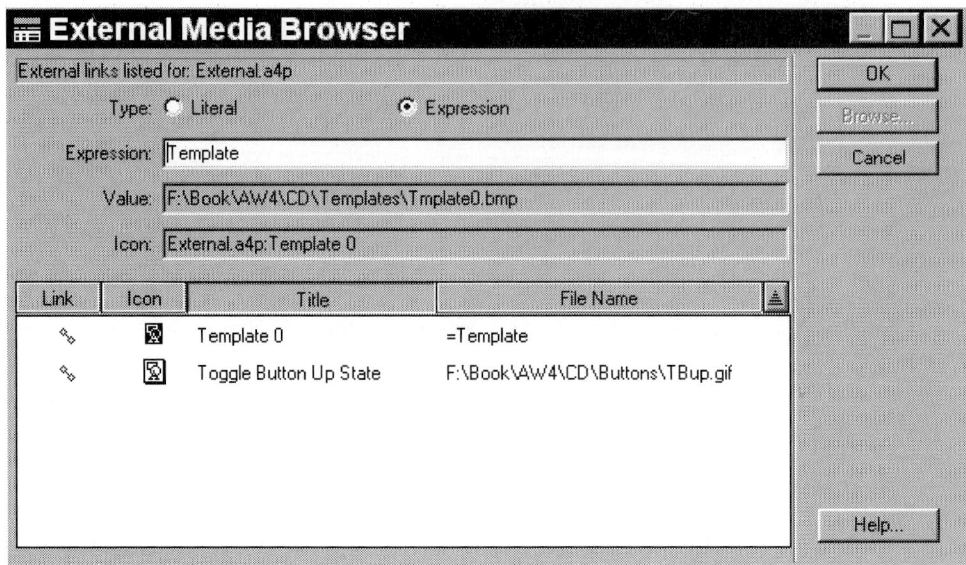

Figure 2.4. Using the External Media Browser and Variables to Link Media to Icons. Note use of the variable (`Template`).

A New Variable dialog box opened (shown in Figure 2.5) and we entered the path to the image as the variable's value (F:\Book\AW4\CD\Templates\Tmplate0.BMP).

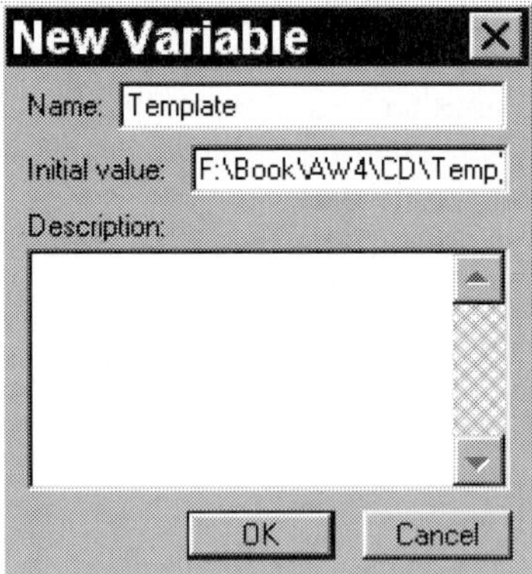

Figure 2.5. Using the New Variable Dialog Box to Provide a Value for the Template Variable.

The use of external media greatly facilitates distributed content using CD-ROM and the Internet. It also makes content management easier while developing the initial piece on your hard drive or over a Local Area Network.

Let's see how to use both embedded and linked graphics as we next explore the display icon.

USING THE DISPLAY ICON

Use the display icon to add both text and graphical content. We begin by discussing the supported types of graphics, then how to add and manage graphical and text content.

General Functionality

Text and graphics objects are added and edited in the Presentation window. The Presentation window isn't intended to replace powerful graphics and imaging applications, such as Illustrator, Freehand, and Photoshop. However, the features of the Presentation window are sufficient to create simple graphic objects. Graphics that are more complex need to be imported into Authorware from other applications.

To add a display icon, choose it from the Icon Palette, then drag it to the flowline. When it's first placed on the flowline, it's empty and given the label "Untitled". Clicking the mouse cursor over the label will put the label into edit mode. Any descriptive name can now be given to it.

To add content to the display icon, the Presentation window must be opened. This can be done by either double-clicking the display icon on the flowline, or by running the project. When the Presentation window opens, the toolbox will be visible. You can use the toolbox to create new graphics and text, or import existing images and text.

Working With Graphics and Text Objects

Graphic images can be added to a display icon by either of two techniques. This section looks first at using the Clipboard application and then at importing existing images created in other packages.

Using the Clipboard

Images can be either pasted from the Clipboard or they can be imported. The decision of which of these to use is usually a matter of workflow. It is very common for authors to have a graphics package and Authorware open concurrently. As images are completed in the graphics package, they are copied to the clipboard and directly pasted into the Presentation window.

Importing Images

It is also common for teams to work on a project. One person on the team will create the graphics and save them as external files and another will author. In this case, the images must be imported. Choose _F_ile from the menu bar, then _I_mport, and then enter or select the appropriate file-type in the Import which file dialog box, shown in Figure 2.6. This dialog box works like a standard Windows browser in the upper left and has a preview window on the right. After working through the directory structure to locate the appropriate file, the file is highlighted with a single mouse click and brought into the Presentation window with the Open button.

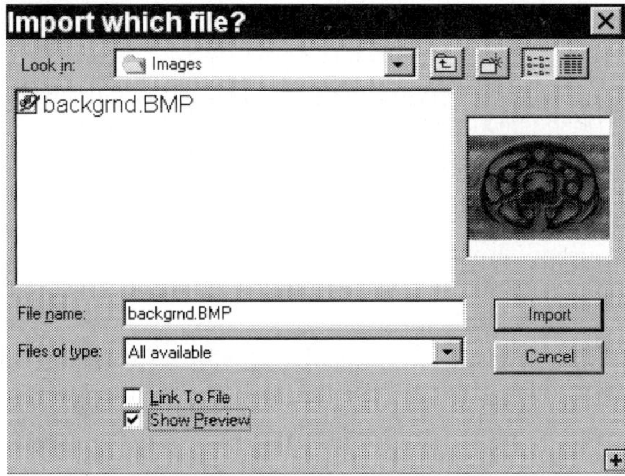

Figure 2.6.   The Import Which File Dialog Box. It displays file name and type to the left and, if the Show _P_review box is checked, a thumbnail to the right.

    Batch Importing If you click on the small plus sign near the lower right corner of the Import which file dialog box, the dialog box expands. As you specify a file to import, you then push the Add button in the nwly expanded portion of the dialog box. Figure 2.7 shows we are about to import two images into a new piece.

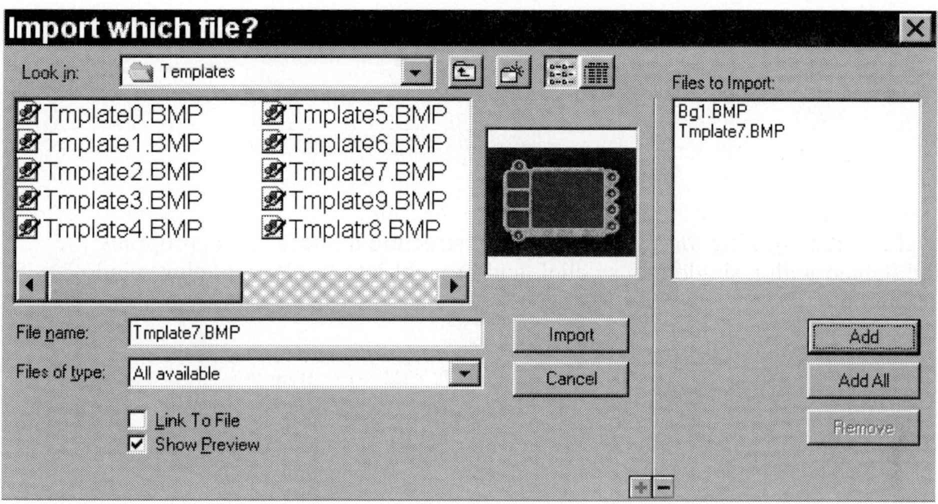

Figure 2.7. The Expanded File Import Dialog Box. The right-hand section indicates we are about to import two files.

If you try to replicate what we show in Figure 2.7, then run the resulting piece, you'll find that the **Bg1.BMP** file doesn't show in the Presentation window. To see it, you need to first open the display icon and move the **Tmplate7.BMP** image so you can see the underlying image. Next, move the **Bg1.BMP** image in front of the **Tmplate7.BMP** image by selecting **Bg1.BMP**, then selecting Modify>Bring to Front. Finally, use the handles to resize the **Bg1.BMP** image.

Sample File To see the result, you can open and run the **Import2.a4p** file in the Chapter 2 folder on your CD-ROM.

Link to File If this box is checked, the graphic will be linked, rather than embedded, as described in the previous section.

Cropping To crop an image, select the image in the Presentation window, and then select Modify>Image Properties. The dialog box in Figure 2.8 will open.

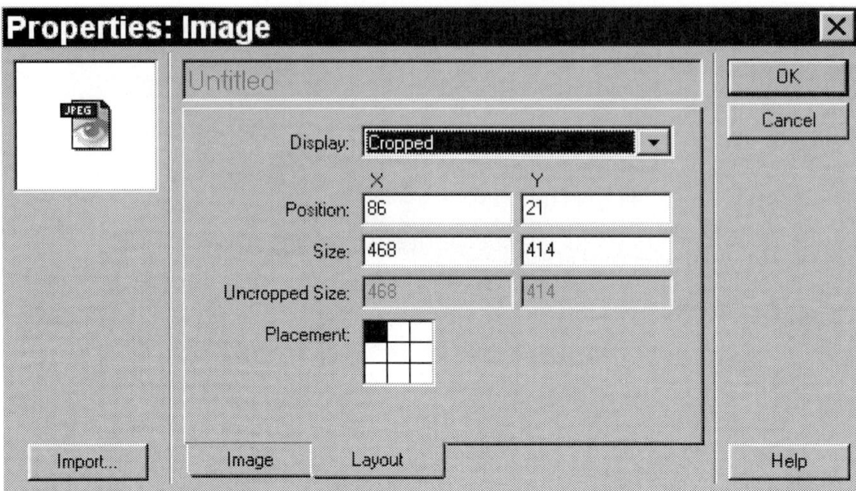

Figure 2.8. Using the Properties: Image Dialog Box to crop an Image. Click the Layout tab to perform the actual cropping.

Push the Layout tab and then select Cropped from the Display drop-down list. Finally, enter new values in the X and Y fields. As you enter the values, you can immediately see the effect on the image as it is cropped to reflect the new values. Check one of the nine boxes at the bottom of Figure 2.8 to display different sections of the cropped image. Figure 2.9 shows the effect of two of the nine crop location boxes.

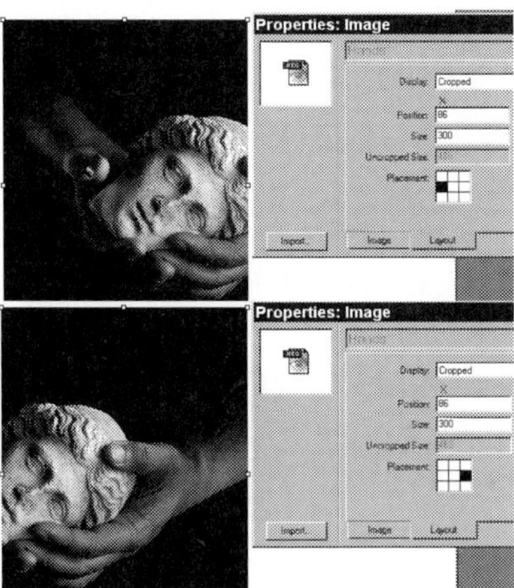

Figure 2.9. The Same Image with Different Crop Locations Specified.

Instead of cropping in the manner just described, once the image is in the display icon, you can select the object, then use the selection handles to crop.

Scaling Images In most cases, the size of the image is too large or too small to fit the Presentation window, or is simply the wrong size for your purposes. To change the size of an imported image, use the Scaled option in the Display drop-down list. In Figure 2.10 we have scaled an object by 30% in both the X and Y directions.

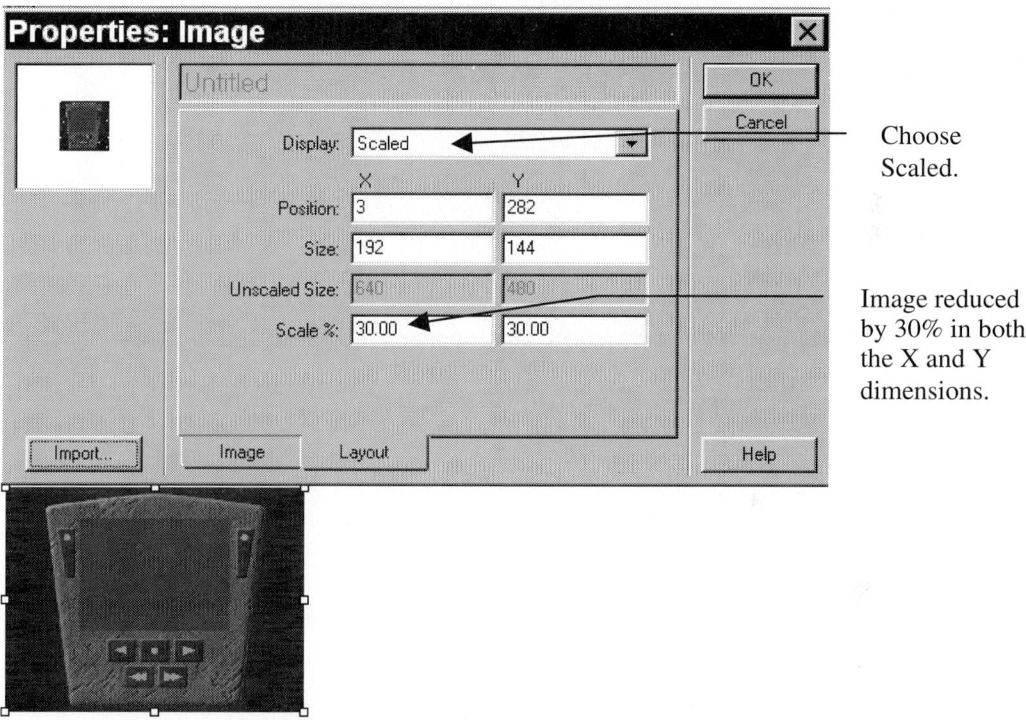

Choose Scaled.

Image reduced by 30% in both the X and Y dimensions.

Figure 2.10. Scaling an Imported Image.

Moving Objects

If you select an object and hold down the left mouse button without moving the mouse, the cursor changes into a hand. When the cursor is hand-shaped you can move an object anywhere within the Presentation window. If an object is moved before the cursor changes, only the object's outline moves when you move the mouse. In either case the object's placement is determined when the mouse button is released. Pressing the Shift key while dragging an object constrains its movement to vertical, horizontal, and 45-degree angles.

Using the Grid

It is often desirable to align objects to the same horizontal or vertical pixel. This is a some-what difficult chore with the large number of pixels that make up the Presentation window. Authorware provides a grid in the Presentation window that serves as a visual guide to aid in alignment tasks. A *grid* is a series of horizontal and vertical lines. You can show the grid to facilitate drawing or aligning objects within the same icon or objects in several icons. To activate the grid, select View>Grid. This displays a reference grid with reference marks 32 pixels apart, as shown in Figure 2.11. The actual grid lines are 16 pixels apart, but only every other one is referenced on the grid.

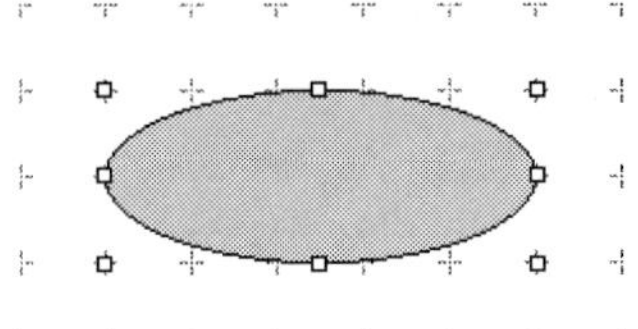

Figure 2.11.   The Reference Marks That Appear When The Grid Is Displayed. Each mark is 32 pixels from its predecessor. There are additional invisible grid lines half way between the marks.

To facilitate the placement of objects, you may find it useful to make objects ***snap to the grid***; that is, only permit an object to have a boundary on one of the grid lines. To do this choose View>Snap to grid. This causes objects to jump to the nearest 16-pixel grouping.

Changing an Object's Layer

Another mechanism to arrange objects within a display icon is the Modify>Bring to Front and Modify>Send to Back feature. With this feature, overlapping objects in the same icon can be placed in front of or behind one another. This is a helpful feature to arrange objects when placing text objects over a frame or when drop-shadowing text. We referred to this in our earlier discussion about batch importing. There the problem was one object completely covered the other. By using the Bring to Front and Scaled options for the multi-colored im-age (**Bg1.BMP**), we were able to see it in its desired location. You might want to retry the batch retrieval and subsequent scaling and layer changing at this time.

Aligning Objects

With its six options, the Align Objects Toolbox (see Figure 2.12) provides a quick and accu-rate mechanism to align objects. It provides the ability to align objects to the left, the right, to the top or bottom. It also provides options to space objects equidistantly on either a verti-cal or horizontal axis.

To use the alignment palette, select all objects to be aligned, the select <u>A</u>lign (Ctrl+Alt+K) from the <u>M</u>odify menu and then choose the desired alignment option. The object that is located furthest in the alignment direction chosen provides the reference to which the other objects are aligned. For example, when using the top align option, the selected object located closest to the top of the display will dictate the height of the other objects.

The vertical equidistant spacing option uses the top-most and bottom-most objects to define the outer limits of all selected objects. Other objects are spaced evenly between them on their centers. For the horizontal option, the left-most and right-most locations define the limits.

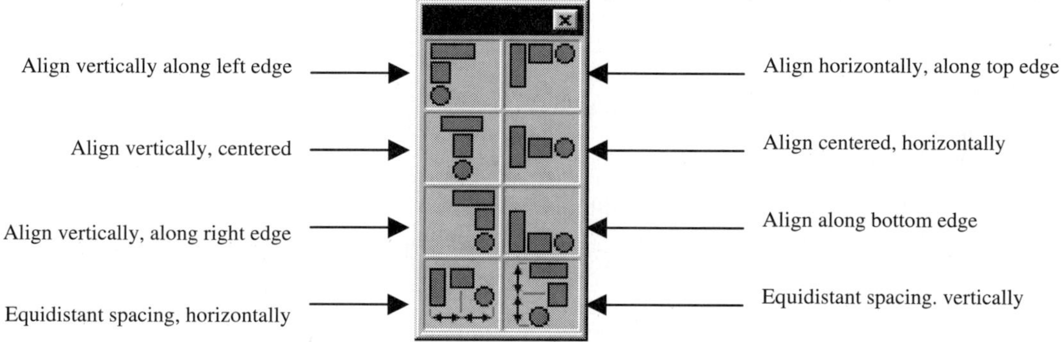

Figure 2.12. The Alignment Toolbox. To view this toolbox, select the objects, then choose <u>M</u>odify><u>A</u>lign (Ctrl+Alt+K).

Grouping Objects

When manipulating objects in the Presentation window, there are times when multiple objects need to be kept together. This may be to speed alignment, to move all objects as a unit, or to otherwise simultaneously process all the objects. Authorware allows object grouping and ungrouping. To group, all desired objects are selected and <u>G</u>roup is chosen from the <u>M</u>odify menu (or use Ctrl+G). Once objects are grouped they are treated as a single object: The group has only one set of handles in place of each object's individual ones.

Your Turn
❏ Start a new piece.
❏ Add a display icon and name it Background.
❏ Open Background's Presentation window by double-clicking on the icon.
❏ Choose <u>F</u>ile><u>I</u>mport and import the **Tmplate0** bitmap in the Templates folder on your CD-ROM.

❑ Link your Background display icon to the **Tmplate0** bitmap. If you didn't link to the image, you will have to delete the Background display icon, and start over. To delete an icon, select it, then push the cut icon on the toolbar ( )

❑ Scale the **Tmplate0** bitmap so it fills your Presentation window. Try scaling the Y direction to 90%. You can fine-tune your scaling in the Presentation window by selecting one of the handles and dragging in the desired direction.

❑ Switch to the flowline.

❑ Add a second display icon and name it Buttons.

❑ Double-click the Buttons icon.

❑ You are going to add buttons to the background you imported previously. However, the background isn't visible, so you don't know where to place the buttons you are about to import.

❑ Close the Presentation window.

❑ Run your piece.

❑ The Buttons icon will open its Presentation window because its content is empty. In addition, the Background bit map will now be visible.

❑ As a shortcut, you can use shift-double-click to view the contents of previous icons while adding content to new ones. We'll see this technique again a bit later.

❑ Import FirstUp, Lastup, Nextup, and Prevup bit maps from the Images\Buttons folder on your CD.

❑ They're all on top of each other. The Prevup button should be the only one visible because it was the last one to be imported.

❑ Select the Prevup button.

❑ Send it to the back. Which button is now "on top"?

❑ Bring the Prevup button to the front.

❑ Rearrange the FirstUp and Lastup buttons so that FirstUp is above Lastup.

❑ Arrange the Nextup and Prevup buttons near the lower right corner, one above the other.

❑ Use Shift+Click to select all four buttons.

❑ Align them along their left-most edges.

❑ Move the Lastup button a bit to the left.

❑ Notice that neither the FirstUp button, nor the other two, move.

❑ Realign all buttons along their left-most edges.

❑ Select the four buttons.

❑ Group them.

❑ Move any button to the left or right.

❑ All buttons move together because they are grouped. You don't have to save your work.

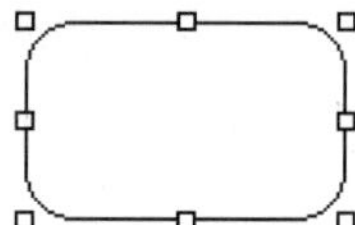

The Presentation window Toolbox

The presentation toolbox contains eight different tools. These tools allow for the creation and manipulation of text and graphic objects. A single click over any icon in the toolbox will select that icon as the active one. By default the selection tool is highlighted as the active tool.

The Pointer (Selection) Tool

Objects in the Presentation window have two states when Authorware is in edit mode: *selected* or *unselected*. In the selected state, the object will appear to have an outline of small black squares around it. These squares are called *handles*. Selected objects are active. That is, they are the only things affected by the actions of the author. New authors require some time to get accustomed to selecting active objects because at any given time the Presentation window can show multiple objects from several different display icons.

The pointer tool acts as a toggle switch to change objects from selected to unselected. This toggling is accomplished by single clicking repeatedly on the same object or by clicking on different objects. Authorware follows Windows conventions when using the pointer tool and the Shift keyboard key. Holding the Shift key down while using the pointer tool will select multiple objects. Multiple objects can also be selected by clicking above and to the left of the leftmost object, then dragging over the other objects, while continuing to hold down the mouse button.

The pointer tool can also be used to move objects. To move objects using the selection tool:

1. Choose the selection tool.
2. Select the object by clicking on it. You will see several *selection handles*, appearing as small boxes, outline the object, as in the following drawing:

3. Click on any portion of any line, but not a selection handle, and not in the interior of the object.
4. Drag and drop.

 **Your Turn**
❑ Open a new project.
❑ Add a new display icon.

❏ Name it "Icon 1" by selecting the current name ("Untitled") and then changing it.

❏ Open the blank Presentation window by pushing the Restart button, by pressing Ctrl+R, or by double-clicking on the icon on the flowline.

❏ Add a rectangle by first selecting the rectangle tool, then clicking in the general area where you want the upper left corner to be.

❏ Now drag down and to the right, while holding down the mouse button.

❏ Release the button when the rectangle is sized to your satisfaction.

❏ Move the rectangle near the upper left corner of the Presentation window.

❏ Save your work as **Mywork2a.**

If you had trouble moving the rectangle, remember:

1. Select it.

2. Click along an edge.

3. Drag and drop.

As you do this, note that the original object remains where it was while the dragging operation is active. Once you release the button, the original object is erased.

The Text Tool A

Creating Text Objects To add text, choose the text tool from the toolbox. Moving the cursor to the desired position and left clicking will set where the text is to begin. The text-width line pictured below will be visible.

**When the text-width line is visible, text can be entered, imported, or pasted. The blinking cursor bar beneath the text-width line marks the insertion point for text entry. The line's length can be adjusted by moving the selection handles at either end of the line.

Text Formatting A paragraph is defined to be any text up to a hard return. If you entered your name three times, with an [Enter]/[Return] at the end of each name, you'd have three paragraphs. Paragraph properties include margins, indents, tabs, and alignment.

Normally, the left margin is set to where ever you begin typing; the right margin is defined to be the longest line. The *margins* are adjusted by moving the selection handles at either end of the text object. To *set a tab*, select the paragraph then click just above the ruler where you want to set the tab. They are indicted by small triangles on the text-width line. If you want a decimal tab, click the triangle and the tab indicator will change shape.

In the example in Figure 2.13, a tab has been added and used to enter the second line.

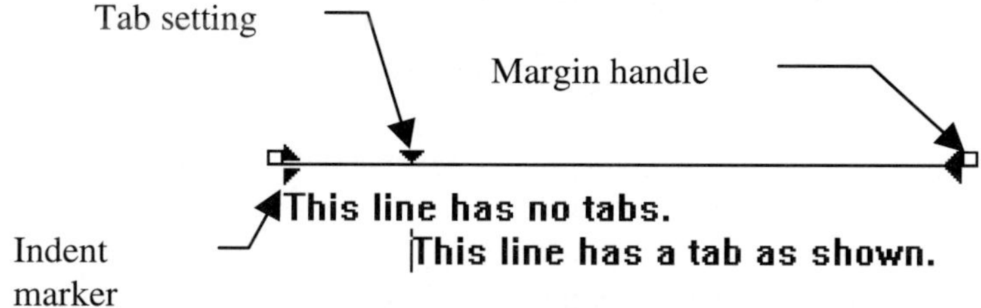

Figure 2.13. A Text Object With A Tab Set And Used. The second line was entered
this way: The tab key was struck, then the text entered.

You can also indent text. First, select the paragraph to be reformatted. The left edge of
the paragraph (anything up to a hard return is a paragraph) is indented by moving the top
half of the triangle toward the right. To move a top portion of a triangle but not the bottom
half, use Shift-drag. Moving the opposite triangle adjusts the right side of the paragraph. By
dragging the bottom left triangle, just the first line is indented.

In the example in Figure 2.14, two paragraphs were entered, separated by a return. The
first paragraph was selected and the first line triangle moved right, The procedure was repeated for the second paragraph.

Figure 2.14. Use Of Indents with Multiple Paragraphs.

Importing Text To import existing text, open the Presentation window, choose File
Import and then enter or select the appropriate file-type in the Import which file dialog box,
shown in Figure 2.15. There are two standard text types that appear in the dialog box: Rich
Text Format (RTF), and Text (TXT). However, you can import any ASCII text file, regardless of file extension.

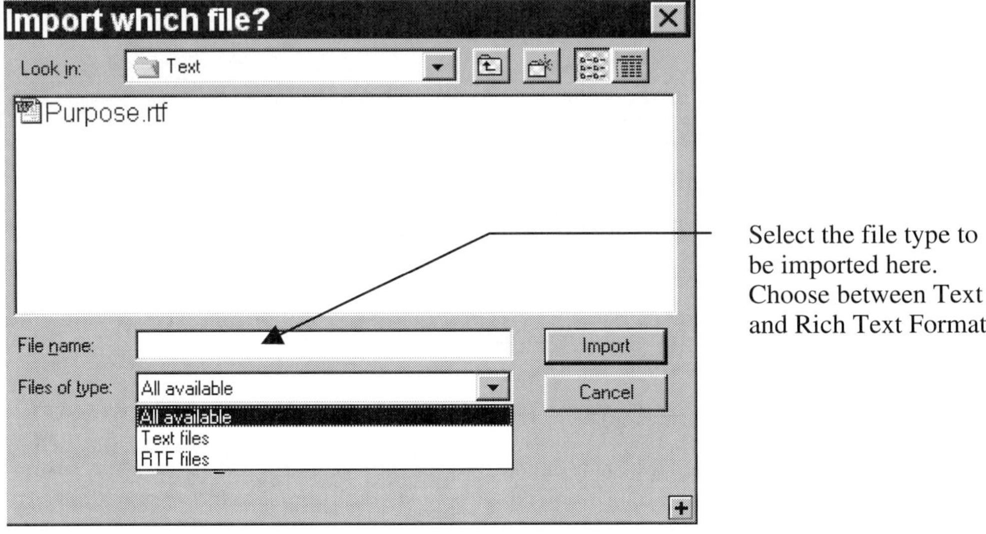

Select the file type to be imported here. Choose between Text and Rich Text Format.

Figure 2.15. The File Import Dialog Box.

If the text is RTF and there are page breaks, or if the text is longer than a page in length, the RTF Import dialog box shown in Figure 2.16 will appear.

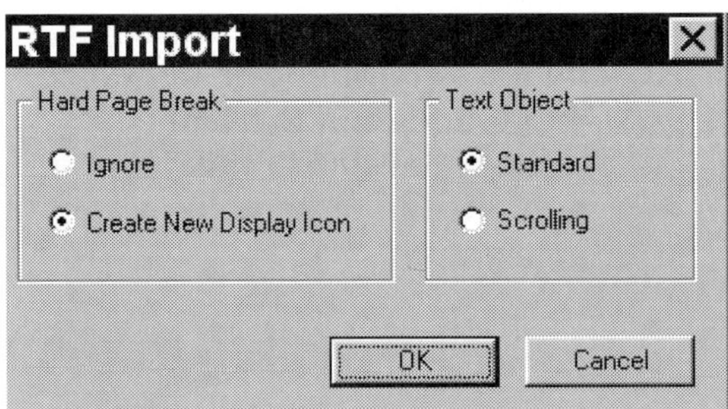

Figure 2.16. The RTF Import Dialog Box.

Choose Ignore to have Authorware use the display icon that's currently open to store all text. If you select Create New Display Icon, Authorware will create separate icons for each "hard-coded" RTF page break. The Standard radio button makes the text appear normally, while the other choice creates scroll bars for the text.

Pasting Text The procedure we just followed works equally well for pasting text, except that you do not need to create a text object first, Authorware does this automatically. This makes it easy to cut and paste from a word processor into Authorware. In fact, because of the many advanced features of word processors, it is preferable when creating large text objects to use such applications, then use an Edit/Copy Edit/Paste sequence to insert the text into your project. Figure 2.17 shows text that was created in Microsoft Word and then pasted into Authorware.

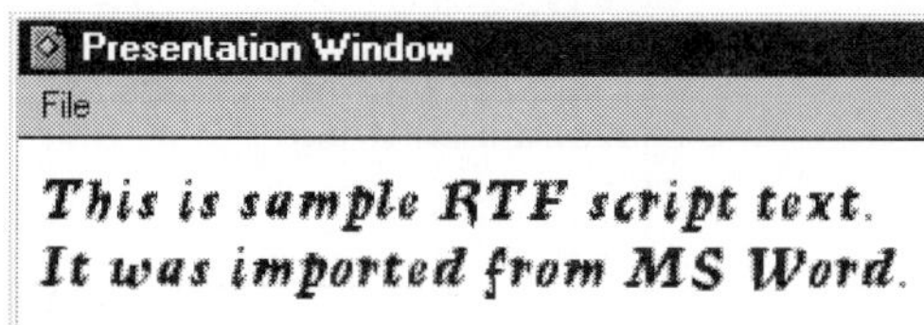

Figure 2.17. Text Pasted into a Presentation Window from Microsoft Word.

Changing Font Characteristics and Making Text Scroll A text font can be selected before or after keying in the text. To change fonts, select the text object, then choose Text>Font. (See Figure 2.18 for the complete list of choices under the Text menu.)

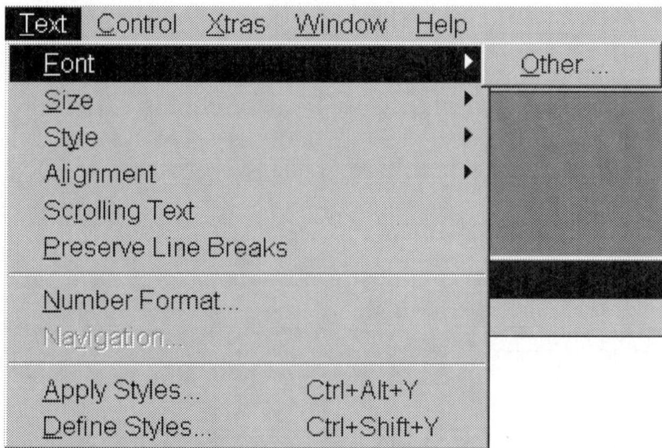

Figure 2.18. The Text Menu with All Options Shown.

A list of currently loaded fonts will appear. To select one, just point and click. Choose Other to add a new one to the drop-down list. This feature keeps track of all fonts used in a project so that they can be selected quickly instead of scrolling through the entire font list. After selecting Other, you will see the Font dialog box, shown in Figure 2.19. From the Font drop-down list, select the desired font. Sample text will display the selected font with whichever other font parameters that are currently selected. Clicking OK registers the font for use with the current project.

Figure 2.19. The Font Dialog Box.

The Size, Style, and Alignment formatting features are selected in a similar way from the Text drop-down menu. Select the text object, then choose the Text menu item followed by Size or Style. These features control other text properties typically associated with a word processor.

For longer strings of text that need to reside in the same icon, a scroll box is available. To make text scroll, select the text object, then choose Text> Scrolling Text. The scroll box that is created becomes a new object, and the text becomes a string inside of it. By selecting the scroll box object, handles will appear that can be used to change its width and height.

Applying Text Styles Figure 2.20 shows the customary styles that are available with most Windows applications.

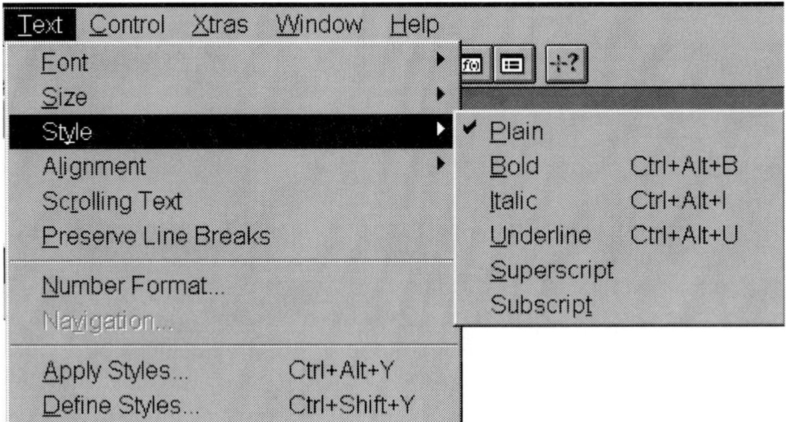

Figure 2.20. Customary Windows Styles are Available Through the Text>Styles Command.

In addition, to save time when formatting text objects, Authorware provides several format styles. You can even add your own style. Format styles allow the author to determine a whole set of properties for text objects that are used repeatedly for other text objects in a project. After a style is established, a text object can be created and the style applied to it. The object will immediately take on all the style properties. The several mouse clicks saved for each object over the course of a project can generate considerable savings of. If the style is changed, all objects given that style will change accordingly. This is another benefit of styles

The Define Styles dialog box, shown in Figure 2.21, contains all text properties in one area. To view it, select Text>Define Styles. Pushing the Add button will create a style called "New Style". The style name should be changed in the box in the lower left of the window where it is highlighted. Style names should be descriptive, like "Section Titles" or "Question Text". After naming the style, select the appropriate parameters.

The sample text window in the upper right corner displays text based on the chosen parameters. Clicking on the Modify button registers all chosen parameters to the style. This button is also used to edit styles any time over the project. Styles not being used in a project can be removed by first selecting them in the style list box and clicking on the Remove button. The option box labeled Interactivity will be covered in Chapter 9.

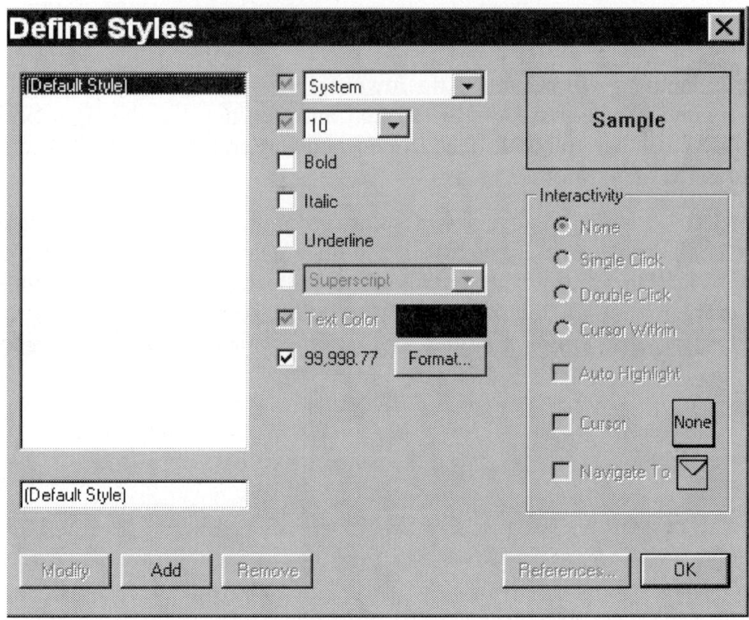

Figure 2.21. The Define Styles Dialog Box.

The Color Palette   The color of text and other objects added to the Presentation window have components that can be changed. To add to or change color of an object, select the object, then choose <u>W</u>indow>I<u>n</u>spectors><u>C</u>olors (or Ctrl+K). The color palette in Figure 2.22 appears. Authorware provides three color components for coloring objects. They are the Pen, Foreground, and Background.

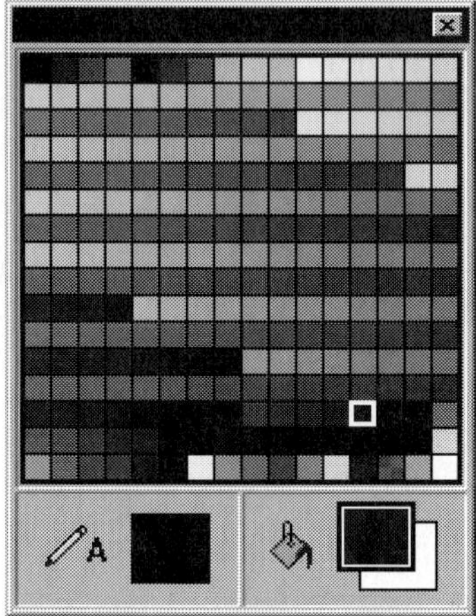

Figure 2.22. The Color Palette.

Clicking on the color swatch in the lower left beside the pencil icon and then a color in the palette, updates the color for selected text and outlines. To the right beside the bucket icon, there are swatches for both background and foreground colors. These color swatches are changed in the same way.

The Modes Palette A text object's background can have one of five different mode properties. These properties are controlled with the modes palette. The modes palette is called up by selecting <u>M</u>odes from the <u>W</u>indow>I<u>n</u>spectors menu. It is shown in Figure 2.23. Properties in the mode palette control how the object is displayed and how it interacts with other objects. The most common modes for text objects are Opaque and Transparent.

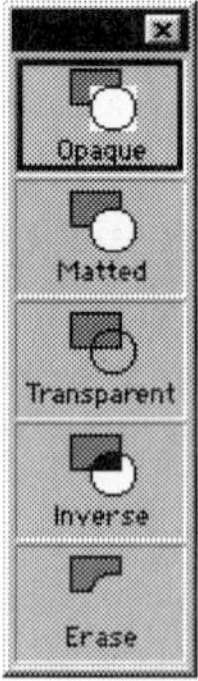

Figure 2.23. The Modes Palette Dialog Box.

An *opaque* object covers its background. Such objects display quickest and consume the least memory. A *matted* object acts like an opaque one, but white space is removed from the edges of the object. A *transparent* object permits its background to show through. *Inverse* objects display inverted colors if shown against a nonwhite background. If the background is white, the colors are not inverted. Finally, *erase* objects show only the project background through their outline.

Drawing Tools

The other six tools in the toolbox are all used for creating graphic objects. These tools also have additional palettes, such as Line and Fill, which can change object appearance.

The same steps are used for using all drawing tools except the polygon tool.

- Choose the tool.
- Place the cursor in the desired starting area of the object.
- Hold down the left mouse button and drag to the desired stopping point.

The Straight (Restricted) Line Tool The Straight or Restricted Line Tool is used to give additional control when drawing line objects. Using this tool, lines are restricted to horizontal, vertical or 45-degree increments in between. This tool is especially helpful when creating grids and adding depth to text boxes. When the standard line characteristics aren't exactly what you want, you can change them by using the Line Palette, shown in Figure 2.24. The palette is made visible by selecting Window>Inspectors> Lines (or Ctrl+L).

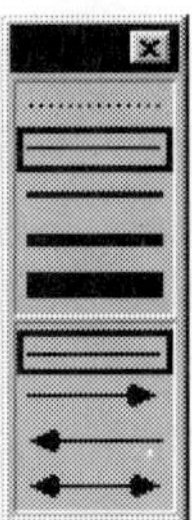

Figure 2.24. The Line Palette. Activate it by Choosing Window>Inspectors>Lines.

Lines drawn with any of Authorware's toolbox draw objects have several properties. The Line Palette controls line thickness and type. Any line can be made thicker or thinner until transparent. As you will see, transparent lines are useful when using the Oval, Rectangle, Rounded Rectangle, and Polygon drawing tools. Only lines created with the Restricted and Diagonal Line tools can utilize the arrow types on the line palette. Line color can be changed using the color palette's pen color feature.

The Diagonal Line Tool ⬚ The Diagonal Line Tool shares all the properties of the Straight Line Tool with the exception of its drawing restrictions. This tool gives the author the most freedom of any tool in the toolbox. Lines of any length and angle can be created with it.

The Oval and Rectangle Tools ⬚ ⬚ The Oval and Rectangle Tools function identically. The difference between them is the shapes they create. They can each operate freely or restricted by holding down the shift key. When restricted, the Oval Tool will create only circles and the Rectangle Tool only squares. As well as having color and line properties, these objects also have fill capabilities.

We've worked a bit with the rectangle tool already, when we constructed **Mywork2a**. If this file isn't open, do open it at this time.

☞ Your Turn

- ❏ Turn on the grid (remember to open **Mywork2a** if it isn't already open).
- ❏ Draw a circle having a diameter of about four reference marks. Fill it with the color red.
- ❏ Fill the rectangle you previously created with the color blue.
- ❏ Move the circle so it is above the rectangle. Now we'll practice selecting, aligning and moving multiple objects.
- ❏ Move the circle above and to the right of the rectangle.
- ❏ Now select both objects.
- ❏ Align them so the circle and the rectangle are aligned along their tops.
- ❏ Save your work.

The Fill Palette Any draw object created using the Oval, Rectangle, Rounded Rectangle or Polygon drawing tools has a fill property. The fill property is controlled via the Fill Palette shown in Figure 2.25. It's opened by selecting Window>Inspectors>Fills. The most commonly used options in the Fill Palette are None, Transparent, and Solid. These are the first three selections in the first column in Figure 2.25.

With None is selected, the object can always be seen through. The Transparent selection is actually the color white and the object's mode selection will determine how it is displayed. The Solid selection displays the fill color selected in the color palette. All other options of the Fill Palette are various patterns of the transparent and solid fills. Objects given these patterns, retain both the Transparent and Solid implementation.

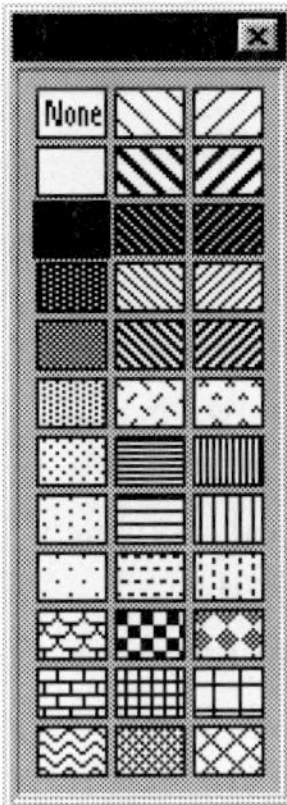

Figure 2.25. The Fill Palette.

In Figure 2.26 are three examples of an oval object with its line mode set to thickest and fill set to solid. The second oval has its line property set to transparent and its fill set to none, while the third has the line set to thick and fill to none.

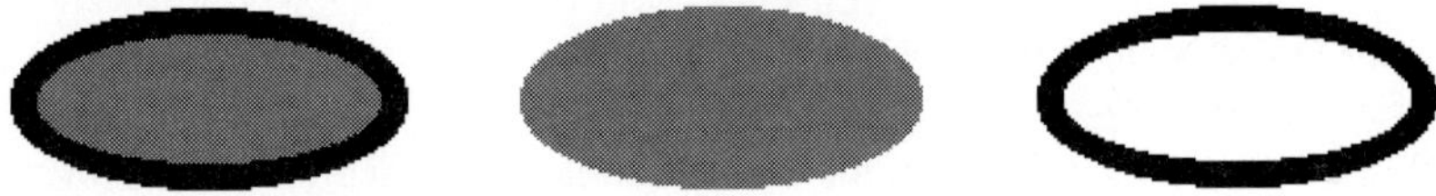

Figure 2.26. Examples Of The Same Object With Different Combinations of Fills And Lines.

The Rounded Rectangle Tool The Rounded Rectangle Tool is somewhat of a combination of the Oval and Rectangle Tools. When a rounded rectangle object and the Rounded Rectangle Tool are selected, an extra handle appears inside the object. This handle can be used to manipulate the roundness of the perimeter edges. Based on the handle position, the object can be transformed into at any shape between a rectangle and an oval (see Figure 2.27).

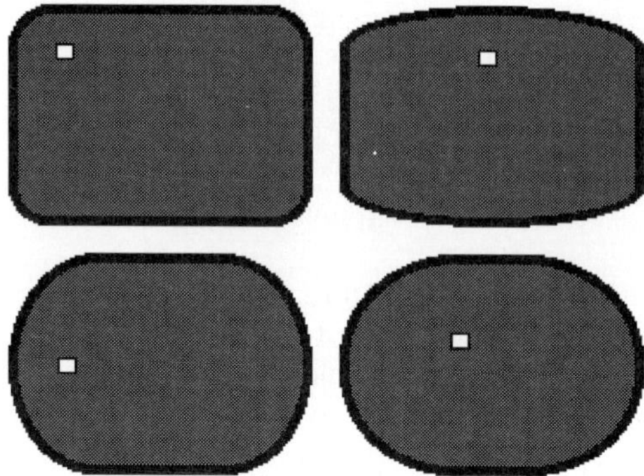

Figure 2.27. Uses for the Rounded Rectangle Tool. Note the different positions of the handles and the corresponding shapes created from the same base object.

The Polygon Tool The Polygon Tool is used to create objects with multiple sides. You might use this to draw a check mark that is placed next to a choice made by a user, or a customized button. Each time you click, you define another point along an edge. There are two basic ways to use this tool:

- Usually, the last click will be in the same location as your first. When this is the case the shape closes with a line around its exterior.

- Double-clicking the mouse instead of single clicking will close the object without an exterior line between the last two points.

Figure 2.28 illustrates these points.

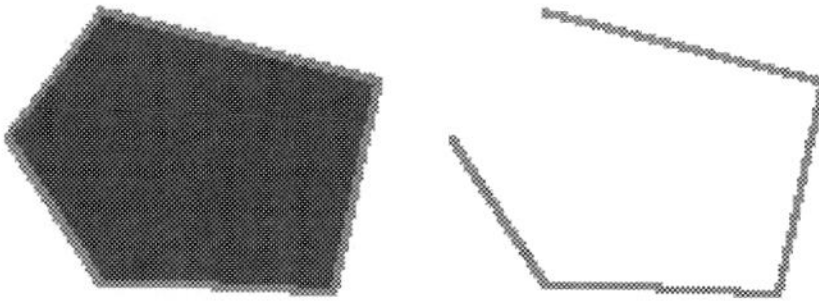

Figure 2.28. The Polygon Tool. The first object was started and closed on the same point. The second was closed with a double-click and filled "none".

CHANGING DISPLAY ICON CHARACTERISTICS

Associated with icons are three major characteristics: transitions, layers, and position. Layers determine the position of the icon's contents relative to other icons, and transitions refer to special effects as icon content is displayed or erased. Recall that we briefly discussed Transition effects in Chapter 1.

We provide icon property values through the Icon Properties dialog box, shown in Figure 2.29. In that figure we have chosen to display information about a display icon, thus the name you see in the title bar of the dialog box. To open it, select the icon, then choose the Modify>Icon>Properties menu item.

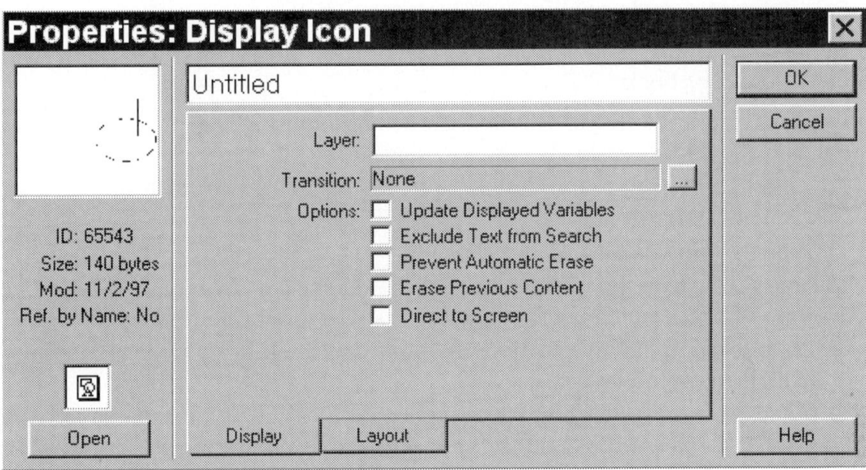

Figure 2.29. The Properties Display Icon Dialog Box. Open it by selecting the icon, then choosing the Modify>Icon>Properties menu item.

The Display Tab

The Display tab is used to change the layer, transition, and several display characteristics of objects in the Presentation window. First, let's review layers. Layers can be associated with objects and icons.

Setting an Object's Layer

Objects are assigned layer numbers in the order in which they are added to the display. To change an object's layer:

- Select the object.

- Choose <u>M</u>odify><u>S</u>end to Back or <u>M</u>odify><u>B</u>ring to Front.

Icons can also be assigned layers through the Layer field in the Display Icon Properties dialog box we saw in Figure 2.29. The higher the icon layer value, the closer the objects within the display icon are to the front. This is used extensively with buttons. We want buttons to always be visible, so we assign icons containing buttons high layer values.

Setting an Icon's Layer

To change an icon's layer value:

- Select the icon on the flowline.

- Choose the <u>M</u>odify><u>I</u>con><u>P</u>roperties menu item. This opens the Icon Properties dialog box (see Figure 2.29).

- Enter a value in the Layer text box, shown in Figure 2.29. The value can be between 0 and 255.

☞ Your Turn
❑ Open **Mywork2a.a4p**.
❑ Drag the box on top of the ellipse. What happened? Why didn't the box end up on top? It was added before the ellipse, so it is on the bottom layer.
❑ Try to change the layer of just the box. Use the <u>M</u>odify><u>I</u>con><u>P</u>roperties menu item, then enter a layer value.
❑ It doesn't work as all objects in the icon are assigned the same layer value. All you can do is use the <u>S</u>end to Back or <u>B</u>ring to Front options- You can't specify an exact layer value to an object
❑ A work-around is to place each object in a separate icon, then assign suitable layer values to each icon.
❑ Remove the ellipse from the display, add a second display named Icon2, then draw the ellipse in that icon.
❑ Assign the layer values of the two icons so the box is on top of the ellipse.
❑ Add a third icon (Icon3) and add a triangle (use the Polygon Tool). Color it yellow, and place it on a layer between the other two objects.
❑ Move all three objects around and place them on top of each other. Which is on top? In the middle? Do you understand why?
❑ Save your work again.

Transitions

There are a number of options that determine how the content of a display icon is first displayed or transitioned on the screen. The Transition button on the Icon Properties dialog box (see Figure 2.29) gives the author the opportunity to make the presentation of elements more dramatic and effective by changing how objects appear and for how long. The Transition dialog box shown in Figure 2.30 sorts transitions by category. Authorware was designed to have a number on transitions developed internally (hence the internal category) and to provide an open architecture for development of transition by third parties.

The Duration field in the Transition dialog box determines the length of time in seconds a transition will take to complete. In the Smoothness field, transition granularity is specified. A lower value will result in the smoother transition. Using higher values results in coarser transitions. The Affects option determines whether the transition updates the entire window or just an area governed by the size of all the objects in the transitioning display icon. A preview of the transition with all the selected options can be seen at any time by clicking on the Apply button.

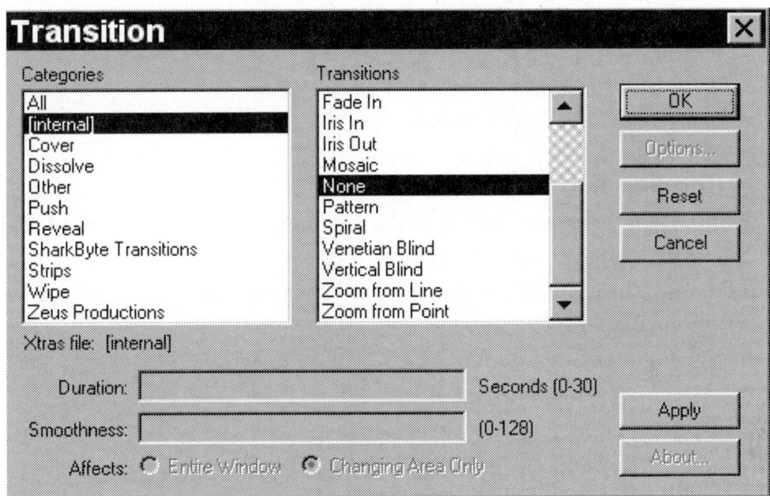

Figure 2.30. The Transition Dialog Box.

Sample File If you want to preview what you're going to do, open the **Pencil.a4w** file in the Chapter2 folder on your CD-ROM.

Your Turn

❑ Start a new project.

❑ Add a display icon and name it Pencil.

❑ You are going to create a pencil, so begin by drawing the pencil's tip using the polygon tool.

❑ Use the Rectangle Tool to add the barrel of the pencil.

❑ Add another rectangle as the eraser.

❑ Fill the tip in black.

❑ Use a yellow fill pattern for the barrel.

❏ Color the eraser a pink color.
❏ Add a new display icon and call it Text.
❏ Add a scrolling text box to the right of the pencil.
❏ Add this text:

"This is a pencil.
It was drawn using only the *toolbox*, which is available within the Presentation window.
It was drawn using the Polygon and Rectangle Tools".

❏ Make the word "pencil" red and the word "toolbox" blue.
❏ Select the Text icon.
❏ Choose <u>M</u>odify><u>I</u>con><u>P</u>roperties.
❏ Select [internal], Iris In.
❏ Change the duration to 3 seconds.
❏ Add another display icon.
❏ Name it Import.
❏ Import the **Purpose.rtf** file in the Chapter2\Text folder on the CD-ROM.
❏ Change the text from scrolling to standard.
❏ Position the text so it's near the top of your piece.
❏ Run the piece.
❏ Save your work as **Pencil.**

Options

There are five options that can be turned on or left off.

Update Displayed Variables When we cover variables we'll return to this feature then because you will see more use for it at that time. A variable is an item whose value can changed. If the variable's name is enclosed in braces {Score}, for example, and if the Update Displayed Variables checkbox is checked, then whenever the variable's value changes, the new value will be automatically displayed. While it slows down performance, it is usually a good idea to check this box.

Exclude Text from Search One of Authorware's powerful features is the ability to search icons for text. Checking the Exclude Text from Search box excludes text within the selected icon from the scope of the search.

Prevent Automatic Erasure When Authorware exits from many icon-types, it automatically erases objects in the Presentation window. Check the Prevent Automatic Erasure box to prevent this from occurring. Be forewarned, however, you'll find that icons seem to erase when you don't want them to, and don't seem to erase when you do want them to. Properly controlling the appearance or disappearance of icons content can be frustrating. Many other icon-types also have options that control the automatic erasure of icon content, so look at the properties of thew individual icon as well as at this property, while you're debugging your piece.

Erase Previous Content This option erases objects still visible, that were added to the Presentation window by previous display icons.

Direct to Screen This option displays objects in the selected icon in front of all others. In effect, it sends all objects in the selected icon to the front (highest layer).

The Layout Tab

Most of these options will be reviewed in Chapter 3, when we discuss moveable objects.

Positioning

Most of the time we want objects to stay where we construct them, but there are exceptions. The Positioning field defines where objects can be moved, if at all. There are four positioning options: No Change, On Screen, In Area, and On Path.

No Change Use No Change when you want Authorware to leave all objects in the display icon right where they were when you or the user last exited the piece.

On Screen The On Screen option permits the object to be moved anywhere but must always remain on the screen. The position can be specified through X,Y coordinates or by dragging to the desired location.

In Area Use the In Area option to force the object(s) to always be within a rectangular area you define as the author.

On Path Choose this option to force the object(s) to follow a pre-set path you define.

Base Initial and End

These three sets of X and Y coordinate values define the boundaries of the allowable area where the object can be moved, and the initial location of objects in the display icon's content. For example, you might define a rectangle and place the object initially in the center of the rectangle. All of these properties will be revisited in Chapter 3.

USING THE ERASE ICON 

The erase icon is used to remove other icons (and their contents) from the Presentation window. When an erase icon is opened, it also opens the Presentation window. The icon of any object clicked on in the Presentation window will be added the erase icon's list of icons to erase. When the erase icon is encountered on the flowline, it reads through the list and erases all appropriate icons with whatever erase options are selected.

The Erase Icon Dialog Box

An erase icon's dialog box (shown in Figure 2.31) contains options that control what happens when the icon is encountered. The transition effects work the same when erasing objects as they do in displaying them. Transition options are applied concurrently to all icons in the erase list.

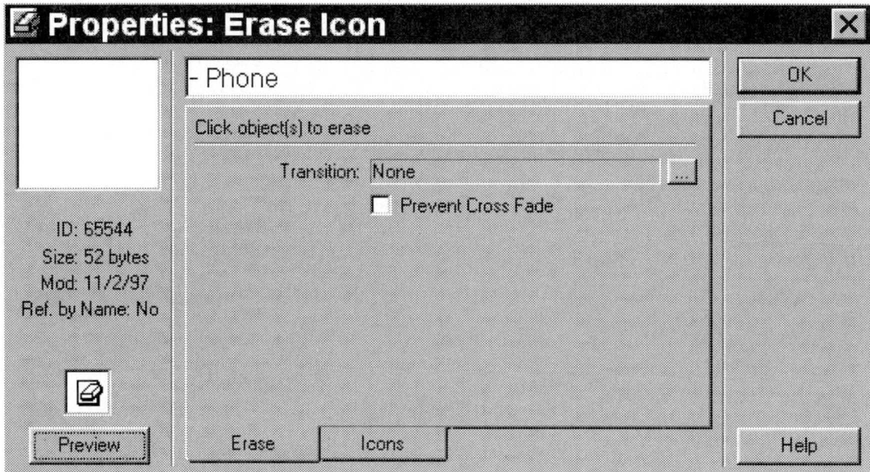

Figure 2.31. The Erase Icon Properties Dialog Box.

The Erase Tab

Prevent Cross-Fade Choosing Prevent Cross-Fade will ensure a complete erasure of the icon content before displaying the objects associated with the next icon in the flowline. This option ensures that images from two or more icons are not visible at the same time.

Transition This option displays the Transitions dialog box discussed earlier in this chapter.

The Icons Tab

Push this tab to reveal Figure 2.32. It's the fields within this tab where we specify which icons to erase or not erase.

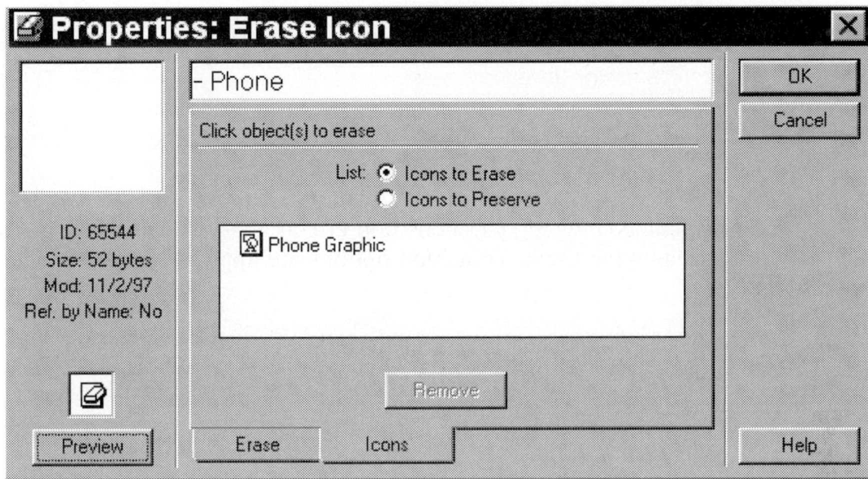

Figure 2.32. The Icons Tab of the Erase Icon Dialog Box.

A frequent approach to multimedia creation is to first add a display icon containing a common background. Other objects are then added to that background in successive icons. In most cases, it wouldn't be desirable to erase the background, instead, erasing objects that appear on top of the background is preferable. In this example, choosing the Background icon as the one to not erase (Icons to Preserve) would create the desired effect.

Remove Button Push the Remove button to delete an icon from the list of icons previously chosen as a candidate for erasure. Assume you have selected five icons to erase. Now you change your mind about the third one. Click on the third one, then push the Remove button, and the contents of that third icon will no longer be erased.

USING THE WAIT ICON 

The wait icon is the simplest form of interaction. It stops the program flow until a condition it is anticipating is met. The condition can be based on user responses such as a mouse click anywhere on the screen, pressing any key on the keyboard or clicking on a button it generates labeled "Continue". These are all options given in the Wait Icon Properties dialog box, shown in Figure 2.33.

Besides waiting for a Mouse Click or Key Press event to terminate the wait, Authorware can also be made to pause for a certain interval of time. The time limit is set in the dialog box, as you can see from Figure 2.33. The Time Limit field can accept either an actual number or a variable. When the Show Countdown box is checked, the Presentation window presents a small clock icon that ticks away the remaining time.

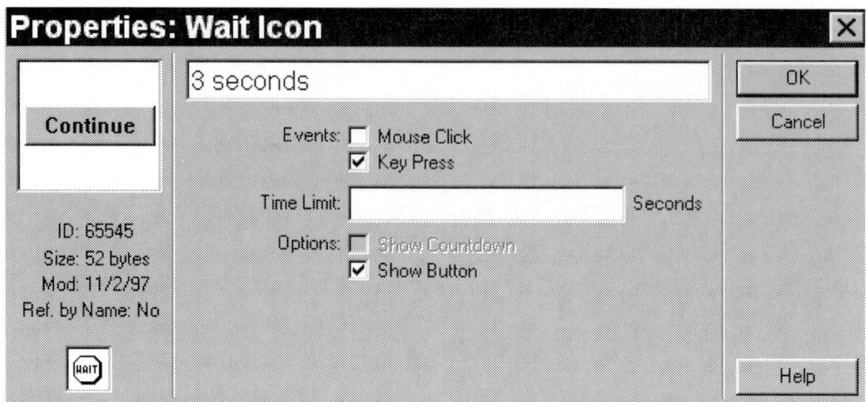

Figure 2.33. The Wait Icon (Wait Options) Dialog Box.

If you don't want to show the Continue button, deselect the Show Button check box.

USING THE MAP ICON

The map icon is used to group icons into a single icon. It is through using it that we overcome the physical limit imposed on the length of the flowline, and it provides a way to organize icons that have a common purpose.

Grouping and the Map Icon

After starting an Authorware project, it is possible to quickly run out of room in the main flowline window. The map icon was designed to alleviate this problem. A map icon bundles any number of selected icons, including other map icons, into a single icon.

There are two ways to populate a map icon. The first method is to place a map icon on the flowline and then double-click on it to display a new flowline window. Icons can now be dragged or pasted from one flowline window to the next. The other technique is accomplished by selecting a group of icons and then choosing Group from the Modify menu. In this manner, a map icon will be left in the place of the previously selected icons.

In order to keep track of all the different flowline windows, window levels are specified (see Figure 2.34). The main flowline window is at Level 1. Each subsequent map icon adds a level. A map, in a map, on the main flowline would be considered in Level 3.

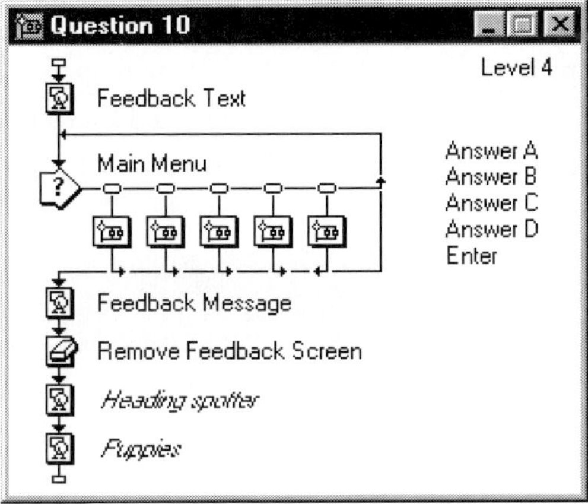

Figure 2.34. An Exploded Map Icon. This map is in Level 4, three layers down from the main flowline.

AN INTRODUCTION TO LIBRARIES

Authorware libraries provide a mechanism to keep projects organized and efficient. A *library* is a file kept outside of the Authorware code file into which icons can be stored. The files have a .a4l extension. Once in a library, icons can be used repeatedly in the code file adding small amounts of storage space. The benefits of the relationship of the code file to the library are:

- When common elements are updated in a library, they are immediately updated in the entire project.
- Libraries can organize files by data type.
- Libraries can be shared by multiple authors concurrently when working on large projects with many common elements.
- Total application file sizes are more efficient.
- Application executable file size can be kept smaller and therefore will generally run faster and better.

Creating a New Library

Libraries can only contain display, interaction, sound, movie, and calculation icons. To create a new library, follow these steps:

- Select File>New>Library (Ctrl+Alt+N).
- The Library window, shown in Figure 2.35, will open.
- Drag icons from the flowline to the just opened Library window.
- To save the library, select the Library window by clicking in its title bar area, then choose File> Save. Authorware will assign a .a4l extension.

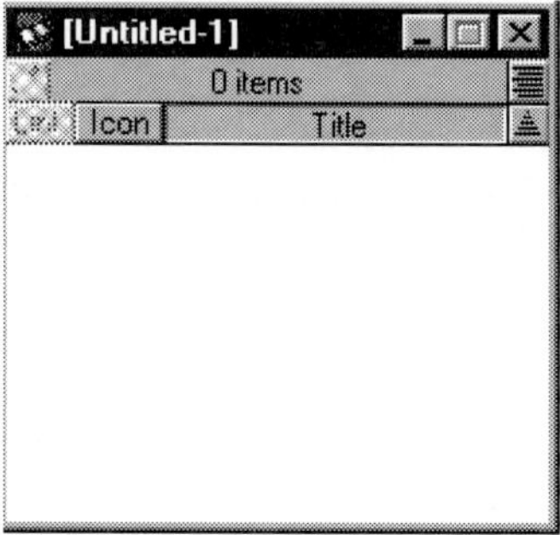

Figure   2.35. An   Untitled   Library   Window.   It   is   opened   by   selecting   the File>New>Library menu command.

Using Existing Libraries

To open an existing library, follow these steps:

- Choose the File>Open>Library menu command.
- This opens the Open Library dialog box, shown in Figure 2.36.

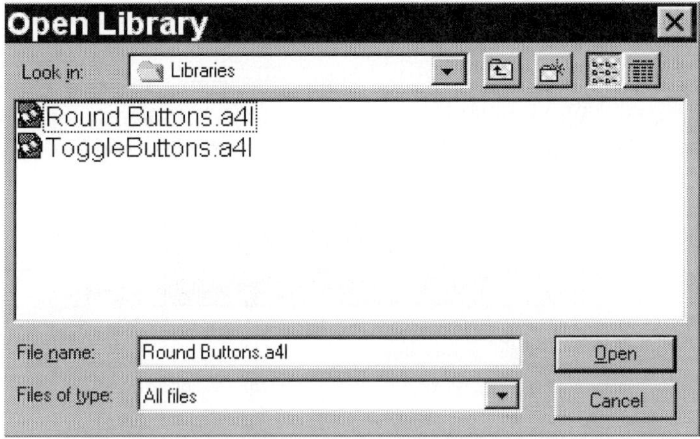

Figure 2.36. The Open Library Dialog Box. Use it to select the library file to open.

Adding Content from a Library

Once a library is open, icons can be dragged from it to the to the flowline. Icons added to the flowline from a library cannot be edited. They must be edited in the library. This is because Authorware creates "links" in the code file that points to the actual icon in the library. This is an important point, one that students often overlook.

Editing a Library Icon

As we just stated, you cannot edit the content of an icon that was dragged from the Library to the flowline. Instead, you must double-click on the icon in the library. The Presentation window for that icon will open and you can make any necessary changes. Alternatively, you can also use Edit/Copy Edit/Paste to select the icon from the library and paste onto the flowline. Icons added this way can be edited, but you have severed the link between the library and the flowline, negating most of the benefits of having a library.

An Authorware project can have many libraries. The Libraries option under the Window menu displays all libraries that the current project has links to. Whether or not a library is displayed on the interface, its links are kept intact.

Library Window

Library windows (shown in Figure 2.37) provide many options to view and organize icons. Each icon can have a title and an information string. The icon in the top right of the window toggles the displayed view from titles only (▤) to titles and information (▤). Icons can be sorted by linked and unlinked icon type, title, creation date, and link name. Switching among the sorting options is accomplished by clicking on the appropriate button in the library window header. For each of these options, the icons can be sorted in increasing (⊟) or decreasing order (⊟) by pushing the appropriate icon, found just to the right of the sort category buttons. When sharing a library, the pencil icon in the top left corner of the window must be set to the locked position (⊠). This locks the library so that no changes can be made to it.

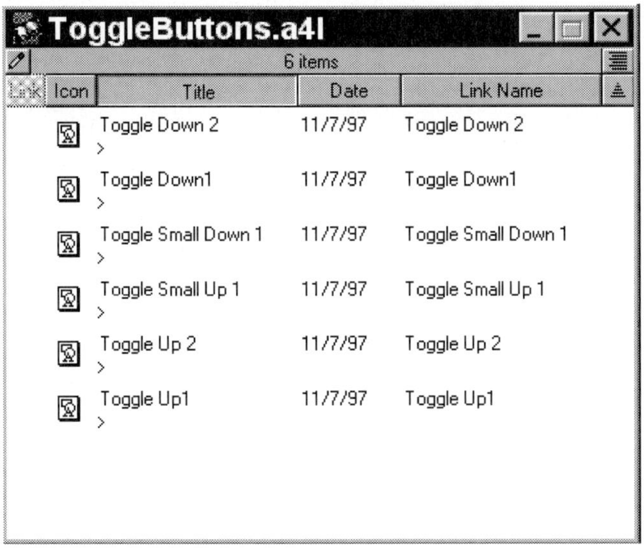

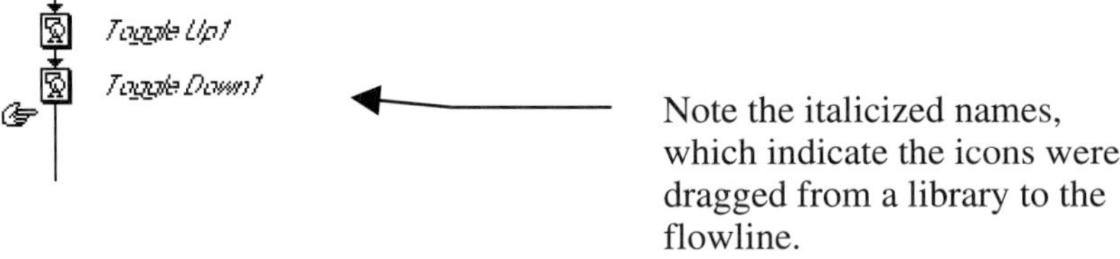

Figure 2.37. A Library Window. This library is ToggleButtons.a4l.

When you drag an icon from the library to your flowline, its name will be italicized, as you can see in Figure 2.38. When an icon is linked to an icon on the flowline, a link symbol (⌗) appears beneath the Link column in the Library window.

Note the italicized names, which indicate the icons were dragged from a library to the flowline.

Figure 2.38. Icon Names are Italicized if the Icons came from a Library.

Sample File You can preview what you're going to do next by running the **Erase.a4p** file in the Chapter2 folder on the CD-ROM.

Your Turn

❑ Start a new piece.

❑ Add a display icon and name it Background.

❑ Import the **Backgrnd** bitmap in the Chapter2\Images folder.

❑ Add a display icon and name it Title.

❑ Use Shift+double-click to open the Title icon's Presentation window and add this white transparent text near the top of the background: "An exercise in waiting and erasing". It's important that you make the text transparent (use the modes inspector) so it shows on top of the image.

❑ Add a wait icon. Set it up so it waits 3 seconds, shows the countdown clock, and doesn't display a button.

❑ Add an erase icon named "- Title". Make it erase the title using the transition Zoom to Line in four seconds.

❑ Add another display icon. Name it "By".

❑ Add your name near the bottom of the Presentation window using this format "By: Your Name". Again use white transparent text. Use a font other than the default one, and make it 12-point bold.

❑ Wait three seconds, then erase your name using a wait then an erase icon. Don't show the countdown clock this time. Call the erase icon "-By".

❑ Select the icons between and including Title and "-By".

❑ Group them into a map icon under the name Intro. The Intro map flowline should look this way:

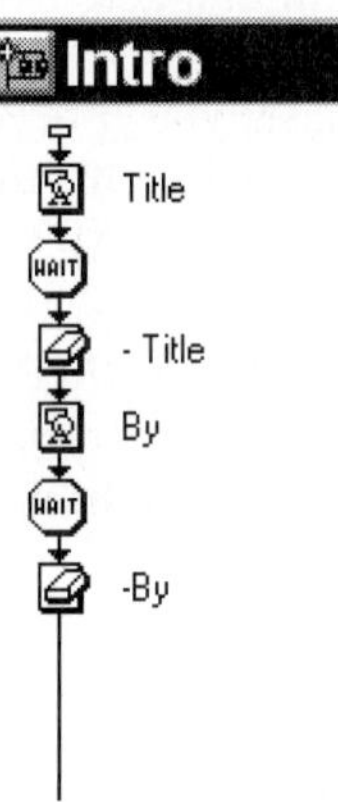

❑ Open the RoundButtons library in the Libraries folder on your CD-ROM.

❑ Drag the *Round Up 1* member to your flowline right after the Intro map icon.

❑ Run the piece

❑ Notice that the button isn't transparent. Make the image transparent by following the next three bulleted steps.

- Double-click the *Round Up 1* icon in the Library dialog box.
- Choose the Mode inspector (Ctrl+M).
- Select the Transparent option.

❑ Position the button so it is in the lower left corner of the background.

❑ Your flowline should look this way:

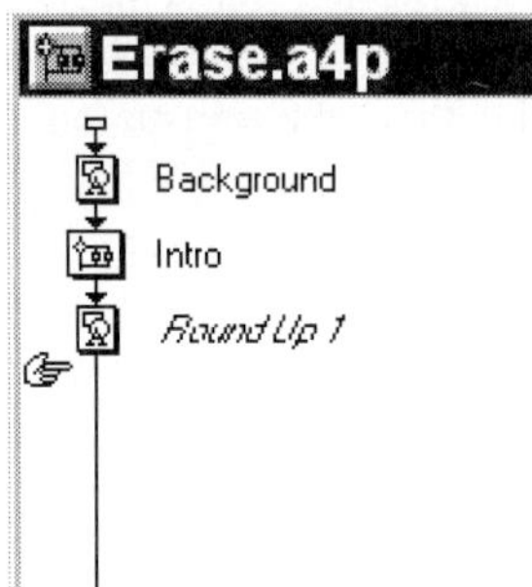

❑ Save your work as **Erase.**

❑ When asked if you want Authorware to save the changes to the RoundButtons library, you'll have to say no, unless you've copied the Library folder to your hard drive. This is because you cannot write to a CD-ROM.

The final activity for this chapter is to add to the continuing digital video piece began in the previous chapter. So far, all we've done is specify the overall characteristics of the file. Recall we called it DigVid1. If you are using the working model version of Authorware you couldn't save your work at the end of the last chapter. In that case, you'll need to open **DigVid.a4p** in the Chapter1 folder. Otherwise open your copy of DigVid1 at this time.

Your Turn

❑ Add a display icon, name it Template, and import **Tmplate7.BMP** from the Templates folder on the CD-ROM.

❑ Add a second display icon, name it Panel, and import **Panel7a.bmp** from the Backgrounds folder on the CD-ROM.

❑ Crop the image to 377 X 52 pixels.

❑ Place the panel above the template.

❑ Center the panel.

❑ Open the Panel display icon.

❑ Open the Lines inspector and choose a thick line.

❑ Select the Rounded Rectangle tool.

❑ Draw a rounded rectangle around the resized panel. Size the two objects so the rounded rectangle looks as though it's a border around the panel.

❑ Use the color inspector to make the line a dark blue.

❑ Open the RoundButtons library.

❑ Double-click the Round Up 1 member and make it transparent.

❑ Drag the Round Up 1 library member to the flowline.

❑ Position the button so it covers the opening in the upper left corner of the template.

❑ Drag another display icon to the flowline and name it Title.

❑ Open the Title icon and add this dark blue 25-point text inside the panel "Digital Video". Use the same blue you used for the lines. Make the text transparent and use a transition of your choice.

❑ Save your work as **DigVid2**.

SUMMARY

You have seen how to use display icons to add and import graphics and text. When several objects appear on the same Presentation window, they are assigned layer values corresponding to the sequence in which they were added. The layer values of both objects on the screen and icon layers can be modified. It is often advantageous to show grid lines and make objects snap to the grid. Use the align option to make objects align in a common fashion.

The contents of icons are displayed one after another until all the icons on the flowline are executed. To pause the display, use the wait icon. To remove an icon's contents from the display, use the erase icon. When the flowline gets too long, group two or more icons into map icons.

Use libraries to store assets that are used multiple times in one or more presentations. Each time you add a graphic to a display icon, it consumes additional disk space. Items dragged from libraries multiple times are only stored once. This not only saves storage space but also makes maintenance easier because only one copy of the asset must be changed.

Study Exercises

2.1 Create a new project called C2Q1. Add a display, a wait and an erase icon, followed by a second display icon Draw your own graphics in the first display icon. Color some of the objects. Move them around. What happens when you drag one object on top of another? After 7 seconds, erase the objects. Add some text in the second display icon. Make the text scroll.

2.2 Create a new project called C2Q2. Drag a display icon and open the Presentation window and use the Rounded Rectangle Tool to draw a red button. Create a drop shadow around it. Label it Next. (Hint: copy and paste the original button. Move the new button down and color it black. Slide the black button beneath the original but "nudge" it two pixels down and two to the right using the cursor/arrow keys. You will also need to place the black version of your button to a layer beneath the red one by using Attributes Send to back).

2.3 Create a new project called C2Q3. Add a display icon and create a circle, a square, and an ellipse. Color each a different color. Add an erase icon and erase just the circle. What happened? Why? Fix the problem so the circle can be erased, while leaving the square and the ellipse.

2.4 Create a new piece named C2Q3. Add two display icons, one named BG, one named Buttons. Import the Tmplate8 bitmap. Scale it so it fits an 640 X 480 Presentation window. Into the Buttons icon, import TBUp4 and Tbup GIF images. Make them transparent and move the buttons so one fits in each of the first two round holes on the right side, as shown below.

Finally, use a third display icon to create a small white square that covers the rectangle in the center of Tmplate8.

Movement

Now that we have the capability to create and remove objects from the display, if we animate objects and allow the user to interact with them, our programs will come alive. There are several ways to show animation or movement in an Authorware piece. The most common method uses the motion icon. A motion icon lets Authorware move an object using a predetermined set of parameters. A second approach uses objects in a display icon. This approach invites the user to interact with the objects in the program. This chapter looks at the different motion types, user initiated movement, and introduces you to packaging a project into an application.

At the conclusion of this chapter, you will be able to:

- Setup a series of icons on the flowline for an animation sequence.
- Animate display icon objects using a motion icon.
- Select the appropriate motion type for a situation.
- Create objects that move in response to user interaction.

- Create an Authorware executable.

THE MOTION ICON - ANIMATING

Authorware provides a variety of animation options within the motion icon. They are broken down into two types — Direct Motion and Along Paths. A motion icon moves digital movies or display icon objects. In its simplest form, animation or movement is accomplished by dragging an object while in author mode. Authorware tracks the movement and records it automatically. All objects in the selected icon being moved are animated, so if you want to move a single object, place it in its own icon.

Authorware provides a variety of animation or motion types within the motion icon, but all are created using the same basic process:

- Add a display object icon with the item(s) to be moved.
- Add a motion icon.
- Specify the motion parameters.

Common Dialog Box Elements

As you might guess, each motion type has its own set of unique parameters. However, there are several common parameters that we discuss next. When you first open a motion icon, you see a dialog box like the one in Figure 3.1. This dialog box contains parameters common to most motion types.

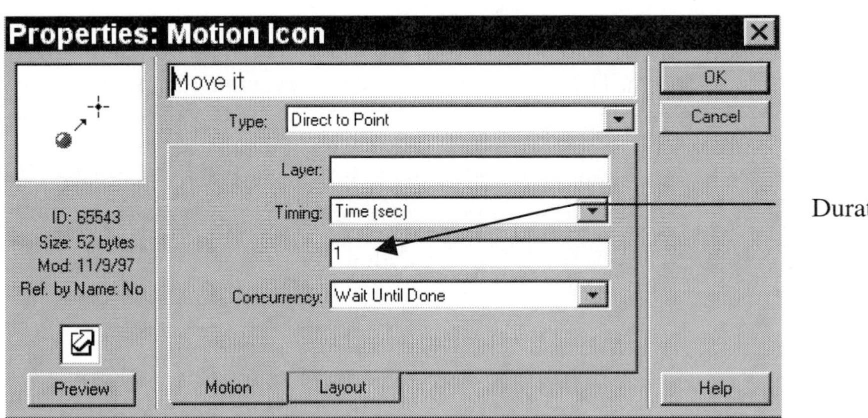

Figure 3.1. The Direct to Point Motion Dialog Box.

This dialog box gives the author the ability to control all aspects of object movement. Let's examine the parameters common to all motion types, beginning with the Type drop-down list.

The Type Drop-Down List

Open the Type drop-down list (see Figure 3.1) to reveal Figure 3.2.

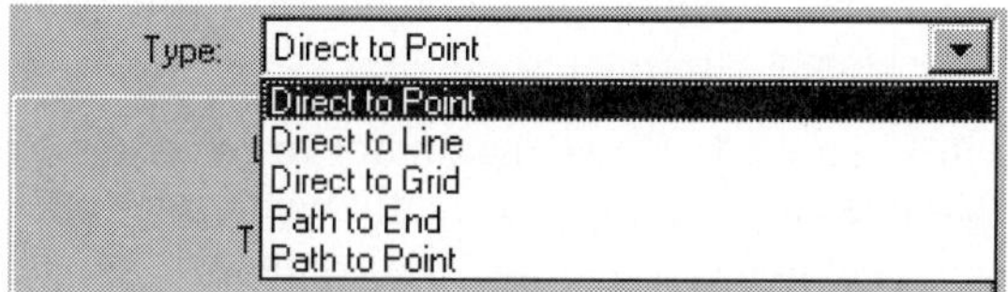

Figure 3.2. The Motion Type Dialog Box.

The Type drop-down list allows the author to switch among five types of object movement. Direct to Point is the default type and will be selected when the Type drop-down list opens. Other options include: Direct To Line, Direct to Grid, Path to End, and Path to Point.

Layer Box

Enter the layer number for the icon being moved. The default value is zero. Animated objects are always shown on top of stationary ones. When several motion icons are active at the same time, the objects associated with the higher layer values will animate on top of those with lower layer values. For example, if you had three motion icons with corresponding layer values of 5, 2 and 10, the objects in the third icon would move on top of those in the first. All objects in the second icon would appear below all others.

Timing Drop-Down List

There are two timing options; Time and Rate. Notice in Figure 3.1 that the option for Time is selected. This means that the object to be animated should take 1 second. If Rate is selected instead, the value entered in the duration text box will be interpreted as "how long it should take to move the object one inch." Monitors have from 72 to 90 pixels per inch. Thus, a setting of 7 means to move the icon contents one inch every 7 seconds. To see the results of altering this (or any) value, push the Preview button.

Concurrency Drop-Down List

The two common timing options are Wait Until Done and Concurrent. The default is Wait Until Done, which means the animation must finish before the next icon is run. If you set the value to Concurrent, the motion begins, then the content of the next icon is executed. That next icon might be another motion icon so you can run several animations at the same time. If you place a sound icon after the motion icon, you can play music or a sound effect while the motion is occurring.

We should point out that some motion types have a third concurrency option — Perpetual, which enables you to move objects even after an icon is exited.

Preview

The Preview button in Figure 3.1 allows the author to replay and review the motion as defined by the current parameters. This is quite useful when fine-tuning your presentation. You can make changes to the parameters, then test the results without having to run the complete program or exit the motion icon.

Duration

Enter the desired duration of the animation in this text box. Note the default units is in seconds, so a value of 8 would mean the animation would run for 8 seconds.

Direct Motion Types

The Layout tab reveals additional parameters. However, these parameters are unique to the chosen type of motion so we'll look at the Layout tab for each motion-type as we discuss that type. If you look at Figure 3.2 again, you'll notice there are two general motion categories: Direct and Path. We begin by discussing the Direct options.

Direct to Point

The default motion type, Direct to Point, causes Authorware to move the selected object(s) along a straight line from its starting point to its end point in the specified amount of time. This means the object will always move along the same path from beginning to end.

To create a Direct to Point animation, follow these steps:

1. Add a display icon that contains the object to be moved.
2. Add a motion icon.
3. Run the piece from the display icon.
4. The dialog box for the Motion Icon Properties opens, as shown in Figure 3.3. The Motion tab will be selected initially.
5. Select Direct to Point as the Type option (the default).
6. Enter a value for Duration, and select a Concurrency option.

7. Push the Layout tab, which opens the dialog box in Figure 3.3.

8. Click on the object to be moved and drag it to its desired final location.

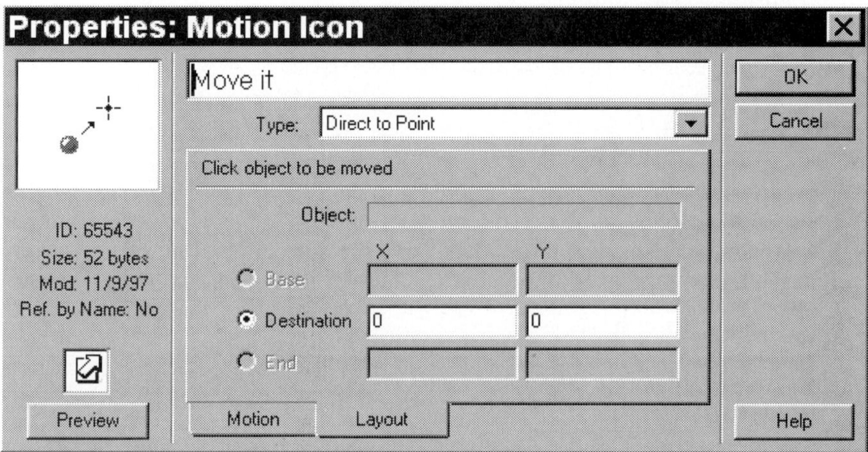

Figure 3.3. The Direct to Point Layout Tab.

Notice in Figure 3.3 that only the Destination fields are active. The X and Y Destination values are relative to the upper left corner of the Presentation window (point 0,0). This means a Destination value of 320,240 would move the selected object one-half of the way down and one-half of the way across the (default) Presentation window. If you are more comfortable with dragging and dropping, you can simply move the selected object to its desired final location, and Authorware will fill in the X,Y values for you. Let's try it.

Sample File To preview the Direct to Point animation, open the **Motion.a4p** file in the Chapter3 folder on the CD-ROM. Place the stop flag just after the Direct To Point icon. Restart from the Flag. Watch the red ball move along a predetermined path to a designated end point. Close the file and start a new piece.

Your Turn

❑ Create a new piece.

❑ Add a display icon and name it Red Ball.

❑ Open its Presentation window and draw a red ball (a circle with a red fill) near the upper left corner.

❑ Add a motion icon.

❑ Name it Direct to Point.

❑ Run the piece and when the Motion Icon Properties dialog box opens, choose Direct to Point as the type.

❑ Push the Layout tab.

❏ Click on the red ball.
❏ Drag the red ball down and to the right.
❏ Push the Preview button to see the effect.
❏ Push the Done button.
❏ Save your work as **Motion.a4p**.

Direct to Line

Like the previous option, this moves an object in a straight line. However, whereas the Direct to Point option moves an object at a predetermined rate along a predetermined path, this option uses a variable or expression to determine the current location of the object along the path. Figure 3.4 shows an example of the Layout tab settings associated with the Direct to Line option.

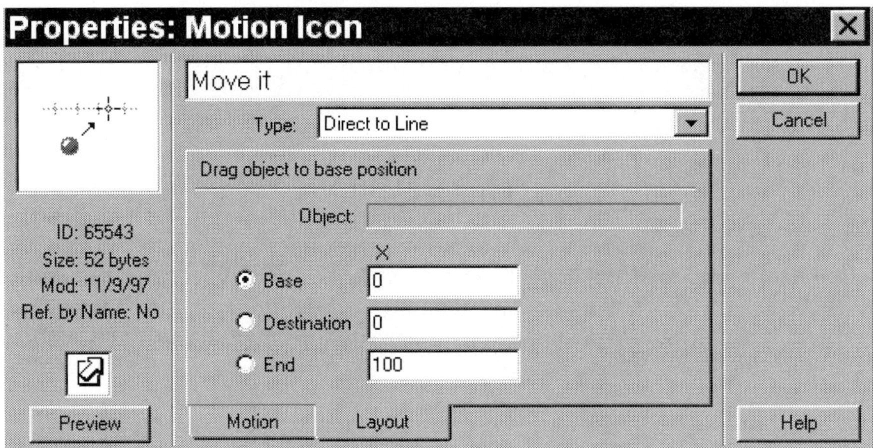

Figure 3.4. An Example of a Direct to Line Motion Type Dialog Box. Use this option to move an object based on a calculation (variable or expression).

As we explained, direct to line makes Authorware move an object along a straight line based on an expression or variable. The lowest value taken on by the variable or expression is called its **base value,** while the highest value is called its **end point**. The final required component is the variable or expression whose value determines the current location of the object along the line. Enter the variable's name in the Destination field.

Follow these steps for creating a direct to line animation:

1. Add a motion icon to the flowline.

2. Open the motion icon.

3. Select the Layout tab.

4. Choose Direct to Line as the motion type

5. Select the object to be animated.

6. Position the object to be animated at its base (starting) location.

7. If the object is already at the desired base location, simply click on the object to signify this fact.

8. Push the End radio button.

9. Drag the object to the desired end position of the line.

10. You will see a line drawn in the Presentation window, which represents the path the object will follow.

11. Push the Destination radio button.

12. Enter a value within the range specified by the base and end values (0 and 1000, by default), 50 for example. Alternatively, enter a variable, expression or function name in the Destination field.

13. The object will position itself along the path proportional to the current value in the Destination box. In the example, the position would be one-half of the distance because 50 is mid-way between 0 and 100.

It's unlikely you would want to always position the object mid-way along a path. Usually, you want to control the location of the object under program control. To do this, enter a variable or expression in the Destination text box.

Sample File To preview the Direct to Line motion, open the **Motion.a4p** file in the Chapter3 folder of the CD-ROM. Position the start flag just before the Green Ball icon, and place the stop flag just after the Direct to Line icon. Run the piece and observe the green ball. It seems to move just as the red ball did. Now double-click on the Direct to Line icon. Push the Layout tab in the Motion Icon Properties dialog box and enter a value of 25 in the Destination field. Push the Done button and watch the green ball. You've told Authorware to move the ball to the location along the path that's 1/4 of the way. Experiment with different values in the Destination box. Let's see how to create this motion. First, close the **Motion.a4p** you opened from the CD-ROM and open your version.

Your Turn

❏ Add a display icon and name it Green Ball.

❏ Open the Presentation window (Shift+double-click on the icon) and draw a green ball.

❏ Add a motion icon and name it Direct to Line.

❏ Run the piece from the start.

❏ When the motion icon properties dialog box opens, select Direct to Line.

❏ Push the Layout tab.

❏ Click on the green ball to designate it's at the start point (move it if you want a different starting point).

❏ Push the End button.
❏ Drag the green ball along a straight line.
❏ This designates the end point.
❏ Save your work (continue to use the **Motion.a4p** file name).
❏ Your Presentation window should now look like Figure 3.5.

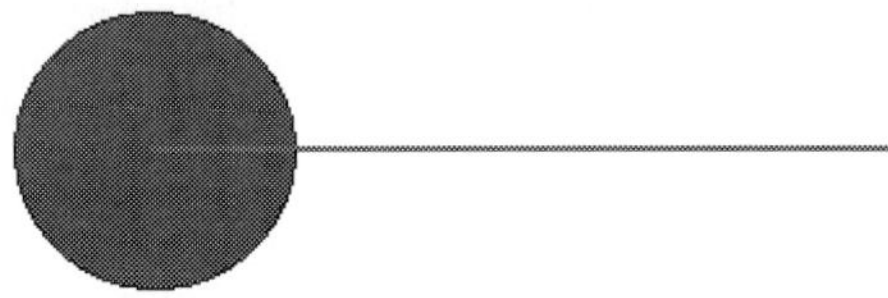

Figure 3.5. The Line that Represents the Path to be Followed when the Direct to Line Path is Defined.

❏ Enter a value of 25 in the Destination box. The Red ball should move to a point about 25% of the way along the path.
❏ Enter a value of 50. Then enter 100.
❏ Enter a value of 150. What happened? The red ball jumped to the end point, even though you exceeded the end point value.

When the end point values are exceeded, there are several options. The default is to stop at the end points. To see this, and the other options, double-click your Direct to Line icon. Then push the Motion tab. You will see a new field, Beyond Range, which can be seen in Figure 3.6.

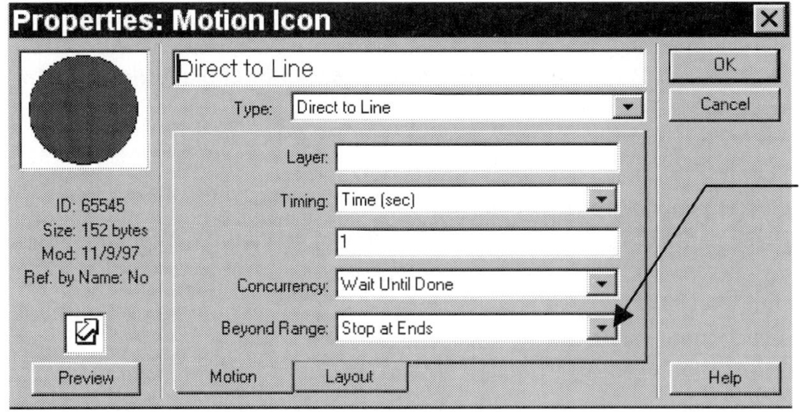

Figure 3.6. The Beyond Range Field. It isn't available for Direct to Point motion, but is for the other motion types.

Beyond Range The beyond range drop-down window parameter specifies what to do if the value of the Destination variable or expression falls outside the range specified by the base and end point values.

Consider a testing example. Imagine a slider that shows the progress of the test taker as each question is answered. Assume when the project was first created there were 50 questions and the base/end points set at 0 and 50. Now assume 10 more questions have been added but no one has changed the end point value. The variable tracking how many questions have been answered will move from 0 to 1 to 2 up to 50, then 51, 52, . . . What should Authorware do when the user begins the 51st question? Use the Beyond Range property to specify the desired action. There are several options. To view these options, open the drop-down list. The first option (the default) is "Stop at Ends".

Stop at Ends If the variable's value or the expression exceeds either extreme, this option moves the selected object to the nearest end point (base or end). Using the previous example, if the user is answering the 51st question, the object would be positioned at the location based on the variable value equaling 50, the closest end point. Once the student completed more than 50 questions, the gauge wouldn't move anymore because the variable would exceed the end point and Authorware was instructed to "stop at the end point". The next option is "Loop".

Loop Much like the previous example, the loop choice moves the selected object to a location based on the variable's value. However, now think of the line as if it were a loop process. If the end points are 0 and 100, then a value of 150 would be like one complete loop plus 50 on the second loop, so the effective location would correspond to a value of 50. Specifically, the exact location is calculated as: Value minus Length. Assume the base is 0 the end 100 and the value of the variable 150. The length is thus 100 (100 minus 0) and the location of the object will be 150 minus (100 minus 0) = 50.

Go past Ends This option causes the object to be moved to a scaled location, just like with the loop option, but if necessary, the object will be moved beyond its end point.

Timing Options Two of the timing choices here are the same as before; Concurrent and Wait Until Done. A third option is Perpetual.

Use Concurrent timing when you want the motion to begin and have Authorware immediately proceed to the next icon. If Wait Until Done is selected, Authorware will not proceed to the next icon until the current movement is completed.

The Perpetual option forces Authorware to continue to monitor the value of the variable even after exiting the motion icon. The object will be moved as long as it continues to appear in the Presentation Window. Motion will continue until the object is erased or another motion icon gains its control.

In the next exercise, we'll use a variable to control the location of a yellow ball. The motion will be perpetual so we can continue to move the ball, even after control passes to other icons. This requires that we create a variable and then change its value several times. As it changes value, the ball should move accordingly. The exercise will introduce you to variables and give you another opportunity to review the motion types we've covered thus far.

Sample File To preview your work, open the **Motion.a4p** file in the Chapter3 folder on the CD-ROM. Run from the beginning of the file and pay attention to the yellow ball. Nothing seems to be happening! That's because the ball is controlled by a variable, `location`. Select Window>Variables, then look for **Motion.a4p** in the Category drop-down list. Select `location` and enter a value of 25 in the Current value box. The ball should move about 1/4 of the way along a path. Enter 50, then 100. You should push the Done button between each entered value. You'll have to keep opening the dialog box to enter the next value. This motion is perpetual, and the location of the ball is determined by the value of a variable. Let's see how to build this. Close the CD-ROM version of **Motion.a4p** and open your version.

Your Turn

❑ Drag a map icon to the flowline and call it Variable Motion.
❑ Open the map and add a display and a motion icon. Name them Show Ball and Move Ball.
❑ Open the Show Ball icon and draw a yellow ball.
❑ Attach a calculation to the Show Ball icon by selecting the icon, then striking Ctrl+= (Control plus the equals sign).
❑ Inside the calculation dialog box that opens, shown in Figure 3.7, enter `location:=0`. (This could have been any name, we simply chose `location`.)

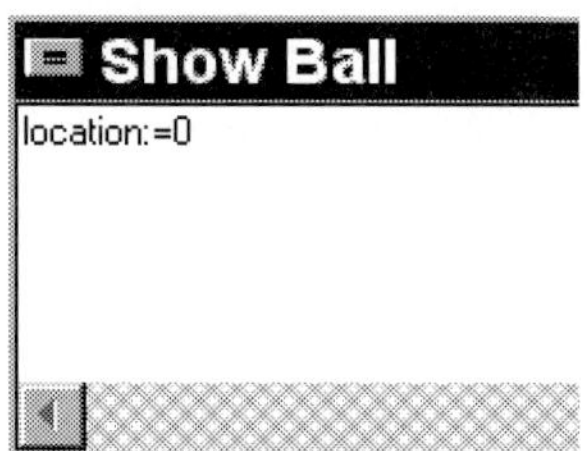

Figure 3.7. Specifying a Calculation. This assigns a value of zero to the (new) variable, location.

The statement shown in Figure 3.7 is an ***assignment statement.*** It assigns a value to a variable, in this case `location`. When the Show Ball calculation dialog box closes, you will notice a small "=" attached to the Show Ball icon. This indicates a calculation is attached to it. Alternatively, we could have added a calculation icon to a location prior to Show Ball, but the above method saves us a step.

❑ Close the box and a dialog box will pop-up.
❑ Push Yes.
❑ A New Variable dialog box opens where you enter an initial value and a description, as in Figure 3.8.

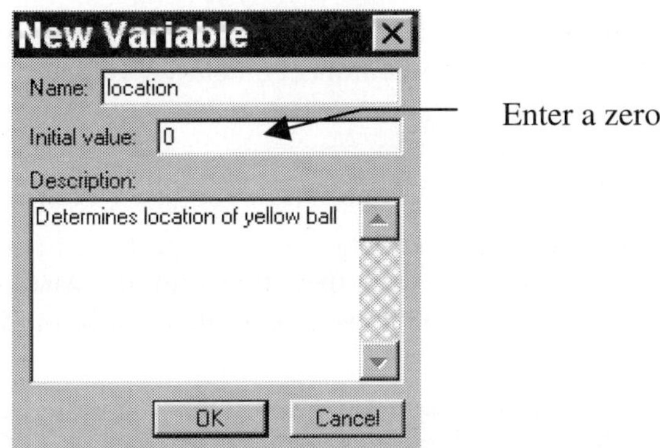

Figure 3.8. Specifying Values for a New Variable.

❏ Add the description and initial values as shown in the New Variable dialog box we just examined.

❏ Open the Variables dialog box, shown in Figure 3.9, by selecting <u>W</u>indow><u>V</u>ariables (Ctrl+Shift+V).

❏ Choose the Motion.a4p line in the Category drop-down list, then click on the `location` variable.

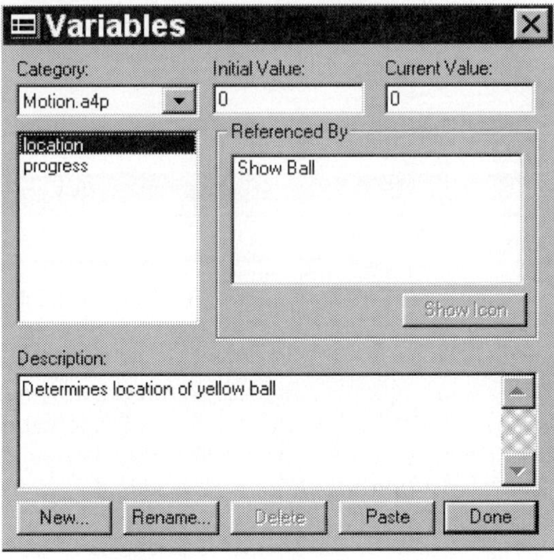

Figure 3.9. The Variables Dialog Box. It can show all Authorware variables or only selected subcategories.

❏ Notice the Initial Value is zero as is the Current Value. The Current Value can be changed within this dialog box, or under program control. We will change the value and watch the impact on our movement.

❏ Drag the start flag to just before the Variable Motion map icon.

❏ Restart from the flag.

❏ The Motion Icon properties dialog box will open.

❏ Select Direct to Line.

❏ Set concurrency to Perpetual (within the Motion tab), and enter `location` as the variable to control the motion, as we have done in Figures 3.10 and 3.11.

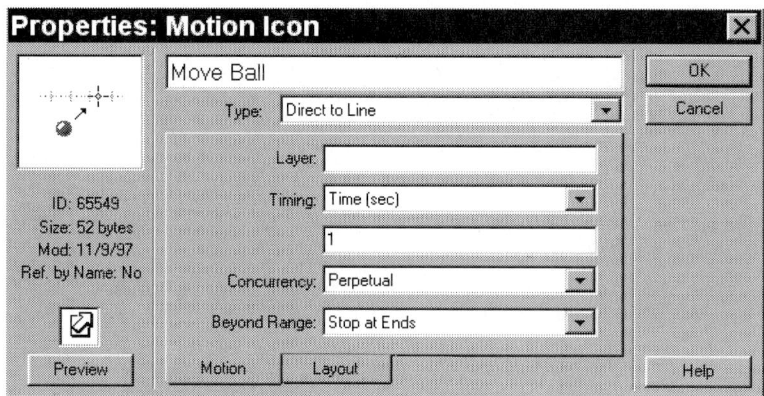

Figure 3.10. The Motion Tab for the Move Ball Icon.

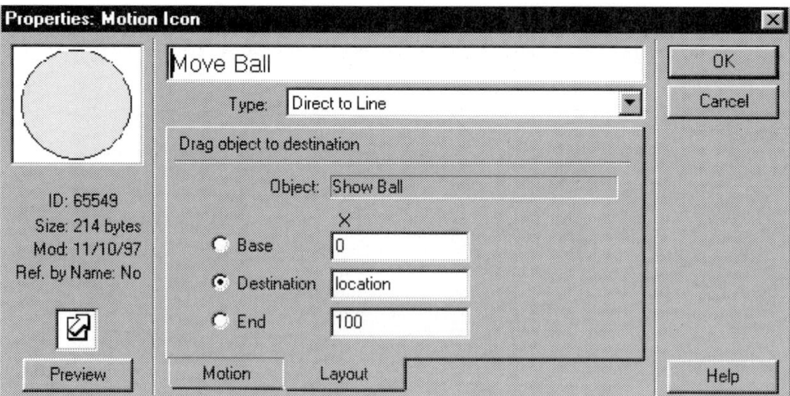

Figure 3.11. The Layout Tab for the Move Ball Icon. Set the variable's name to `location` in the Destination field.

Let's review a moment: The motion will continue, even when we exit (note the Perpetual setting). The path we create will be represented at its end points by values of 0 and 100 (Base and End). To determine the exact location of the object (the ball), Authorware checks the value of a variable we created, location. Finally, if the value of location exceeds 100 or is less than zero, the object is to be placed at the corresponding end point (Stop at Ends). We next need to create the path (define the end points).

❏ With the Move Ball motion dialog box open, drag the ball to its starting position (near the left border).
❏ Click the Base radio button.
❏ Click the End radio button.
❏ Move the ball to the rightmost position.
❏ You have just defined the path.
❏ Push OK when satisfied with the path. Now we need to change the value location and the position of the ball should change accordingly.
❏ Open the Variables dialog box and locate the location variable.
❏ Change the value in the Current Value area to 10.
❏ Click the Done button and watch the ball move accordingly.
❏ Experiment with location values of 25, 50, 75, 100, and 200. (You'll need to keep opening the variables dialog box).
❏ Save your work.

Direct to Grid

Use Direct to Grid motion to position an object within a rectangle, based on the value of two variables or expressions. Recall that we express an object's location in two dimensions by means of two parameters: X (horizontal) and Y (vertical).

To create a Direct to Grid motion, follow these steps:

1. Add a motion icon to the flowline.
2. Double-click the motion icon.
3. Choose Direct to Grid as the motion type.
4. The Direct to Grid motion dialog box, shown in Figure 3.11 opens. The Motion tab will be selected.
5. Enter a duration value and a Concurrency option.
6. Push the Layout tab. The dialog box in Figure 3.12 will open.
7. Select the object to be animated. This object should be inside a display icon that is located higher-up along the flowline.
8. Position the object to be animated at its base (starting) location.
9. If the object is already at the desired base location, simply click on the object to signify this fact.

10. Push the End radio button.

11. Drag the object to the opposite corner: If you started with the lower left corner as the base, drag to the upper right corner.

12. You will see a rectangle drawn in the Presentation window, which represents the path the object will follow.

13. Push the Destination radio button.

14. Enter values, variables, expressions, or Authorware functions in the X and Y boxes. The values entered represent the current location of the object.

15. The object will position itself along the rectangle at the X,Y coordinate specified by the Destination X and Y values.

Figure 3.12 shows the Motion tab of the dialog box for the Direct to Grid motion type.

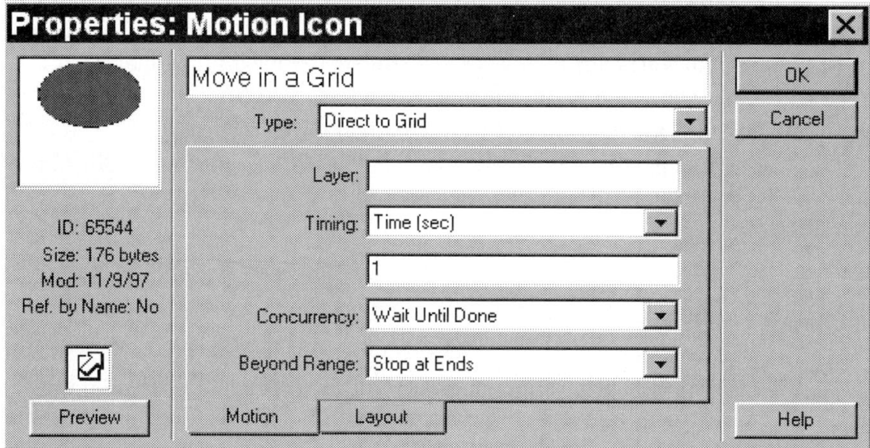

Figure 3.12. The Motion Tab for the Direct to Grid Motion Type.

Figure 3.13 shows the Layout tab for Direct to Grid motion type.

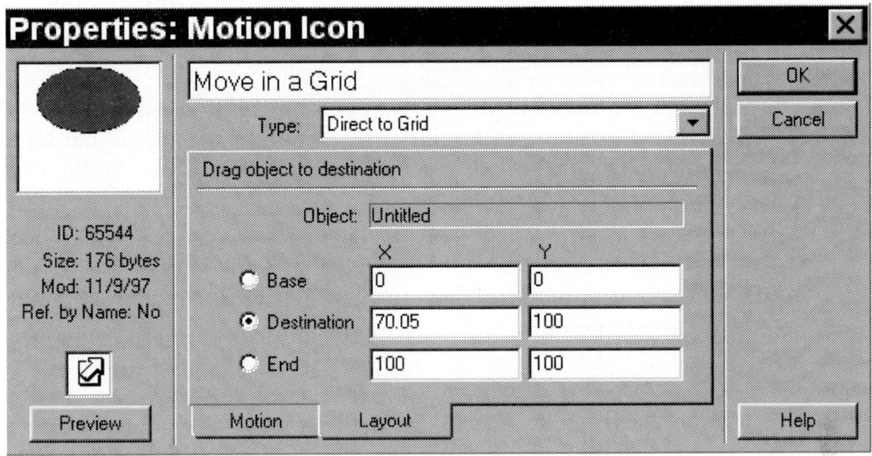

Figure 3.13. The Layout Tab for Direct to Grid Motion Types.

The concurrency, beyond range, duration, and layer parameters are as before. The new parameters include Destination X and Y values.

Destination X and Y Values Enter the variable or expression that determines the X and Y values of the current location of the object. As these two variables change values, the object will move within the grid as defined by the base and end points.

Base and End X and Y Values Here is where we define the grid. Begin by clicking the base button. The dialog box prompts you to drag the object to the upper left corner of the rectangle. Now click the end button and drag the object to the lower right corner. The rectangle shown in Figure 3.14 will be visible when the mouse button is released.

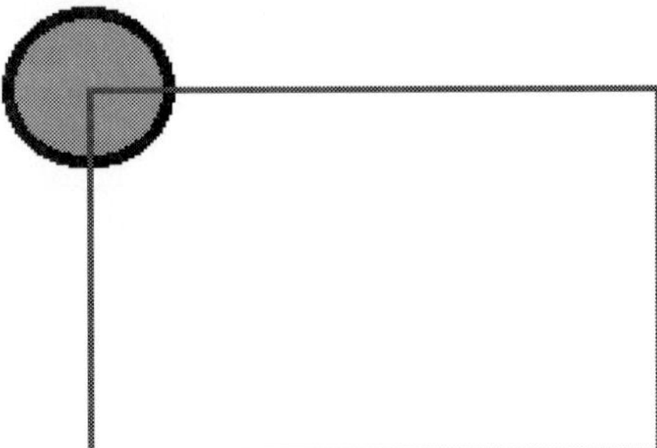

Figure 3.14. The Rectangle That Defines the Direct To Grid Area. The object being moved is the small circle in the upper left corner.

Next, you have to provide end-point values for the horizontal (X) and vertical (Y) values. The default values are 0,100 for both of them. This means the horizontal values will range from 0 to 100, as will the vertical.

We'll continue with the exercise we began earlier in the section on Direct to Point.

Sample File To preview your work, open the **Motion.a4p** file in the Chapter3 folder on the CD-ROM. Restart from the flag. Move your cursor around the screen. Watch how the red ball moves accordingly. Let's see how to build this. Close the file from the CD-ROM and open your version of **Motion.a4p**.

Your Turn

❑ Add a motion icon, name it Direct to Grid, and change its type to Direct to Grid.
❑ Specify its Base and End points by following the steps outlined in the section on Direct to Grid above. You should now see the rectangular area over which the ball will move.
❑ Specify CursorX and CursorY as the Destination variables. These variables specify the location of the cursor in pixels, as measured from the upper left corner of the Presentation window. As the cursor moves, the value of each of these two variables changes accordingly.
❑ Set the Concurrency to Perpetual.
❑ Specify a duration of .5 seconds.
❑ Run your piece and move the cursor, and watch as the ball moves along your rectangular path.
❑ Save your work as **Motion.a4p**.

We've now covered the direct options. Next we'll cover the along path choices.

Along Path Motion Types

The last two motion types are similar to two we've already discussed. The only difference is that instead of linear paths, the object can follow paths that twist and turn. Instead of a line, perhaps you want the object to bounce across the screen like a bouncing ball, or follow a stair-step as you move the object from one step to another. Instead of creating a single line, or end-point you create lines with several segments. Let's look at these last two motion types.

Path To End

The To End motion option moves an object from its starting location along a specified path to its predetermined destination. The object always moves from its start point to its end point.

To set up a Path to End animation:

1. Add a display icon that contains the object to be moved.

2. Add a motion icon.

3. Run the piece from the display icon (use the start flag).

4. When the Motion Icon Properties dialog box opens, select Path to End as the Type option.

5. Enter a suitable value for Duration, and select a Concurrency option. Typically, we select Wait Until Done as the Concurrency option. This way the piece pauses until the animation finishes, then control passes to the next icon.

6. Push the Layout tab, which is shown in Figure 3.15.

7. Click on the object to be moved and drag it to an intermediate location. Release the mouse and drag the object to the next position. Repeat until the object is at its final location.

8. Note the small triangles, called *control points*, and the path that is created (see Figure 3.16 for an example.)

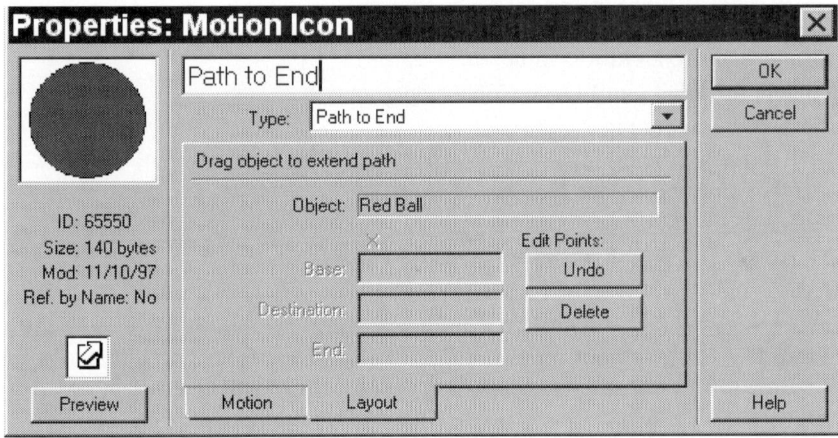

Figure 3.15. The Layout Tab for Path to End Motion Types. The only enabled option is to drag and drop the object several times.

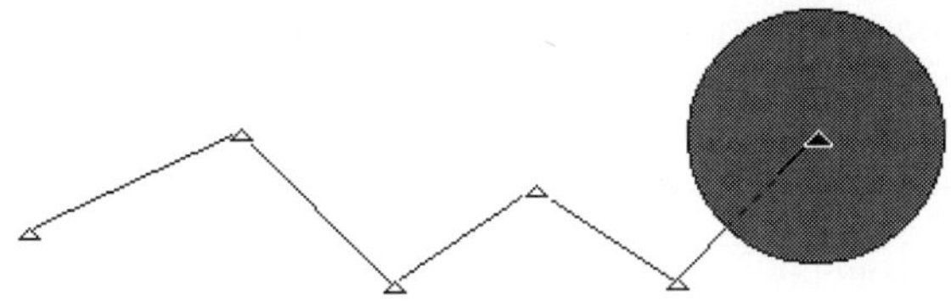

Figure 3.16. The Path and Control Points (Triangles) that Designate a Path to End Motion Path.

You can use the Undo and Delete buttons to edit the control points (triangles). Let's look at an example.

Sample File To preview what we're going to do, open the **Motion.a4p** file in the Chapter3 folder on the CD-ROM. Place the start flag just before the Blue Ball icon and re-start from the flag. Notice how the blue ball bounces around the screen and settles in a final location. When you're finished, open your version of **Motion.a4p**.

Your Turn

- ❑ Add a display icon, name it Blue Ball, and then select it and enter Shift+double-click to open its Presentation window.
- ❑ Create a blue ball.
- ❑ Add a motion icon to your flowline, and name it Path to End.
- ❑ Position the start flag before the Blue Ball icon and restart from the flag.
- ❑ When the Motion Icon Properties dialog box opens, choose Path to End as the type.
- ❑ Enter 8 as the Duration value.
- ❑ Select the Wait Until Done Concurrency option.
- ❑ Push the Layout tab.
- ❑ Click on the blue ball. Note the small triangle. Drag the ball to a new location and release the mouse button.
- ❑ Repeat several times.
- ❑ Push the OK button when finished.
- ❑ Move the start flag back to the icon palette.
- ❑ Run your piece. A few final comments about the red and yellow balls: Notice that if you move your mouse, the red ball moves. Recall we created a perpetual animation to accomplish this. Also, your yellow ball doesn't move at all. You need to give the location variable a new value to move the yellow ball.
- ❑ Save your work (as **Motion.a4p**).

Path To Point

This option moves an object from its start point along a path to its destination, based on variables or expressions. To set up such animation, follow these steps:

1. Add a display icon that contains the object to be moved.

2. Add a motion icon.

3. Run the piece from the display icon.

4. When the Layout tab for Motion icon opens, select Path to Point as the Type.

5. Enter a value for Duration, and select a Concurrency option.

6. Push the Layout tab.

7. Click on the object to be moved and drag it to its first intermediate location.

8. Click on the object to be moved and drag it to another intermediate location. Release the mouse and drag the object to the next position. Repeat until the object is at its final location.

9. Enter variables, expressions, or function names in the Destination X and Y boxes.

You can adjust the path by dragging the triangles to new locations. Use the Delete button in the Layout tab to remove control points.

Let's add a black ball and use the `CursorX` function to control it as it moves along a path.

Sample File To preview what we're going to do, open the **Motion.a4p** file in the Chapter3 folder on the CD-ROM. Place the start flag just before the Black Ball icon and restart from the flag. Move the cursor left and right and watch how the black ball responds. Close the file and open your **Motion.a4p** file.

Your Turn

❏ Add a display icon, named Black Ball, and then open it and draw a black ball.
❏ Add a motion icon and choose Path to Point as the type.
❏ Choose a duration of 6 seconds and select the perpetual concurrency option. (We want the animation to continue even after control exits the motion icon)
❏ Push the Layout tab and drag and drop the black ball several times, as you did in previous exercises.
❏ Enter `CursorX` as the Destination variable.
❏ Push the Done button.
❏ Place the start flag just prior to the Black Ball icon
❏ Restart from the flag.
❏ Move your mouse and watch the black ball move along the path.
❏ Save your work. We are finished with the Motion piece so you can close it at this time.

USER MOVEABLE OBJECTS

Thus far, the objects that moved were done so automatically or under the control of a variable or expression. There is another way to move objects: Allow the user to do so. Perhaps you'd like to set up an interaction where the user must move a graphic over a word in response to a question, or slide the handle of a slider that represents time. The position of the slider would represent the time period for the related data. Let's see how to set up such movements.

The Icon Properties Layout Dialog Box

To set up such a movement, select the object, and then choose <u>M</u>odify><u>I</u>con><u>P</u>roperties. You will then see the dialog box shown in Figure 3.17.

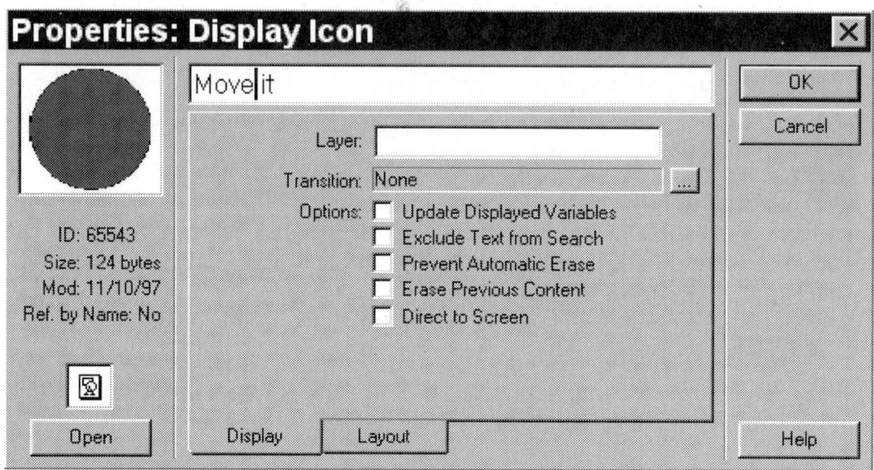

Figure 3.17. The Icon Properties Dialog Box. We will use its Layout tab to establish parameters for user-movable objects.

Push the Layout tab to reveal Figure 3.18.

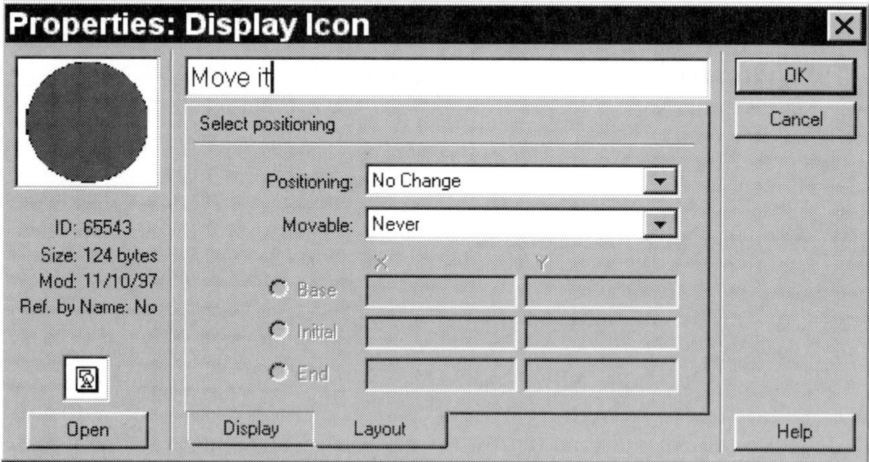

Figure 3.18. The Layout Tab. Use the settings in here to set up the user-movable properties.

Positioning

There are four Positioning options: No Change, On Screen, On Path, and In Area. These options can be seen in Figure 3.19.

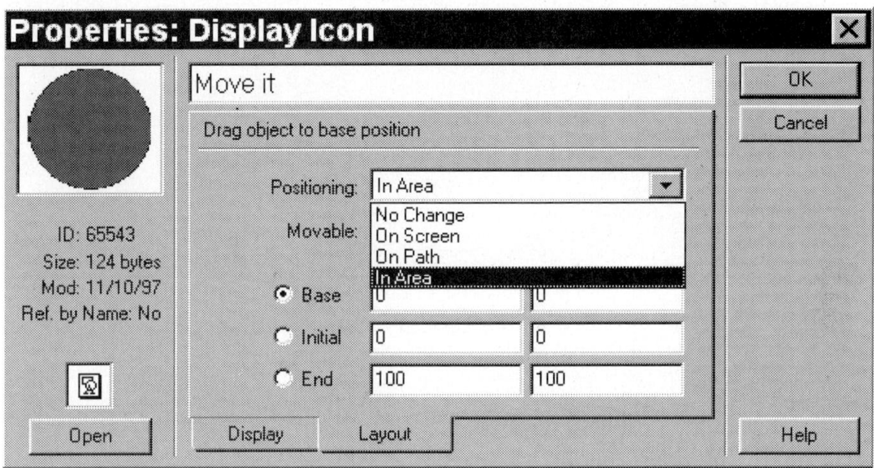

Figure 3.19. The Positioning Options. To see them, open the Positioning drop-down list.

These four options specify where the object is permitted to appear when the Presentation window opens. As you will see later in this chapter, the Movable options specify where the object may be moved after its initial position is determined. Normally you must establish values for both of these options to properly define your animation. Let's return now to the initial positioning options.

No Change If No Change is chosen, the object will appear at the same location as where it was created or imported. This is the default option.

On Screen If you specify On Screen, the object's initial position (specified by the value or expression or variable in the Initial field) can be anywhere, as long as that location is visible in the Presentation window.

On Path Choose the On Path option in the Positioning drop-down list to define a path for the initial location. The object can be initially positioned anywhere along that path. This option might be specified as part of a slider definition, where the user drags a slider handle along a straight line. The On Path Positioning option would specify that the handle can initially be located anywhere along the defined path.

If the On Path option is selected, the dialog box for the Layout tab changes to that of Figure 3.20.

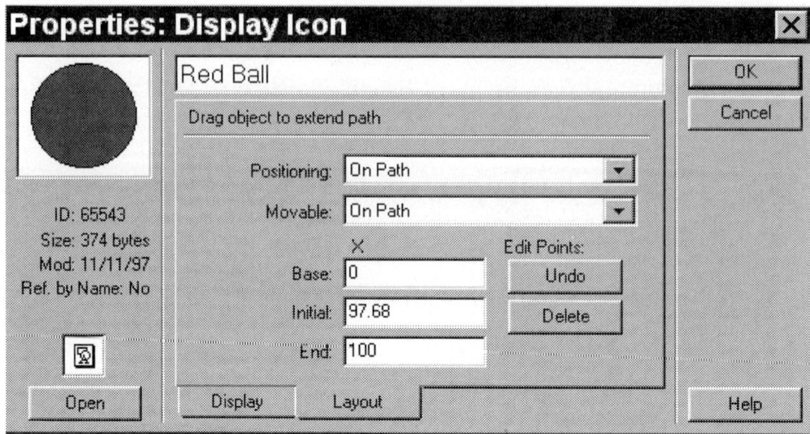

Figure 3.20. The Icon Properties Layout Tab Associated With The On Path Movable Object Property.

As you define the path, a line will become visible, which represents the allowable motion path, as shown in Figure 3.21.

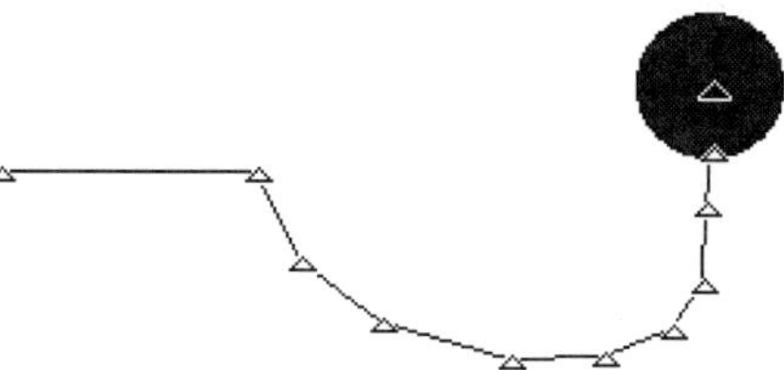

Figure 3.21. The Control Points that Define the Path of an Object.

To create the path, repeatedly drag the object, then release the mouse button. Each time you do so, another control marker appears. To switch from linear segments to curved ones, double-click on the appropriate control points. The segment will change to a curved one, as shown in Figure 3.22.

Figure 3.22. A Curved Path Segment. To accomplish this, double-click on the control point for the segment you wish to make curved.

Initial Value In Figure 3.20, we can place a variable or expression in the field labeled Initial, if we want to control the position of the object. For example, assume you have a slider handle that controls the location of the ball. As the handle is moved, the ball moves accordingly. The variable you use might be called `SliderHandle`. That would be the value you would enter in the field.

Edit Points Buttons Use these buttons to edit the path. To delete a control point, select it, then push the Delete button. Use the Undo button to remove the effects of the previous action.

Defining an On Path Initial Location To set up a path as an allowable initial location follow the steps below.

1. Drag a display icon to the flowline (if the object to be animated is already in a display icon, this step isn't necessary).
2. Select Modify>Icon>Properties.
3. Push the Layout tab in the Icon Properties dialog box.
4. Select the On Path option from the Positioning drop-down list.
5. Click the object to be animated.
6. Drag the object to an intermediate location and release the mouse.
7. Continue until you have fully defined the object's path.
8. Double-click any control points associated with line segments you want to convert to curves.
9. To control the initial location under program control, enter a variable, expression, or function in the Initial field.

☞ Your Turn

❏ Start a new piece.
❏ Add a display icon and name it Green Ball.
❏ Open the Green Ball icon and draw a small circle and color it green.
❏ Close the Presentation window
❏ Select the icon.
❏ Select Modify>Icon>Properties.
❏ Push the Layout tab.
❏ Select the On Path Positioning option.
❏ Drag and drop the green ball several times, being careful to move the object and not the control points.
❏ Make the green ball bounce off the walls and stop about where it started.
❏ Push OK when finished.
❏ Run your piece.
❏ Not very impressive, is it!

❏ The problem is that all you've done is specify an allowable starting position. Open the Icon Properties dialog box and enter a value of 25 for the initial value. Close the Icon Properties dialog box and run your piece again. Watch where the green ball is positioned when the Presentation window opens.

❏ Try to move the ball—you can move it anywhere because you are in author mode. Once the piece is packaged, the object won't be moveable at all because the moveable option is set to Never. As you will see, it takes both of these options to properly control a moveable object.

Let's finish the Positioning choices, then we'll discuss the Moveable field.

In Area If this option is chosen, the object is always located within an area you define using an expanded Layout dialog box that appears, and is shown in Figure 3.23.

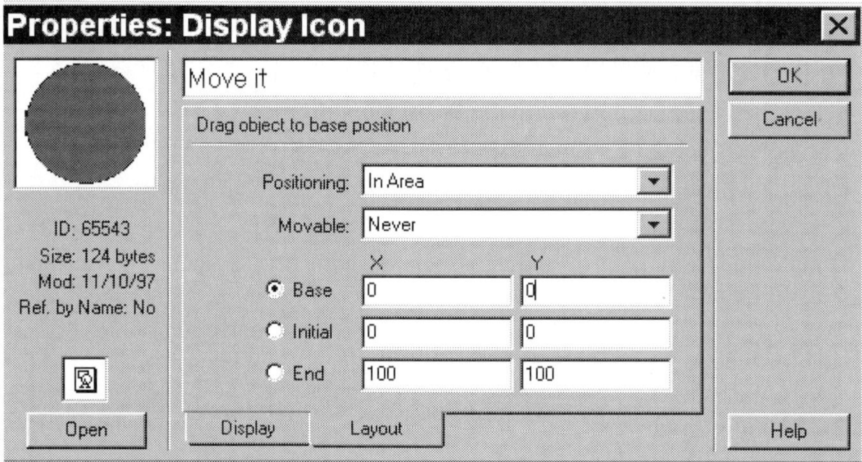

Figure 3.23. An Example of the Dialog Box Associated with the Layout Tab for the In Area Motion Type. This will appear when you choose In Area as the Positioning option.

The initial horizontal and vertical values of the object's position are specified by the value of two variables that are placed in the two X Y Initial fields. The Base and End parameters establish boundaries for the moveable object.

To define the area over which an object can be moved, first drag the image to one of the corners of the allowable area: the upper left corner is customary. This is called the ***Base*** location.

Next, specify the end position: Push the end radio button, and then drag the object to the opposite corner (the lower right corner, if you are following our suggestions) You should see a gray rectangle that defines the moveable area. You can see this in Figure 3.24.

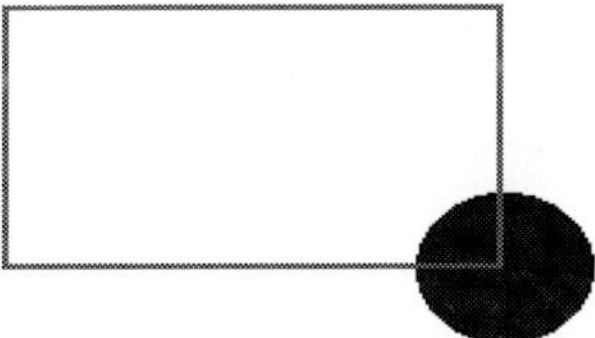

Figure 3.24. The End Position

Movable

Note there are four options here: Never, Anywhere, on Screen and Along Path Only. Collectively they determine if the user can move the selected object, once it has been placed in the Presentation window according to the Positioning option.

Never Choosing Never means the object isn't moveable. Note that while in author mode the object is movable.

Making Objects Nonmovable While in Authoring Mode If you want to prevent movement of an object while you are authoring the piece, do the following:

- Select the icon containing the object.
- Enter Ctrl+= (or use Icon>Calculation).
- Enter `Movable:=FALSE` inside the Calculation window that opens.

Now the object isn't moveable when the piece is running. If you open the Presentation window for the icon, you can move the object as needed.

Anywhere Choose Anywhere to enable the user to move the object anywhere, even off the screen.

On Screen Choose on screen to permit the user to move the object anywhere, as long as it's visible in the Presentation window.

In Area/Path Only You should select this option to limit movement of the object to the path you defined in the Positioning section.

We are going to next create a project that combines a user moveable object (a handle on a slider) and a motion icon. As the handle of the slider is moved left to right, it will control the movement of a second object, a ball, which will move along a predetermined path defined by a motion icon.

Sample File To preview the next exercise, open the **Slider.a4p** file in the Chapter3 folder on the CD-ROM. Move the slider right and left and watch the ball. Try to move the slider beyond the rightmost edge: You'll find you cannot. Close the file and let's see how to build it.

☞ Your Turn

❑ Create a new piece, called **Slider**.

❑ Add a display icon called Red Ball and add a red circle, filled with a red color of your choice.

❑ Now we're ready for the slider. Here's what it will look like when we're finished:

❑ As the handle is moved to the right, the ball will move proportionally to the distance the slider handle has moved. Conversely, as the handle is moved left, the red ball will move back a distance proportional to the distance the handle traveled.

❑ Drag a map icon to the end of the flowline.

❑ Label it Slider.

❑ Open the Slider map icon.

❑ If not already open, open the **Slider.a4l** library by selecting File> Open>Library.

❑ It's in the Libraries folder on your CD-ROM.

❑ Drag the *Slider (Track)* and *Slider (Knob)* icons to the flowline.

❑ Rename the *Slider (Knob)* icon to simply Handle.

❑ Run your title: You will see the slider and its handle.

❑ Position the handle so it's at its left most location. This is the starting point of the path we will define.

❑ Restrict the path that the handle can take to the beginning and ending of the bar:

❑ Select the Handle icon.

❑ Choose Modify>Icon>Properties.

❑ Make sure Positioning and Moveable are set to On Path.

❑ You will see a small triangle in the center of the handle . In addition, the dialog box expands its size.

❑ Drag the handle to its farthest location on the right. Be sure to drag the handle, not the small triangle.

❑ If you look carefully, you can see the path you just created.

❏ Notice the path from the starting point to the ending point

❏ Now we need to define the movement of the ball. Because we want the ball to move along an irregular path based on the location of the handle, we'll need to choose the Direct to Point motion type.

❏ When an object moves along a path, the variable `PathPosition` contains its current value. The value of `PathPosition` will always be between the Base and End Values. We can use this fact to use the handle's position to control the ball. Let's see how.

❏ Drag a motion icon to the Slider map icon.

❏ Label it Move the Ball.

❏ Push the Restart button.

❏ When control reaches the Move the Ball motion icon, choose Path to Point as the motion type.

❏ Set the Concurrency to Perpetual. This way, Authorware will continue to monitor the variable associated with the motion, and move the ball accordingly. Even if we transfer control to another icon, we will still be able to move the ball.

❏ Enter `PathPosition@"Handle"` as the Destination value. This says to position the ball at the location specified by the Handle icon.

❏ Click on the ball and move it a small distance.

❏ Release the mouse, and drag and drop the balls to another location.

❏ Repeat this process, creating a path of the type we saw earlier in this chapter.

❏ Your Presentation window should look like the one below:

❏ Click OK when finished.

❏ Save your work as **Slider.a4p**.

❏ Run your title.

As it runs, move the slider to the right and the red ball should move along its defined path proportionally to the handle's position. Try moving the slider to the left: the ball follows!

CREATING AN APPLICATION

By now you can add graphical and text objects, erase and animate them. You should be able to create linear pieces. A linear piece runs from icon to icon in a linear fashion. Suppose you create such a project. How can someone who doesn't have Authorware run your project? The answer lies in a concept Authorware calls ***packaging***. With packaging, a user of your project doesn't require a development copy of Authorware to run your project. Instead, a runtime version of Authorware can be included along with your project. This runtime, while not permitting changes to be made to your project, does allow the user to run it. Let's explore the process for creating packages.

After a title is completed, it must be packaged into a runtime version. The code file and all libraries need to be transformed into the distribution format. To package a project, start by selecting File>Package. You will see the dialog box shown in Figure 3.25.

Figure 3.25. The Package Dialog Box

You must decide which options to include in the runtime. First, decide if you want to include the runtime executable, RunA4W. There are two versions of the program, a 16-bit version for Windows 3.X and a 32-bit version for Windows 95/98 and Windows NT. The 16-bt version is named **RunA4W16.exe** and the 32-bit version is named **RunA4W32.exe.** You select the version by opening the drop-down list box you see in Figure 3.25, and selecting either of the two Windows options you will see. When you push the Save File button, an executable (16 or 32-bit) will be created for you. The user can then run your piece without any additional files.

If you elect not to include either version of RunA4W, a special version of your title having the extension of .APP will be created. In this case, the user must run RunA4W and when a dialog box asks which title to open, specify the .APP file. If the application uses several Authorware files, you only need include the RunA4W file once.

Resolve Broken Links at Runtime

The next decision involves what to do about broken links. Links are created between icons in libraries and icons in the flowline. A link is broken when an icon on the flowline references a library icon whose icon ID has changed. Normally you will check the Resolve Broken Links at Runtime option.

Package all Libraries Internally

Recall that libraries contain frequently used icons. If this option is checked, only those icons referred to by the piece are included. There is no need to include the library on the disk when the title is distributed.

Use Default Names When Packaging

If this is selected, Windows titles packaged with the RunA4W file will have the EXE extension. If the runtime isn't included, the file will have an A4R extension. Packaged libraries are assigned extensions of .A4E.

Save Files and Package

Pressing this button starts the packaging process. Exactly what happens depends on choices you previously made. For example, if you didn't select Package All Libraries Internally, Authorware will pop-up a dialog box asking you about Package Library options.

Ordinarily you should package your work with only those library icons that you referred to, include RunA4W, and use default names.

 **Your Turn**
❑ Package **Slider** for your platform. Run the application on a computer other than the one you authored it on and make sure it runs properly.

The final task is to add to the DigVid2 file we last saved in Chapter2. You can open that file at this time or use the one on your CD-ROM. The final version is saved as DigVid3 in the Chapter3 folder, but you should open the DigVid2 version in the Chapter2 folder so you can follow along.

Your Turn
❑ Open **DigVid2**.
❑ Add a display icon named Directions.
❑ Use Shift-Double-click and open Directions.
❑ Choose the Text tool and set the margins so they stay inside the main portion of the template, as shown below.

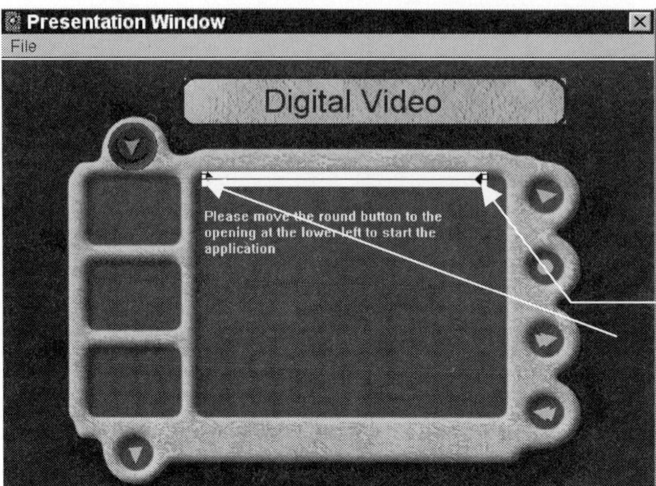

Set margins
this way.

❑ Add the text "Please move the round button to the opening at the lower left to start the application". Skip several lines, then enter "Press any key when you have finished". Use 10-point yellow text and use a shade as close to the yellow border as you can.

❑ Select the *Round Up 1* icon.

❑ Choose Modify>Icon>Properties.

❑ Set Positioing and Moveable to On Path.

❑ Click on the button and drag it to the opening at the lower left.

❑ Add an erase icon and name it -Text..

❑ Enter Shift-double-click and open the -Text icon.

❑ Click on the text you added in the Directions icon, then choose the Dissolve Bits transition.

❑ Set the dissolve to take 3 seconds.

❑ Add a Wait icon and deselect the Show button box. Do check the Key Press option box.

❑ Run your piece.

❑ If it seems to work properly, save your work as **DigVid3**.

SUMMARY

Authorware provides two methods for moving objects: Using a motion icon, or using positioning, which is an Icon Property. There are five types of motions, grouped into Direct and Along Path. The three Direct motion types are: Direct to Point, Direct to Line, and Direct to Grid. The two path types are Path to End and Path to Point.

In addition to specifying the type of motion or animation, you can also specify duration and concurrency. Concurrency options include Wait Until Done, Continue and Perpetual. Choose Continue to have Authorware jump to the next icon while the animation is occurring. Choose Wait Until Done to pause the running of your piece until the animation finishes. Finally, choose Perpetual to have the animation continue even after control passes to another icon.

Objects can be moved along predetermined paths or their movement can be based on calculations or variables. Use the variable `PathPosition` to control movement of one object through movement of a second. When objects are free to be moved by the user, they might be moved off the screen. To prevent this, you can restrict movement to rectangular areas.

In addition to creating motion using the motion icon, you can use an icon property to enable the user to move the object. We call this positioning. There are two main properties: Positioning, which establishes an initial location, and Movable, which specifies what how the user can move the object after its initial position.

To save your piece so anyone can run it, without having to own Authorware, use the packaging facility. Be sure to choose the proper version when packaging: For Windows 3.X, for Windows NT or 95/98, or choose to package without a RunA4W.

Study Exercises

3.1 You can animate an object perpetually by using settings like this:

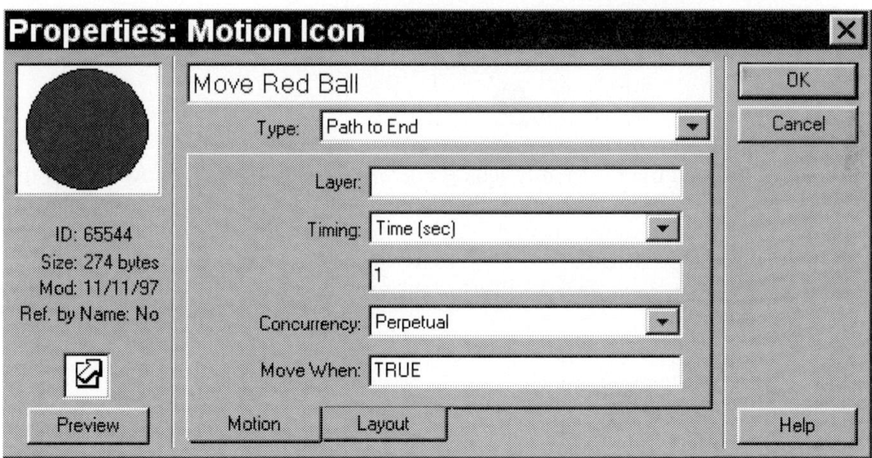

The Type is Path to End, the Concurrency is Perpetual and the motion is to continue as long as TRUE is true! Suffice it to say this is always true. Create a new piece called C3Q1. You are to animate two circles, one red, one blue. Make them orbit around each other perpetually, in opposite directions.

3.2. This exercise will use positioning (forcing an object to move within a certain area) and a motion icon of the Direct to Grid type. You will draw a small square, and then restrict a small red ball to move within the confines of that square. As the ball is moved within the rectangular area, another graphic will move accordingly: Move the ball up and the graphic moves up; move the ball down and the graphic moves down.

The X and Y coordinates of an icon (the small ball, for example) can be determined by using two variables: `PositionX` and `PositionY`. Let's see how to use them to create our next piece.

Create a new title called C3Q2. Add the following icons:

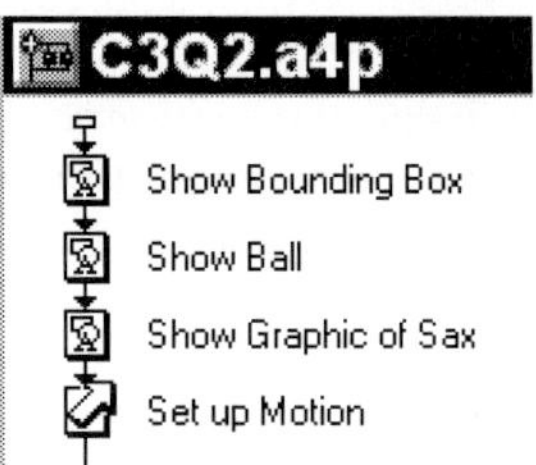

Open the Presentation window for the first icon and draw a small black square. Use the Lines Inspector and make the border a bit heavier. Use shift-double-click and open the Show Ball Presentation window. Draw a small red ball near the lower left corner of the bounding box as shown below.

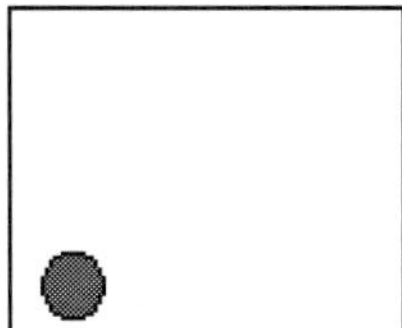

Select the small red ball and use the <u>M</u>odify <u>I</u>con <u>P</u>roperties menu to limit the movement of the ball to the black square area. (Hint: Be sure to choose Positioning as In Area, and Movable as In area Only) In the text box for the X Initial value, enter: `PositionX@"Show Ball"`. Similarly, for the Y value enter: `PositionY@"Show Ball"`. Use the dialog box below as a help.

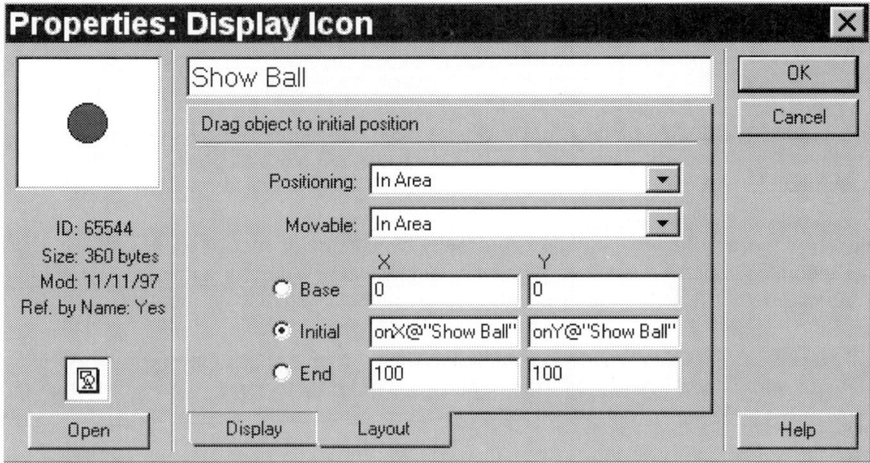

This will assign the X and Y coordinate values to the values of `PositionX` and `PositionY`.

Next, find the graphic called M_sax in the Images folder in the Chapter3 folder on your CD-ROM. Import it into the Show graphic of Sax icon. Now for the Set Up Motion icon. Set its type to Direct to Grid. As X and Y values use the same settings you used for the small red ball (Remember `PositionX` and `PositionY`?).

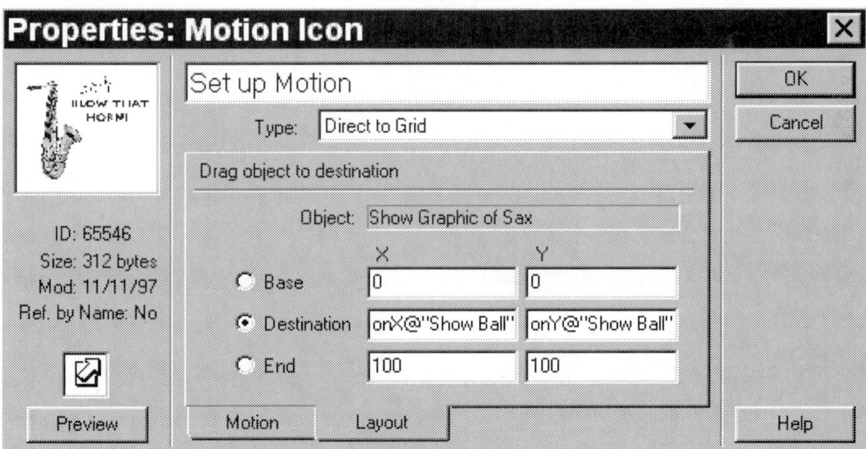

 Define a rectangular area over which the graphic of the saxophone can be moved. Make it fairly large. You can follow the same routine you used for setting paths earlier in the chapter.

To test your piece, run the title and move the red ball it should only move in a rectangular area, As the ball moves, the saxophone should move accordingly.

Last, you'll change the cursor to a hand. Select the Set up motion icon, then choose <u>M</u>odify> <u>I</u>con> <u>C</u>alculations (or use Ctrl+=). Add this line to the calculation dialog box that opens: `Setcursor(6)`.

3.3. Create a new piece called C3Q3. Add a display icon and draw a black ball. Add other icons to animate the black ball in a complete circle requiring 7 seconds, and make the black ball turn yellow after one revolution.

3.4 Create a new piece called C3Q4. Add two display icons and one motion icon. Use the crop facility within the Import function to illustrate a plunger going inside a syringe. Use the Syringe graphic in the \Chapter3\Images folder. Use both images, but crop the plunger and place it into your second icon.

3.5 Modify question 4 to add a yellow rectangle between the plunger and the syringe. As the plunger moves down, more and more of the yellow should disappear. Call this piece C3Q5.

An Introduction to Interactions

*T*here are several ways to alter the linear execution of an Authorware presentation: decision icons enable the author to decide what path to take; and framework, navigation and interaction icons enable end-users to decide what to do when. This chapter looks at the interaction icon.

Interaction icons enable the user to branch based on objects such as buttons, hot spots, menus, and so on. An interaction consists of an interaction icon, and one or more response types and result icons, which represent actions to take.

This chapter looks at the interaction icon and the dialog box that is shared by all interactions. It then briefly examines the eleven interaction types.

At the conclusion of the chapter, you will be able to:

- State the eleven types of interactions.

- Identify the components of an interaction.

- Describe the elements or options of the interaction options dialog box.

- Describe and discuss the purposes of the common elements of every interaction type.

THE INTERACTION ICON

Multimedia projects that display information in a linear fashion are sometimes called "page turners". A button may be used, or the next piece of information presented automatically, but the information is presented in a continuous, linear fashion — one piece of information after another.

Contrast this with a project that has navigation buttons that take you anywhere, hot text that when clicked displays additional media content, quizzes and tests with multiple-choice and fill-in-the-blank questions, menus that provide additional navigational paths and so on. These kinds of interactions separate the mundane from the exciting, the uninspired from the inspirational projects.

Authorware provides for several types of interactions. Each has a common set of properties, plus ones unique to the interaction type. We begin by exploring the common elements.

The Anatomy of an Interaction

An interaction icon effectively combines the results of three other icons: display, wait, and erase. A complete interaction consists of several parts, one of which is the interaction icon itself. As shown in Figure 4.1, an interaction consists of an interaction icon, which presents the text, hot object and so on, one or more possible user-interaction objects, or *response types*, and a set of *result icons*, a series of possible actions to take, one result set for each response type. The final component of an interaction is the *result path,* which determines where control passes when the user responds to a given interaction.

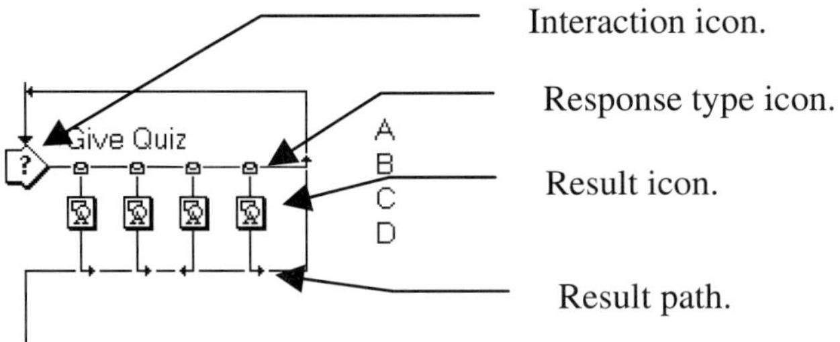

Figure 4.1. A Typical Interaction. The components include the interaction icon; a set of response types with associated results and exit paths.

Typical response types include buttons, text input and hot spots, but there are many others available as well: ten in all.

A button interaction might look like Figure 4.2.

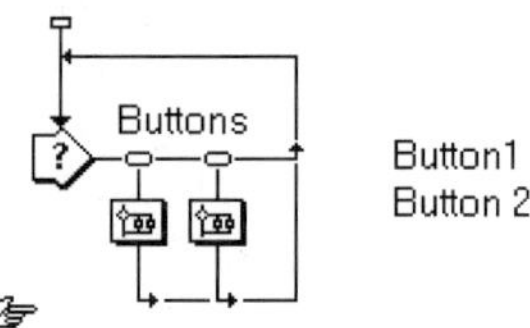

Figure 4.2. A Typical Button Interaction.

When an interaction icon is encountered, text and graphics inside the icon are shown. This part is similar to the display icon. Here is where you might show quiz questions, a graphic with clickable objects (also called hot objects), a graphic with areas you would like to make clickable, and so on. Buttons are also added through the creation of the response types. In Figure 4.2, two buttons would be created, one called "Button 1" and the other "Button 2". When an interaction icon is encountered, Authorware then waits for the user to respond.

When a response is detected, a mouse click or a keypress, for example, Authorware looks at the result icons to the right of the interaction icon, also called *target responses*, to see if the response matches any of the result icons. Each result icon represents a possible response, and the response type symbol might be considered a switch. If the user response matches the target response, the switch is closed and control passes to the set of actions you associate with that response type.

In the example in Figure 4.2, Authorware would determine which button was pressed. Once that was determined, Authorware would execute the contents of the associated result icon, one of two map icons in the figure.

As another example, assume the interaction is to be a multiple-choice quiz. The target response icons might look for keypresses for the letters "A", "B", C", or "D". The response type would be keypress, and there would therefore be four response types. The corresponding response icons might be sound icons, each of which says, for example, "A" is incorrect, please try again". If "C" is the correct response, the result path for that response would lead out of the interaction, while the others would point back to the interaction icon (called Try Again).

Figure 4.3 shows what that interaction might look like:

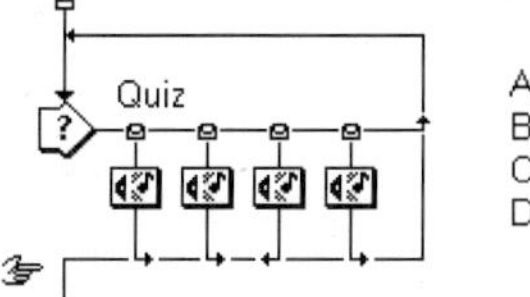

Figure 4.3. A Typical Keypress Interaction. Choice "C" is the correct answer.

As an interaction is exited, a wait (continue) button can be displayed, and the information displayed within the interaction icon, plus any added by the response types or result icons, erased. Remember: an interaction can be considered a display icon (show the interaction), a wait icon (show a Continue button after the interaction), and an erase icon (erase the information displayed through the interaction).

Catchall

If a given target response doesn't match the user response, the switch remains open, and control is passed to the next response icon on the right for matching. What if none of the anticipated responses is received? This should not occur. You should have a response for each possible input. The solution is to create a *catchall*, a response that intercepts all inputs not explicitly anticipated.

As an example, assume you are presenting a European map with several hot spots. The user is to click on a country that's a member of the United Kingdom. If the user clicks on area that isn't "hot", France, Germany, and so on, you want to display a help screen. In this case, the catchall would be the European area of the map. Or consider the situation where there are four possible answers to a keypress interaction (A-D). Here you should provide a catchall for all other keypresses (E, F, and so on) and display a suitable error message. We'll see how to create such catchalls for many of the interactions, as we discuss them individually in the next chapter.

Next, let's examine the interaction icon itself . All interactions begin with this icon.

The Interaction Dialog Box

Figure 4.4 shows the dialog box associated with a typical interaction icon. To view it, add an interaction and then choose <u>M</u>odify><u>I</u>con><u>P</u>roperties.

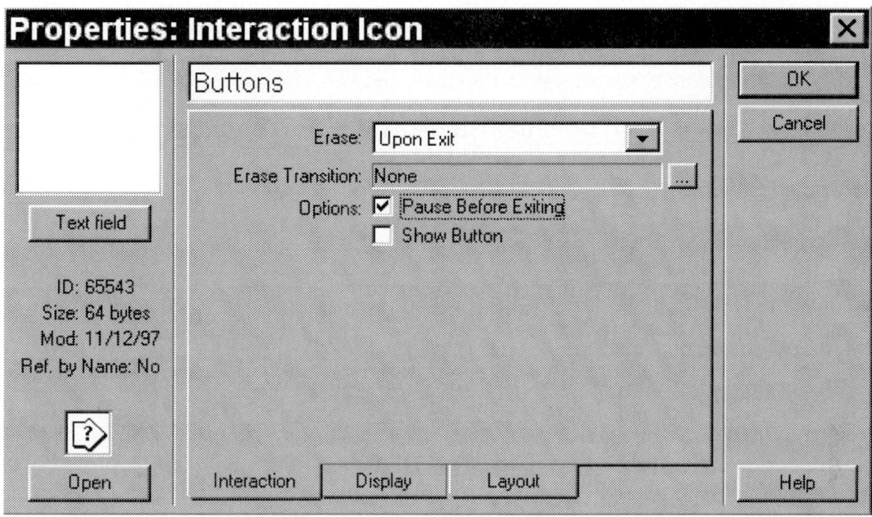

Figure 4.4. The Dialog Box Associated With an Interaction Icon. Only the Interaction tab options are shown.

Pause Before Exiting and Show Button Check Boxes

One of the target response icons in an interaction must exit the interaction. This is how the user leaves the interaction and progresses to the next icon on the main flowline. Normally you don't want the exit process to occur immediately. Instead you might display text, or play a sound. You must pause the exiting process until the sound is played or until the text can be read. To do this, you need to check the Pause Before Exiting box.

If you do check the Pause Before Exiting box, the interaction will temporarily stop, waiting for the user to click the mouse or press any key. However, there is no message to that effect, so the user might not know what to do! Therefore, you will probably want to also check the Show Button box. This will cause Authorware to display a "continue" button as the interaction is exited. As a rule, if you check the Pause Before Exiting checkbox, you should also check the Show Button checkbox.

Erase Interaction

Interaction content that appears in the Presentation window comes from the interaction icon and possibly from the result icons. The interaction icon might display a quiz question and each response icon a possible feedback message. The choice you make here determines whether to erase the content derived from the interaction icon alone.

There are three choices in the Erase Interaction drop-down list: On Exit, After Each Entry, and Don't Erase.

The On-Exit Erase Option This option will erase any content added through the interaction icon. Figure 4.5 shows typical content for a keypress interaction.

What was the name of the first computer?

A. Apple II
B. EDVAC
C. ENIAC
D. None of the above

Figure 4.5. Content For a Typical Keypress Example. Choice "C" is correct.

If the On Exit choice is made, the question will be erased when the user makes the correct choice, and the interaction exits. Note, however, any feedback displayed from within the response icon associated with the correct response will not be erased. For example, you might provide a message that displays "Very Good". This feedback would not be erased. This erasure must be handled in another way, which we discuss later.

The After Each Entry Option Choosing After Each Entry will cause Authorware to erase the screen after the user makes a choice, presses a button, and so on. If we applied this option to the flowline in Figure 4.5, every time the user pressed a key (the correct or an incorrect key) the text would be erased, then re-displayed. If the correct response were entered (the one that exits the interaction), the content would be permanently erased, so you wouldn't need an additional erase icon after the interaction.

The Don't Erase Option The Don't Erase option causes the content of the interaction icon to stay in the Presentation Window under all circumstances. In this case, if you need to erase the Presentation Window display, you'll need to add an erase icon as the first icon encountered after such an interaction. Figure 4.6 shows such a flowline.

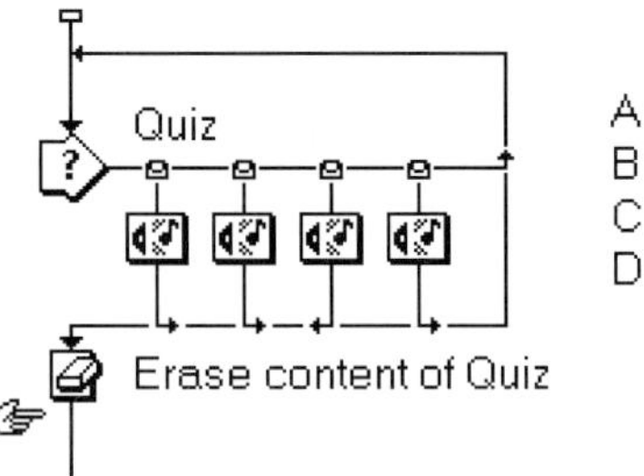

Figure 4.6. A Flowline That Uses the Don't Erase On Exit Option To Erase Interaction Content.

Erase Transition

We have seen transitions before. If this button is pushed, you will see a long list of transitions that you can choose among to apply to the Presentation window as its contents are erased. It's the same list you saw for the erase icon. Figure 4.7 shows the dialog box for the erase transitions.

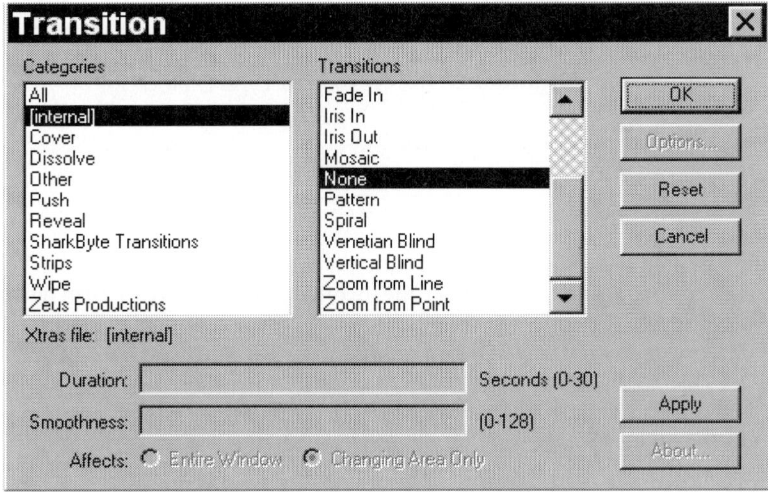

Figure 4.7. The Erase Transition Dialog Box.

RESPONSE TYPES

When you set up an interaction icon, you attach a result, or target, icon to its right. As you add the first icon, Authorware will prompt for a type. Once you choose a type, any additional icon you add are assumed to be of the same type. Of course, you can change types, thus allowing you the possibility of mixing response types within the same interaction.

Let's next examine the eleven response types. When you add the initial result icon, you'll see the dialog box in Figure 4.8.

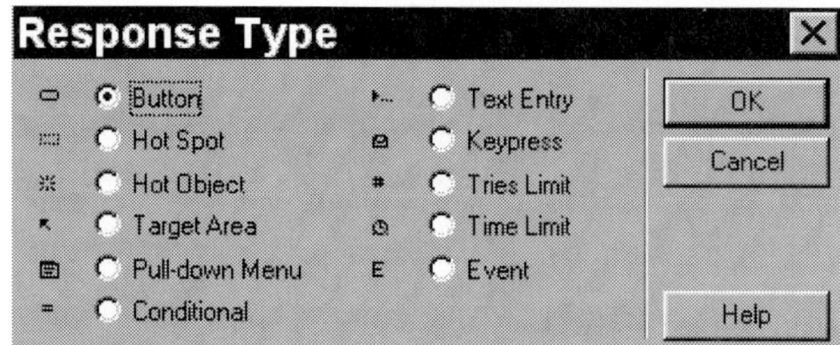

Figure 4.8. The Response Type Dialog Box.

Buttons

Buttons are commonly used to transfer control or offer a series of choices. When pushed, a button causes Authorware to branch to the result icon attached to that button. The result might be a dialog box, a sound, a digital video, or even a jump to a completely new sub-topic. It's the use of responses like buttons that enable you to create pieces that are truly interactive.

While there is a default button object style, Authorware has an easy way to customize buttons and even add a sound effect, which plays when the button is pushed.

Hot Spots

Hot spots are rectangular portions of a display associated with corresponding sets of actions to take. The actions can be triggered by clicking, double-clicking or by simply moving the cursor over the hot spot. The cursor shape can be altered while over the hot spot. An example of a hot spot interaction would be a map of London. You might create hot spots over the Tower of London, Westminster Abbey, and Tower Bridge. If the mouse were clicked while over the Tower hot spot, the user would be presented with another image, which might offer an overview of the Tower of London and new hot spots indicating suggested Tower locations to visit.

Hot Objects

A hot object is like a hot spot, but the entire object is hot meaning the user can click, double-click, or simply move the cursor over the object. Hot object areas do not have to be rectangular. Digital movies can be made into hot objects. Hot objects must be in their own icons; they cannot be part of a compound display icon. If you want to make several objects hot, all having the same feedback, place them in the same icon.

Target Areas

Use a target area if you want a user to drag an object to a specified area. For example, you might use an icon that depicts a "You-are-here" situation for an airport. As the user drags the icon to various airline logos, maps appear showing the frustrated traveler how to get to that airline within the terminal. Alternatively, you might be giving a quiz where the student is shown a quotation plus photos of several possible authors. The student must drag the photo of the author to the quotation.

A target area is always rectangular, and, while in author mode, Authorware shows an X inside it. When you create one of these you can also define boundaries to prevent the user from moving the object off the screen.

Pull-Down Menus

Use a pull-down menu to enable users to make a selection from a menu appearing at the top of the Presentation window. Each menu requires its own interaction icon. Menu separators that group similar commands, as well as hot keys can also be defined. We usually make pull-down menu interactions perpetual, so that when control leaves the menu icon, the menus created by it stay active.

Conditionals

Use a conditional interaction to display content based on some condition. For example, after three wrong tries, a help dialog box is shown. Conditionals are also used to filter input — only permitting numeric entries, for example. A common use of conditionals is to create hot text; that is, text that when clicked displays additional content.

Text Entries

Text entry responses can be range from the simple to the complex. These might be used to ask for the user's name, or to ask who was the author of *Gone With the Wind*. In the first example, we want to take no action. In the second example, we want to match what is entered against the correct answer. We need to anticipate incorrect spellings and different methods of capitalization. Authorware also provides the ability to use wild cards, to match n words, to ignore punctuation and extra words, and to specify a particular answer sequence.

Keypress Responses

Suppose you are presenting a multiple-choice test with possible answers of A, B or C. You need to determine which key was pressed, and provide appropriate feedback. In this example, you would use a keypress response. You can not only check for normal keystrokes, but also Control, Alt, Esc, function keys, and so on. As with Text Entry interactions, you should check for and accept both upper and lower case answers.

Tries Limit

Use this to force Authorware to branch after a certain number of tries, even if the user hasn't matched a correct response.

Time Limit

If used, this will force Authorware to branch after a specified amount of time. You might consider this if you were giving a timed test. A useful option is the ability to show the remaining time.

Event

Third-party vendors can write *Xtras*, extensions to Authorware. In addition, Authorware can utilize Microsoft objects called ActiveX controls. In general there are two types of Xtras: *sprites* and *scripting*.

With the other response types, Authorware waits for the user to interact with the piece—push a mouse button, enter a letter or word, and so on. With Xtras, the added code tells Authorware an event has occurred. If a sprite Xtra is used, the event occurs when the user interacts with the object created by the Xtra.

COMMON RESPONSE TYPE OPTIONS

If a new response type is added, or an existing one opened, a dialog box will be displayed presenting options that apply to that response type. While Figure 4.9 shows the options for a button interaction, all eleven response types share some common options. It is those common options that we discuss in this section.

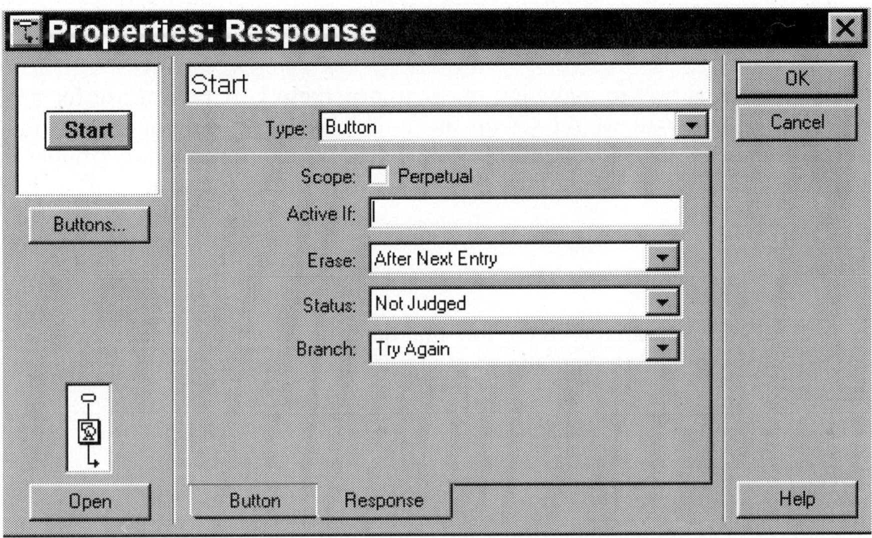

Figure 4.9 The Button Options Dialog Box. This is a typical interaction dialog box with many options shared among the ten possible interaction types.

Among the common components are:

- Type
- Scope
- Active If
- Erase (feedback)
- Status (response tracking)
- Branching (exit)

Type

When you add the first response icon to the interaction, Authorware will prompt you with a dialog box as to which of the eleven types you want. As you add each succeeding response icon, Authorware will assume it's to be of the same type as the previous one. Use the Type drop-down to select a different response type.

Scope

Check the Perpetual box to make the interaction perpetual. A typical use for this is with a help button. Authorware would set up the interaction, then continue down the flowline. However, the help button would stay active and ready for the user to push. Usually, Authorware pauses the piece until the user responds to the interaction.

Active If

Enter an expression or variable in the box that determines when the interaction is active. For example, perhaps you don't want the "Next" button to be active if there are no more icons to display.

Erase

This specifies what to erase after displaying the content of the result, or feedback, icon. For example, you might create a help button as a response. Once the help is displayed you would erase the contents. There are four options:

- Before Next Entry
- After Next Entry
- Upon Exit
- Don't Erase

Before Next Entry

Select this option to make Authorware erase the result icon's display before redisplaying the interaction display, which prompts the user for another response. Be sure to include a wait icon in the result or else the user won't have time to view the content prior to erasure.

Sample File To see an example of a Before Next Entry piece, run the file **Feedbk1.a4p** in the Chapter4 folder on the CD-ROM. Push the Text button and watch what happens. When the button is pushed, control passes to the Text icon, which displays a suitable message (also called the *feedback* or *response*). Because the button's feedback option is set to erase the feedback ("Text is an important communications medium often used with multimedia") prior to next entry, the message displays as desired. It is then erased before the next entry (another button push) can occur. Consequently the text displays so fast it cannot be read. Obviously, this was the incorrect choice. Let's look at the next one.

After Next Entry

Select this option to make Authorware erase the result icon's content *after* the user makes another response (a mouse click, keypress, etc.).

Sample File To view such an interaction, run the **Feedbk2.a4p** file in Chapter4's folder. As before, push the Text button. Now the message stays visible. In fact, it will remain visible until you make another selection (try the Computer button). What happened when you pushed the Computer button? The message displayed as we wanted, but because it was designated as the "correct" response, the interaction exits and control is sent back to the main flowline, as shown by Figure 4.10.

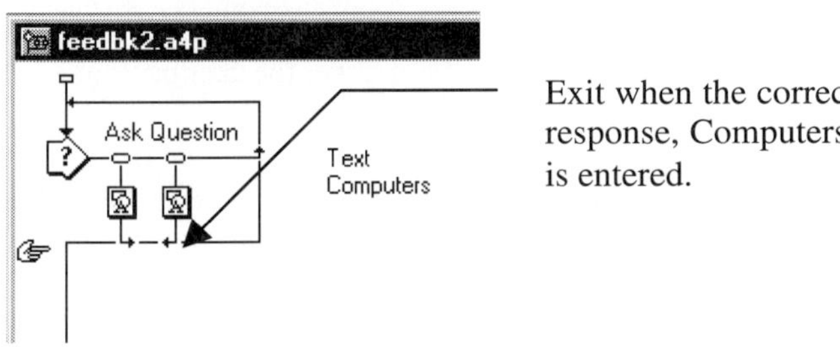

Figure 4.10. The Feedbk2 Flowline.

Why did the question and the response both erase? For the answer, open the interaction icon properties. Figure 4.11 shows what you'll see.

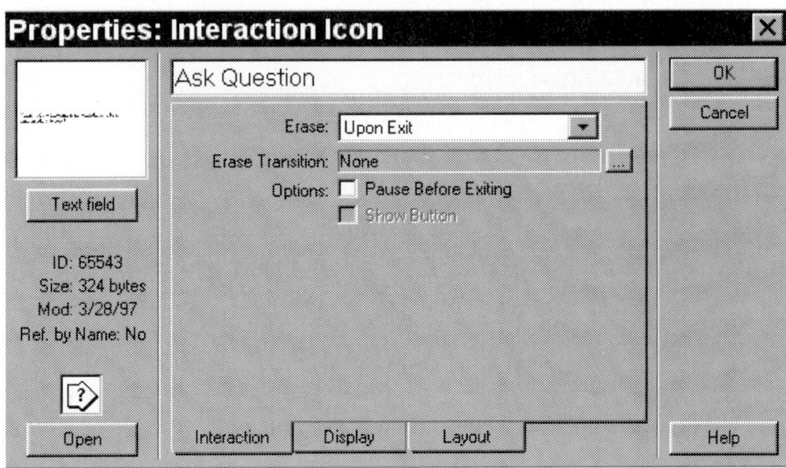

Figure 4.11. The Icon Properties Associated with the Ask Question Interaction.

The Erase Interaction option is set to "Upon Exit". This will erase the question posed within the interaction icon. The erase "After Next Entry" option erased the feedback message. Normally the feedback isn't erased when set this way until you make another entry. The exception is when the response is the correct one. In that case, setting the option to erase feedback "After Next Entry" will cause the feedback to be erased as the interaction is exited.

On Exit

If this option is selected, Authorware leaves the result icon's display on the screen until the interaction is exited. This means if the user selects another response (clicks another button, clicks another hot spot, etc.) the current display is still shown, resulting in the potential for overlapping displays. This sounds like it might solve our problem.

Sample File Run **Feedbk3.a4p** and push the Computer button. We set its erase option to "Upon Exit". It still doesn't work! Maybe we should not erase the feedback at all. That's the last option.

Don't Erase

Select this option to leave responses on the screen until an erase icon removes them.

Sample File Run **Feedbk4.a4p** and see if this solves our problem. Push the Text button. That works as expected. The Computer button's feedback is set to "Don't Erase". Push it. What happens? The interaction (the question) erases, but not the question.

One solution is to not erase either the question or the response within the interaction. Instead, use a wait icon and an erase icon to delete them both.

Sample File You can see our solution in **Feedbk5.a4p**. Pay particular attention to the Erase Interaction setting in the Ask Question icon and to the Erase Feedback choice in the Computer button response type icon.

Status

Use this option if you want Authorware to judge each interaction and compute performance statistics for you. Perhaps you are creating a quiz or training title and need to track each user's performance. In cases such as these, you would assign one of the two options, Correct Response, or Wrong Response, to each response. A third choice, Not Judged, is used when you do not need to track right and wrong answers.

Correct Response

Assign the Correct Response option to the path that constitutes the correct answer or response. Only one response should be designated as being correct. The other choices would be set to Wrong Response.

Wrong Response

Set the response tracking option to Wrong Response for all the incorrect choices. Both of these options are relevant for response types that ask a question, or do, in fact, have a correct and incorrect answer or response. Assume you have a multiple-choice question with four possible answers. Assume "B" is the correct one. The user answers by pushing a button. You would create an interaction icon with four button result icons, as shown in Figure 4.12.

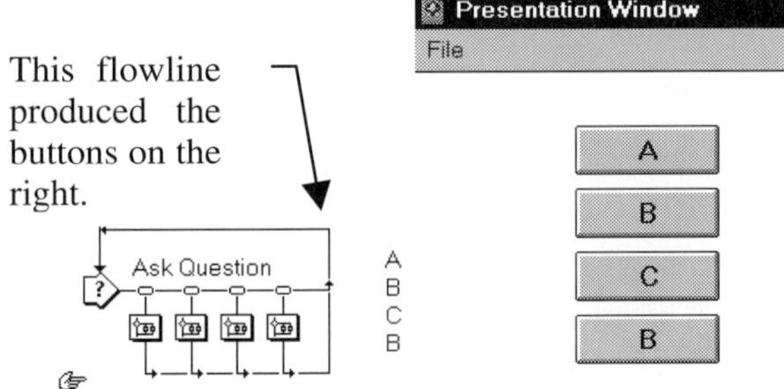

Figure 4.12. Creating a Four-Button Interaction.

For the first, third and fourth button response, set the option to Wrong Response, as shown in Figure 4.13.

Figure 4.13. Designating a Response as Being Incorrect.

For the second result icon, set the option to Correct Response. As you can see in Figure 4.14, a plus sign (+) sign will appear next to the correct response(s), while a minus sign (-) appears next to the incorrect ones.

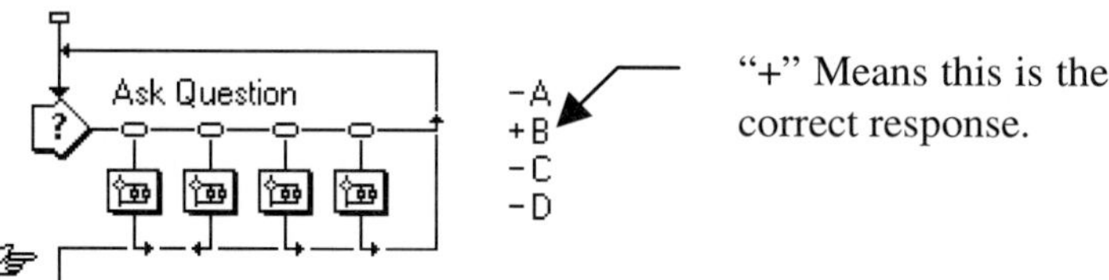

Figure 4.14 Correct and Incorrect Response Designations. A "+" indicates a correct response, a "-" an incorrect one.

Sample File The complete example shown in Figure 4.14 can be found in the **Responses.a4p** file in the Chapter4 folder.

Not Judged

This is the third option, and it is appropriate when you do not want Authorware to track correct and incorrect responses. For example, a button to display help wouldn't be a candidate for judgment.

Exit Branching

This specifies what Authorware should do after getting a correct or incorrect response. Authorware will move along the interactions, checking what was entered against each possible response. When it detects a match, it runs the icons in the result. Now a decision must be made about what to do next.

There are four choices:

- Try Again
- Continue
- Exit Interaction
- Return

Try Again

If Try Again is chosen, Authorware will loop back to the interaction icon and wait. The result is shown in Figure 4.15.

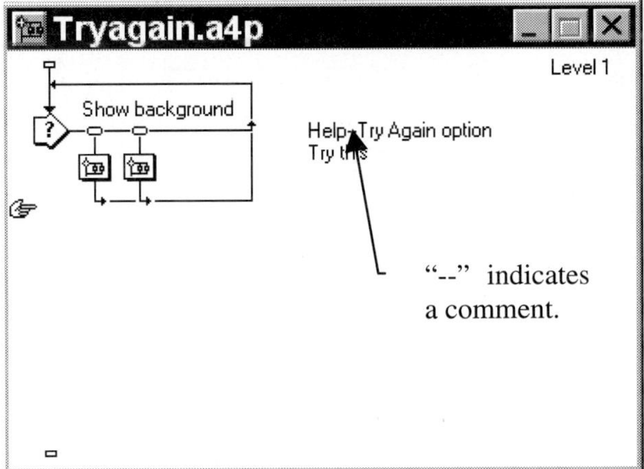

Figure 4.15 A Flowline Where Both Responses Are Designated as Try Again. A comment is also included.

Notice the small branching arrows leaving the Help and the "Try this" map icons. These are interpreted as: "If there are additional icons to the right, skip them and pass control to the interaction icon (named Show background).

Sample File "Run the **Tryagain.a4p** file in the Chapter4 folder to see the complete example. We should note that despite the messages to the contrary, the example doesn't contain any hot spots. It's intended to merely show the flowline for responses designated with the Exit Branching option "Try Again"

Continue

Use Continue to have Authorware continue checking icons to the right for possible additional matches.

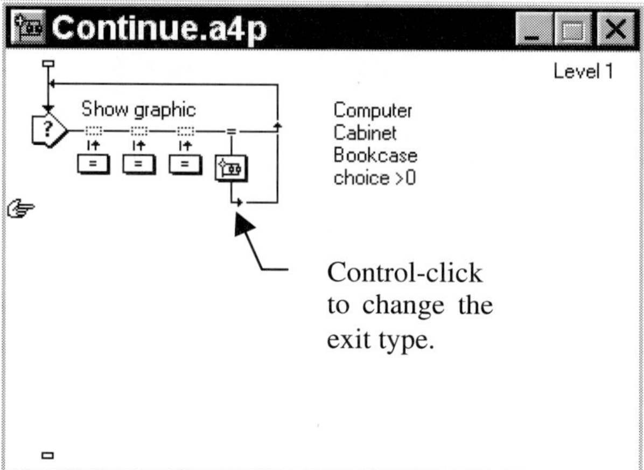

Figure 4.16 The **Continue.a4p** Example From the Chapter4 Folder on the CD-ROM.

See the small arrows above, pointing back up to the response types? These are interpreted as meaning: "After doing whatever is in the result icon, go back and continue checking for other possible correct responses. "

You can change the branching type by control-left clicking on the exit branch within the design window.

Sample File To see the complete example of this, run the **Continue** file in the Chapter4 folder. It uses conditional result icons attached to hot spots and a conditional interaction type. We'll discuss the example again in the next chapter, once we understand more about specific interaction types.

In general, the piece sets up three hot spots, one over each blue object. If a blue object is selected by clicking on it, a variable is set to 1,2 or 3, depending on which object was selected. Because of the Continue Exit Branching option, after an object is clicked, control returns to the interaction flowline and eventually gets to the last response type —the conditional.

It checks to see if the variable is greater than zero. If it is, it executes the attached icon, which displays a message, waits, and then erases the message. If the looping option for the three blue hot spots had been set to Try Again, control wouldn't get to the conditional response icon, and the message wouldn't appear.

Exit Interaction

The TF example in Figure 4.17 shows an Exit Interaction exit type. The path from the "F" icon leads to a wait icon.

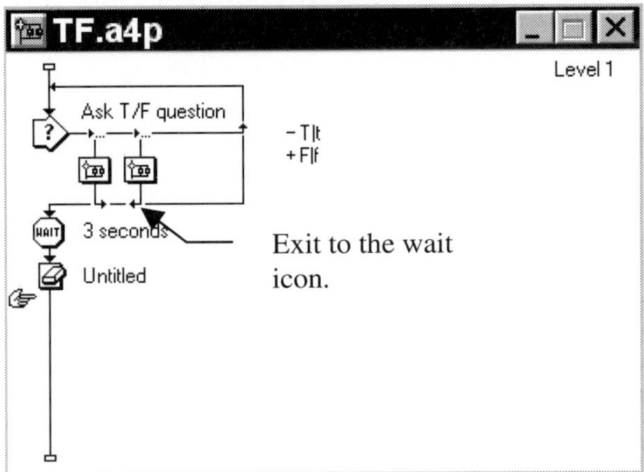

Figure 4.17. The Flowline for the **TF.a4p** Project.

Choose Exit Interaction to make Authorware move to the next icon on the main flowline (not the next icon within the interaction). This is the option usually associated with the correct response because you want to provide some positive feedback, then move on to a new question or topic.

Now the branching arrow on the second response exits the interaction.

Sample File If you want to see the complete example, it's in the Chapter4 folder, and named **TF.a4p**. If sets up a True/False question as a text interaction and designates False ("F" or "f") as the correct response. Don't be concerned about the text response type, just be sure you understand the consequences of selecting Exit Interaction as the Exit Branching choice.

Return

This option is only available with the "Perpetual" option, which is associated with Hot Object, Button, Hot Spot, Target Area, Pull-down menus and conditional interactions.

Perpetual Responses A perpetual response is one that remains active, even if the interaction is exited. You might use this to make pull-down menus and buttons available throughout the title. When a user matches a perpetual response, and Authorware detects a Return branch, control will pass to the icon following the one that was being presented when the user matched the perpetual response. The first section in the next chapter shows how to create a perpetual button.

SUMMARY

Authorware provides a robust collection of eleven types of interactions. Each of the ten requires an interaction icon, a response type, a result icon, and a branching arrow. Each of the ten types shares a common Interaction Options dialog box, which is viewed by double-clicking the interaction icon. This chapter explored the contents of that dialog box in detail.

Study Exercises

4.1 Assume you have a composite image derived from the content of several icons. The user can see ten irregularly shaped items. You would like each of them to be interactive. Which of the eleven interaction types would you choose, and why?

Mouse-Driven Interactions

*I*n the last chapter, we looked at the structure of a typical interaction. It consists of an interaction icon, one of eleven different response types, some response icons and paths to take if the response is right or wrong. This chapter looks in detail at interactions that use the mouse: buttons, hot spots, hot areas and target areas.

Buttons are the means to conventional navigation. You've probably seen multimedia titles that have buttons labeled "next", "previous", and so on. Pushing such buttons invoke further actions, such as advancing to another page.

A hot spot is a rectangular area, which if clicked, invokes a response—some new graphics, a sound, or a jump to another section of the project. A hot object is similar, but whereas hot spots are rectangular, a hot object doesn't have this restriction: The entire object is clickable. Finally, a target area involves moving an object from one location to another. Usually, one of the destination areas is designated as being "correct" For example, you might create a child's game where the child is asked to drag the object to the correct spelling of the object.

At the conclusion of the chapter, you will be able to:

- Use the Button Options properties to limit when a button is active.
- Create custom buttons.
- Associate sound with buttons.
- Use buttons to control events
- Create and use hot spots.
- Create and use hot object responses.
- Create and use target area responses.

BUTTONS

We begin with the most familiar interactions; those based on buttons. Almost all interactive multimedia titles include navigation buttons to move forward, backward, and so on.

Guidelines

Don't fall into the trap of simply using forward and backward buttons on each page. If you do so, you're using a traditional linear page-turning book metaphor. Think interactively. Use hot spots and objects, make the title a cinematic experience, not a book with a computer as a page turner!

Creating Your Own Buttons

This section will show you how to create your own buttons within Authorware. While Authorware contains many predrawn buttons, you can also create your own by following these steps:

1. Draw a rounded rectangle (or rectangle, or use the polygon tool).
2. Add a fill color.
3. Select it.
4. Copy it.
5. Paste it.
6. Color it black.

7. Place it on top of the original button.

8. Use the arrow keys to nudge the black version down two and over two pixels to the right.

9. Select the black image.

10. Use <u>A</u>ttributes><u>S</u>end to Back.

11. Add text to the button.

12. Make the text transparent.

13. Drag over all three objects to select them all.

14. Group them by selecting <u>M</u>odify><u>G</u>roup.

15. Move the button to its desired location.

The light will appear to be coming from the upper left corner of your screen. To achieve a polished, professional look, you should have at least two "looks" or states to your button: One before the button is pressed, and another while it's pressed. You should also associate a sound with the button-push. These features are added using the button editor.

THE BUTTON EDITOR

The Button Editor enables you to associate different look to a button, depending on its state. A button in its "up" (unselected) state should appear different from its "down" (selected) state. To view the Button Library dialog box (shown in Figure 5.4), follow these steps:

1. Add an interaction icon to the flowline.

2. Add a response icon. For a "Help" button, you would probably want to display text, so a display icon would the appropriate choice. For a "Quit" button you need to invoke a calculation icon containing an Authorware function, so you would attach a calculation icon. (See Figure 5.1 for a complete flowline.)

3. Specify "Button" as the type (it's the default).

4. Double-click the response type icon ('ᵞ').

5. You will then see the Button Response Properties dialog box, shown in Figure 5.2. Notice the first tab says, "Button", corresponding to our choice for response type.

6. The current button definition is shown graphically in the upper left corner of Figure 5.2.

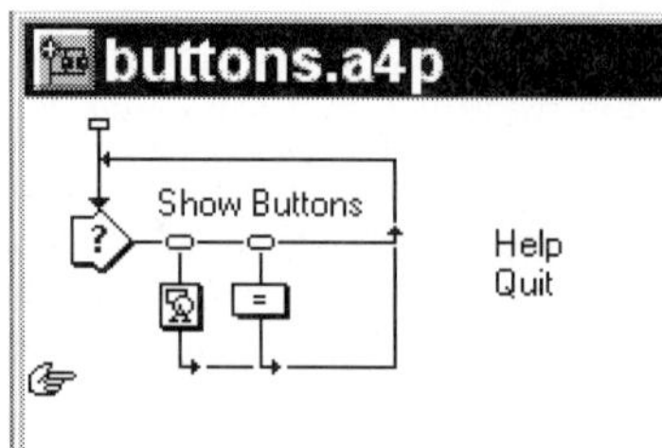

Figure 5.1. A Flowline Containing Two Button Responses.

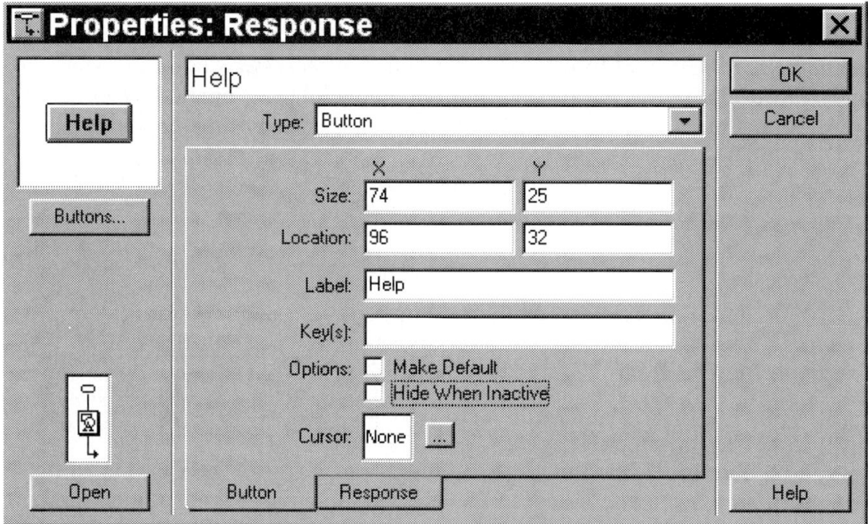

Figure 5.2. The Button Response Properties Dialog Box. To view this, double-click on the button response type icon within an interaction.

Push that button ("Help" above) to view Buttons dialog box, shown in Figure 5.3. This dialog box shows the current list of available button styles for the piece.

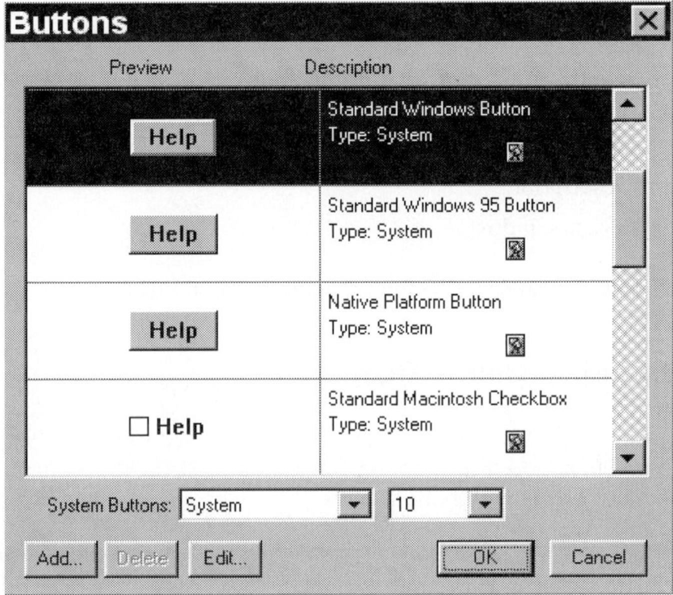

Figure 5.3. The Buttons Dialog Box. Use it to select a button style, font family and font size.

The button captions in Figure 5.3 are all the same, and match the response icon's name (see Figure 5.1 for the response icon names). If we had double-clicked on the response type icon for the Quit button, all captions in Figure 5.3 would have read "Quit". The dialog box merely shows the author the set of available button-types.

To change the characteristics of an existing button-type, push the Edit button. To add a new button, push the Add button. In either case, the Button Editor, shown in Figure 5.4, will open. If you choose to edit one of the standard buttons, you will be asked if you would like to create a copy to work with. It's generally a good idea to do so, so you don't lose any of the original standard button types.

The Button Editor Dialog Box

The Button Editor dialog box, shown in Figure 5.4, is used to add or change the following button properties:

- Captioning.
- Providing for up-to four different "looks": one each for up, down, inactive or when the cursor rolls over the button.
- Applying a sound to the button as it is pushed.
- Specifying the location of the button caption.

- Adding a graphic instead of a caption.

The components of the Button Editor include:

- The States window.
- Button Description.
- Button Assets window.

The next section will describe these components.

The Button Editor Dialog Box

The three sections of the Button Editor dialog box are used to specify which graphics to associate with each state, add a description for each button (note this is not the button's caption), and associate sounds with button states.

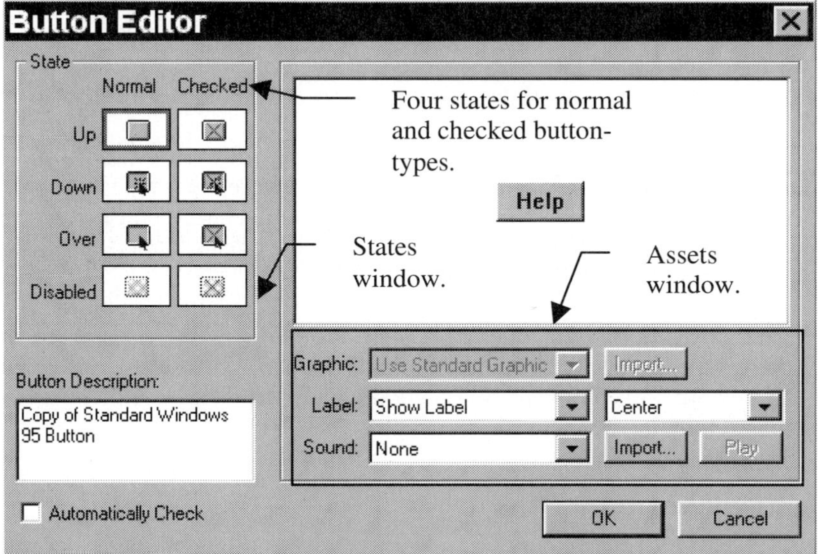

Figure 5.4 The Button Editor Dialog Box. Here is where we define the properties of a new button or change properties of existing ones.

States Window

Each button has four possible *states* or *conditions*. This means you can customize user feedback in many creative ways. For example, you could have one button graphic for its up state, another for its down state, and yet another if it's inactive.

One of the characteristics of interactive multimedia is the ability to provide feedback. Differentiate active from inactive buttons and buttons that have been pushed from those that haven't. Add an audio click as a button is pushed. Use the different media. Use your creative skills, make use of the *multi* in multimedia!

Let's look at the purpose of each of the four Normal button states:

- *Up* is the state when the button is unused. That is, the button has not been pushed.

- *Down* is the way the button will look when pushed. A common technique is to somehow highlight the button when it has been pushed. When the mouse is released, the button returns to its up state. If you want sound to play as the button is pushed, attach the sound effect to the down state.

- *Over* is the way the button should appear when the mouse is positioned over the button. Sometimes this is called a *rollover*.

- *Disabled* is the way you want the button to appear when it is not available. A common practice is to dim such buttons.

To apply a button look to a state, select the state, and then import the button graphic that will apply to that state. For example, you might use an imaging program to create a button called Help-up. A second button, called Help-down, would also be created. They would differ from each other slightly. Perhaps the "down" version would be darkened, or have the light appear to come from a different angle.

Let's now look at the other fields within the Button Editor shown in Figure 5.4, beginning with the Button Description field.

Button Description

Use the Button Description text box to enter up to 80 characters of descriptive text. This is **not** the text to be used on the button: that text is its *label*. The Automatically Check option creates buttons that toggle between checked and unchecked, and is used with radio buttons and check boxes.

Button Asset Window

Here is where the creative work begins. Within this section, we define the graphic and associated sound for each state.

Button Display Window The large white area is where the button is previewed. It will be blank when you first enter this dialog box, provided you have chosen to add a new button. If you are editing an existing button, it will be shown in this area.

Button Graphic Click in this drop-down menu area to import a graphic to be used as a button. The usual Authorware graphic formats are supported (see Chapter 3).

Button Label This is the text that optionally appears on the button. Using this field, you might specify a different caption for each state, or chose to delete a caption in one of the four states. The label is actually entered into the Button Name field in the Button Options dialog box (see Figure 5.1).

Suppose you want the label (caption) to disappear when the button is pushed. To accomplish this you would choose the up state then select Show Label. Next select the down state and choose None, as shown in Figure 5.5.

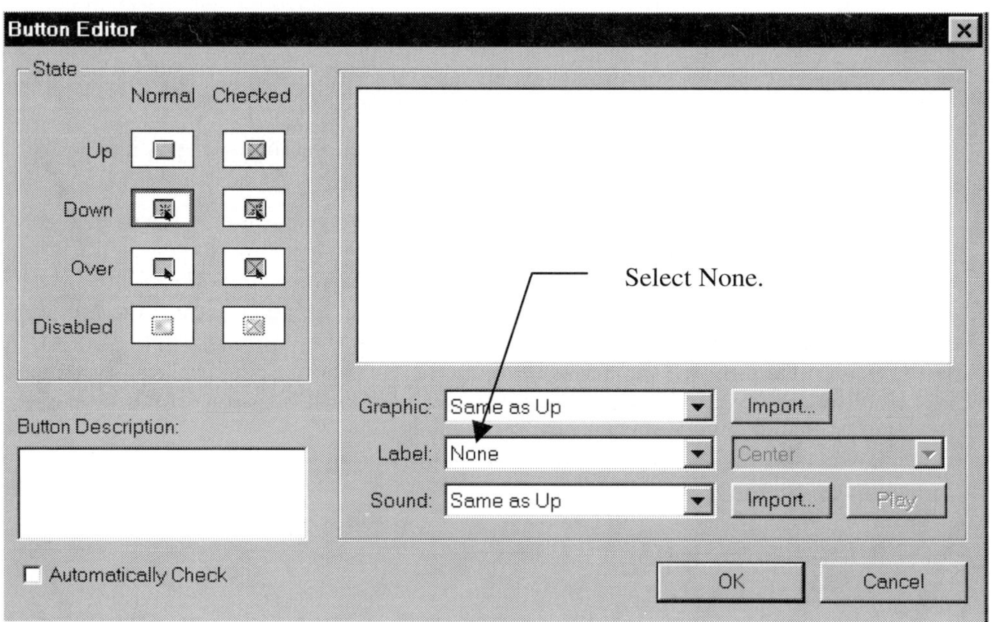

Figure 5.5. Settings to Eliminate A Caption While a Button is in its Down State. Set the Label option to None.

Associating Sounds with States: the Sound Property Use this drop down list to specify when to display a sound that was imported for the button. Each of the states may or may not have an associated sound to play.

Click the Sound Import button to import a sound to associate with a button. Figure 5.6 shows the resulting Load Sound dialog box.

Click the Play button on the Button Editor dialog box to hear the sound you've imported.

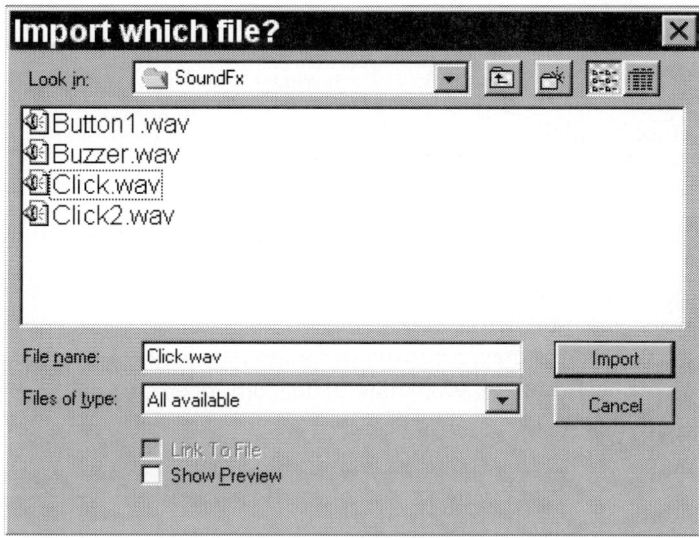

Figure 5.6. The Load Sound Dialog Box. Specify the file name, and then push the Import button.

This concludes the discussion about the button editor. Let's add a button to the library to reinforce what we've learned.

Sample File We are going to create two buttons, each having two states and an audible sound as the button is released. To preview this exercise, open the **Buttons.a4p** file in the Chapter5 folder on the CD-ROM. Push the toggle button and look for the words to appear. Run from the start and push the Quit button. Let's see how this was constructed.

Your Turn

❑ Start a new piece.

❑ Add a display icon and name it Background.

❑ Open the Background icon and import the **Tmplate4.BMP** from the Templates folder on the CD-ROM.

❑ Scale the image to 90% in the Y direction.

❑ Add an interaction icon and name it Buttons.

❑ Attach two display icons and name them Start and Quit.

❑ Your flowline should look like the following:

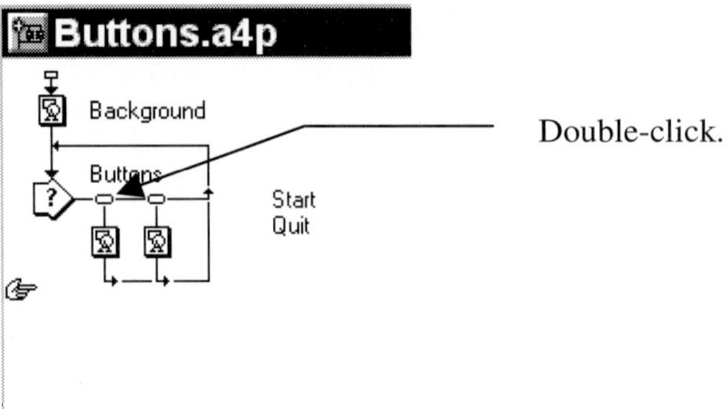

❑ Double-click on the Start button response type icon.

❑ When the Response Properties dialog box opens, push the Buttons button, as shown below.

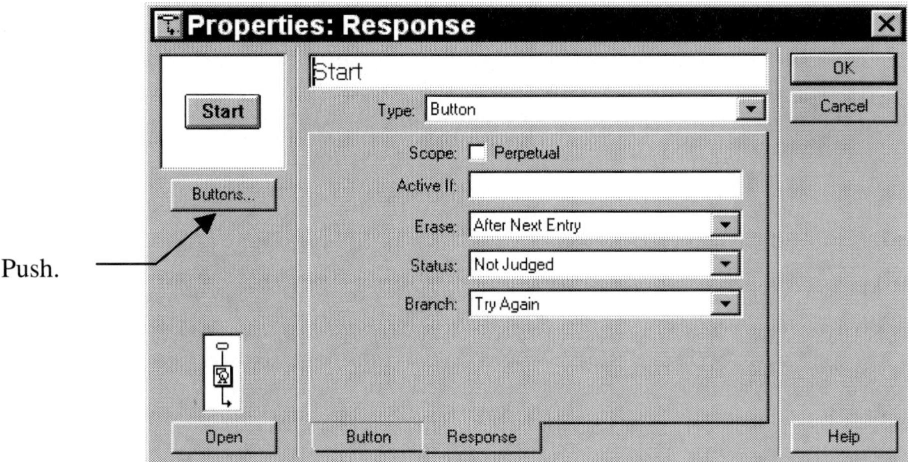

❑ The Buttons dialog box opens. Because we are going to create a new button, push the Add button, as shown in the figure below.

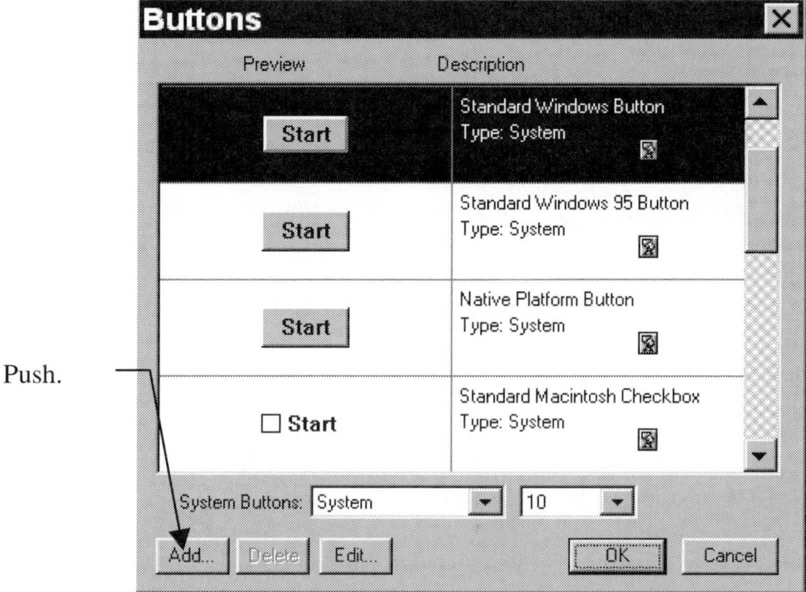

Push.

❏ The button editor will open, as you can see from the figure below.

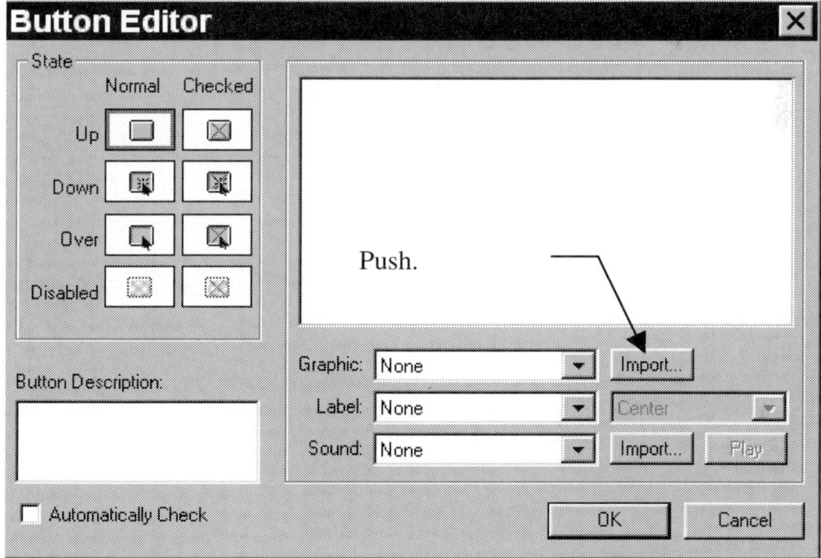

❏ Click the Up normal state button.
❏ Push the Import button next to the Graphic field and select the **TbUp** image in the Images\Buttons folder on your CD-ROM.

❑ Push the Import Sound button and when the Import Which File dialog box opens, select the **Click.wav** file as the sound. It is in the Sounds folder on your CD-ROM.

❑ Push the Down Normal button and import the **TbDn** button, using the steps from importing the **TbUp** button.

❑ Make the button perpetual.

❑ Now do the same for the Quit button. This time use **Quit-up** and **Quit-dn** images.

❑ Choose **Buzzer.wav** as the button sound.

❑ Move the buttons so they cover the round areas near the lower right corner of the Background.

❑ Now you need to add content to the display icons.

❑ Open the Start display button and this white 20-point bold, italicized, transparent text "Get ready to enter Cyberworld!!!"

❑ Open the Quit display and create a small red box with 14-point white transparent text " Are You sure you want to Quit" inside the box.

❑ Run your piece.

❑ Push your toggle button. The Cyberworld text should display and audible feedback should signify that the button has been pushed.

❑ Push your Quit button and the white text on the red background should display.

❑ Listen for the click each time you click.

❑ Save your work as **Buttons.a4p**.

Now that you've seen how to add a button to the library, let's look in more depth at button interactions.

BUTTON INTERACTIONS

When you add a button interaction to the flowline, Authorware automatically creates a default button in a default location in the Presentation window. The button's name will match that of the icon used to create the button. Similar to all interactions, when the button is clicked, the contents of the associated result (target) icon are executed. By default a button's look and name consist of a traditional button shape with a name matching that of the icon that created it. These facts are shown in Figure 5.7.

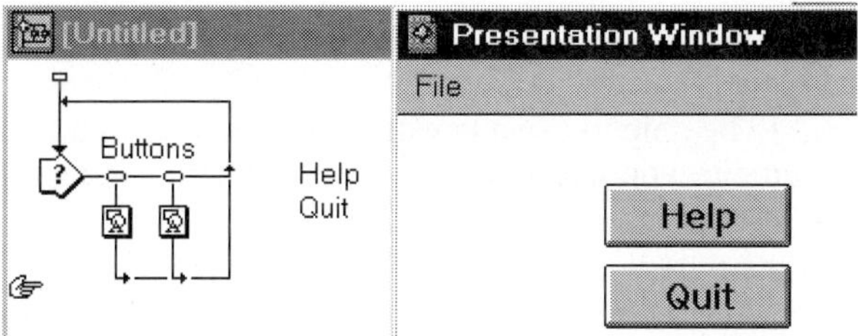

Figure 5.7. An Example Showing That Button and Icon Names Will Be the Same.

In Figure 5.7 we created two button responses, Help and Quit. Authorware created two buttons, one for each icon. The button labels match their respective icon names.

Opening the Response (button) Properties dialog box permits you to change the name, as well as many other button properties. Do this by double-clicking the response type icon. The Response (button) Properties dialog box is shown in Figure 5.8.

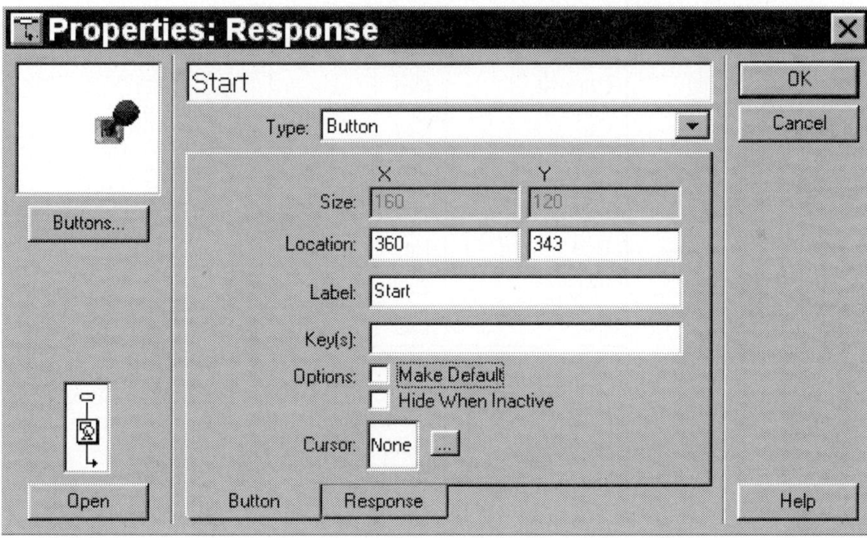

Figure 5.8. The Properties Dialog Box for Button Responses. To view it, double-click the button response type icon within the interaction.

Changing the Button Name

Recall that the title you assign to the icon on the flowline becomes the button's label. The button will be automatically sized to accommodate this title. If you alter the name here, the icon's title will change accordingly.

Assigning Hot Keys to Buttons: The Key(s) Field

You might find it useful to be able to use a keystroke (a hot key) in addition to being able to push the button. For example, you might want to use Ctrl-Q for the Quit button and Ctrl-H for the Help button.

You should accommodate upper and lower case by using the "or" separator ("|"). To allow H or h, enter: H|h. To also allow Alt-H, use AltH|Alth|H|h. Function keys are referred to as F1, F2, ...F15. Table 5.1 lists the keys and their corresponding names.

Table 5.1 Authorware Key Names.

Key Name	Windows Key
Alt	Alt
Backspace	Backspace
Break	Break
Clear	none
Cmd	Ctrl
Control	Ctrl
Ctrl	Ctrl
Del or Delete	Del or Delete
DownArrow	down arrow
End	End
Enter	Enter
Esc	Esc
F1, F2, ...F15	F1, F2,...F15
Help	none
Home	Home
Ins or Insert	Insert or Ins
LeftArrow	left arrow
PageDown	PgDn
PageUp	Pg Up
Pause	Pause
Print	Print
Return	Enter
RightArrow	right arrow
Shift	Shift
SysReq	SysReq

Table 5.1. Authorware Key Names (continued)

Tab	Tab
UpArrow	Up Arrow

Making a Button Perpetual: The Perpetual Checkbox

This option makes the button active, even if the interaction is exited. Don't forget to erase when the button when it is no longer needed.

Sample File If you open the **Active.a4p** file in the Chapter5 folder on the CD-ROM, and run the application, you will see a perpetual button named Change State. If this button is pushed, it changes the state (value) of a variable from 0 to 1 or 1 to 0. Following is the flowline for the file.

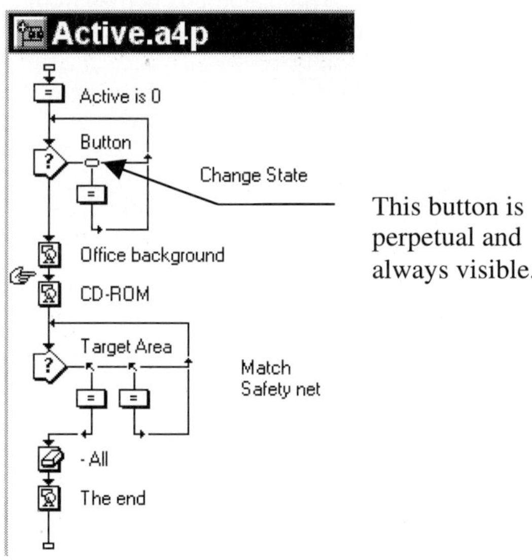

This button is perpetual and always visible.

If you double-click the button response symbol, and then click the Response tab, you'll see the button's current options, as shown in Figure 5.9.

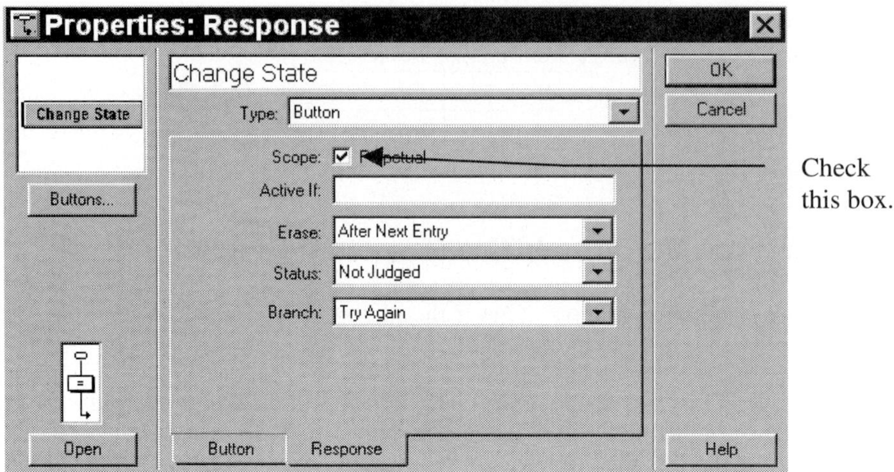

Figure 5.9. Settings To Make A Button Perpetual. The dialog box comes from the **Active.a4p** file in the Chapter5 folder on the CD-ROM.

Unfortunately, although the button is active at all times, it may not be visible. To make a button always visible and active:

- Set the button's active state to Perpetual.
- Select the interaction icon containing the button.
- Choose <u>M</u>odify><u>I</u>con><u>P</u>roperties.
- Adjust the layer value so that it is higher than other layers.

The properties for the Button icon are shown in Figure 5.10.

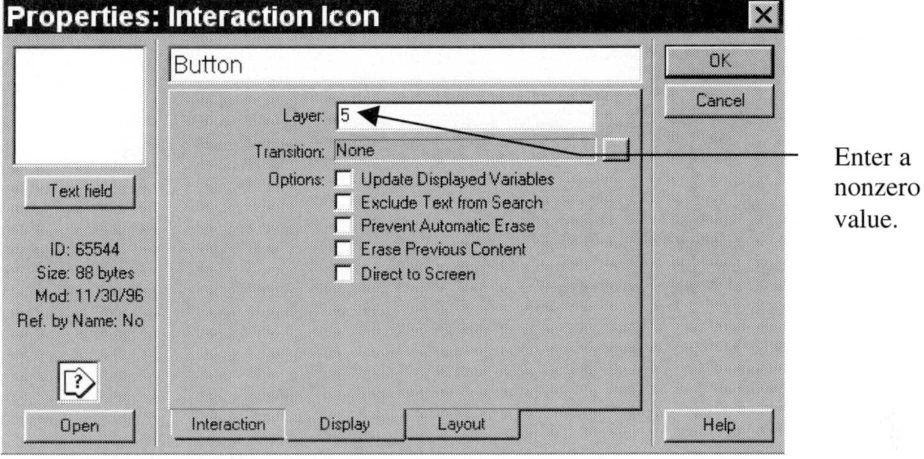

Figure 5.10. The Display Properties for the Button Icon in Figure 5.9. The layer value is set to a value greater than zero, thus the button is always visible.

Creating a Perpetual Quit Button

Follow the steps that follow to create a Quit button that is always active.

1. Create an interaction with a button response type.
2. Attach a calculation icon to the interaction icon.
3. Open the calculation icon and add: `Quit(0)` as the single statement. This means to exit to the Program Manager with Windows 3.X, and to the Desktop with Windows 95 computers.
4. Select the interaction icon and set its layer to 10 (actually any number above zero). This will keep the button on the top layer.

Sample File The **Perpetual.a4p** file in the Chapter5 folder contains a complete example of a perpetual Quit button.

Controlling the Active State of a Button: The Active if Field

Suppose you only want the button to be active under a certain condition. In that case, you would specify the condition here (see figure 5.9). In the example that follows, we use a variable, called `Counter`. As long as its value is within a set of limits, the button remains active. If the variable exceeds the limits, the button is dimmed (made inactive). The Active If field can be seen in Figure 5.9, and that's where we'll enter the variable.

Sample File Open the **Actbutn.a4p** file in the Chapter5 folder. Its flowline is shown in Figure 5.11.

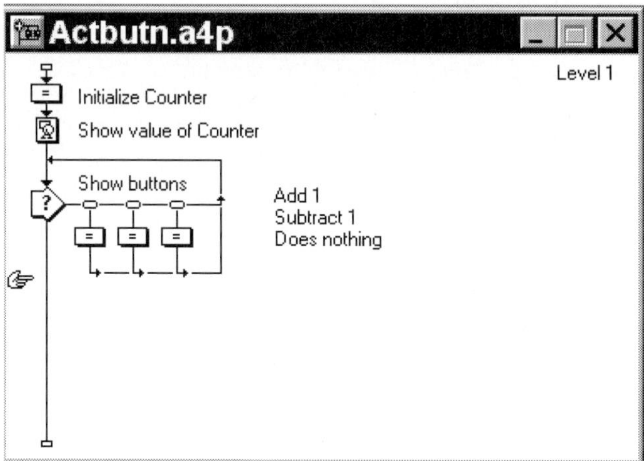

Figure 5.11. The Flowline for **Actbutn.a4p**. It has three buttons. One adds 1 to a variable, Counter, while a second subtracts 1. The final button does nothing but switches between active and inactive states depending on the value of Counter.

Run the project and repeatedly push the Add 1 button. It adds 1 to Counter. Eventually Counter will exceed an upper limit (9), which causes the "Does Nothing" button to dim. The response for Add 1 is a calculation icon having the content shown below.

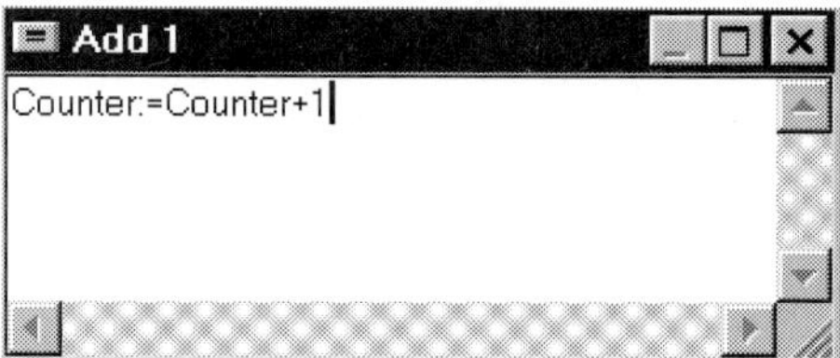

Figure 5.12. The Contents of the Calculation Icon Associated with the Add 1 Button in Figure 5.11.

It adds 1 to the current value of Counter. Subtract 1 does the opposite - it subtracts 1 from Counter. If pushed repeatedly, the value of Counter falls below two, and the button named "Does nothing" is again dimmed.

The key to making the "Does nothing" button active or inactive lies in the Response properties for the Does Nothing button, shown in Figure 5.13.

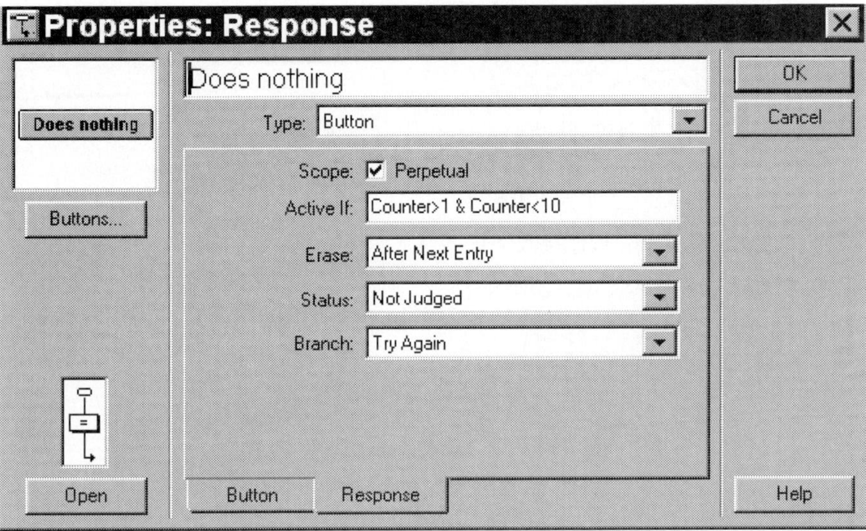

Figure 5.13. An Example Showing A Condition, Which If True Specifies When A Button Is Active. As long as the value of `Counter` is between 2 and 9, the "Does Nothing" button is active.

Look at the Active if text box entry. It says the button is usable (active) as long as the value of `Counter` is between 2 and 9 ("&" means and).

Specifying How to Show an Inactive Button: The Options Field

There are two options in Figure 5.8, which specify how to show an inactive button: dim the button (the default) or hide it. In Figure 5.14, you can see we chose to make the button dim when the value of `Counter` wasn't within the specified limits. This is because we did not check the Hide option button.

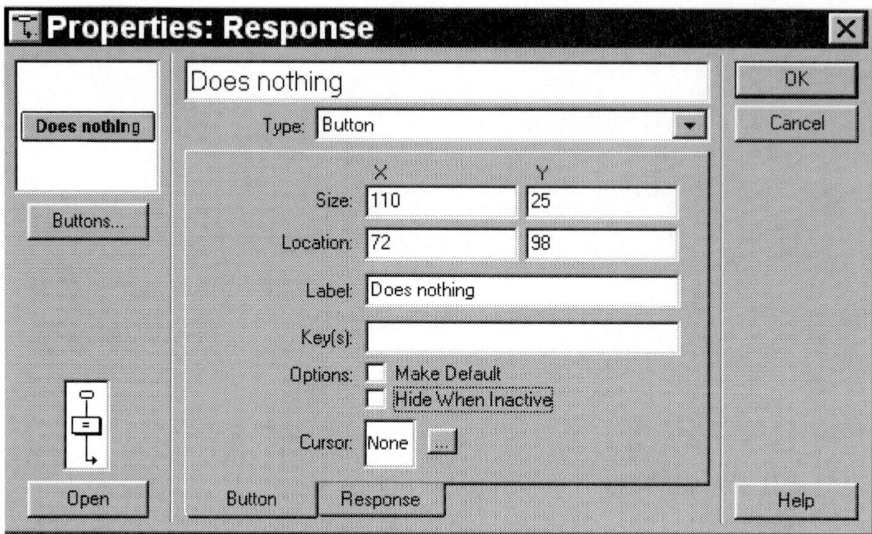

Figure 5.14. The Button Properties for the Does Nothing Button. The Options section is used to specify whether to dim the button if inactive (the default) or to hide the button.

Showing a Default Button

If you are presenting a series of buttons and want one to be the default (that is, it will be pushed if the Enter or Return key is used), check the Make Default button for the default button only. A heavy line will be drawn around the button.

Specifying a Custom Cursor

If you want the cursor to change shape while over your button, push the Cursor button, and then choose a cursor shape from the list. You can add your own custom cursors to the list by using programs specifically designed for this purpose.

Specifying a Button's Position and Size

You can specify pixel values to precisely locate a button. However, it is much easier to simply drag and drop. That is, use your mouse to drag your button to its desired location, then release the mouse button.

Specifying the Button Type

Clicking on the "Buttons" button or the preview button in Figure 5.14 displays what the default button looks like, or allows you to select another button type via the Button Library, which we discussed earlier.

This concludes the discussion about buttons. They will probably be your most often used interaction type, but surely not the only type. Hot spots are another frequently used interaction type, and are discussed in the next section.

HOT SPOT INTERACTIONS

Hot spots are rectangular areas over which the user can click, double-click, or simply move the cursor. As the hot spot is activated, the contents of the associated result icon are executed. To create a hot spot:

1. If necessary, add an interaction icon to the flowline.

2. Attach a response icon to the interaction icon. When the Response Type dialog box opens, select Hot Spot. Then push the OK button.

3. Name the icons.

4. Add the graphic containing the areas to be made hot. Typically, this is added to the interaction icon. To add the graphic double-click the icon. When the Presentation window opens, either import a graphic or use the toolbox to add content. Close the Presentation window.

5. Add a target response icon—a display icon, for example, as shown in the figure below.

6. Double-click the hot spot response type symbol to view the Hot Spot Properties dialog box as shown in Figure 5.15.

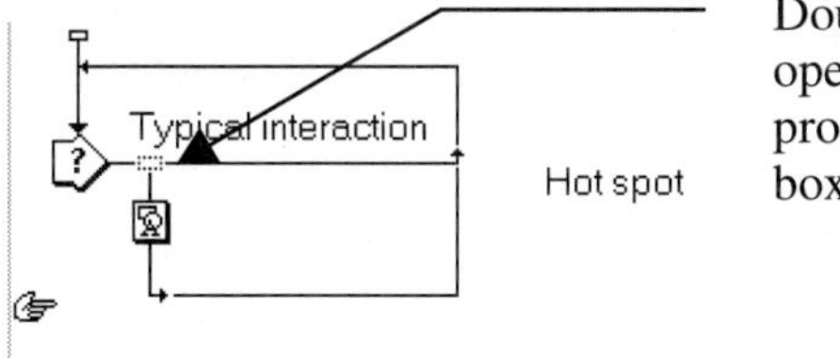

7. Enter appropriate values for the dialog box options shown in Figure 5.15.

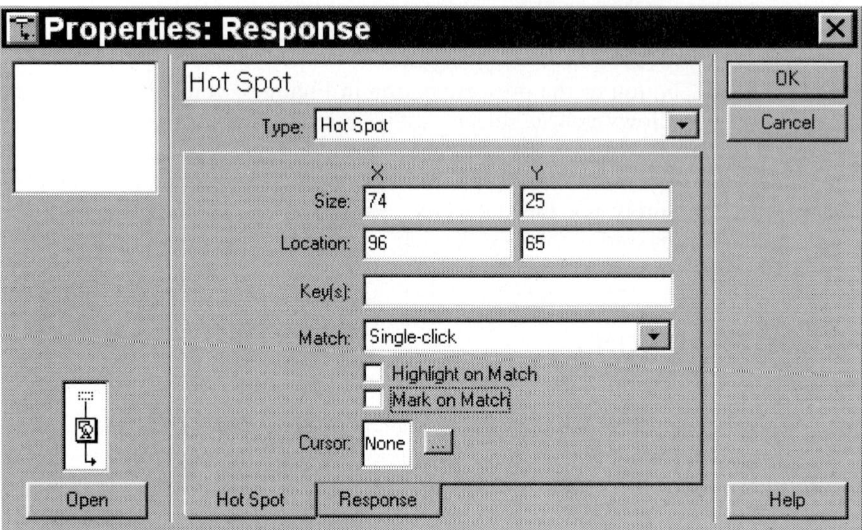

Figure 5.15. The Hot Spot Properties Dialog Box. To open it, double-click the hot spot response type symbol.

8. While the Hot Spot Properties dialog box is open, you will see a small dotted rectangle, shown in Figure 5.16, within the Presentation window. This box defines the default hot spot area on the screen. You might need to move the dialog box to see the hot spot area.

Figure 5.16. The Rectangular Area that Defines a Hot Spot.

9. Move and size the hot spot rectangle so it covers the area you wish to make interactive.
10. Add the content to the response icon.

Let's next look at some of the settings in the Hot Spot properties dialog box. Because the Response tab is the same as that which we saw with buttons, we'll concentrate on the Hot Spot tab.

The Hot Spot Properties Dialog Box

The Title, Key(s), Cursor, Location and Size, plus all the settings in the Response tab are used the same way as with the button response, which we discussed above. Let's examine the other options.

Auto Highlighting Hot Spots: Highlight on Match

If you choose the Highlight on Match option, Authorware will display inverse colors, if the hot spot is matched (selected).

Indicating a Match Has Been Made: Mark on Match

If you use this option, you will see a small square along the left side of each hot spot. When the response is matched (clicked, double-clicked or simply by moving the cursor over the hot spot), the square will be filled in.

Figure 5.17 shows the square prior to selecting a hot spot, and Figure 5.18 how the small square looks after selecting the hot spot.

Figure 5.17. An Unselected Hot Spot, when the Mark on Match Option is Selected.

Figure 5.18. A Selected Hot Spot.

Match

The Match drop-down list determines how the user will select the hot spot. The options are:

- Single-click.
- Double-click.
- Cursor in area.

Specifying the Hot Spot Area

The default hot spot area will be shown like the figure below.

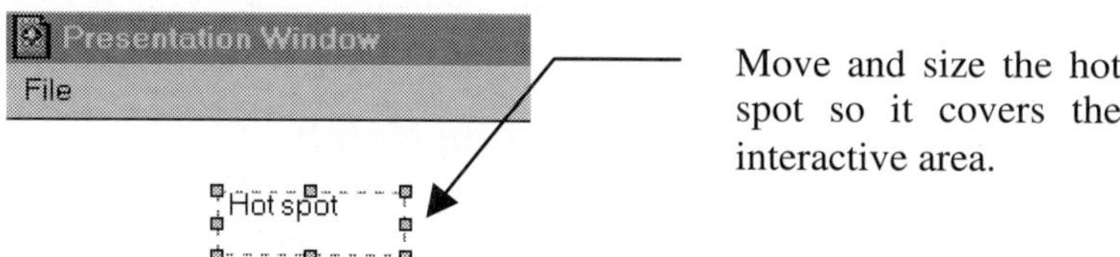

Move and size the hot spot so it covers the interactive area.

To move and size the area, use the mouse to drag the rectangular area to its destination, then size it.

Sample File See the **HotSpot.a4p** file in the Chapter 5 folder on the CD-ROM, if you want to see the completed example that follows. Run the piece and move the cursor over the tulips. There should be a message saying "Amsterdam is known for its tulips." Let's how this piece was created.

Your Turn

❏ Close the **HotSpot** file and start a new piece.

❏ Add an interaction icon to the flowline.

❏ Drag a display icon to the right of the interaction icon and choose Hot Spot as the type

❏ Name the icons: give the interaction icon the name Hot Spot Example and name the Display icon Tulips. Next, add the graphic content to the interaction icon itself.

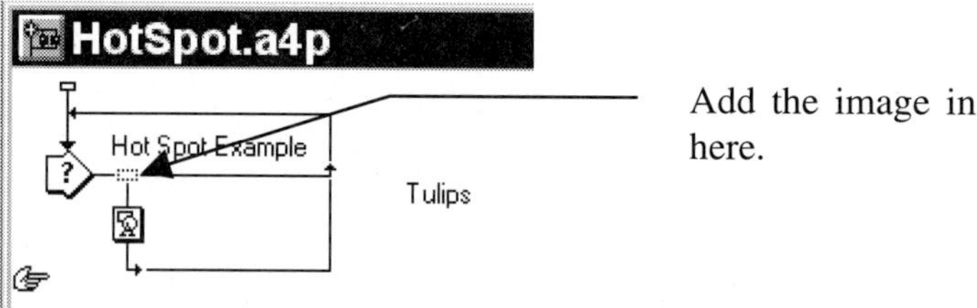

Add the image in here.

❏ Add the image containing the future hot spot: Double-click the Hot Spot Example interaction icon, when the Presentation window opens, choose <u>F</u>ile><u>I</u>mport and select the **Amstrdam.bmp** bitmap image from the Chapter5\Images folder on your CD-ROM.

❏ Double-click the hot spot response symbol to open the Hot Spot Properties dialog box.

❏ Specify the hot spot options. Start by selecting the In Area Match option in the Hot Spot tab dialog box as shown below.

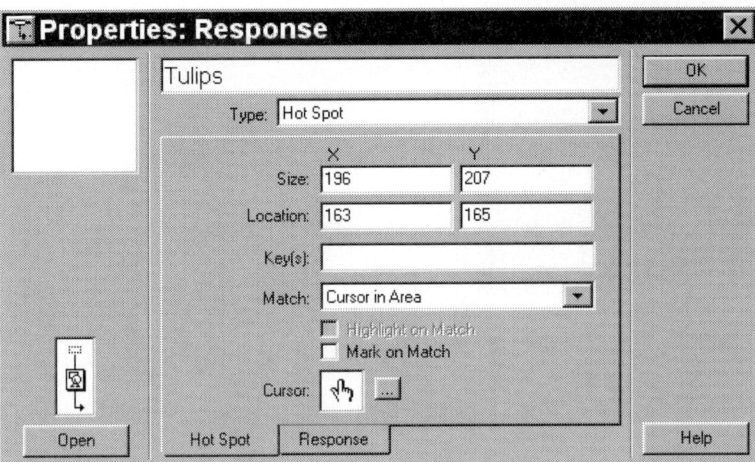

❏ Choose the Response tab to reveal the next figure.

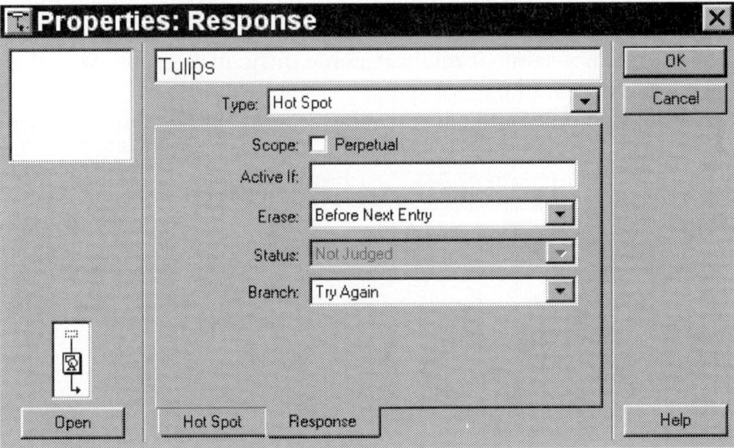

❏ Choose the Before Next Entry Erase option.

❏ Adjust the hot spot rectangle so it covers the desired hot area: In our case the tulips, as shown by the next figure.

❏ Add the response content. Open the display icon and add this text: Amsterdam is known for its tulips.

❏ Test your piece, and if it's working correctly, save it as **HotSpot.a4p**.

You should also create a "catchall" hot spot. This is to catch the user who clicks in areas not designated as being hot. As we've seen previously, a catchall is always the last icon within an interaction. To create a hot spot catchall, add a display or map response as the last position on the right. Then use the hot spot rectangle to designate the entire screen as the hot spot. Add appropriate text to the response icon(s).

As you add additional hot spots, it might become difficult to remember where they all are. Striking Ctrl-Alt will display all the hot spots.

In the HotSpot project, you would add a display icon as shown in the following figure:

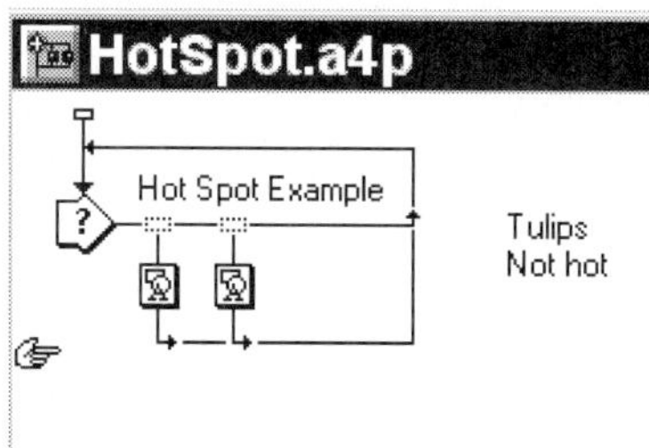

Next you would set the Not hot options and size the hot spot so it covers the complete screen.

Sample File You can view this by opening and then running **HotSpot2.a4p** in the Chapter5 folder. If you do open the file, move the mouse around and watch the message saying the current spot isn't hot.

The catchall works because Authorware evaluates interactions from left to right. If a planned-for hot spot is selected, Authorware detects a match. Because branching is set to Try Again, control returns to the interaction and never gets to the catchall.

However, if no correct hot spot is clicked, control passes to the catchall. Catchalls only work if branching is set to Try Again for all icons to the left of the catchall. If Continue is used instead, Authorware will respond to the matching response, but control will also flow to the catchall, resulting in an incorrect feedback.

Hot spots are commonly used when you want to designate several rectangular areas as being interactive. If you want to make a complete object interactive, or hot, use a hot object interaction.

HOT OBJECT INTERACTIONS

Recall hot objects are functionally equivalent to hot spots. The major difference is the hot area isn't restricted to being rectangular: Entire objects become interactive. The dialog box for hot objects is similar to that of hot spots.

The Hot Object Properties dialog box is shown in Figure 5.19.

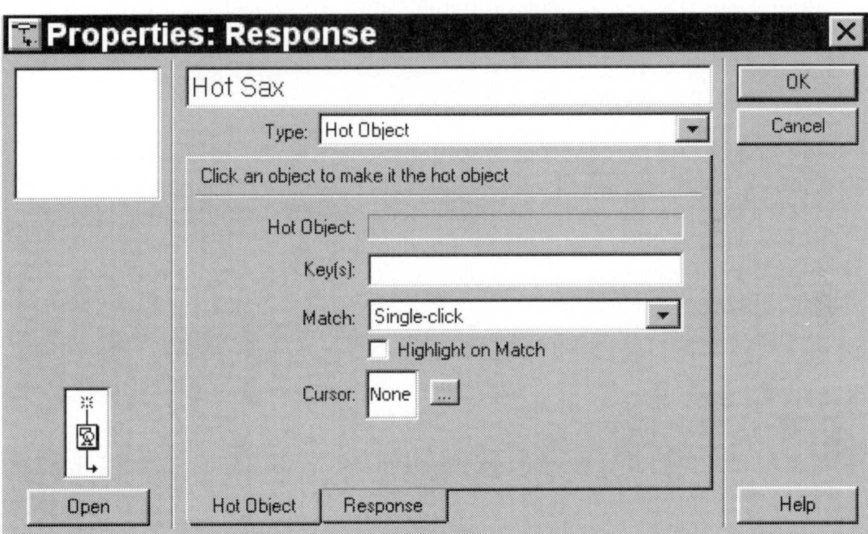

Figure 5.19. The Hot Object Properties Dialog Box.

The only difference from the hot spot properties dialog box is the inclusion of the message you can see at the top: "Click an object to make it the hot object." You are being prompted to click the object in the Presentation window to be made interactive. Once you choose an object as being the hot one, the dialog box changes to be like that shown in Figure 5.20.

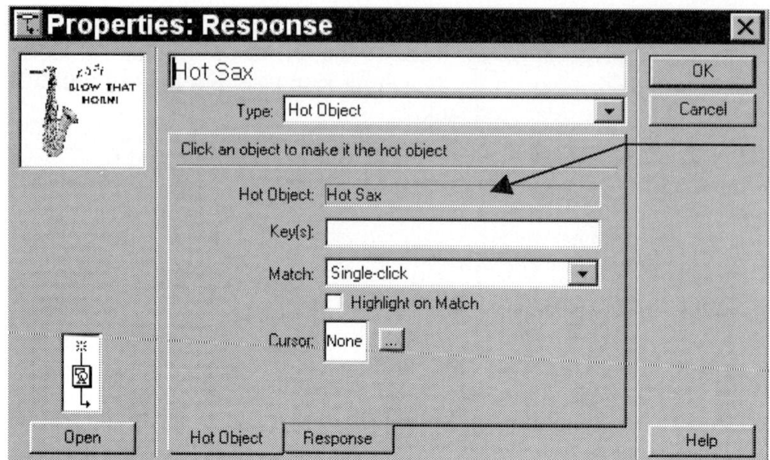

Name of the icon containing the hot object.

Figure 5.20. The Hot Object Properties after an Object is Chosen as being the Hot One.

Let's build a project that uses hot objects.

Sample File To preview this next interaction, open the **Lighthous.a4p** file in the Chapter5 folder on the CD ROM. Move the mouse over the moon and watch what happens. Now move the mouse away from the moon. Let's see how to build this project.

The task is to display a graphic of a house with all its doors closed. We'll add a background from a library and place the house image over it. Next, we'll draw a moon that will become the hot object. When the cursor passes over the moon, the lights in the house will come on and the doors will open. If the **Lighthous.a4p** piece is open, close it at this time.

Your Turn
❏ Start a new project.
❏ Add the Mottled image from the Backgrounds library in the Libraries folder on your CD-ROM.
❏ Add a display icon named Doors Closed.

❏ Run your piece and when the empty icon opens, import the image of a house with its lights off and doors closed. The file's name is **offclsd**, and it is in the Chapter5\Images folder on your CD-ROM. The house should be in the middle of the frame. Don't move it.
❏ Add another display icon.

❑ Label it Moon.

❑ Shift-double-click the Moon icon to open it along with the complete Presentation window content.

❑ Draw a white circle using the ellipse tool from the toolbox (Recall: Use shift-click to draw a circle). Your Presentation window should look like that in the figure that follows.

❑ Add an empty interaction icon below your Moon icon.

❑ Label it Turn on the Lights.

❑ Attach a display icon to the Turn on the Lights interaction icon.

❑ Choose Hot Object as the type.

❑ Push OK.

❑ Label it Hot moon.

❑ Double-click the response type.

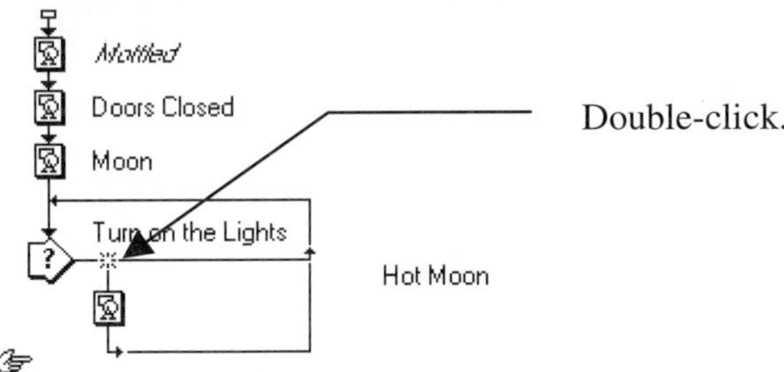

❑ You are being prompted to click on the object to be made hot.

❑ Click on the moon you drew earlier. The status line at the top will now say Hot Object Moon. Note that Moon is the name of the icon that contains the moon.

❏ Note: We could have drawn the moon inside the Turn on the Lights interaction icon. We merely chose this method to demonstrate the fact there are usually several ways to accomplish the same thing. Authorware is a versatile software package.

❏ Next, we want to show a different cursor while over the hot object, so push the Cursor button.

❏ Select the "hand" Standard cursor and push the OK button to close the Cursors dialog box.

❏ Next, choose which type of mouse interaction should activate the hot object. Choose the Match option, Cursor on Object. This means as soon as the cursor passes over the moon, the match is made.

❏ Push the Response tab and set the Erase Feedback option to Don't Erase. Otherwise, the new image (the house with its lights on) will disappear.

❏ Click the OK button in the Hot Object Properties dialog box.

Figures 5.21 and 5.22 show the completed Hot Object Properties dialog boxes.

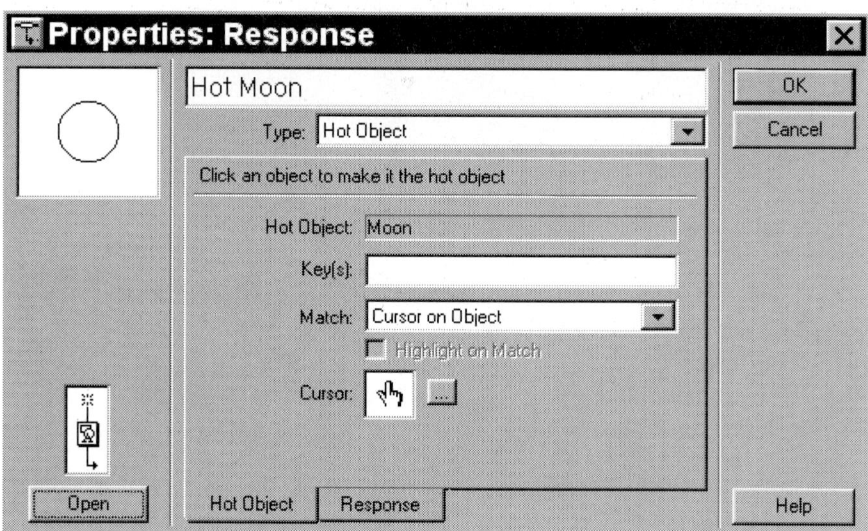

Figure 5.21. Final Settings for the Hot Object Tab for the Hot Moon Icon.

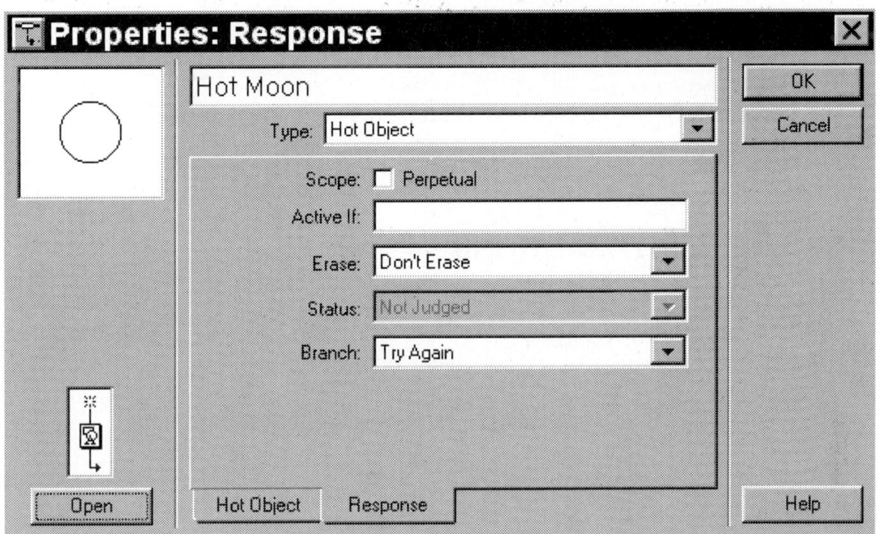

Figure 5.22. Final Settings for the Response Tab for the Hot Moon Icon.

Now we need to specify what to do if the hot object is selected. We want to give the illusion that the lights in the house have been turned on. We do this by displaying another bit map, which is similar to the closed-door graphic, but has lights on.

❏ Press the Restart button.
❏ Move the cursor over the moon.
❏ When the empty display icon (Hot Moon) is encountered, the Presentation window will open.
❏ Import the **onclsd** bitmap file from the \Chapter5\Images folder.

Run your piece and position the mouse over the moon — the lights should go on! The moon also disappears. Why?

The moon we manually added to the graphic of the house with the lights out obviously isn't on the graphic we just imported. How can we fix this?

We could simply add the moon to the Hot Moon icon. An alternative is to flip back and forth between the two images. As the cursor moves away from the moon, show the previous version of the image, in effect erasing the "feedback" (the image of the house with its lights on) before Authorware checks for the next interaction. To do this:

❏ Open the response type.
❏ Set the Erase Feedback option to Before Next Entry.
❏ Save your work as **Lighthous.a4p**.
❏ Run the project again. Now as the cursor enters the moon area, the lights go on. As it leaves the area, the lights go out again. This is because we erase the feed-

back (the new image that shows the house with the lights on) before the next entry. That is, before the user moves the cursor over the hot object.

The third, and final, mouse-driven interaction is known as a Target Area interaction. We discuss this type next.

TARGET AREA INTERACTIONS

The purpose of a target area interaction is to drag an object to a predetermined location. There are two main components: The object being dragged, and the specified destination area.

You create a target area interaction, by following these steps:

1. Place the object to be moved in a display icon that precedes the Target Area interaction.
2. Set up an interaction.
3. Add a response icon.
4. Specify the type as being Target Area.
5. Specify the options in the Target Area Properties dialog box.

The Target Area Options Dialog Box

The Target Area Properties dialog box is shown in Figure 5.23.

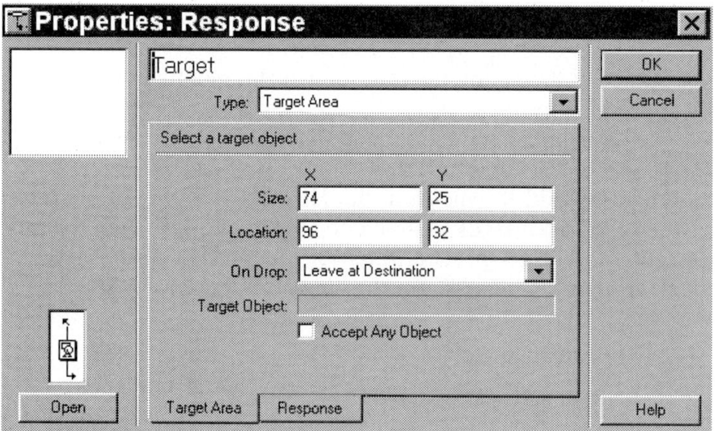

Figure 5.23. The Target Area Options Dialog Box.

There are two new options: a destination drop-down (On Drop) and an Accept Any Object checkbox.

Destination Drop-Down Options

This option specifies what to do when the object is dropped at its final location. There are three options: Leave (the default), Put Back, and Snap to Center.

Leave Use of this option will cause the object to be left at the location specified by the user at the conclusion of the drag and drop operation.

Put Back This option will return the object to it original location. Use this option if the interaction is a test or quiz having a correct answer. If the object is dragged to the wrong location, this option will move the object back to its original location. Use this option in conjunction with Try Again branching.

Snap to Center This option will snap the object to the center of the target area. Suppose the target area is quite large. Using this option, once the user lets go, the object will be placed in the exact center. You might find this useful to designate a correct response.

The Accept Any Object Checkbox

Ordinarily, you set up a target response so one particular object must be dragged to a given location. If this option is selected, any object can be dragged to the target area and can therefore trigger the associated response. We will use this option when we construct a safety net in the exercise that follows.

Specifying the Target Area

When the Target Area Options dialog box first opens, you will see a default rectangle in the Presentation window having the same name as the icon attached to the Target Area response type, as you can see from the figure below.

The dialog box will also prompt you to move the object to the target area. Be sure to do this: Don't merely size and move the rectangle. Once the object is moved, then size the target area appropriately. We'll see an example of this in the next exercise.

Once complete, the new project will check to see if a magnifying glass is over a target area: a silhouetted image of a family. If it is, an erase icon is executed and the image of the family removed from the Presentation window.

Sample File Open the **Target.a4p** file in the Chapter5 folder on the CD-ROM. Drag the silhouetted family anywhere but on top of the magnifying glass. Drop the image. It returns to its original position. Now drop it on the magnifying glass. The family is erased. Close the **Target.a4p** file and let's see how it was constructed.

Your Turn

❏ Start a new piece.

❏ Add a display icon, open the Chapter5\Images folder, and import the **childsil** bitmap. Make its mode transparent.

❏ Add another display icon, and import the object to be moved: the magnifying glass. Its name is **maglass**. Name the display icon Magnify Glass.

❏ Add an interaction icon with an associated erase icon, named Erase Family. Name the interaction icon Target. Choose Target Area as the response type.

❏ Run the project and the Target Area Properties dialog box will open. Notice the message: "Drag the object to the target position. Also, note the dotted rectangle in the Presentation window. It marks the current target location. Its label matches that of the icon: "Erase Family".

❏ Click the family.

❏ Drag the family over the magnifying glass.

❏ Resize the rectangle so it covers the family.

❏ Choose Exit Interaction as the Branch option because this is the correct response —we want to exit the interaction and pass control to the next icon (which will be an erase icon.)

❏ Leave the Erase option as Don't Erase.

❏ Run the project and drag the family over the magnifying glass.

❏ When the empty erase icon opens, choose to erase the family by clicking on it.

❏ Apply a transition erase effect. As you can see from the figure below, we chose a Spiral effect.

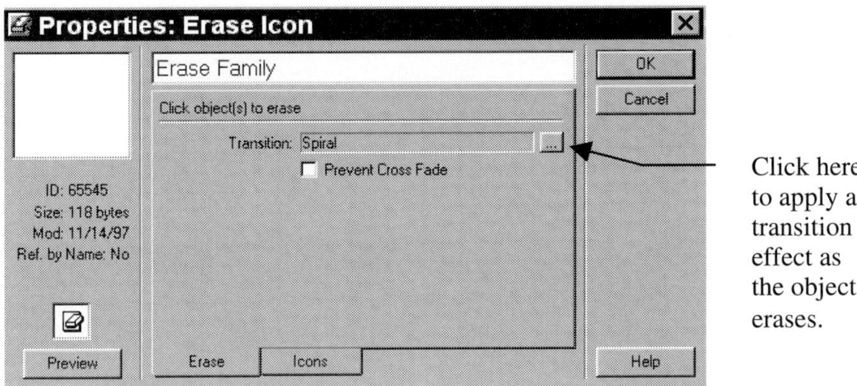

Click here
to apply a
transition
effect as
the object
erases.

Add an erase icon that deletes all objects when the user makes a correct response.
❏ Save your work as **Target.a4p**.

An enhancement to our piece would be the following: If the user drags the family glass over the target area, leave it there. If the family is dragged a location other than the correct one, return it to its original location. This is an occasion when we need to use the Put Back destination option in the Target Area Properties dialog box.

Consider another example where the user must drag images of wine bottles to the countries where each is produced. If the user is correct, the bottle stays, but if incorrect, the bottle is returned to its original location.

Creating a Catchall or Safety net

To create a catchall:

1. Drag an icon to the right of the correct target area response type.

2. Name the icon (safety net or catchall would be appropriate).

3. Run the piece.

4. When the Target Area Properties dialog box opens, check the Accept any Object box.

5. Select the Put Back option.

6. Re-size the rectangle so it covers the entire screen.

 **Your Turn**

❏ Attach a display icon named Catchall to the Move to the Magnify interaction icon. Your flowline should now look like the figure below.

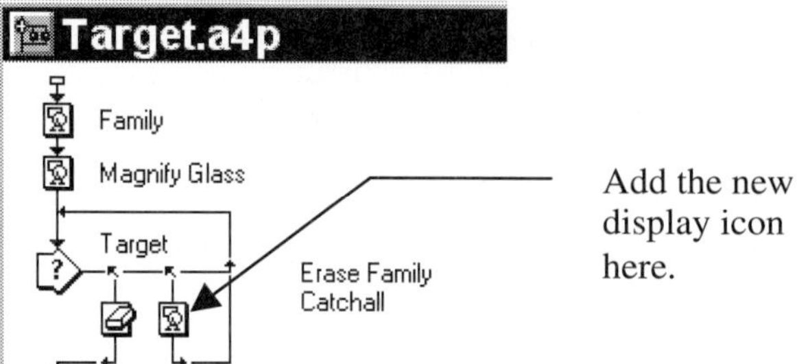

Add the new display icon here.

❏ Run the piece and drag the family to any location other than the correct one. Be careful not to accidentally move the background.

❏ When the Target Area Response Properties dialog box opens, set the properties as they are in the figure below.

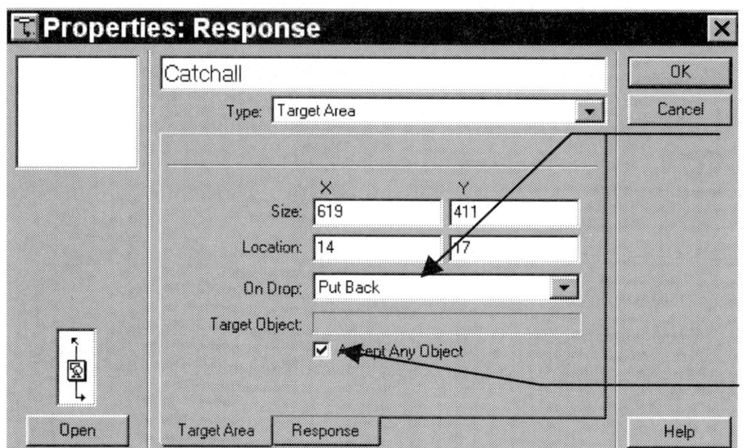

Return the magnifying glass to its original location.

Consider anything a match.

❏ Be sure to check the Accept Any Object box, so that clicks anywhere are considered a match.

❏ Resize the target area rectangle so it covers the entire screen, as shown by the figure below.

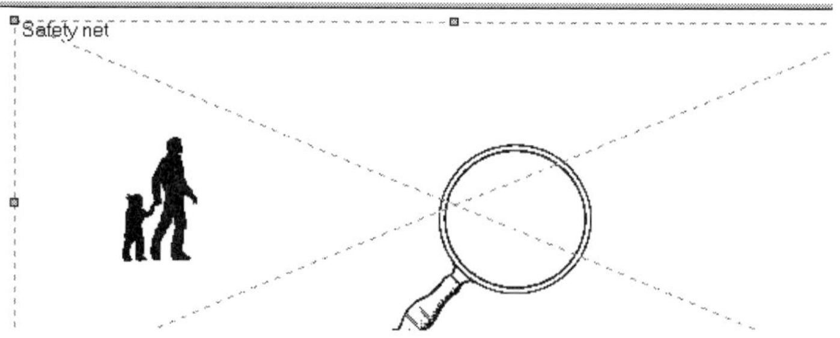

❑ Open the Safety net display icon and add this text in 14 point red "Please try again". Be sure the text doesn't obscure existing text or any other object.
❑ Save your work as **Target.a4p**.
❑ Run the piece.

One of the problems you may have encountered is moving the wrong object, an object you don't ever want to move. The solution is to make that object nonmovable. Let's make the magnifying glass nonmovable.

Making an Object Nonmovable

To prevent a user from moving an object while the piece is running (While in author mode the object is always movable):

- Select the icon containing the object.
- Select <u>M</u>odify><u>I</u>con><u>C</u>alculation.
- Enter `Moveable:=FALSE` in the Calculation window.

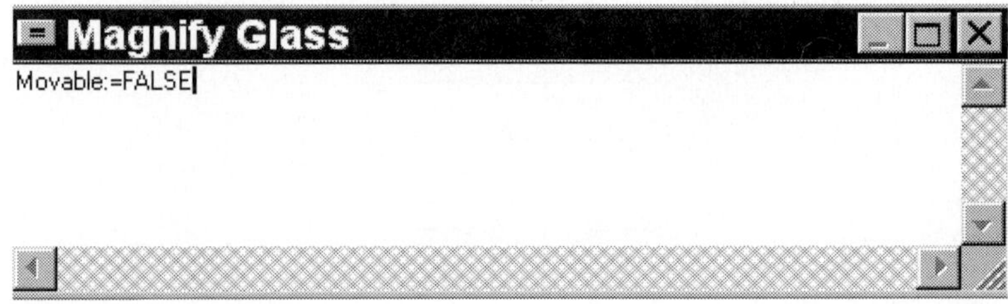

Your Turn
❑ Select the Magnify Glass icon.
❑ Choose <u>M</u>odify><u>I</u>con><u>C</u>alculation.
❑ Enter the following:

❑ Run your piece and try to move the magnifying glass: You'll find you cannot.
❑ Save your work.

There are many enhancements and options available with target areas. For example, you can limit when the process is active, designate whether the match was right or wrong, limit the number of tries or limit the amount of time to get the match correct. The latter two options are covered in the next chapter, the former two we briefly discuss next.

Limiting When a Target Area is Active

To establish a condition that controls whether a target area is active:

1. Choose or create a variable or expression that if true establishes the active state of the target area.
2. Enter the variable name or expression in the Active if box in the Target Area Properties dialog box.
3. Establish a mechanism for setting the variable or expression to its two states (True and False).

Preventing an Object from Being Moved Off the Screen

At present, there's nothing to prevent the user from moving the family completely off the screen. We briefly looked at how to prevent this in general terms in Chapter 4. Let's see how to apply the concept to prevent moving the family off the screen. This is done through a setting in the Modify>Icon> Properties dialog box (see Figure 5.24). To implement this:

1. Select the icon with the moveable object.
2. Choose Modify>Icon>Properties.
3. Push the Layout tab.
4. Select the Movable On Screen option (see Figure 5.24).

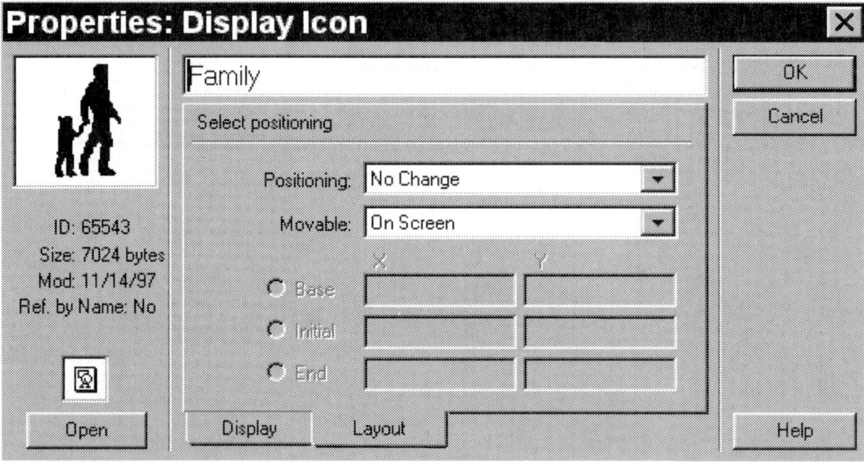

Figure 5.24. Preventing an Object from Being Moved Off the Screen.

Sample File Open the file named **Active.a4p** again. Run it. You should see a main screen with a button named Change State, a debug message that constantly displays the value of a variable we created, named `Active`, and a CD-ROM image, which is to be moved to the item that uses it (the computer). This is a target area project.

USING A VARIABLE TO FACILITATE DEBUGGING:

In the Presentation window, place the variable's name inside braces ("{" and "}") (To see this: Select the Office Background icon, then use the text tool to highlight the Target Area text).

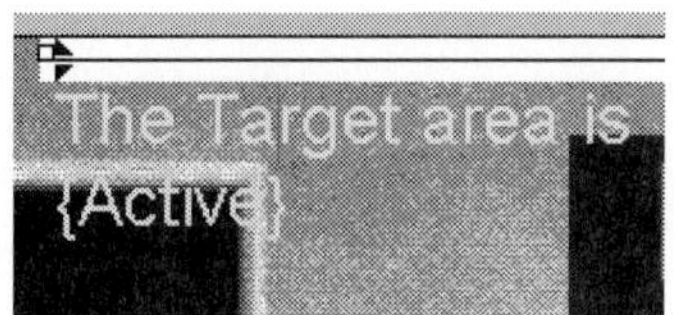

1. Select the icon containing the variable's name.
2. Select <u>M</u>odify>Icon><u>P</u>roperties.
3. Check the two boxes as shown in Figure 5.25.

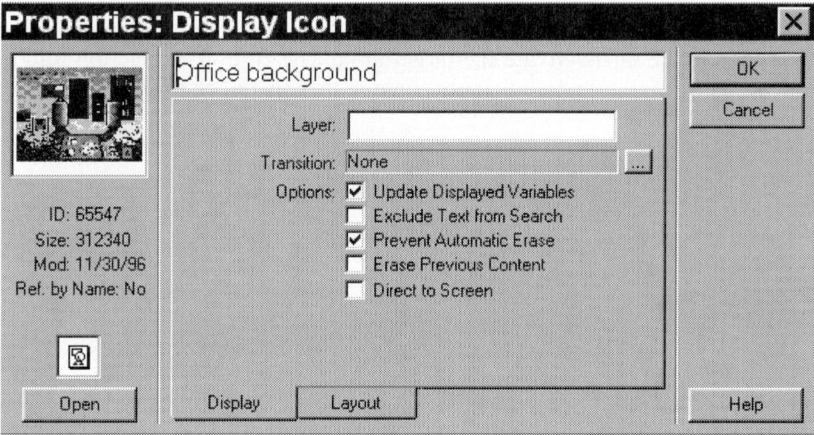

Figure 5.25. Making Sure a Variable's Value is always Updated and Visible. Check the two boxes: Update Displayed Variables and Prevent Automatic Erasure.

Figure 5.26 shows the complete flowline for the **Active.a4p** piece.

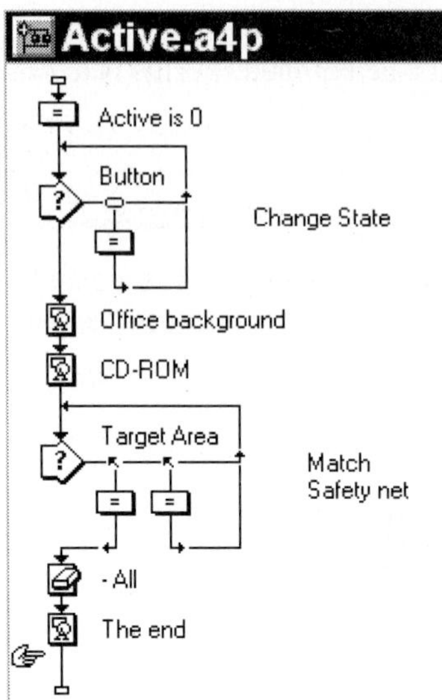

Figure 5.26. The **Active.a4p** Flowline.

It begins by using a calculation icon to set a variable, `Active`, to zero. It is this variable, that we use to activate or inactivate the target area. The Button interaction toggles that value of `Active`, using the calculation icon content in Change State. The calculation is shown in the figure below.

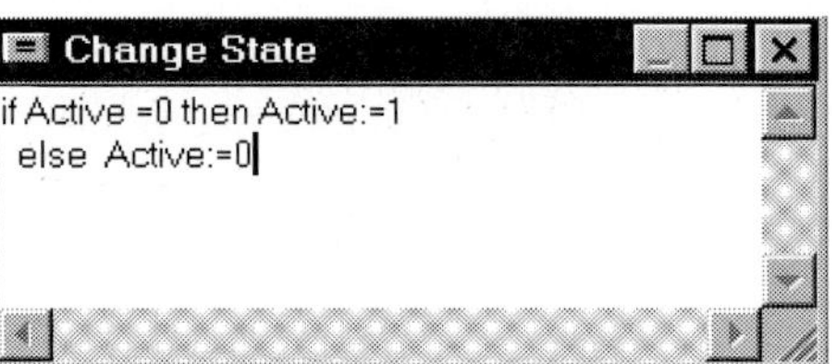

The next two icons display the background(an image of an office) and the CD-ROM, which is the object to be moved. The target area interaction has two responses: a correct one and a safety net. Open the Match response type icon. Then push the Response tab. You should see Figure 5.27.

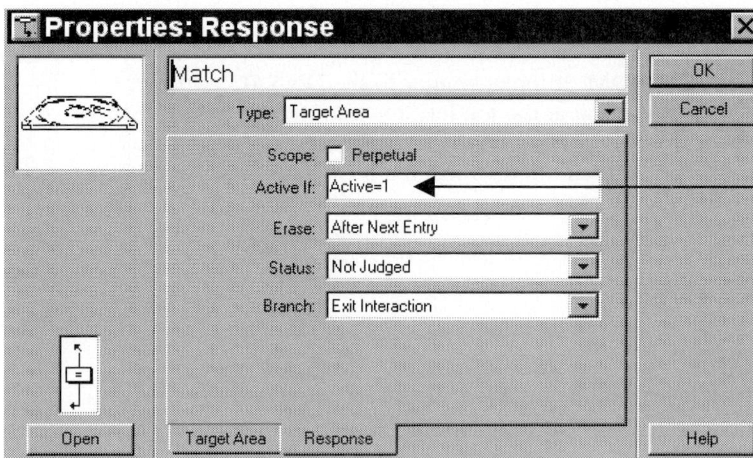

Interaction is available, as long as `Active` equals one.

Figure 5.27. The Match icon's Dialog Box. It defines when the icon is active, and how to handle correct and incorrect matches.

The interaction (a target area) is available only if the value of `Active` is set to one. By pushing the button on the screen, the value of Active switches between 0 and 1. Also, note the interaction exits when the match is made. Then everything is erased and an end message displayed.

When the user drags the CD-ROM to an incorrect location, we want to "do nothing"; just return it to its original location. As a result, we attached a calculation icon as the Safety net response icon, which contains only a comment, as shown by the figure below.

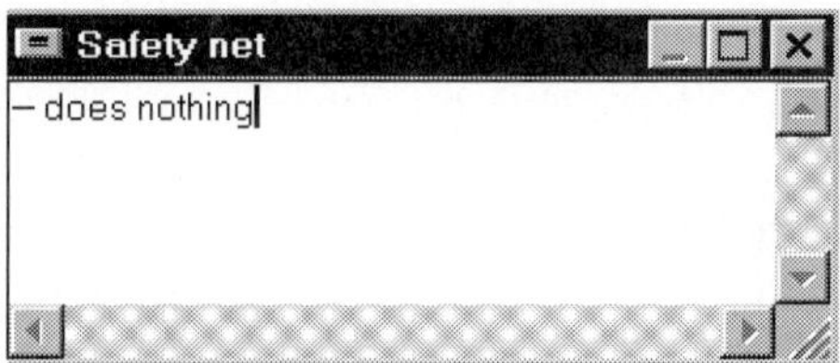

We used the same approach for the correct match.

Run the piece, set the `Active` variable to zero (use the button) and drag the CD-ROM image onto that of the computer. Nothing happens. Now push the button again, be sure the `Active` value is one, and place the CD-ROM image at its correct destination. Now the screen clears and the piece ends.

As has been the custom, we'll finish the chapter by adding to the digital video piece we've been working on.

Sample File To preview what we're going to do, open **DigVid5.a4p** in the Chapter5 folder on the CD-ROM. It looks similar to the **DigVid3.a4p** piece we last worked with in Chapter 3. Drag the button at the top left down to the lower left, then strike any key. Move your mouse over the two buttons on the right side. Notice that a description becomes visible as the mouse rolls over the buttons. Push the Start button—a sound is heard. Push the Quit button, and the piece ends. Let's see how to modify **DigVid3.a4p** so it works like the piece we just visited.

Your Turn

❏ Open **DigVid3.a4p**. If you couldn't save your solution, open ours in the Chapter3 folder.

❏ Add an interaction icon with two calculation icons as responses.

❏ Name the interaction Buttons and select button as the type for both calculations.

❏ Name the calculation icons Start and Quit. Your flowline should like the figure that follows below.

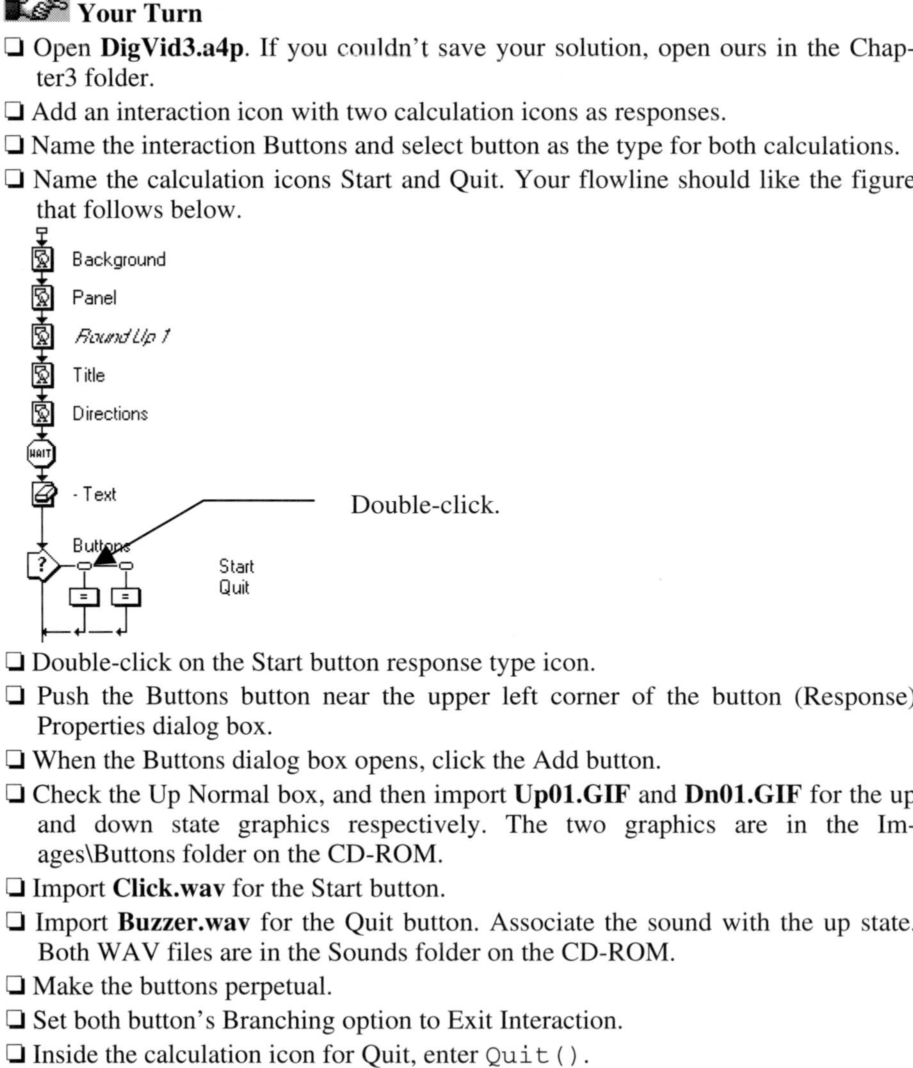

❏ Double-click on the Start button response type icon.

❏ Push the Buttons button near the upper left corner of the button (Response) Properties dialog box.

❏ When the Buttons dialog box opens, click the Add button.

❏ Check the Up Normal box, and then import **Up01.GIF** and **Dn01.GIF** for the up and down state graphics respectively. The two graphics are in the Images\Buttons folder on the CD-ROM.

❏ Import **Click.wav** for the Start button.

❏ Import **Buzzer.wav** for the Quit button. Associate the sound with the up state. Both WAV files are in the Sounds folder on the CD-ROM.

❏ Make the buttons perpetual.

❏ Set both button's Branching option to Exit Interaction.

❏ Inside the calculation icon for Quit, enter `Quit()`.

❑ Enter"--this is a comment" inside the Start button's calculation icon.

❑ Now we'll add the rollovers.

❑ Add another interaction icon and name it Rollover.

❑ Attach two hot spots. The first is a map icon and the second a display. Name them Begin and Quit Message. Your flowline should now look like the one that follows.

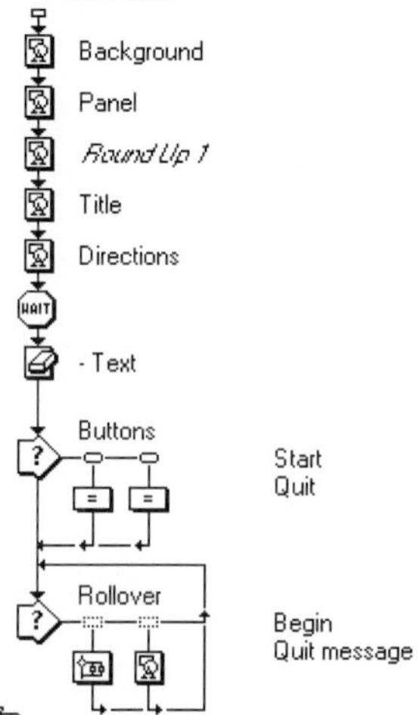

❑ Open the response type icon for each hot spot and move and size the hot spots so each covers its associated button. The hot spots over the Start and Quit buttons should look like the figure that follows.

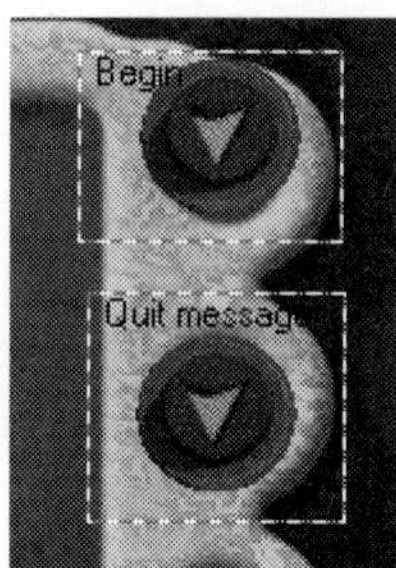

❑ Set the hot spot properties to Match Cursor in Area.

❑ Choose the Hand cursor.

❑ Choose Erase After Next Entry as the feedback value.

❑ The next figure shows the Hot Spot tab settings for the Begin hot spot properties.

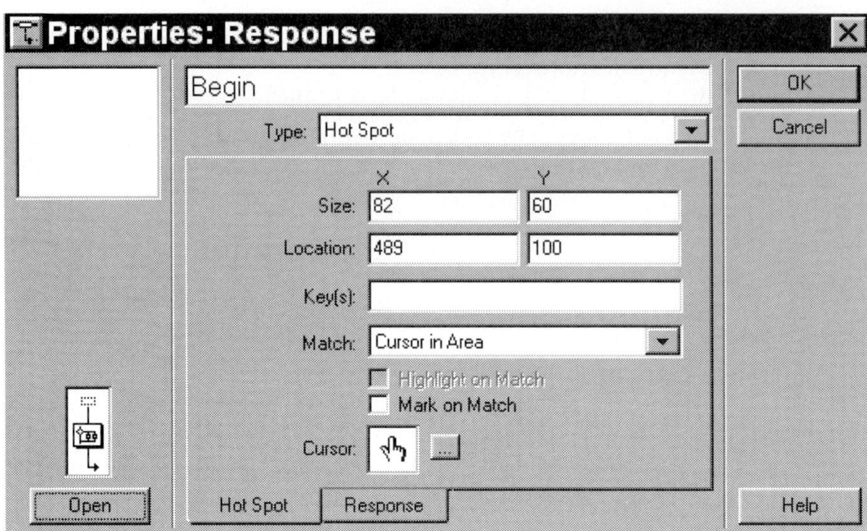

❏ Open the map icon for the Begin button and add a display icon named Show Start Message.

❏ Open the display and add the word "Start" in yellow text. It should appear next to the button as the mouse rolls over it, as shown by the figure below.

❏ Do the same for Quit, but make the text say "Quit".

❏ Run the piece.

❏ If it works properly, save it as **DigVid5.a4p**.

This concludes the chapter on mouse interactions. The next chapter will examine how to create keyboard and system interactions.

SUMMARY

Authorware provides a robust collection of eleven types of interactions. In this chapter, we looked in-depth at those interactions triggered by a mouse operation: buttons, hot spots, hot areas and target areas.

Buttons are often used to display help messages or to jump to other topics. By setting button layers to high values, they can be made perpetual and thus displayed at all times.

Hot objects and hot areas can be used to implement interactivity. When clicked, a hot object can display a graphic, play a sound or movie, or jump to another topic. Unlike hot spots, hot objects do not have to be rectangular in shape.

Target area responses are used in situations where the user must drag an object from one location to another, most likely in response to a question or to an instruction requesting this be done. Target areas can be made inactive or active through the setting of variables or expressions and the object being dragged can be returned to its original location or left at its destination.

Study Exercises

5.1. Modify the Buttons.a4p piece to include an inactive toggle button. Call your project C5Q1. Choose this button: **TBUp4**. Make the button inactive when a third button, Status is pushed. Use **Button4.GIF** for the up state, and **Button7.GIF** as the down graphic for the Status button. These buttons are in the Images\Buttons folder on the CD-ROM. When the Status button is pushed. It should cycle the toggle (Start) button between active and inactive.

5.2. Modify the Hot Spot example to make the windmill and the tulips hot at the same time. As the cursor moves over the windmills display text saying, "Windmills are picturesque." The text should disappear when the cursor moves away from the hot spot. Call the project C5Q2.

5.3. Create a new piece called C5Q3. The project should display a red ball and a blue square. When the red ball is dragged to the blue square, a message saying "Great" should show. When the ball is dragged anywhere else, a message saying, "Try again" should display.

5.4. Create a new piece called C5Q4. Import Tmplate9.BMP and find three round buttons in the Images\Buttons folder on the CD-ROM. Size them and place them in the three round spots on the right side of the template. Each should have an up and down state and a different sound effect when pushed. Make the first play a wave file from the Sounds folder on the CD-ROM. You'll need to use the sound icon, which we haven't discussed yet." When the second button is pushed display text "Button 2 was pushed". The third should quit the piece.

Keyboard and System Interactions

Chapter 5 looked at interactions that were mouse-driven: button, hot spot, hot object and target area interactions all require a user to use the mouse to trigger the interaction. This chapter looks at the remaining interactions: Pull-down menus, Keypress, Conditional, and Text Entry interactions that limit or restrict other interactions – Time and Tries limits, and Events.

At the conclusion of the chapter, you will be able to:

- Create and use menus.
- Create and use keypress responses.
- Use a conditional response to provide feedback based on a calculation
- Create and use hot text.
- Check for keyboard conditions, such as Caps Lock key being on.
- Use models to reduce the authoring effort.

- Use text entry responses for fill-in-the blank types of interactions.
- Limit the number of incorrect responses.
- Limit the amount of time a user can spend with an interaction.
- Use Event interactions to respond to messages from ActiveX controls.

We begin by discussing pull-down menu interactions.

PULL-DOWN MENUS

Pull-down menus contain commands the user can choose among. Menus typically endure for an entire activity, unlike buttons and hot spots, which generally show on a single graphic. In fact, menus are usually designated as being perpetual; thus, they are available until erased.

For each pull-down menu choice, you must create a separate interaction icon. The name assigned to the interaction becomes the pull-down title, while the icons attached to the interaction become the "commands" on the submenu.

Creating a Pull-down Menu

To create a pull-down menu:

1. Add an interaction icon and name it.
2. Choose an appropriate name because it will become the menu name on the menu bar.
3. Attach response icons and choose Pull-down Menu as their response type.
4. Note that each attached icon becomes a submenu (command) choice.
5. Add content to the attached icons.

Sample File Open the **Menu.a4p** file in the Chapter6 folder. You'll see the flowline from Figure 6.1.

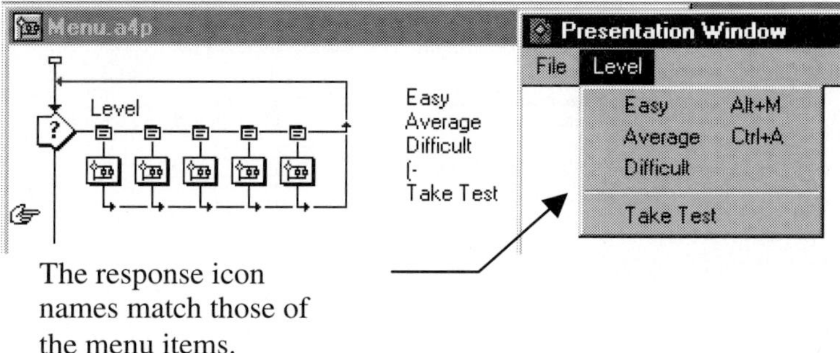

The response icon
names match those of
the menu items.

Figure 6.1. The **Menu.a4p** File. It displays a pull-down menu with a separator.

If you run the title, you will see it displays a four-choice menu, with each command being the result of one of four dialog boxes. There is a ***separator*** between the Difficult and Take Test choices.

Separator Bars

You should group logical commands together, separating the groups by means of a separator bar. To add a separator bar:

1. Drag a display icon to the right of the last command in the previous group.
2. Be sure its response type is set to pull-down menu.
3. Name it "(- "(a left parenthesis followed by a hyphen).

The remaining options pertain to the Menu Options dialog box, shown in Figure 6.2.

The Pull-down Menu Properties Dialog Box

Figure 6.2 shows the Pull-down menu Properties dialog box associated with the Easy icon. As we have seen before, to view this dialog box, double-click the response icon for Easy. The Menu and Response tabs establish the menu name, optional hot keys for invoking the menu choice, an active condition, and the normal feedback options. Let's look at it in more detail.

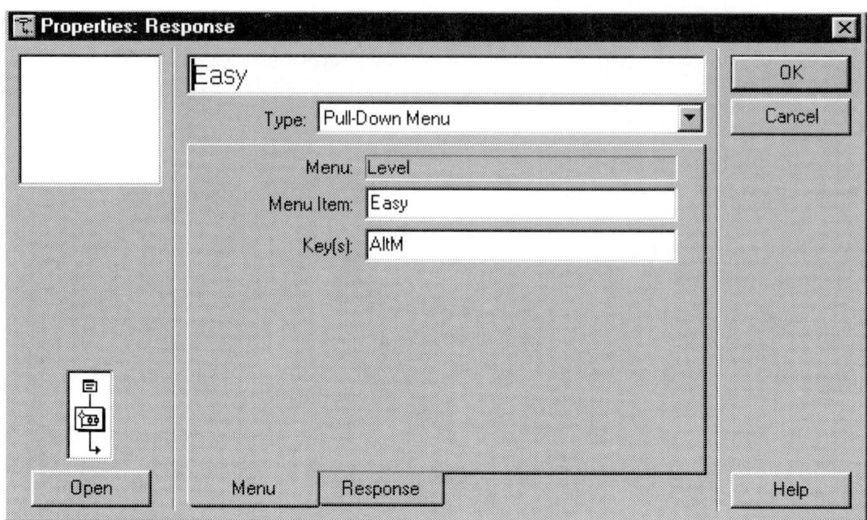

Figure 6.2. The Pull-down Menu Properties Dialog Box.

Menu Item

Each command within a given menu will have a dialog box like that shown in Figure 6.2. The Menu Item Name field value will match that of the icon attached to the Menu response type. In Figure 6.2, both the icon and the Menu Item names do, in fact, match ("Easy").

Key(s): Assigning Shortcut Keys

In many cases, users prefer to use a keyboard command instead of having to make menu selections. To assign a shortcut key to a pull-down menu, enter the key name you want to use as the shortcut. Refer to Table 5.1 to review the standard key names you can use.

Because Authorware doesn't distinguish between uppercase and lowercase, do not use the same letter, once in caps, another in lower case, for two different shortcuts. It's customary to use the Alt key on Windows machines as part of the shortcut key. Thus for the Easy choice in Figure 6.2, we chose Alt-M. The entry was coded as AltM.

The remaining options we have seen before, so we won't discuss them again. Instead, let's build a pull-down menu interaction.

Sample File Open the **Menu2.a4p** file in the Chapter6 folder. Choose the Dogs menu. Notice the subcommands. Do the same for Cats. Let's see how this was constructed.

Your Turn

❏ This will be merely a skeleton of a project. When you're developing a complex project, in many cases it is best if you define the navigation, and then add the content. This is the situation here. We will build a series of menus, each having one or more commands. Attached to each command will be a display icon that merely states "so and so content to go here". Let's begin.

❑ Start a new project.

❑ Create a flowline with three interactions, named Quit, Dogs, and Cats.

❑ For the Quit interaction, as you add a calculation response type, choose pull-down menu as its type.

❑ Attach display icons as responses to Dogs and Cats, and specify perpetual pull-down menus as their type of response. Your flowline will look this way:

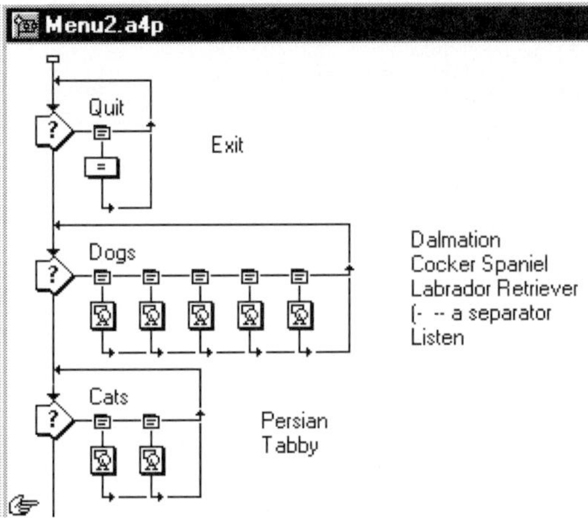

❑ The properties for each of the Menu and Response tab dialog boxes look like the following two figures.

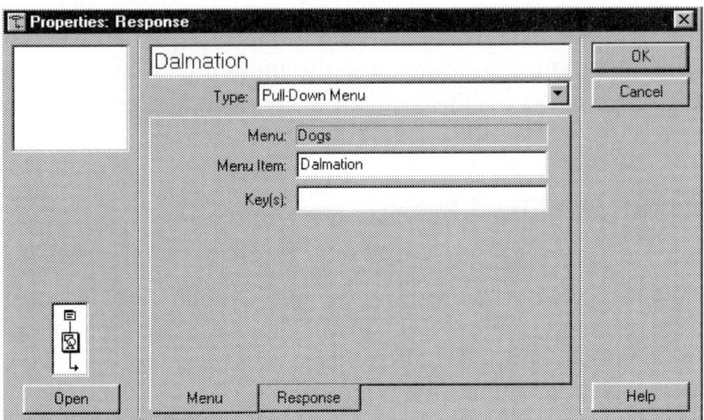

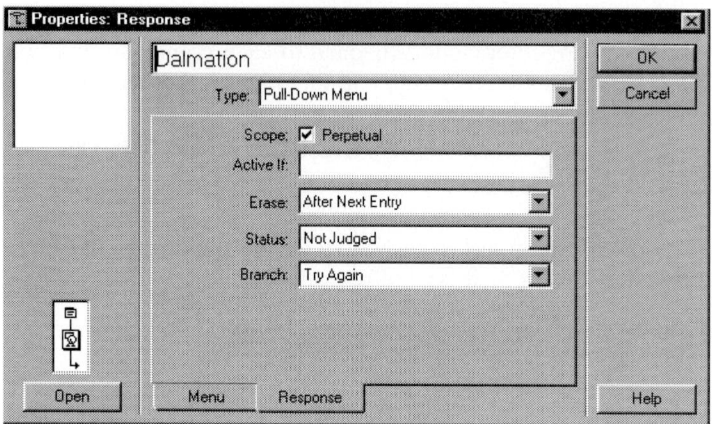

❏ The key point is to check the Perpetual checkbox.

❏ Add `Quit()` inside the calculation icon as shown next:

❏ For all the other display icons, add content, such as "Dalmatian graphic here," Picture of a Persian cat here", and so on.

❏ Add similar content to the "Listen" icon. The text might say "Sound of a Cocker Spaniel barking will go here".

❏ Save your work as **Menu2.a4p.**

If you run your project, you'll see Authorware adds an additional menu item: File. You can replace this by adding an icon with the same name but with content of your choice.

Menus are familiar to most users, occupy little, if any, space, and can be made perpetual, so as the user navigates to other parts of the project, the menu choices remain active.

CONDITIONAL INTERACTIONS

Use a conditional response when you want to have Authorware provide feedback based on a calculation. The paths are followed automatically, based on conditions you set within the conditional properties dialog box. Oftentimes you use a conditional with an Authorware variable. For example, you might want to monitor how long a user has been logged in. To do so, you use the `SessionHours` variable, which returns the length of time the user has been using the current Authorware project. Alternatively, you might want to display a message after each hour. This could also be accomplished through a conditional interaction.

Other uses for conditional interactions include:

- Checking for keyboard toggles (Caps Lock on, Alt key held down, and so on).
- Filtering wrong-type keystrokes (entering numbers as part of a first name, for example).
- Playing a sound while an interaction is active.
- Setting up hot text.

Let's look at the general steps required to create such an interaction, and then look at an example.

Creating a Conditional Response Interaction

To create a conditional response interaction:

1. Add an interaction icon to the flowline.
2. Drag an icon to the right of the interaction icon.
3. Select conditional as the type, then click OK.
4. Double-click the conditional response type symbol ▪.
5. The Conditional Options dialog box opens, as shown in Figure 6.3.

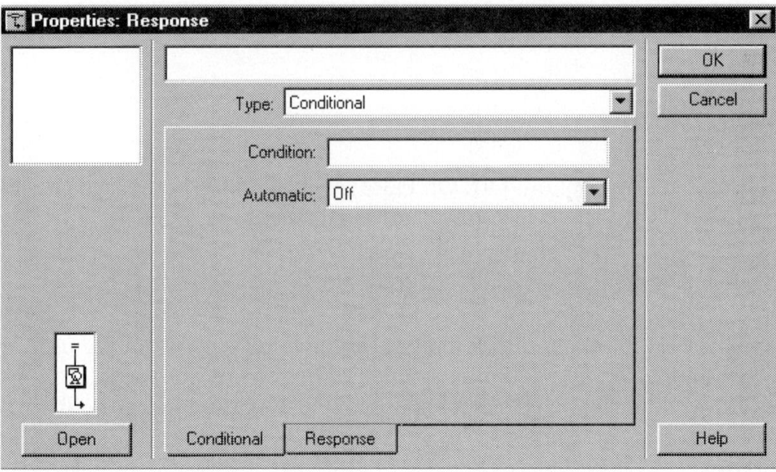

Figure 6.3. The Conditional Properties Dialog Box.

6. Enter the condition or expression to be evaluated in the Condition field.
7. Decide if the interaction is to be perpetual. If so, check the Perpetual box in the Response tab.

8. Choose the desired value for the Automatic field.

9. Select appropriate erase feedback, response judging, and branching options.

10. Click OK to close the dialog box.

The Conditional Properties Dialog Box

Let's explore the new options in the dialog box from Figure 6.3.

The Condition Setting: Specifying when to Follow the Path

You enter an expression, such as `Score>20` into this field. The expressions must evaluate to true or false. Think of it as a question. For example, is the Score greater than 20? If it's true, Authorware will execute the attached response icon; if false, control is passed to the next icon to the right.

The variable or expression may evaluate to 1, "True", "T", "YES" or "ON". Other values equate to False. Examples of valid expressions and variables include:

`CharCount>9` (True if 10 or more characters have been entered).

`WordCount>2`   (True if more than 2 words have been entered).

`TotalWrong > 10` (True if user gets more than 10 wrong answers).

The Automatic Setting

There are three choices for this option: Off, On False to True, and When True. Together they specify how we want Authorware to match a conditional response.

Off

Use this setting to have Authorware check the Condition value only when the user responds to the interaction. Suppose the interaction is a series of buttons or hot spots. Only when the user pushes one of the buttons or selects a hot spot will the condition be checked.

When True

Authorware will carry out the response icon's contents as long as the variable or expression is true. Use this setting when you want Authorware to automatically perform an action.

On False to True

If this option is chosen, Authorware will execute the response icon contents when the variable or expression switches from false to true. This implies the conditional response reacts a single time — when the condition switches from false to true.

Exploring the Automatic Settings

The Automatic setting options can be confusing. Let's look at some examples that experiment with the various values. The examples use a variable, `SessionHours`. We need to explore this variable a bit first.

Sample File To skip creation of the example, you can open and run the **Condt1.a4p** file in the Chapter6 folder on the CD-ROM. It is supposed to display a message ("You have been logged on for less than an hour ") if the user has been logged on for less than an hour. If you run the piece, you'll see it doesn't work. The logic is correct, let's see what's wrong.

Your Turn
- Start a new project.
- Select Window>Variables.
- Choose Category "All", as indicated in Figure 6.4.

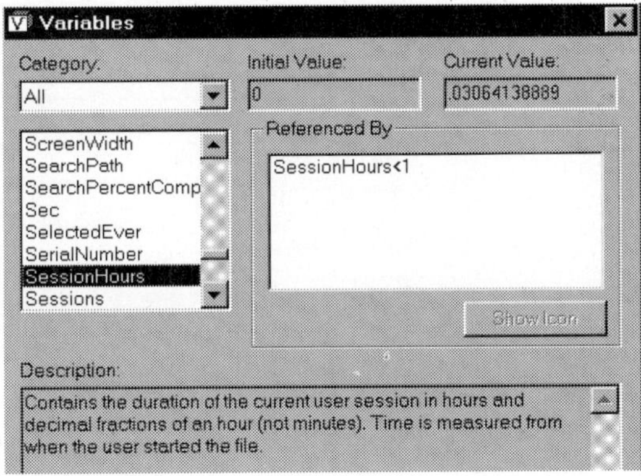

Figure 6.4. The `SessionHours` Variable.

- Select the SessionHours variable.
- Note in Figure 6.4, we had been using the current project for a bit less than an hour. Let's use this variable to display a message, only when the duration is less than hour. The purpose of this short example is to explore the Automatic settings. We begin by leaving the setting to its default: Off.

❏ Add an interaction icon, and call it Test Conditional.

❏ Attach a map icon but don't label it (Authorware will assign the name based on the Condition expression).

❏ Choose Conditional as the type.

❏ Double-click the Conditional response symbol and enter these settings:

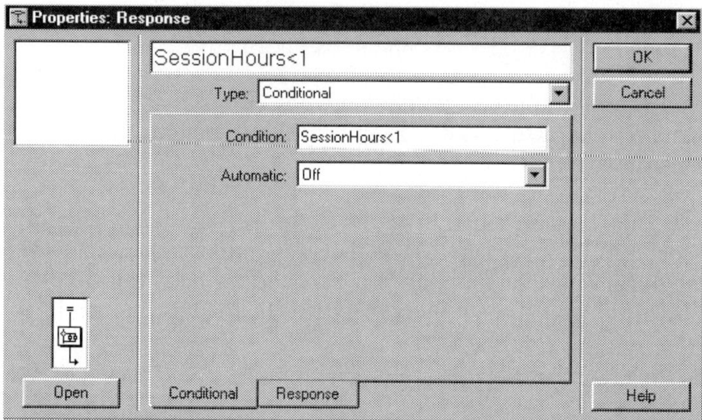

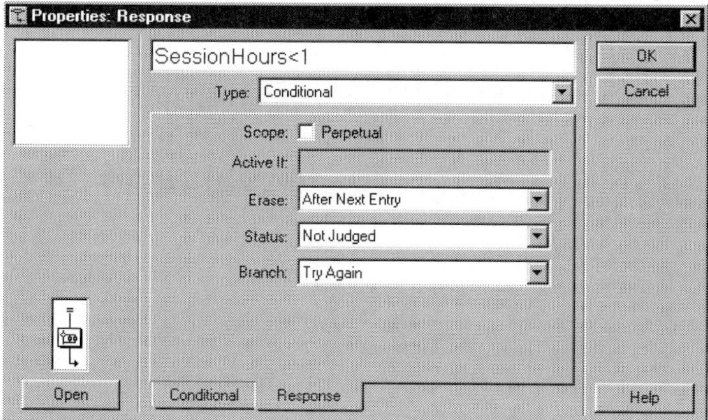

❏ Click OK.

❏ Double-click the map icon and enter this text: "You have been logged on for less than an hour".

❏ Close the icon and run the piece.

Assuming you have been using the current project for less than an hour, you would expect the text to appear. It doesn't. This is because the Automatic is set to Off. The only way this map icon will execute with the Automatic set as it is, is if there is another response type, like a button, attached to the interaction. Let's try that.

We are going to modify the current project by simply adding a button that does nothing.

Sample File If you prefer, you can open the **Condt2.a4p** file in the chapter folder on your CD-ROM.

Your Turn

❏ Attach a button interaction with a conditional response to the Test Conditional interaction. The figure that follows shows the button and the current flowline.

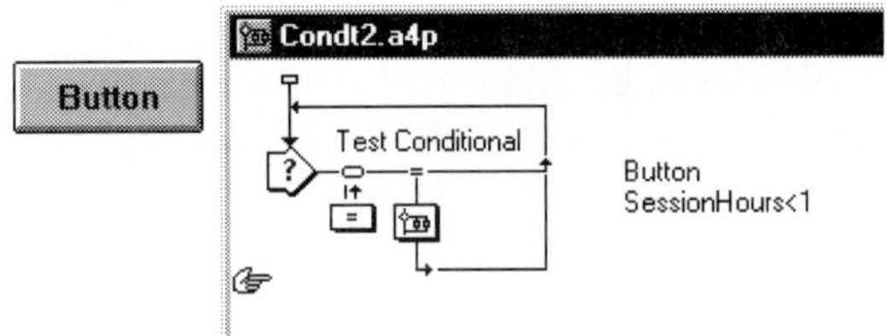

❏ Open the button response symbol and set its branching option to Continue. This way, control will eventually get to the conditional. If set to Try Again, control will by-pass the SessionHours<1 icon.
❏ The calculation icon attached to the button is the familiar "Does nothing" command — a simple comment.
❏ Try the project again. It now works.
❏ Save your works as **Condt2.a4p**.

An alternative solution is to not add the button, but instead change the Automatic value to When True. What do you think would happen if we set the Automatic value to On False to True? The only time the message would appear would be when the user had been using Condt2 for exactly one hour.

Now that we understand the various Automatic settings, it's time to use conditional responses in situations that are more elaborate. The following sections show you how to use conditional interactions to:

- Monitor the number of incorrect responses.
- Determine which of several choices was made.
- Create hot text.
- Filter undesirable data from text entry interactions.
- Monitor keyboard keys.

Using A Conditional Response to Exit an Interaction Based on the Number of Incorrect Responses

Sample File If you want to preview this exercise, open and run the **Wrong.a4p** file in the Chapter6 folder on the CD-ROM. Answer the question incorrectly three times to invoke the conditional response. It presents a question and waits for the user to click on the correct answer. Try clicking the "A" answer three times. A message appears. Now click "A", then "B", then "D" ("C" is the correct answer). Now in addition to a message, the interaction exits because you have three different wrong answers. Let's see how to build this project.

The project includes a conditional that determines how many different incorrect answers a user has entered. While this could be done using the Limit Tries response type, we will use a variable, `WrongChoicesMatched`, to test the number of different incorrect responses. When the number of wrong responses exceeds two, we will exit the interaction. We also want to continuously show the current session length.

Your Turn
❑ Start a new project.
❑ Drag the *Mottled2* icon from the Backgrounds library.
❑ Drag an interaction icon to the flowline and name it Ask Question.
❑ Drop four display icons to the right. Choose hot spots as their type. Name them like this:

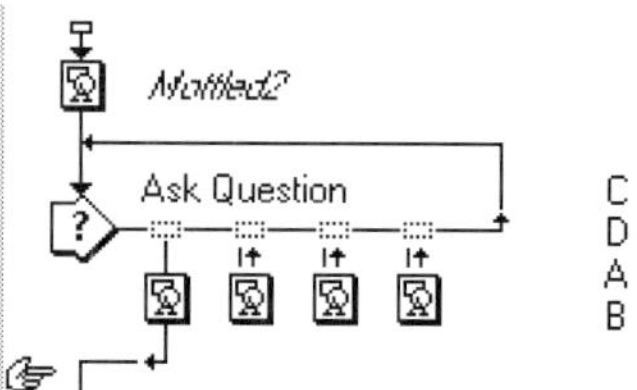

❑ Run from the beginning. The background will display, then your project will halt.
❑ Open the interaction icon using Control-Shift double-click and enter this 18-point text:

What is a codec?
An encryption device
A type of camera
An algorithm for reducing then expanding media files
A method for interlacing displays on a monitor

❑ Near the bottom of the screen, enter in red 12-point text: You have been working for:

❑ We are now going to add a system variable that contains the number of hours and minutes the user has had the current session active.

❑ Add the word `SessionTime` inside braces, like this:

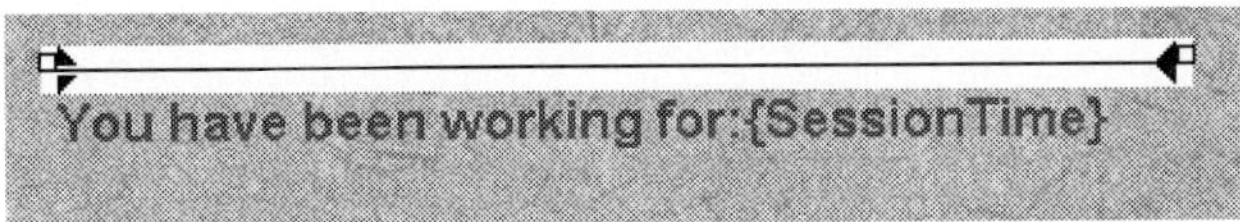

❑ If you click outside the text area you just added, you'll see something like this:

If you run the project, you'll find the value of `SessionTime` isn't continuously updated. The next section shows how to force Authorware to constantly update displayed variables.

Automatic Updating of Displayed Variables

When you are displaying variables you defined, or displaying built-in Authorware variables, you generally want the variable's value to be continuously displayed. That way, as a variable changes value, the current value will always be visible.

To automatically display a variable's latest value:

1. Select the text.
2. Choose <u>M</u>odify><u>I</u>con><u>P</u>roperties.
3. Check the Update Displayed Variables box in the Display tab dialog box that is shown in the figure below.

Next, we'll work with the hot spot response symbols.

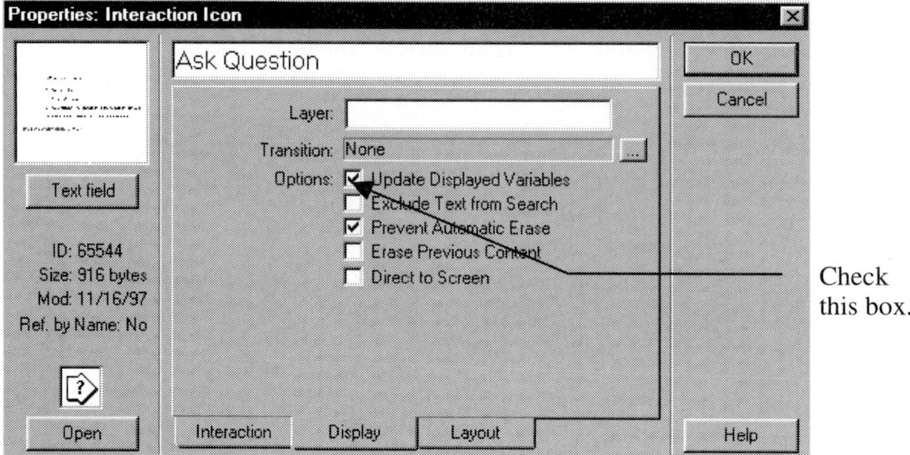

Check
this box.

Specifying Right and Wrong Responses

❑ Open the first response type symbol. This will be for the correct response, C.

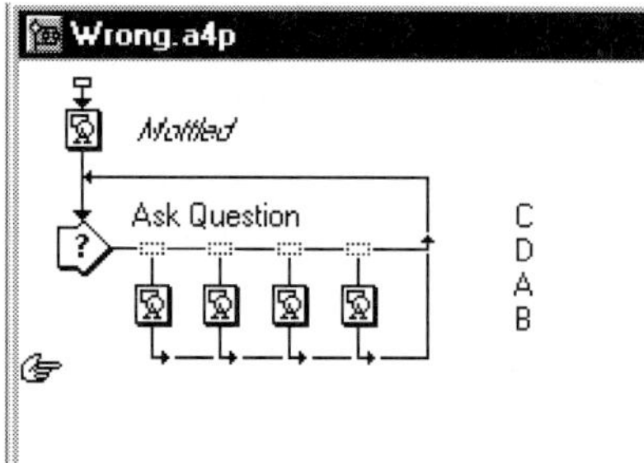

❑ Set the Hot Spot Options for "C", the correct response, as follows:

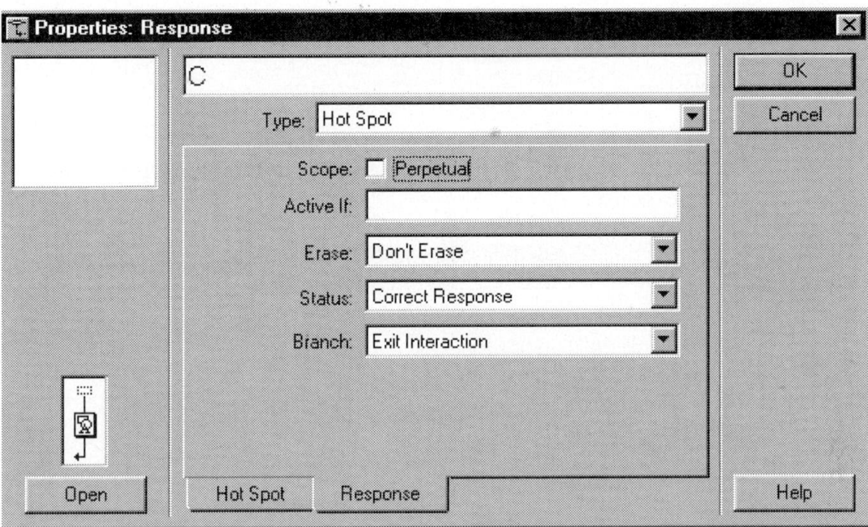

❏ Note that branching is set to Exit interaction because this is the correct response and we want to go on to the next icon. We also chose a custom cursor and checked Highlight on Match, which highlights the choice when it's clicked. This is shown in the figure below.

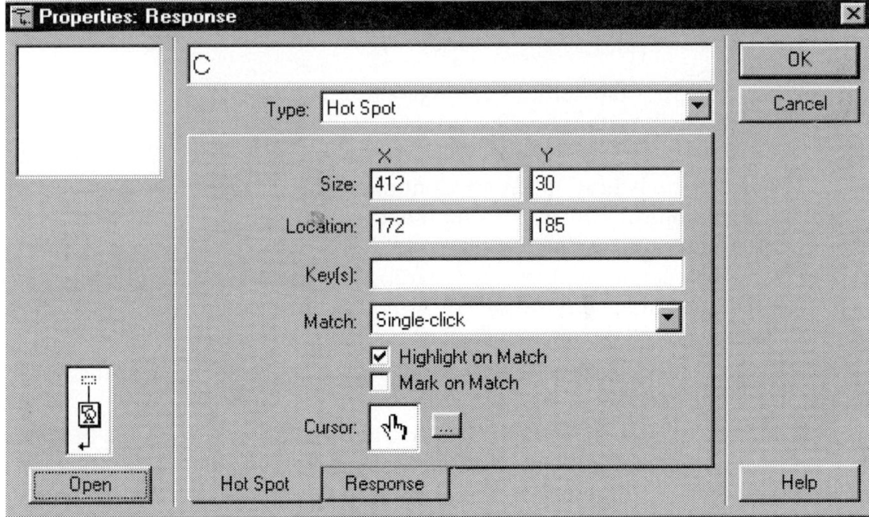

❏ Push the OK button to close the dialog box.
❏ Move and size the hot spot box so it covers the "C" question.

❑ Open the Hot Spot Response properties dialog box for the next three hot spot symbols and set their parameters like those in the following figure, which is for the "D" response.

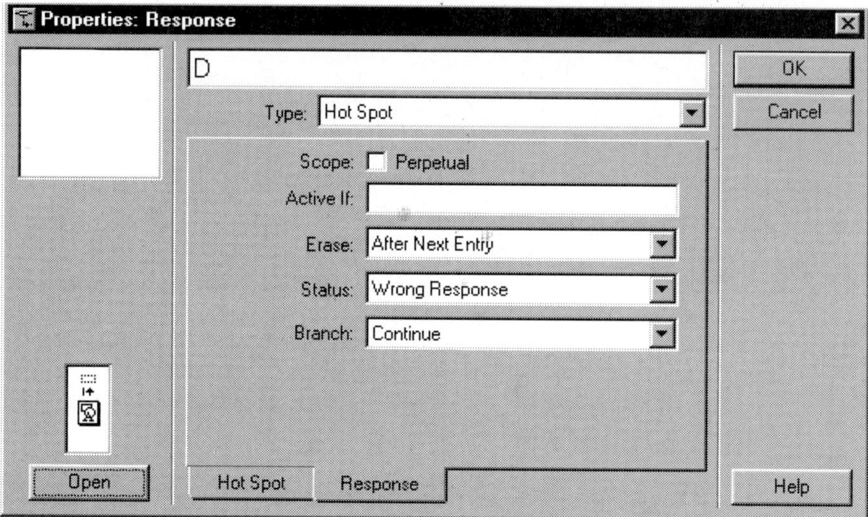

❑ The Hot Spot tab settings are like those for the "C" icon. The only difference among the three will be their titles.

❑ Note the branching is set to Continue. This ensures that after the response is judged, control will pass to the next icon within the interaction, then the next, and so on, until it reaches the conditional (which we haven't added yet) where we will check to see how many wrong answers have been given to this question. If the branching were set to Try Again, control would go from a response immediately back to the interaction icon, skipping the conditional.

❑ Finish choices A and B. Be sure to locate and properly size the hot spot boxes for D, A, and B.

❑ Add a display icon as the fifth Ask Question response. Change the response type to conditional and name it How Many. (Actually, the name is unimportant, as Authorware will rename the icon to be the same as the condition value).

❑ Enter the following as the condition expression:

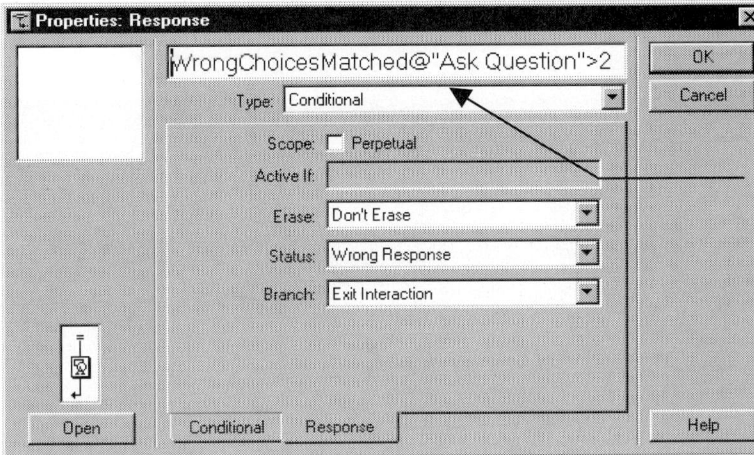

True, if the number of wrong answers exceeds two.

The variable tracks how many unique answers have been made for the interaction named within the quotation marks: In this case, Ask Question. The expression says, if this value exceeds two, consider it a match. In that case, control will pass to the associated display icon where we'll display a message. Now we need to supply the feedback for each response.

Your Turn

❑ Add content and options for the icons according to Table 6.1.

Table 6.1. Settings for the Ask Question interaction Icons

Icon	Message	Erase Feedback	Branching	Judged
A	Sorry. Try again.	After Next Entry	Continue	Incorrect
B	No. That's a Kodak.	After Next Entry	Continue	Incorrect
C	Yes, a codec compresses, then expands sound or video.	Don't Erase	Exit Interaction	Correct
D	Sorry. There is no such device as this.	After Next Entry	Continue	Incorrect
Conditional	The correct answer is "C". A codec compresses then expands sound and video.	Don't Erase	Exit Interaction	Incorrect

❏ Add an erase icon to remove the text left over from the correct answer ("C") and the conditional:

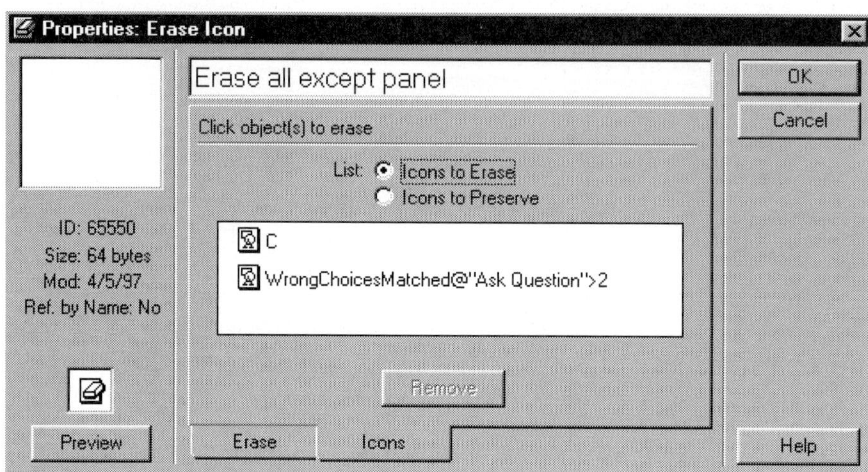

❏ Save your work as **Wrong.a4p**.

Try your project and select A three times. No message appears. Now try "A", "D", then "B". The message appears and the interaction exits. This is because only **different** wrong answers are scored against the variable: repeatedly selecting answer "A" would not trigger the conditional, but selecting three different wrong answers will trigger it.

One problem is that the response displays are erased too quickly after a correct response.

❏ To remedy this, insert a wait icon prior to the erase icon, and set it to wait for 3 seconds without a button.

Using a Conditional Response to Exit an Interaction Based on the Choice Number

You might find use for a conditional and the Authorware variable ChoiceNumber. The value of this variable specifies the relative location of the item chosen by the user. For example, if the user picks choice "B" in our example above, ChoiceNumber would = 4. Thus you might have a conditional with ChoiceNumber =4 as the Condition expression. The associated Hot Spot response icon might say: "No, B is the wrong answer. Try again"

Hot Text (Hypertext)

Hot text works the way buttons do. When a word is clicked, you might provide a definition of that word, or navigate to another section of your title. When text is used as a navigation method, it's called *hypertext*.

Creating Hot Text

To create hot text:

1. Drag a display icon to the flowline.
2. Enter the complete text inside the display icon. Not every word has to be hot. Note the text is placed in a display icon, or an interaction icon.
3. Drag an interaction icon to the flowline.
4. Drag an icon to the right of the interaction icon. One icon per hot word.
5. Choose the icon type that best suits your needs: a sound icon, a map icon etc. When the user clicks on the hot word, the contents of the icon you just added will be executed.
6. Choose Conditional as the response type.
7. Click OK.
8. Double-click the response type symbol and the Conditional Properties dialog box opens.
9. In the Condition text box enter `WordClicked=`.
10. Append the word you want to match. For example, to make the word *codec* hot, enter `WordClicked="codec"`.
11. Set the Automatic setting to On False to True.
12. Choose the desired erase feedback setting.
13. Select the correct Response Tracking option; If you are matching and this is the correct response, set it to Correct Response; otherwise, set it to Wrong Response. If the response is neither right nor wrong, set the value to Not Judged.
14. Select the branching option.

A completed dialog box example might look like this:

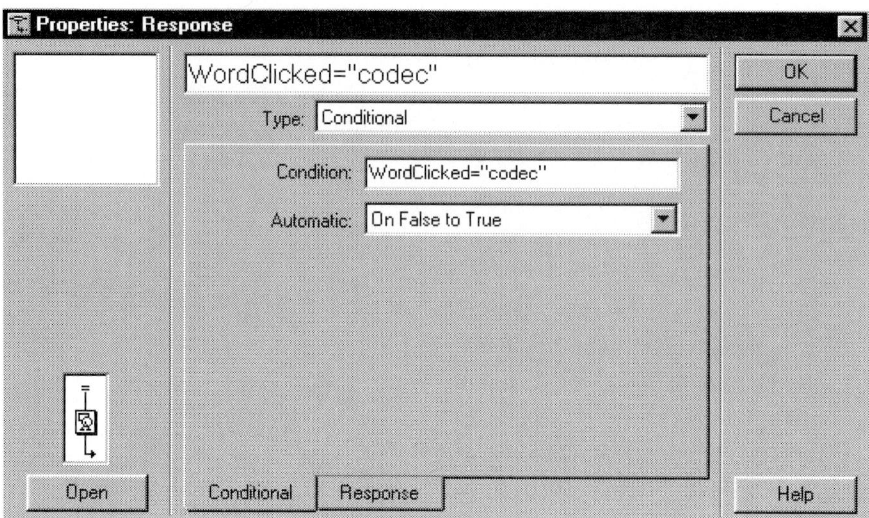

Hot text can be used for matching, or context sensitive help. The next example shows how to implement matching using hot text.

Creating Hot Text: An Example

 **Your Turn**

❑ Open your **Wrong.a4p** project.

❑ Add a map icon to the Ask Question interaction.

❑ The name isn't important, as Authorware will assign one for us. Choose Conditional as the type.

❑ Open the Conditional Properties dialog box by double-clicking the conditional response type icon. Enter these Response tab values:

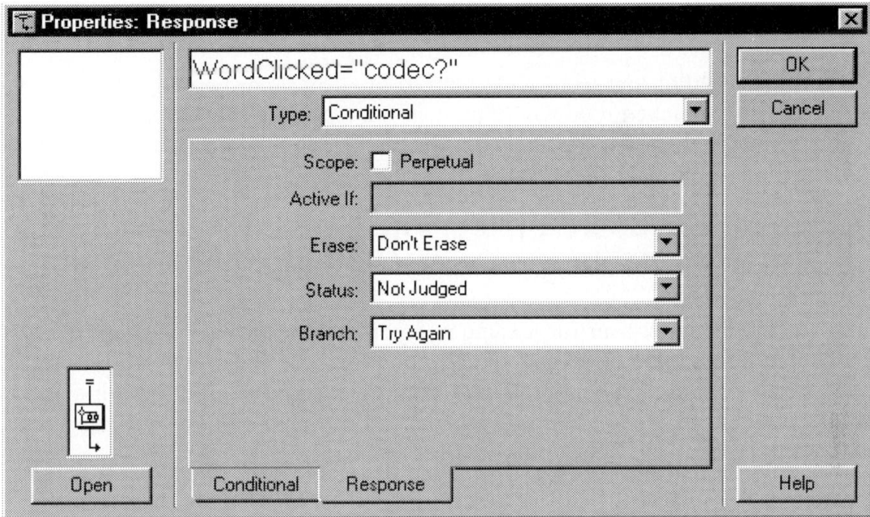

❑ Be sure to include the "?" as part of the "word".

❑ If we had selected When True as the Automatic value, when the user clicked on the word "codec?" the message we're about to display would continue until the interaction was exited. The effect would result in the user perceiving a rapid blinking of the screen. You might test this after we finish with the example.

❑ Open the map icon and add three icons, as indicated by the figure below.

❑ As the text within the Show message icon, enter "Codec stands for Compressor/Decompressor".

❑ Set the wait icon for 3 seconds, no button, and show time remaining.

❑ The erase message icon should remove the text in Show message.

❑ Run your piece and click on the word codec. Your message appears.

❑ Save your work.

Hot Text as a Help Mechanism

How could you use hot text to provide help to the user? You would proceed as above, but when the word was clicked, you would branch to a map icon that displayed a "window" plus some appropriate text. Add a wait icon plus an erase icon that erases all the feedback.

Checking for Keyboard States: The CapsLock, AltDown and other Keyboard-related Variables

Assume you are asking a user for a name and you want to be sure the caps lock isn't down. Inside the conditional, the Condition expression would be CapsLock. CapsLock is a system variable that is set to True when the Caps Lock key is toggled on, False if it's not on. Similar variables include AltDown, ControlDown, and ShiftDown. These will be True when the respective keys are on and False otherwise.

An Introduction to Models

Included on your CD-ROM is a model named AskID, which prompts the user for a unique ID, then if the value is incorrect, permits the user to reenter the ID. It also checks for the Alt and Caps lock keys as we just described. Recall a model is a module or group of icons you can paste in at any time. Unlike library icons, model icons can be edited after they are added to your project.

To make a model available to your piece, use the Insert>Load Model command. Once loaded, the model is pasted onto the flowline by using Insert>Paste Model. Let's see how this is done by creating a new piece.

Your Turn
❑ Move the Paste hand to the beginning of your main flowline.
❑ Select the Insert>Load Model menu choice.
❑ Locate the Models**AskID** model on your CD-ROM.

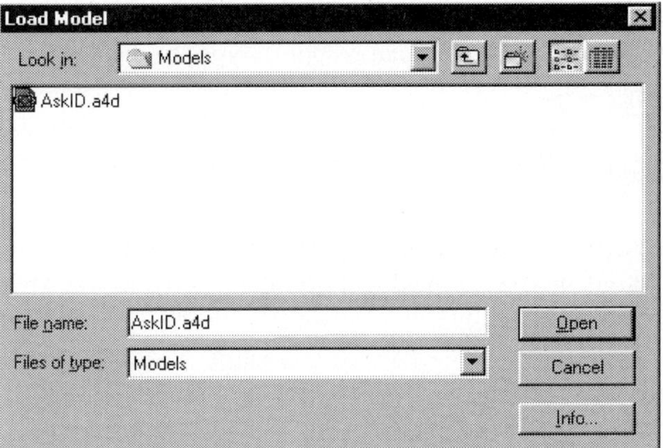

❏ Choose Insert>Paste Model and select the AskID model.

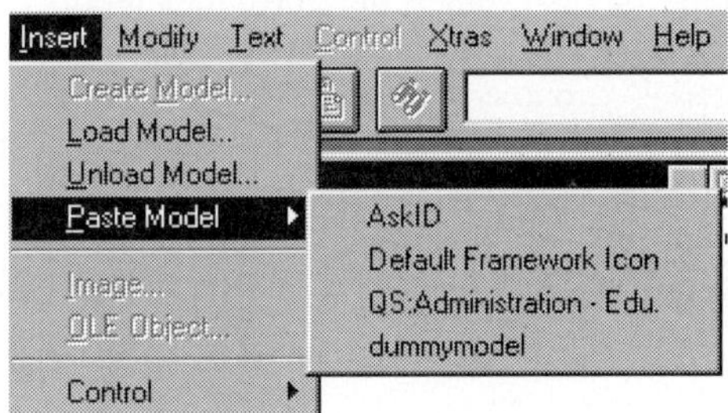

❏ Your flowline now looks like this:

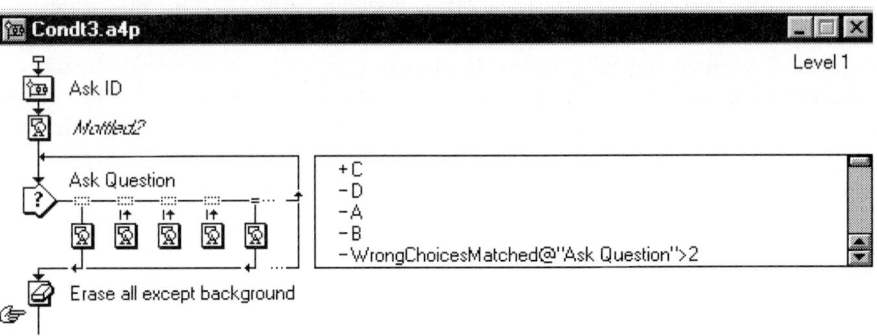

❏ Move the start flag to AskID and run from flag.
❏ Turn Caps Lock on and enter up to 8 characters into the input area.
❏ When prompted if the value is OK, answer No and this time hold down the Alt key as you reenter your name.
❏ Save your work as **Condtn3.a4p**.

If you open the AskID map icon you can see how we used the CapsLock and AltDown variables in the condition portion of the Conditional response types to display warning messages to the user.

Other Conditional Uses

The remaining uses include: Checking for numeric entries, filtering out unwanted text or numbers, and making sure an answer is complete. These only make sense when coupled with a text entry response. As a result, we'll return to these conditional uses after we discuss text entry interactions.

TEXT ENTRY INTERACTIONS

A keypress interaction evaluates which single key is pressed then provides feedback by way of a response icon. In many situations, you need to have the user enter more than a single keystroke. That information can be unjudged — a name for example — or judged as correct or incorrect, such as the answer to a question. In these situations, we use a text entry interaction.

Each text entry interaction can contain only one text entry. Be sure to set up multiple interactions to accommodate multiple text entries. For example, one for name, another for address.

Wildcards

To recognize *any* text, use an asterisk as the expected response. Use this when entering unjudged text, such as a user's name. The asterisk is also used as a catchall to flag unplanned for responses, such as when a multiple choice question has possible answers A-D, and someone enters an "F". In cases such as this, position the asterisk as the last response type. As we have seen, Authorware begins matching from left to right, and if it sees an asterisk it will stop looking at other possible response matches for all icons to the right of the asterisk. This means, Authorware would never reach the correct response!

Flexibility

You should take into account variations in spelling, word order and capitalization. Do this by attaching multiple response icons to the text interaction, each result looking for one of the variations. For example, if the answer is True, allow for true, T, Yes and so on. Use an "or" (|) operator to permit different words meaning the same thing. To make the interaction even friendlier, tell Authorware to ignore capitalization or extra words.

Creating a Text Entry Interaction

To create a text entry interaction:

1. Add an interaction icon to the flowline.
2. Place the question containing the data entry area in the interaction icon.
3. Drag an icon to the right of the interaction icon.
4. Select Text Entry as the type, then click OK.
5. Double-click the Text Entry Response type symbol .
6. Note that the Text Entry Response Properties dialog box opens, as shown in Figure 6.5.

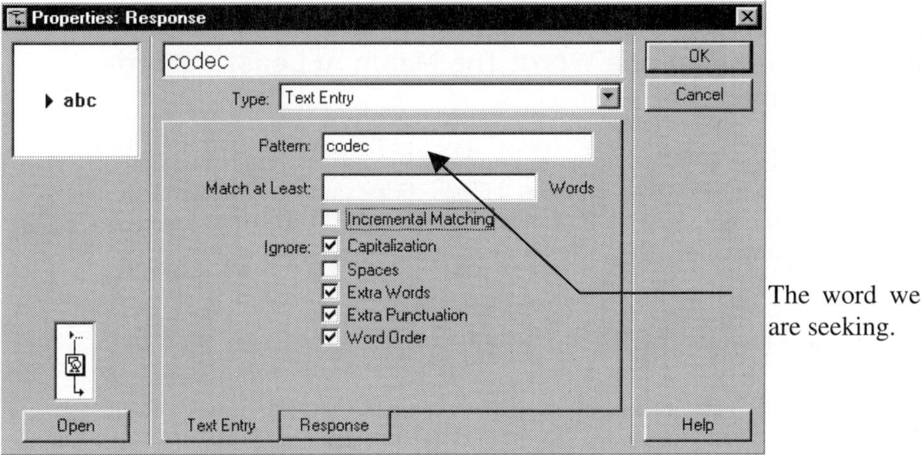

The word we are seeking.

Figure 6.5. The Text Entry Properties Dialog Box.

7. Enter the word(s) to be matched (the correct response) in the Pattern field.
8. Select appropriate erase feedback, response judging and branching options.
9. Click OK to close the dialog box.
10. Adjust the size and placement of the input area by Control double-clicking the interaction icon, then dragging and sizing the field.

The Text Entry Properties Dialog Box

Let's look at the options found in the Text Entry Options dialog box shown in Figure 6.5.

Pattern

Here is where we enter the text we are anticipating. For example, to look for the word "Earth", enter it (without the quotation marks) in this field. A potential problem exists if the user enters "earth", and we're anticipating "Earth".

Permitting One of Several Answers Suppose you want to allow for one of several words. For example: red or green or blue. To do so use the vertical bar ("|"). For the previous example, you would enter: red | green | blue.

Specifying a ? or a * as a Match If you follow the steps we outlined above while looking for a match on the question mark ("?"), you'll find it doesn't work! It's considered a wild card like "*", so Authorware interprets it's presence as a single character, matching anything. To allow for a * or a ? as answers, preface the character with a backslash (\) .

Matching More than one Word: The Match At Least _ Words Option

This option is used to specify the minimum number of words the user must enter. If words are separated by a "|" they are considered as groups. For example, to allow for Spanish or English as valid colors, enter: red white blue | rojo blanco azul in the Pattern field, and specify the user must match at least three words. Authorware will accept the three words in Spanish or English.

Incremental Matching

Suppose you wanted to ask: "Name the first three planets". If you check the Incremental Matching box, the user could try repeatedly to answer the question, getting a portion correct each time. For example, they might enter Mercury the first time, then hit Enter. After seeing some feedback, they might enter Venus and Earth the next time.

The Ignore Entries

To add to the user-friendliness of you project, you might consider making Authorware ignore extra characters or ignore capitalization. This means if we enter "earth" as the word to match, and check the Ignore Capitalization box, the user could enter either "Earth" or "earth".

Text Response Interaction Options

When you control double-click the interaction icon for a text entry interaction, the Interaction Icon Properties dialog box opens. Near the upper left corner is a Text Field button. You can see this in Figure 6.6.

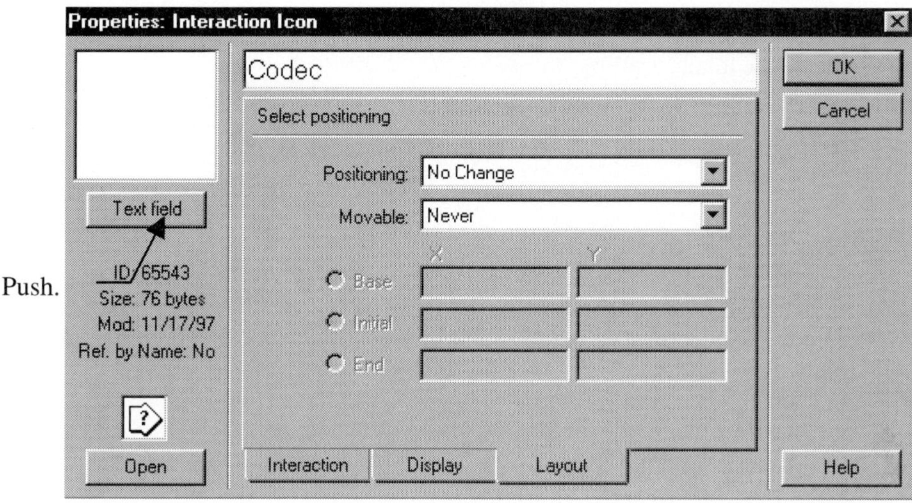

Push.

Figure 6.6. The Interaction Icon Dialog Box for Text Entry Interactions. To open it, Control double-click on the interaction icon.

Push the Text Field button to reveal the Interaction Text Field Properties dialog box, shown in Figure 6.7. There are additional properties in Figure 6.7 we must examine next.

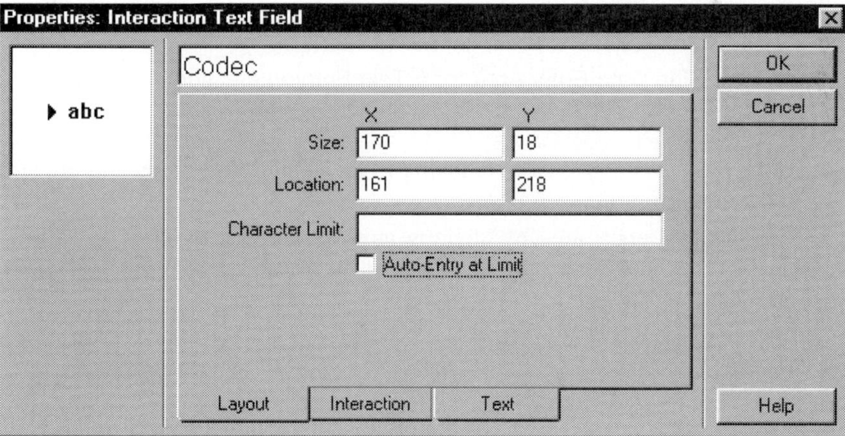

Figure 6.7. The Interaction Text Field Dialog Box. To view this, Control double-click the interaction icon, and then push the Text field button.

Use this expanded dialog box to:

- Specify how many characters to accept.
- Indicate the input location.
- Indicate whether to show an entry marker.
- Specify what keystroke ends the input (Return is the default).

Size and Location

The Size and Location field values specify where the text entry is to occur. An easier way to size and locate the data entry area is to use the Presentation window. To do this, follow the steps that follow.

1. Drag the Start flag to just before the interaction icon.
2. Run the piece from the start flag.
3. Open the Control Panel and push the Pause button.
4. The Presentation window will open.
5. The data entry area will be visible, as shown in Figure 6.8.

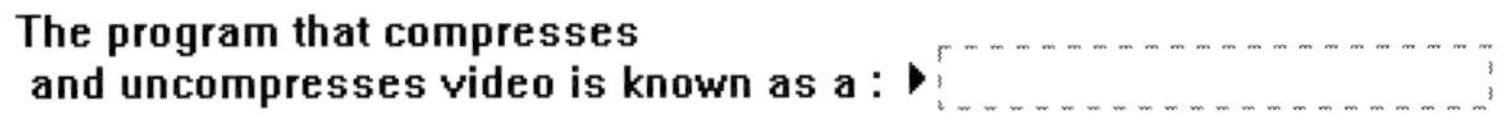

**The program that compresses
  and uncompresses video is known as a :** ▶

Figure 6.8. The Data Entry Area for a Text Entry Interaction. The area can be moved and sized within the Presentation window.

6. Move the data entry area by clicking in the center of the area and dragging it to the new location.
7. Size the data entry area by clicking anywhere inside the area and using the handles to adjust the height and width of the area.

Character Limit

Enter a numeric value or a variable or expression that evaluates to a number. This establishes the maximum number of keystrokes to accept. For example, you might be asking for a Social Security number. The value entered therefore might be 9. If you omit this field, Authorware uses the size of the data entry area to limit the number of keystrokes to permit.

Auto-Entry at Limit

If this box is checked, and the user has entered as many characters as was set as the limit in the Character Limit field, Authorware will automatically accept the value and move on.

Pushing the Interaction tab opens the dialog box in Figure 6.9.

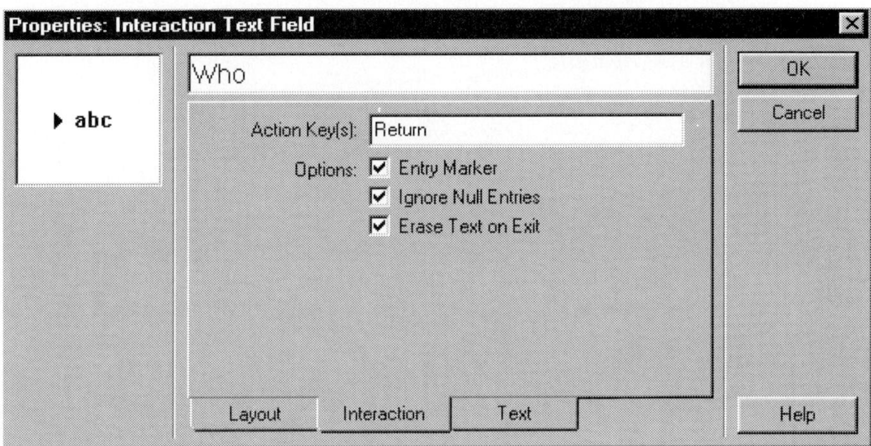

Figure 6.9. The Interaction Tab for Text Entry Interactions.

Entry Marker

The black arrow (see Figure 6.8) indicates the input area for the user. To eliminate this, deselect the Entry Marker option.

Ignore Null Entries

If this box is checked, Authorware will require that at least one character be entered before Authorware checks for a possible match. We normally leave this option checked.

Erase Text on Exit

The text that is entered by the user remains on the screen as long as the interaction is active. When the interaction is exited, the entry is erased. If you deselect the Erase Entry on Exit option, the text remains on the screen until removed by an erase icon.

Pushing the Text tab in Figure 6.9 reveals the dialog box shown in Figure 6.10.

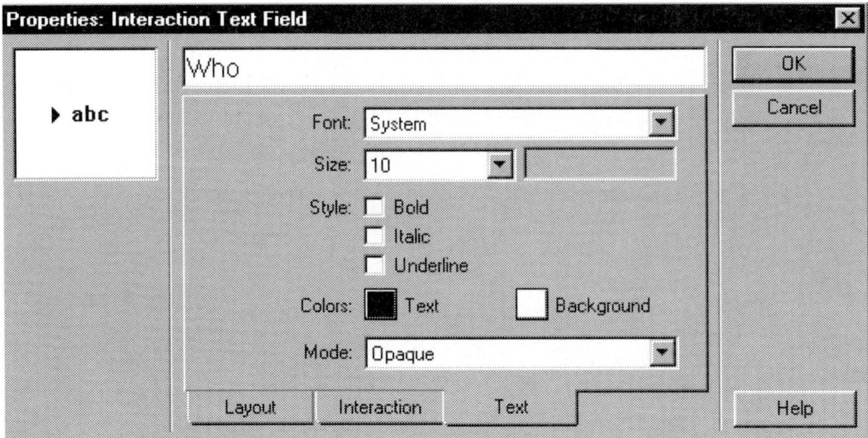

Figure 6.10. The Text Tab for Text Entry Interactions.

Font

Use the Font drop-down list to select the font to be used for the interaction.

Size

Enter a value or select one from the drop-down list to adjust the size of the text.

Style

Check any desirable style options to make the text consist of any combination of bold, italic or underlined properties.

Colors

Use the Text color block to change the color of the text, and the Background block to change the text's background color (the default is white). Pushing either block brings up the Color palette we have seen before.

Mode

Use the Mode drop-down list to select a text display mode. Choose among Opaque, Transparent, Inverse and Erase. These work the same way the Mode Inspector options. The default setting is Opaque. The new option is Erase, which prevents characters from being echoed to the screen as they are entered. This option might be used for password entries.

Let's apply the concepts and definitions we just learned.

Sample File You can preview what we're about to do if you open the **Texntry.a4p** file in the Chapter6 folder of the CD-ROM. Notice the data entry area has the small triangle indicating where the answer is to be entered. Enter Mars. That's the wrong answer. Now enter Venus, the correct answer. The display pauses while you read the feedback, then the interaction is erased. Let's see how to build this piece.

Your Turn

❏ Start a new project.

❏ Drag the *Mottled* icon from the Background library to the flowline. It's in the Libraries folder on your CD-ROM. (Remember to use File>Open>Library to make the library members available to your piece.)

❏ Set up an interaction icon. Name it Text Response Question.

❏ Double-click on the Text Response Question icon to open it so we can enter the question.

❏ Choose the text tool and type in 18 point, black, transparent text:
"Please enter the correct answer. Press Enter when finished"

❏ Use 18-point blue text for the second line:
"The second planet from the Sun is: _______________".

❏ Return to the flowline (Ctrl-1).

❏ Drag a display icon to the right of the interaction icon. The response type dialog box will open.

❏ Choose Text Entry; then click OK.

❏ Don't bother naming the icon because Authorware will assign it the name we are seeking to match (venus).

❏ Double-click the Text Entry response type symbol to open its dialog box.

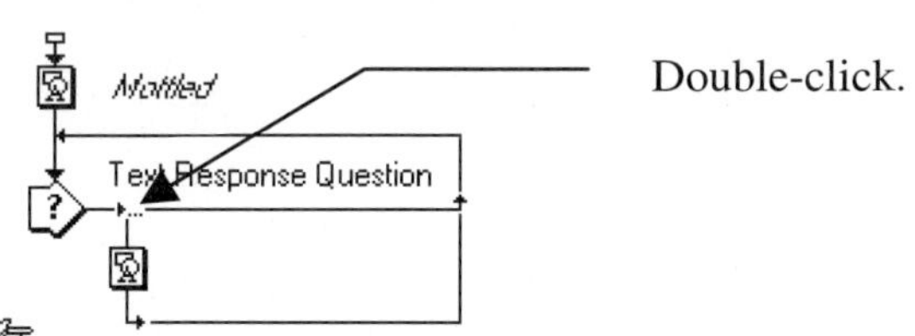

❏ Set the options for the Text Entry Response Options dialog box as we did in Figures 6.11 and 6.12.

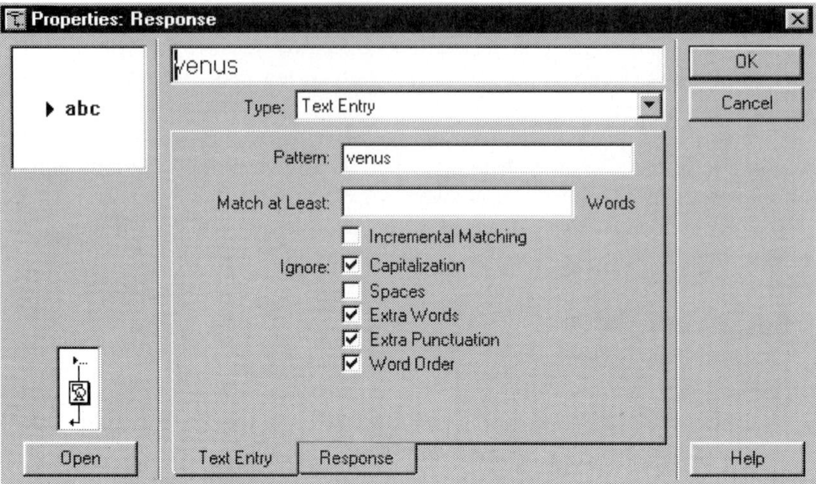

Figure 6.11. The Text Entry Tab Dialog Box For the Correct Response (Venus).

❑ Enter venus in the Pattern text box.
❑ Leave the Ignore options as they are: Authorware should ignore capitalization, spaces, any extra punctuation (like a "." at the end) and any extra words.
❑ Figure 6.12 shows the Response tab settings for the correct response.

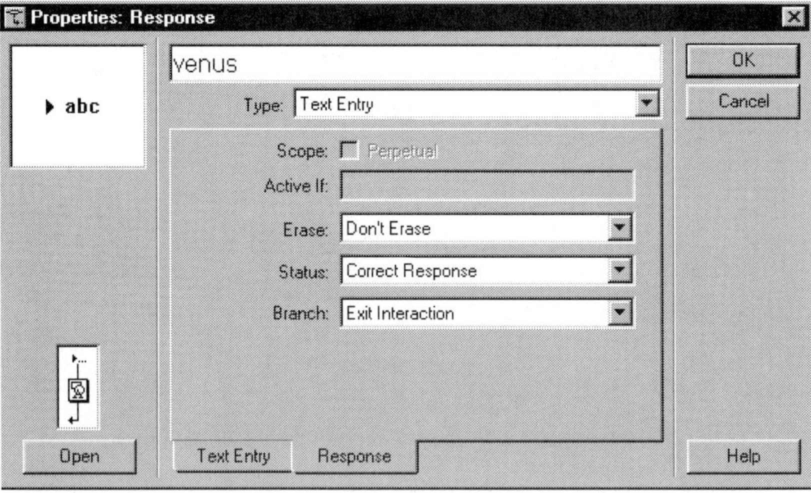

Figure 6.12. The Response Dialog Box for the Correct Response.

❑ Set Branching to Exit Interaction, because this is the correct response.

❏ Choose Don't Erase as the Erase Feedback option because we want the positive feedback to remain on the screen until we erase it.

❏ Click OK to close the dialog box.

❏ Notice the icon's name now matches what we just entered: venus.

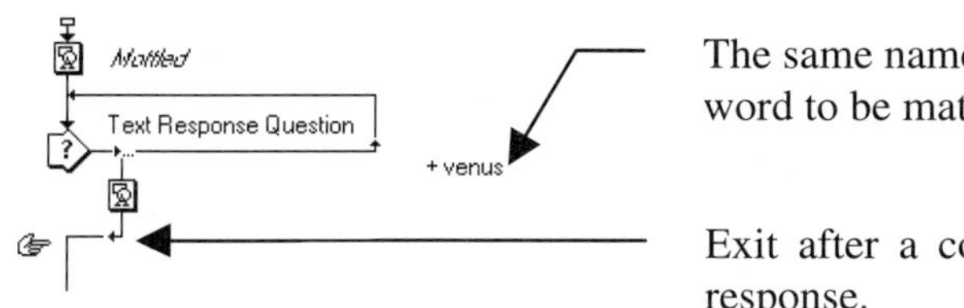

The same name as the word to be matched.

Exit after a correct response.

❏ Open the newly named venus display icon and add the following text in a black 18-point, transparent font: Very good. Venus is the second planet.

❏ Possible wrong answers include earth and mercury. Let's see how to trap responses such as these and provide appropriate feedback.

❏ Drag another display icon to the Text Response Question interaction.

❏ Authorware assumes it's also a text entry response so it doesn't prompt for a response type.

❏ Open the text entry response type symbol ▸....

❏ Enter mercury as the Pattern text, as shown in the following figure.

❏ Set branching to Try Again and set erase feedback to After Next Entry.

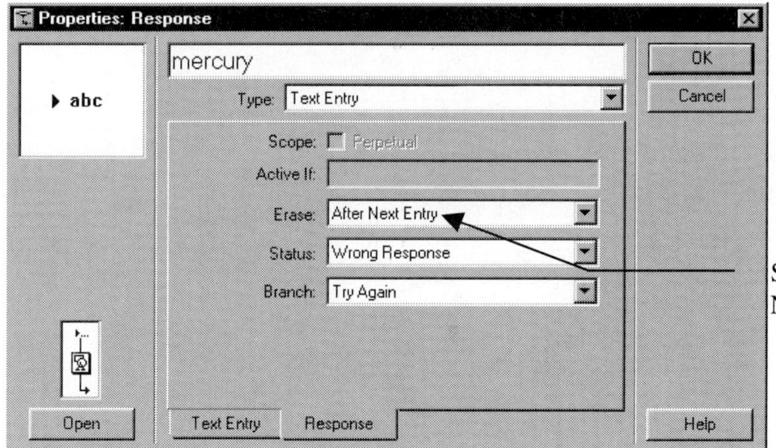

Select After Next Entry.

❏ Set the erase option to After Next Entry. This will erase our feedback when the user next enters text into the text area. Thus, our feedback will remain on the screen until more text is entered. Hopefully you just said to yourself, "What feedback?" That's our next step.

❏ Shift-click the mercury response icon.

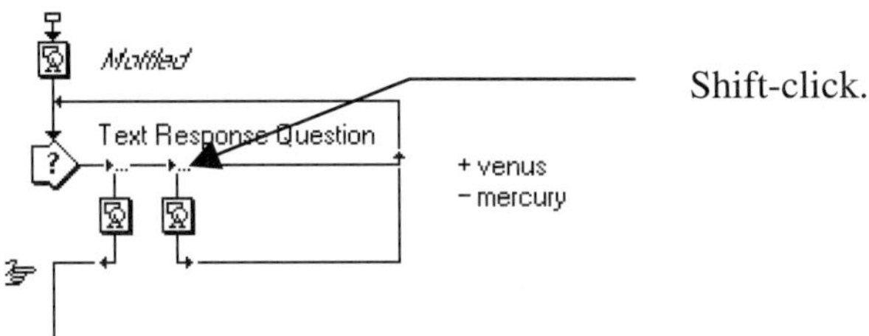

Shift-click.

❏ Enter: "No, Mercury is closest to the Sun. Please try again."
❏ You now must specify where the entry is to take place. You will create a small
rectangular box that covers the area you left blank when you created the interaction.
❏ Control double-click the Text Response Question interaction icon. The interaction icon properties dialog box, shown below, opens.

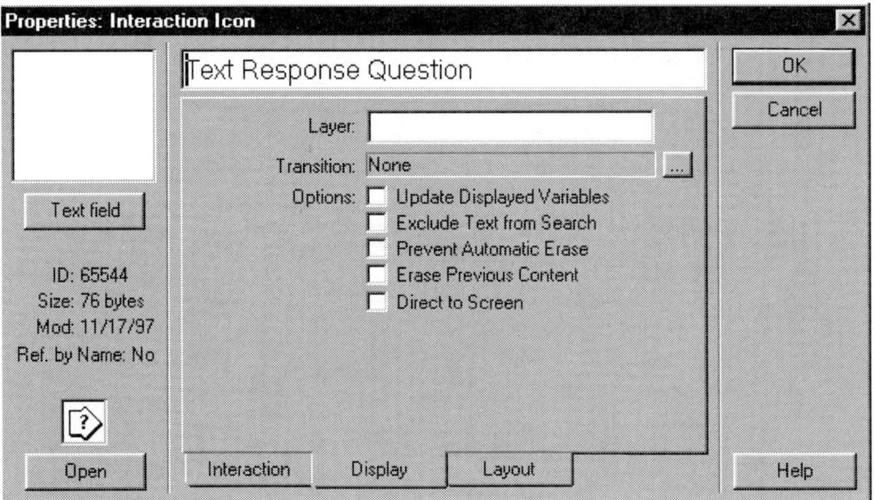

❏ Push the Text field button.
❏ This opens the dialog box, as shown in Figure 6.13.

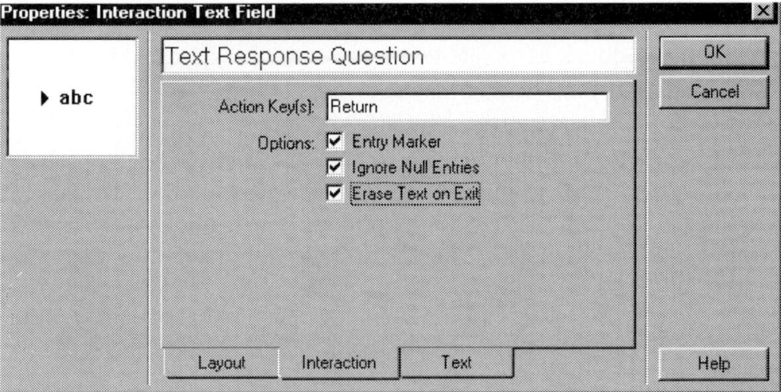

Figure 6.13. The Interaction Tab Dialog Box. It's for the Text Response Question interaction.

❑ Move the dialog box out of the way, then move and size the input area:

The second planet from the Sun is

❑ Leave the Entry Marker and Erase Text on Exit options in their checked state.
❑ We'll use a wild card as the last response to catch any words other than those we checked for.
❑ Complete your Text Response interaction by specifying OK and closing any open dialog boxes.
❑ Drag another display icon to the flowline.
❑ Title it *. This means Authorware is consider any characters in any quantity as a match. What would happen if this icon were first? Control would never pass to the correct answer. Because everything matches "*", Authorware would always use the "*" as the matched response.
❑ Your flowline should now look like this:

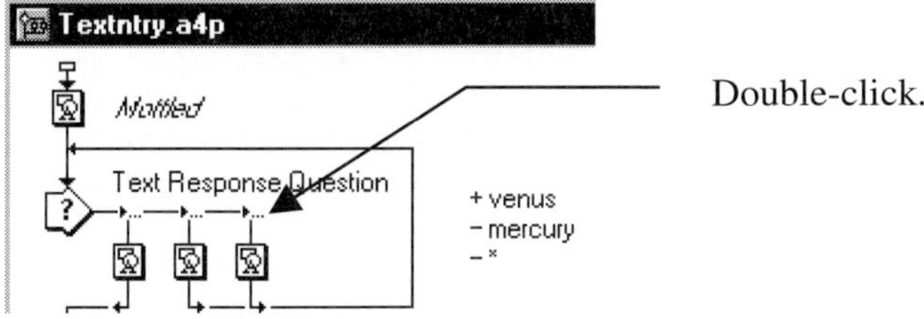

Double-click.

❑ Double-click the response type symbol for *.
❑ Set branching to Try Again and erasure to After Next Entry, then click OK.

❏ Open the * response (display) icon and enter this text: "Please try again." Now let's enter the feedback associated with the correct response.

❏ Run from flag and enter "venus" as the answer.

❏ The feedback displays too fast.

❏ Control double-click on the Text Response Question interaction and check the Pause Before Exit box so the user has a chance to see the feedback before it's erased. Notice you can also display a button. If you run from flag and enter venus as the response, you'll see that the feedback stays on the screen until a key is pressed. It might be a good idea to display a button.

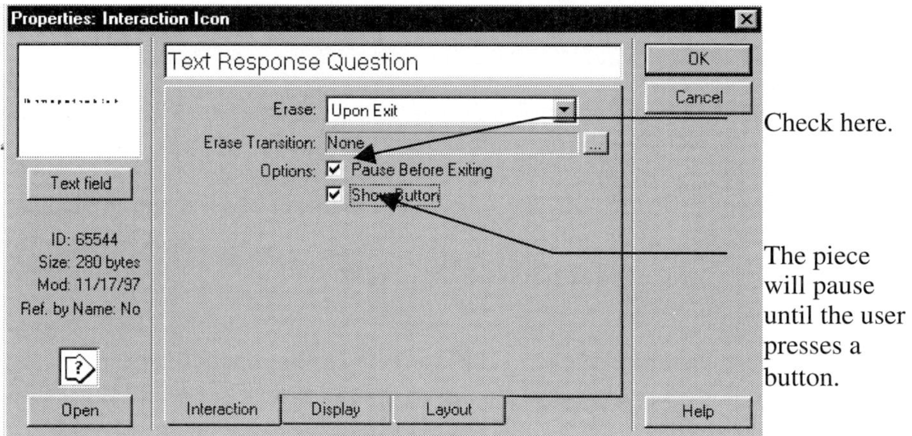

❏ Close the Text Entry Question dialog box.

❏ Save your work as **Textntry.a4p.**

Use text entry responses for open-ended questions that are to be judged, or for text entry, storing the input in variables. They are easy to create and simple to understand. Let's now return to the conditional interaction and add some more functionality to text entry responses.

Checking for Numeric Values: The NumEntry Variable

Suppose you want to ask a question that has a numerical answer. One way to evaluate the response is to use a system variable NumEntry. Authorware stores the first digit of a number in NumEntry. The second and third digits are stored in NumEntry2 and NumEntry3 respectively. We can check any of the digits against a set of values, one value in the set for each possible path.   You could check for a value of 2, 3, and so on, even for ranges, such as less than 9. Let's use these facts in an example.

Sample File To preview the next exercise, open and run the **Numeric.a4p** file in the Chapter6 folder on the CD-ROM. Answer the first question (venus is the correct response), then enter 7 as the answer to the second question. The correct answer is 9 (enter the digits, rather than the words).

Your Turn

❏ Open the **Textntry.a4p** piece and add an interaction icon named How Many Planets?

❏ Set up an interaction icon and name it Ask it.

❏ Open the interaction icon, and add the question:
"How many planets are there?"

❏ Attach a conditional display icon and enter `NumEntry<  9` as the condition value. This checks for a numerical value less than 9. Set Automatic to Off.

❏ Next add another conditional display with `NumEntry=  9` as the Condition value. Mark this as the correct response and use the Exit Interaction branching option. Set Automatic to off.

❏ Add a third conditional display icon for values greater than 9.

❏ Finally add a text entry response with * as the matching value. This is where the user will enter the answer. Notice this must be a text response, not a conditional.

❏ Be sure the first three response types are set to conditional, and the last to text entry.

This one is a
text entry
interaction.

❏ Open each display and add appropriate text.

❏ Position the Start flag at the beginning of the How many planets interaction.

❏ Run your piece.

❏ Enter the correct response.

❏ When the value 9 is entered, the positive feedback message appears but is erased too fast.

❏ Remedy the problem.

❏ Make sure the incorrect responses function properly.

❏ Save your work as **Numeric.a4p.**

Filtering Out Text or Numbers: The NumCount Variable

If you create a conditional and enter `NumCount>0` as the Condition value, any text input field that contains numbers will be filtered out. If you use `WordCount>0`, any text field that contains letters will be filtered out.

Making Sure All Items Are Correct: The AllCorrectMatched Variable

Suppose you don't want the user to go on until he or she has named all of the first three planets. This can be done using a conditional plus the system variable: `AllCorrect-Matched`. When all responses have been matched, `AllCorrectMatched` will be True. It will be False in all other situations.

First set up the interaction icon plus the responses for each correct (and anticipated incorrect) response. Be sure to properly designate the correct and incorrect responses. Then create a conditional response and set the match condition to `AllCorrectMatched`. Each correct response should have Response Tracking set to Correct Response; each Branching option set to Continue (this is necessary so Authorware can see if all responses are correct).

KEYPRESS INTERACTIONS

A keypress interaction presents some information or a graphic, and then waits for a single key to be struck.

Creating a Keypress Interaction

The steps required to create a keypress interaction are similar to those for a button or a hot spot. The steps are:

1. Add an interaction icon to the flowline.
2. Drag an icon to the right of the interaction icon.
3. The Response Type dialog box opens. Choose Keypress, then push the OK button.
4. You don't need to name the result icon as it assumes the name of the key you are waiting for.
5. Double-click the keypress symbol.
6. The Keypress Options dialog box opens.
7. In the Key(s) field, enter the key you want to recognize as a match (Use Table 5.1 to assist with key names).

8. Enter suitable values for the erase feedback, response judging and branching options.

9. Enter content into the result icon.

Let's look at the Keypress Response Properties dialog box; then we'll build a keypress project.

The Keypress Response Properties Dialog Box

Figure 6.14 shows an open Keypress Properties dialog box.

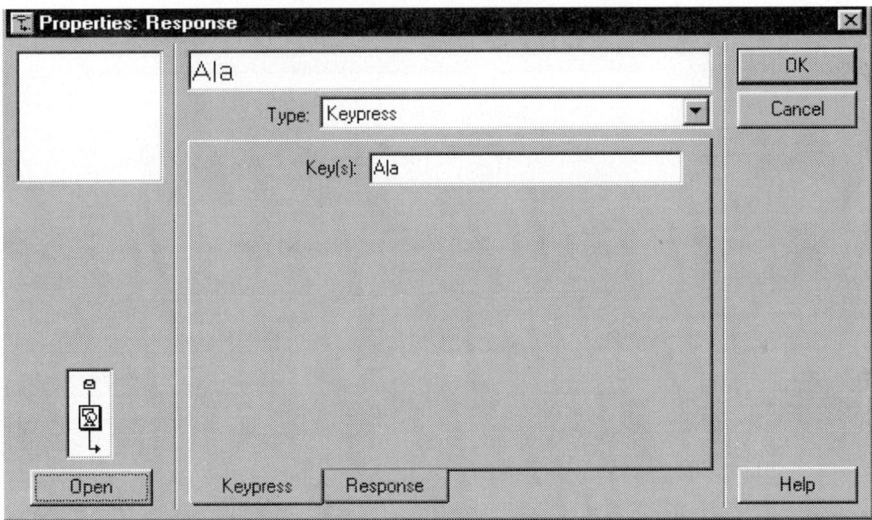

Figure 6.14. The Keypress Response Properties Dialog Box

Because most of the options have been discussed before, we'll only look at the new option: Key(s).

Enter the name of the key you are expecting here. Use table 5.1 for nonstandard key names. If this is a multiple-choice test and "A" is the correct response, enter A as the Key value. As with text entry responses, you should anticipate uppercase and lowercase answers.

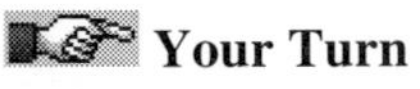 **Sample File** To preview the next exercise, open the **Keypress.a4p** file in the Chapter6 folder on the CD-ROM. Run the piece. The correct answer is "C". Let's see how the piece was constructed.

Your Turn

❑ Start a new project.

❑ Add an interaction icon and name it Multiple.

❑ Attach three display icons. Their types are all the same: Keypress. Name them A, B and C.

❑ Double-click the Multiple icon.

❑ Add this text:

The largest planet is:

A. Earth

B. Mars

C. Jupiter

❑ Open the response type icons for Earth and Mars ("A" and "B") and set their Response options as shown below.

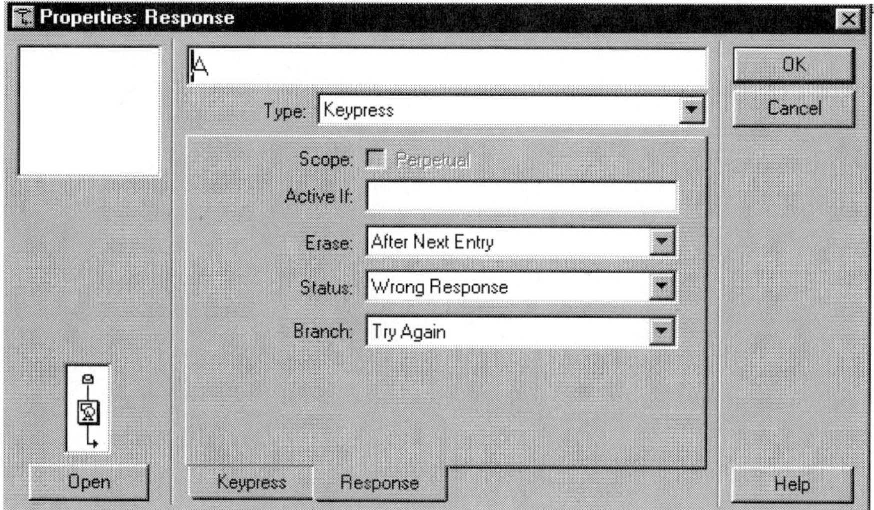

❑ Be sure to look for both upper and lower case "A" in the Keypress tab.

❑ For the correct choice, "C", set Branching to Exit Interaction, and judged to "Correct Response".

❑ Add appropriate text to each display icon.

❑ Your flowline should resemble the figure that follows.

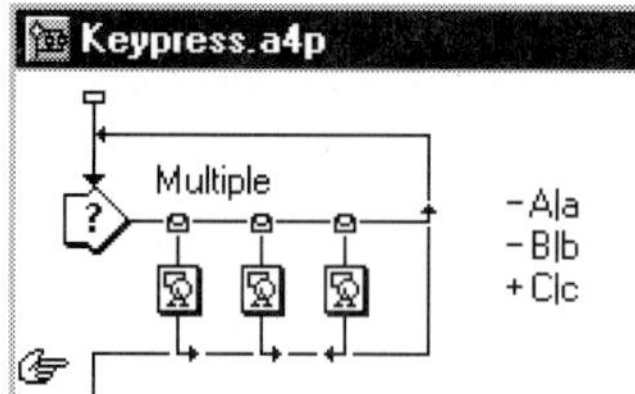

❏ Save your work as **Keypress.a4p.**

Since there are only three choices to make, we might choose to limit the number of wrong answers to two. This can be done using the technique we saw earlier, which involved a conditional and a variable, but it can more easily be done using the Tries Limit interaction type.

TRIES LIMIT

There are times when the user cannot determine the correct answer to a question. In such situations, you might display a help screen after so many tries, or provide the correct answer and proceed. Perhaps you only want the user to have three wrong answers before exiting an interaction. In all of these cases, we can use the Tries Limit interaction to accomplish this.

Authorware keeps track of the number of incorrect response through a variable, `Tries`. Each time a wrong response is detected, `Tries` is incremented by one. When `Tries` exceeds a value you enter in one of the Tries Limit dialog boxes, the interaction responds to the content you provide in the attached response icon.

Let's limit the number of wrong guesses in the text entry example to two.

Your Turn

❏ Open the **Keypress.a4p** project.
❏ Attach another display icon named Tries Limit.
❏ Double-click the response type for the new icon.
❏ Change its type to Tries Limit.
❏ Enter 3 in the Maximum Tries text entry box, as shown in the figure below:

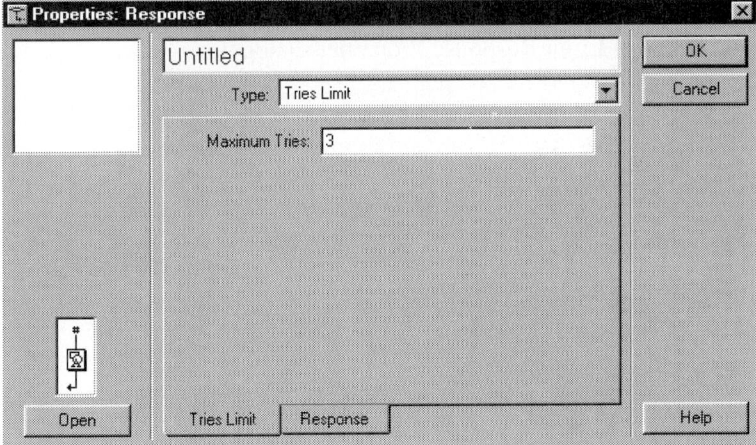

❏ Set the branching to Exit Interaction, because we want to move along after a third wrong guess. That is, two wrong answers is acceptable, three is not.

❏ Authorware will only invoke our response when the number equals three exactly: Not 4, not 5,… We want to present the information in the response icon for all wrong attempts over 2. You can use `Tries >2` as a substitute for the above. Now control comes here as long as the number of tries exceeds two. `Tries` is an Authorware variable.

❏ Your flowline should look like this:

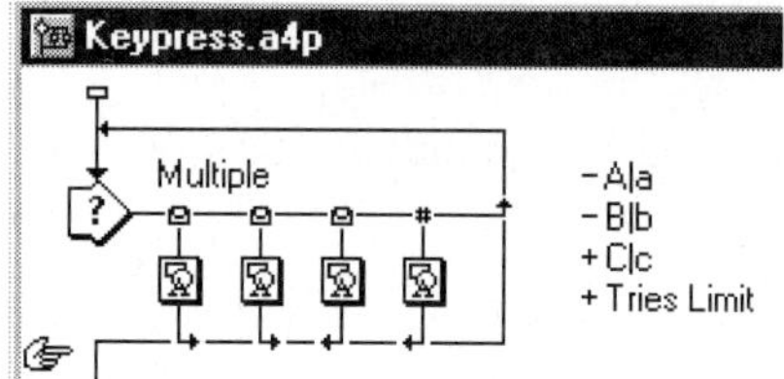

❏ Save your work as **Keylimit.a4p**.

TIME LIMIT INTERACTIONS

Use a time limit response type when you want Authorware to branch to a result icon after a certain amount of time. Inside the dialog box, you specify how long to wait. By checking the Show Time Remaining box, you can display a countdown clock.

The Time Limit Options Dialog Box

Figure 6.15 shows the Time Limit Response Properties dialog box.

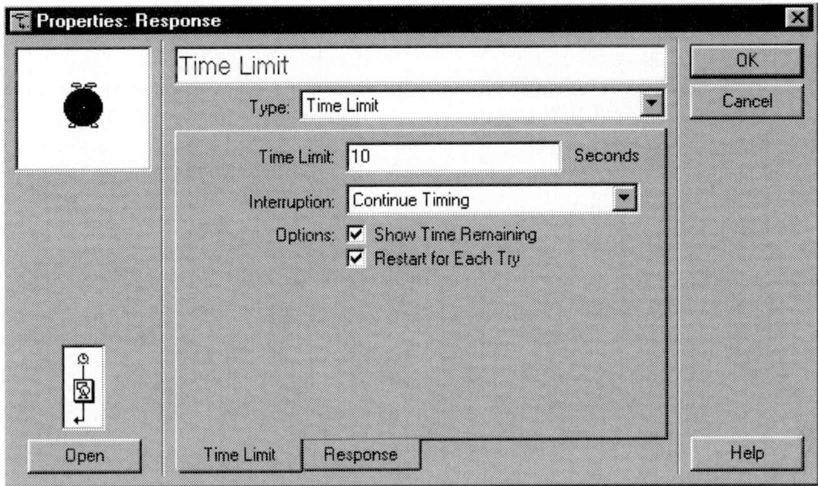

Figure 6.15. The Time Limit Response Properties Dialog Box.

The new options include Time Limit, Show Time Remaining, Restart for Each Try, and Interruption. Let's see what these options do.

Time Limit

Enter the number of seconds the user has to make a response. Suppose you have 100 questions, and entered 10 as the number of seconds. You test your piece and realize users require 15 seconds. You would have to go back in and change all 100 questions. A better solution is to use a variable in this field, then add a calculation icon with the variable set to the desired number of seconds.

Show Time Remaining

If you check this box, a count-down clock will appear, showing the amount of time remaining.

Restart for Each Try

Check this box if you want Authorware to reset the clock after any response. Assume the user waits 10 seconds before a response – the message in an attached display icon would show. If the user waited another 10 seconds, the response would appear again. By checking this box, the clock resets after each try.

Interruption

Use this drop-down box to specify what to do if the user goes to a perpetual interaction, such as a pull-down menu, or a button interaction. There are four options. Refer to the Authorware help for more information.

> ☞ **Your Turn**
>
> ❏ Open your **KeyLimit.a4p** project.
> ❏ Set up a display icon to the right of Tries Limit. Name it Time Limit.
> ❏ Change its type to Time Limit .
> ❏ Click OK to close the dialog box.
> ❏ In the Time Limit text box, enter 10. This limits the user to 10 seconds before giving the feedback in the display icon, where we will enter the text: "Time is up. The answer was C"
> ❏ Set branching to Exit Interaction.
> ❏ Run your piece and wait 10 seconds.
> ❏ When the Time Limit Presentation Window opens, enter the text from above.
> ❏ Run again and wait 10 seconds. Your message appears. Wait 10 more seconds: Nothing happens. We need to reset the clock after each try.
> ❏ Open the response type for Time Limit.
> ❏ Check the Restart For Each Try box.
> ❏ Save your work as **Limits.a4p.**
> ❏ Run your piece. This time the clock should reset after each response.

EVENT INTERACTIONS

The interactions we have examined thus far have responded to events: keys being pressed, time exceeding a threshold value and so on. As the event occurred, some type of interactivity was activated. When you need interactivity not provided by Authorware, you can seek help with third-party vendors who supply Xtras.

There are two types of Xtras: scripts and sprite Xtras. You detect interactions of either Xtra-type through Event responses. The Xtra, and not Authorware, interacts with the user. Xtras respond to interactions by generating events, which communicate to your piece through the Event interaction. Within your Event interaction you instruct Authorware what to do when a particular event is detected as coming form the Xtra.

Like external media, Xtras must be distributed with your piece. They are not embedded with your piece.

Let's add a Microsoft Calendar ActiveX control. ActiveX controls are Microsoft's replacement for OLE (Object Linking and Embedding).

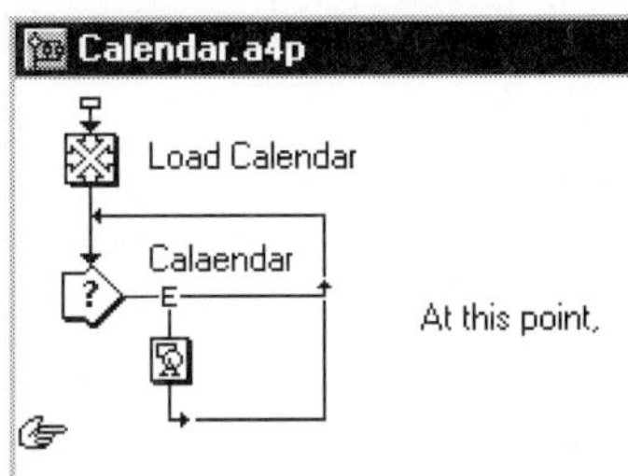
Sample File Open the **Calandar.a4p** file in the Chapter6 folder. Its flowline is shown in Figure 6.16. If you click on any date, a message appears telling you how you might use such an Xtra.

Figure 6.16. The Flowline for the **Calandar.a4p** file, which includes the Microsoft Calendar ActiveX Control.

To build this piece, follow the steps that follow.

1. Select Insert>Control>ActiveX.
2. The Select ActiveX Control dialog box opens, which is shown in Figure 6.17.

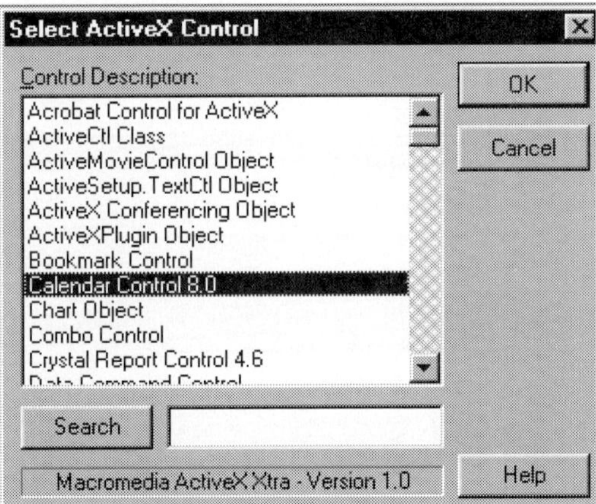

Figure 6.17. The Select ActiveX Control Dialog Box. Use it to choose the ActiveX controls to add to your piece.

3. Choose the Calendar control, as we did in Figure 6.17.
4. ActiveX controls have properties or characteristics that can be changed. When you add the control to your piece, the Properties dialog box for that control opens, as shown in Figure 6.18.

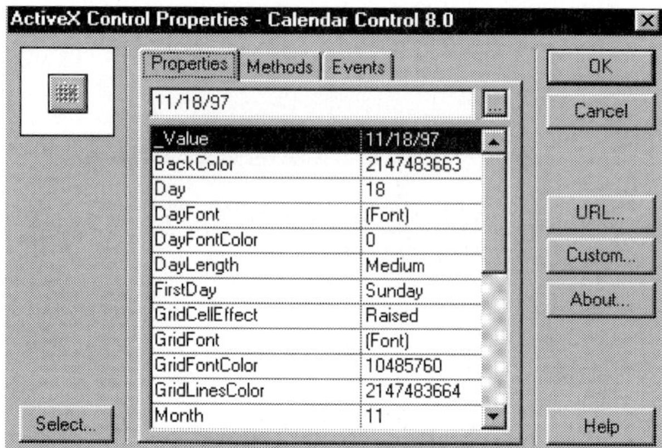

Figure 6.18. The ActiveX Control Properties Dialog Box.

5. Within the Properties tab you can change properties such as which day to show as the first one (the default is Sunday), the default month (the current one is the initial default) and so on.

6. To change a property, select it, and then make the change in the text field at the top of the Properties dialog box.

7. If you click on the Events tab, you can see the list of events to which we can have Authorware respond. Those events are shown in Figure 6.19.

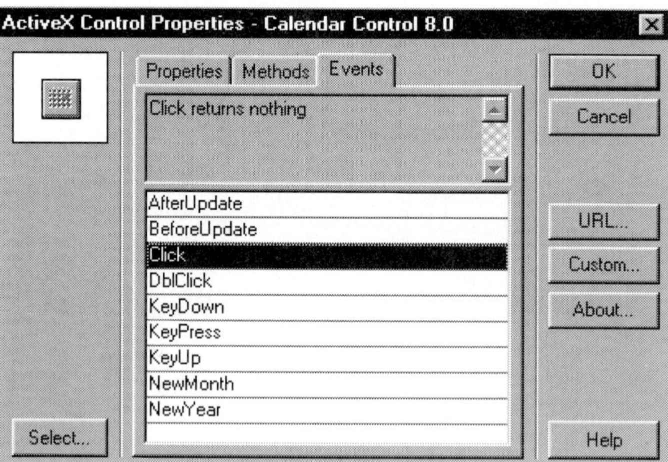

Figure 6.19. The Events Dialog Box for the Calendar ActiveX Control.

8. We decided to have Authorware respond to the Click event. Let's see how that was accomplished.

9. We added an interaction icon and selected Event as the type.

10. Next, we double-clicked on the response type and set up the resulting dialog box like that of Figure 6.20.

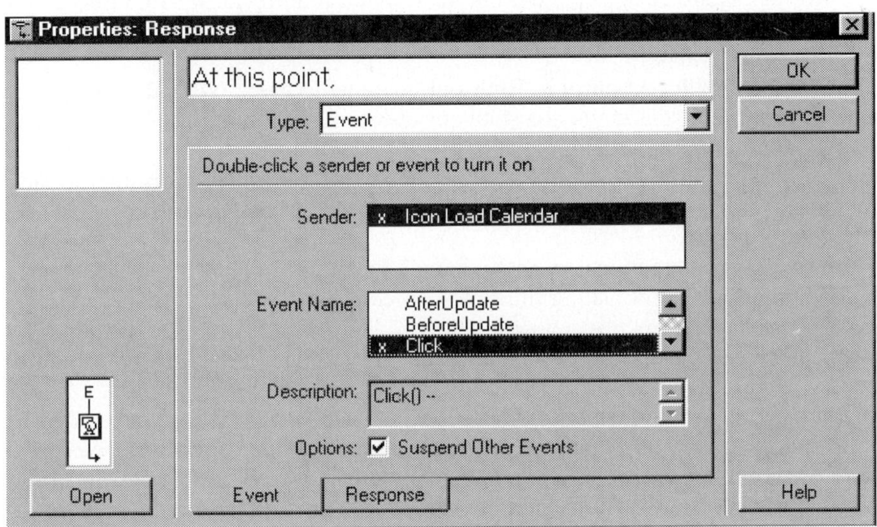

Figure 6.20. The Event Response Dialog Box.

11. The sender of the event is the ActiveX control. We named the icon Load Calendar, and that name appears n the Sender list. Because there might be several ActiveX controls available to your piece, you must indicate to which one you want the event to respond by double-clicking the name of the control.

12. Similarly, because there are many possible events to respond to, double-click the one to be associated with the interaction, Click in Figure 6.20.

13. Lastly, we added the text in the display icon we attached to the interaction.

Event interactions greatly extend the power of Authorware, adding functionality only before possible thorough languages like C++.

This concludes the chapter on keyboard and system interactions. Because of the length of the chapter, we won't add to the digital video piece in this chapter.

SUMMARY

There are several interactions that are triggered by the user interacting with the keyboard, or by an event, such as a time limit expiring. This chapter examined pull-down menus, conditionals, text entry keypress, tries limit, and time limit interactions.

Pull-down menus are easily created, but each menu requires a separate interaction. A separator can be placed between logical submenu choices. Often, menus are made perpetual, so that they are always available.

Use conditionals with text entry to filter out unwanted values. We can also use conditional responses to monitor the keyboard status or check other conditions. Hot text can also be created using conditional interactions.

When you want to limit the number of tries or set a time limit for an interaction, add an icon and choose either Tries Limit to limit the number of wrong answers, or Time Limit to restrict the time available.

We use keypress interactions to gather single-keystroke alphabetic and numeric information. A common use is for asking multiple-choice questions or making selections from menus.

Use text entry responses to collect data about users or as judged responses to questions.

Using ActiveX and other kinds of Xtras, the power of Authorware is extended to accomplish almost any task. Many actions that are not possible in Authorware can be done with ActiveX controls. For example, you could easily create a web browser using Microsoft ActiveX controls. That browser could then be used within an Authorware piece by utilizing the control.

Study Exercises

6.1. Create a new project and call it C6Q1. It should specify a perpetual menu that has two main headings: Exit and My Projects. The Exit menu has one command, Quit, while the other menu option should list at least three of your prior projects. Add each of your projects as individual map icons. To "jump" to an icon from within Authorware use: `GoTo(IconID@"Icon name")`. For example, to jump to a map icon named "Restaurants", create a calculation icon and enter: `GoTo IconID@"Restaurants")`. Your menu should be perpetual.

6.2 Create a text entry project that asks the user to name a popular imaging package. Provide responses for Photoshop and PhotoStyler. Give only one wrong answer and limit the response to 15 seconds. Filter out numeric values and check to be sure that the Caps Lock key is off.

Calculating and Branching

The last three chapters showed how users could interact with an Authorware title. Based on the user's choice, Authorware might display feedback or play a sound or a movie. This chapter looks at the calculation icon and the decision icon. The calculation icon can assign values to system or user-defined variables or utilize built-in functions. While complex, the use of variables enables the developer to create sophisticated and powerful projects that could not be created from use of the icons alone.

The branching icon specifies which path, or how many paths to take. Such an interaction is performed automatically, rather than under the control of the user.

At the conclusion of the chapter, you will be able to:

- Set up a calculation icon.
- Use calculation icons to make objects active or inactive.
- Use calculation icons to control multimedia devices and files.

- Perform mathematical calculations, including the generation of random numbers.
- Use arrays to store and retrieve data.
- Jump among several separate Authorware projects.
- Create looping structures.
- Draw objects.
- Control the Presentation window.
- Jump between Authorware projects.
- Perform system functions such as quitting Authorware.
- Set up and use branching icons.
- Specify how to set up and use sequential and random branching.
- Specify other forms of branching together with repeat options.

AN OVERVIEW OF CALCULATION ICONS

As we have seen in previous chapters, calculation icons are used to assign values to variables. These variables can be Authorware variables, or ones you create. A variable is an object whose value can be changed. Appendix A describes the Authorware variables, while Appendix B lists the built-in functions, which can also be used in calculation icons.

The general syntax for assigning a variable a value is: `VariableName:= expression`. The expression can include references to other variables or to built-in functions. You can insert calculation icons at any point on the flowline. To add content to a calculation icon, double-click on it to open its calculation window where you enter can enter expressions, comments, scripts for If-Then statements, repeat loops and much more. Alternatively, as we have seen in previous chapters, you can attach a calculation to existing icons.

ADDING A CALCULATION TO AN EXISTING ICON

A second way to add a calculation is to attach it to an existing icon. To do this:

1. Select the icon.
2. Select Modify>Icon>Calculation (Ctrl+=).
3. Enter the information in the window that opens.

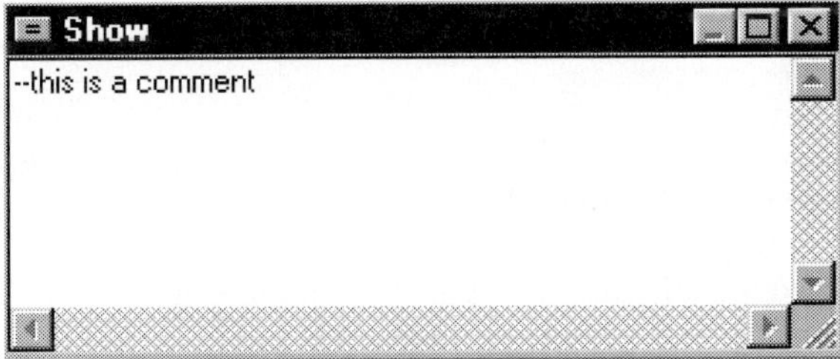

4. Close the window.

5. You will notice a small "=" associated with the icon (see the figure below).

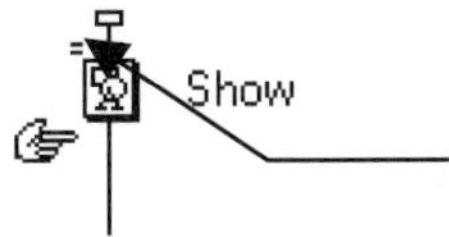

Indicates a calculation is associated with the icon.

TYPICAL USES FOR CALCULATION ICONS

In this chapter, we will see how to use calculation icons to:

- Control the state of interactive objects.
- Play MIDI (Musical Instrument Digital Interface) music.
- Play and record digitized sound.
- Control CD audio.
- Call the Windows Media Control Interface (MCI) to manage multimedia.
- Generate random numbers.
- Perform mathematical computations.
- Control on-screen graphics.
- Control the cursor.
- Control the menu-bar.
- Control how to exit Authorware.

The first use we explore is limiting when a button (or any interactive object) is active.

LIMITING WHEN AN OBJECT IS ACTIVE

There are times when you must make an object unavailable, or inactive. For example, assume you don't want a certain button to be active.

Sample File To do this, use a flowline something like **Active.a4p** in the Chapter7 folder, which you might want to open and run at this time.

Figure 7.1 shows the flowline for the Active piece.

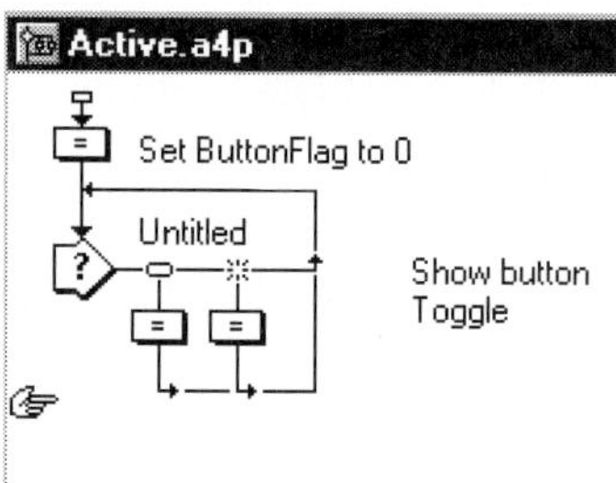

Figure 7.1. The Flowline for **Active.a4p**, a Piece that Uses One Button to Deactivate Another.

Inside an initial calculation icon, you set a variable to "Off", or zero. Let's use `ButtonFlag` as the variable that holds a value of either zero or one. As the statement within the Show button calculation icon, enter: `ButtonFlag:=0`. When you define the button, insert the Active If statement in the Button Properties dialog box, as we did in Figure 7.2.

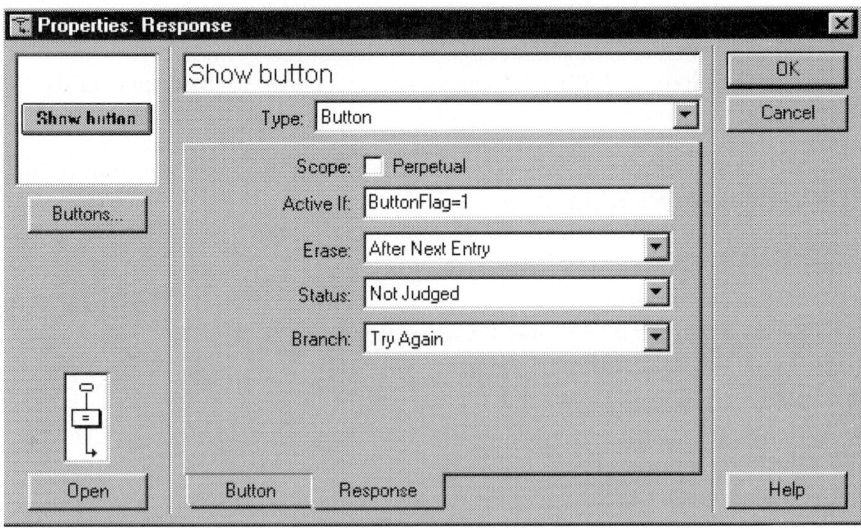

Figure 7.2. Using the Active if Field to Specify when A Button Is Active.

The Active if setting means "show the button as normal when the value of Button-Flag is equal to one." If the value of ButtonFlag is anything else, show the disabled (dim) version of the button. Recall the button editor permits us to have several button graphics, one for each of the four possible states.

If you run the Active project, you can push the red button to toggle the Show Button button between its active and inactive states. Open the Toggle icon and note the statement inside, shown in Figure 7.3.

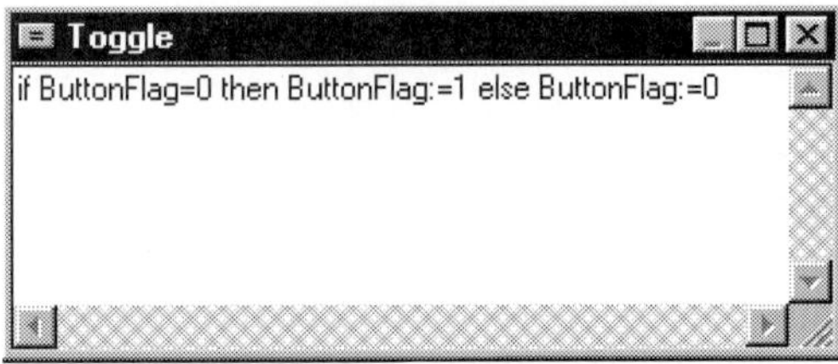

Figure 7.3 The Content of the Calculation Icon Attached to The Toggle Button. It switches values of ButtonFlag between 0 and 1.

Interpret the statement in Figure 7.3 as meaning: "If the value of ButtonFlag equals 0, set it to one. If the value of ButtonFlag is anything else, set its value to 0."

In the exercise that follows, you'll create a button that controls the displaying of a digital movie. The button, named "go", acts as a toggle for a second button. Push "go" once and the second button becomes inactive. Push again, and the second button becomes active. The second button, when active, starts and stops a digital movie. In an effort to reuse earlier knowledge, a motion icon will be used to move an object prior to the display of the "movie".

Sample File If you want to simply follow along with us, open the **Inactive.a4p** piece in the Chapter7\ folder on the CD-ROM.

Your Turn

❑ Start a new project.
❑ Set up a map icon and name it Calculations.
❑ Open the Calculations map icon.
❑ Add a display icon and name it Background.
❑ Import the **Tmplate8** bitmap from the Templates folder on the CD-ROM. Scale the Y dimension to 94%.
❑ Add a calculation icon and name it Set ButtonFlag to zero.
❑ Open the icon and enter `ButtonFlag:=0`.
❑ When the New Variable dialog box opens, enter these values:

❑ Now set up an interaction with two buttons: "Go" and "show movie until ButtonFlag = 0". Choose maps as the response icon types. Name the interaction Show buttons.
❑ Your complete flowline should look like the following figure.

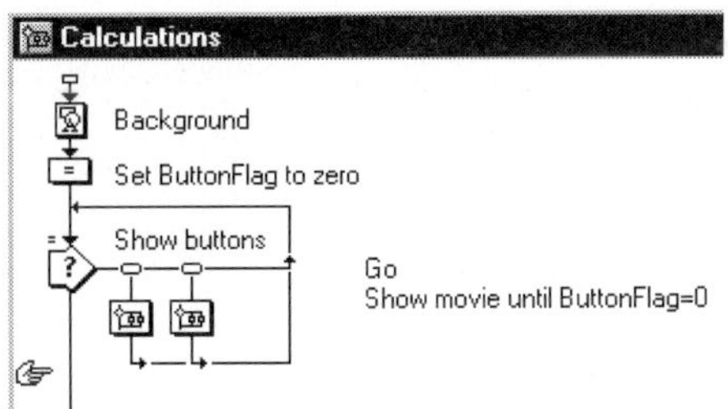

❏ You are going to work with the "Go" button first. This button is always active so you'll associate a single graphic with its up state. To do this, you'll work with custom buttons and the button editor.

❏ Double-click the Go response type icon.

❏ Check the Perpetual box in the Response tab settings.

❏ Click on the sample button in the Type window.

❏ When the Button Library dialog box opens, push the Add button to open the button editor, shown below.

❏ Push the Up Normal button, then the Import button next to Graphic.

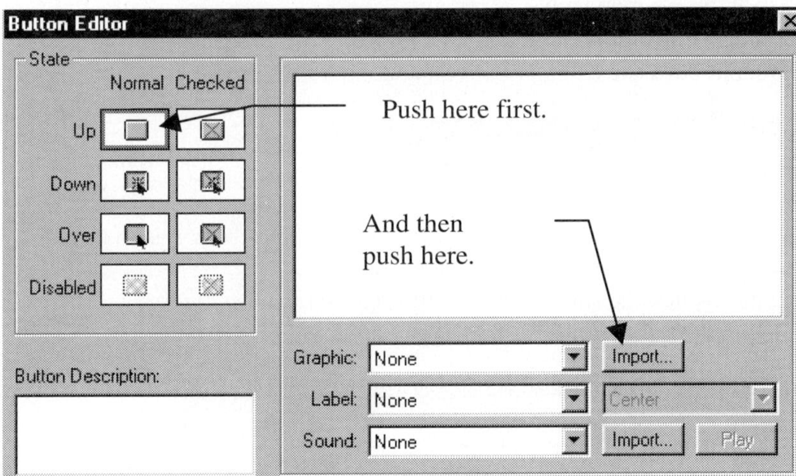

❏ The Import which file dialog box opens.

❏ Click the Show Preview check box.

❏ Choose **TBUp4.gif** in the Images\Buttons folder on the CD-ROM.

❏ Chose **Click.wav** in the Sounds folder as the sound to be associated with the Go button.

❏ Push OK.

❏ Position the "Go" button graphic like this:

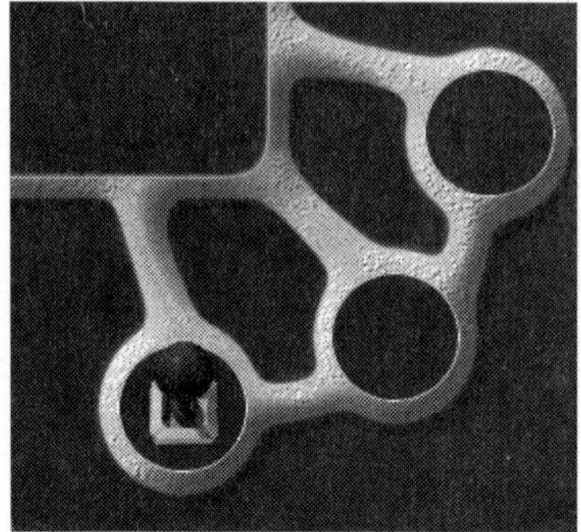

❏ We will place the second button to the right of this one.

❏ When the go button is pushed, it will toggle the value of the `ButtonFlag` variable from one state to the other: From 0 to 1 or 1 to 0. As this occurs, we want to show two different versions of the second button: One version for active, another for inactive. To accomplish this toggling effect we need to attach a calculation icon to the Go button. When the button is "pushed" control will pass to the calculation icon where the toggling of `ButtonFlag` values occurs.

❏ Open the Go map icon.

❏ Set up a calculation icon and name it Toggle ButtonFlag.

❏ Double-click the calculation icon and enter this coding:

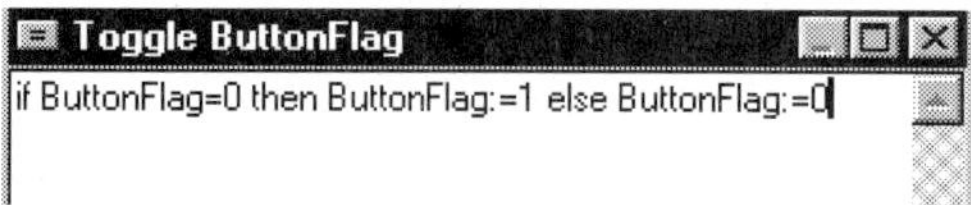

❏ Now it's time to work with the other button. This button is to have an "up" state and a dim (inactive) state. Let's begin.

❏ Double-click the show movie until flag = 0 response type.

❏ Set up the button options this way:

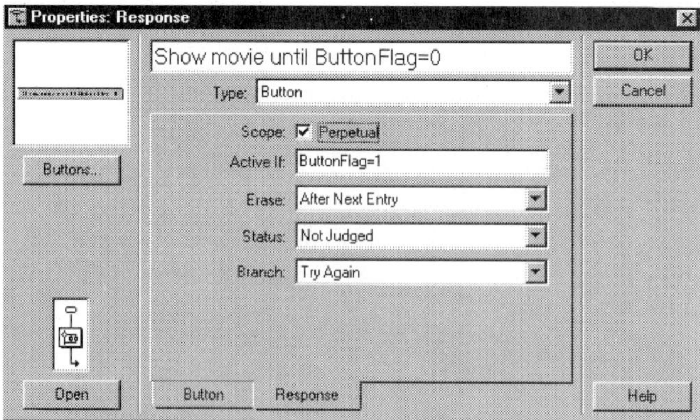

❏ This dialog box says to mark the button as active (available for use) when the value of `ButtonFlag` equals 1. Also, make the button perpetual. When the button is inactive (disabled), we want to show another button.

❏ Push the Button Type button preview.

❏ Import **TBUp03.gif** and **TBDn03.gif** for the up and down graphics, and **TBUp05.gif** as the Inactive graphic. Select **Click2.wav** as the sound for the up state.

❏ Position the second button just to the right of the first one.

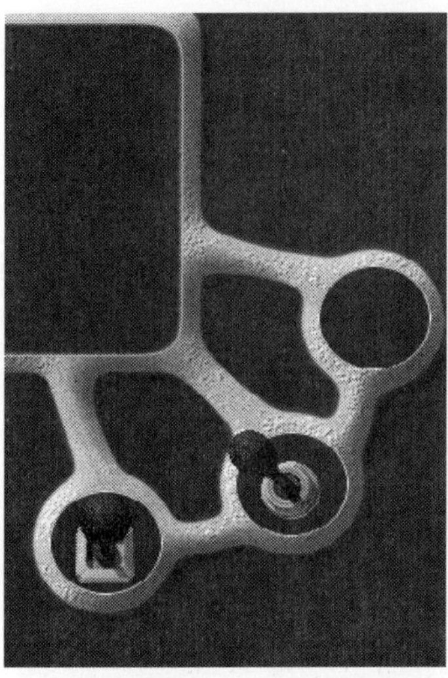

❏ To test your work thus far, run your piece and press the Go button. The button on the right should switch between its up and inactive states as you continue to press the button on the left.

❏ Let's add some feedback regarding the state of the play button.

❏ Open the Calculations map and insert a new display, named Show status, as in the figure that follows.

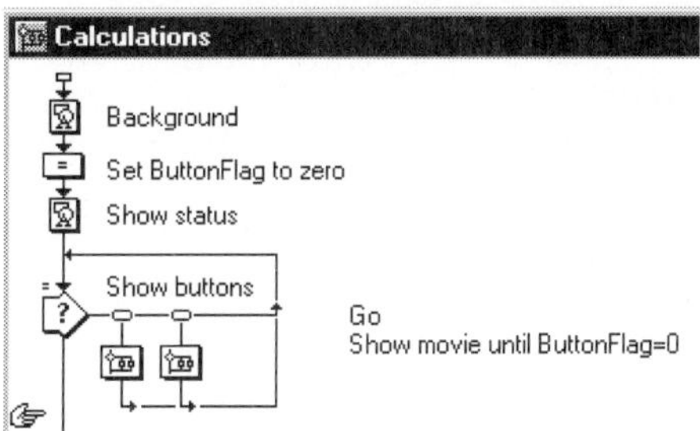

❏ Shift-double-click the new display icon, then enter the text you see in the next figure.

❏ As you can see, we've included a variable, Text. Because Text is a variable, we need to tell Authorware to constantly display the current value. To do this, select the icon, and then choose <u>M</u>odify><u>I</u>con><u>P</u>roperties. Check the Update Displayed Variables and Prevent Automatic Erasure boxes, as indicated in the figure below.

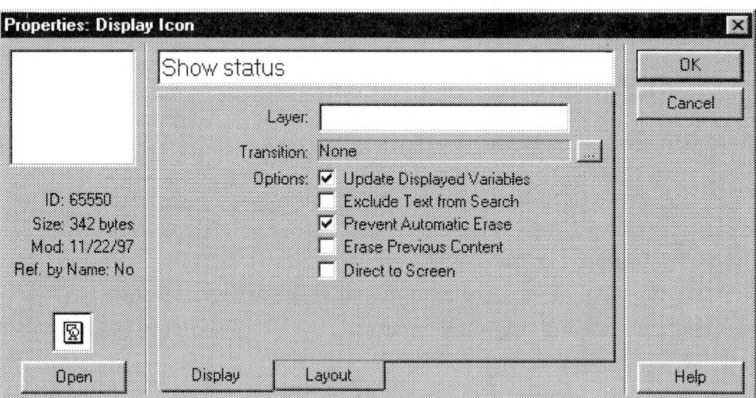

❏ We need to give Text a suitable value.

❏ Enter Ctrl+= on the Show buttons interaction icon and add this calculation:

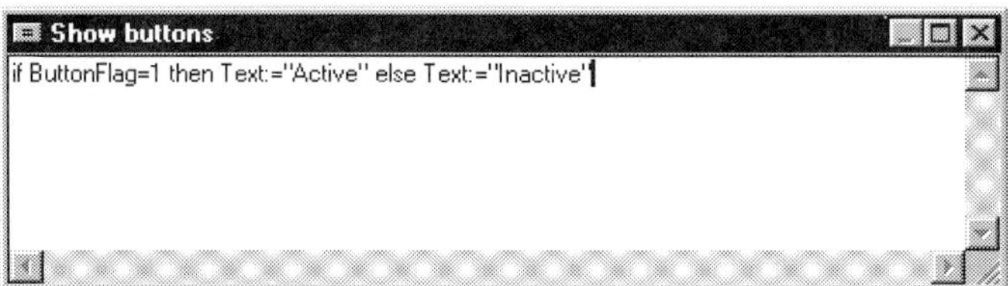

❑ This means that when the value of `ButtonFlag` is equal to 1, set the value of `Text` to Active, otherwise set it to Inactive.

❑ Run your piece and push the play button a few times. The message should change accordingly.

❑ Open the show movie until ButtonFlag=0 map, and set up a movie icon and name it like this:

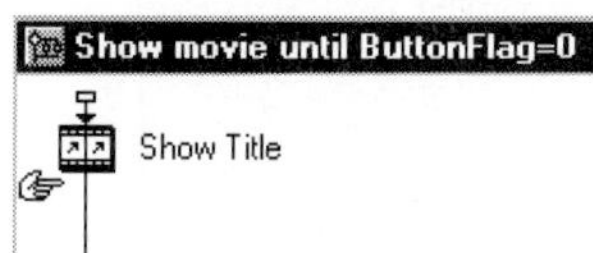

❑ This map icon is going to play a QuickTime movie (**Title.mov**) that is in the Chapter7 folder on your CD-ROM. The movie will play continuously until the variable `ButtonFlag` is set to its 0 state.

❑ Try pushing the Play button when it's in its inactive state. Nothing should happen.

❑ Push your Go button again so the other button appears in its active state.

❑ Push the Play button.

❑ Open the Show Title movie icon and import the Quick Time MOV file named Title from the Chapter7 folder on CD-ROM.

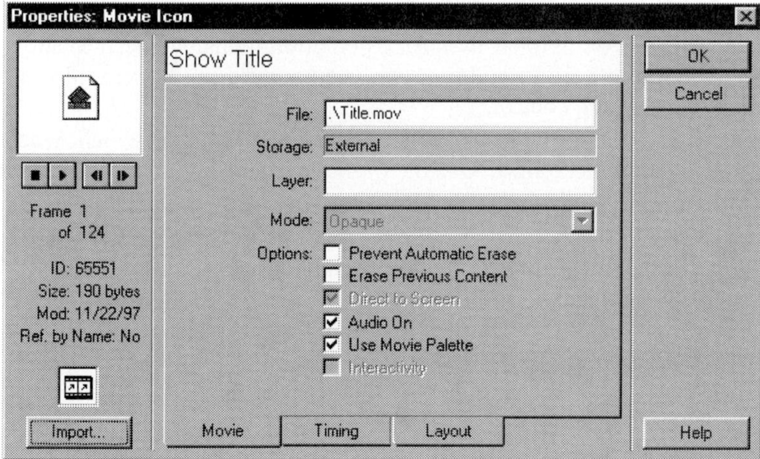

❑ Push the timing tab and enter the values you see in the figure below.

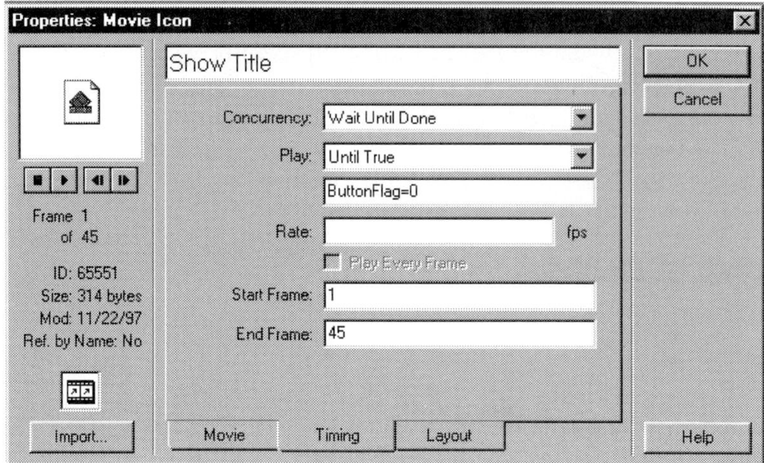

□ Notice we set the Play Until True option so that the stars continue to shine until the value of `ButtonFlag` equals 0. How does this occur? When we push the Go button, the value is toggled from 0 to 1 or 1 to 0. In effect, the left (Go) button will act as a stop button. Let's see what happens when we push the right button.

□ Push the second button. (Be sure the button is in its active state.)

□ Push it.

□ When finished watching, push the Go button and the movie will stop.

□ Before we move on to other uses for calculation icons, we need to add a way for the interaction to exit. In addition, we need some messages to inform the users about what they can control.

□ Add a third button to the screen (attach a calculation icon) which, when pushed, simply exits the interaction. Use the `Quit(0)` calculation we've seen before.

□ Use **Quit-up.gif**, **Quit-dn.gif** and **Button1.wav** as the up, and down graphic and the sound respectively

□ Position your Quit button near the lower right corner.

□ Add an erase icon that erases everything.

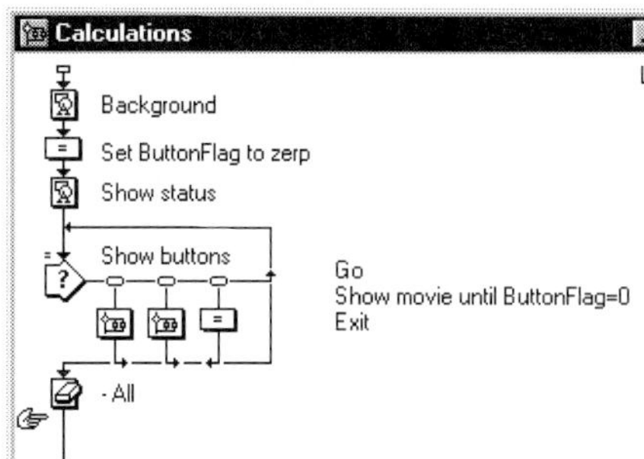

❑ Run your project, test your work, and then push the Quit button.

❑ Select the Show Buttons icon, then select Modify>Icon>Calculation (or Ctrl+=). Here's where we'll set up two more variables to display control messages.

❑ Inside the calculation icon, enter:

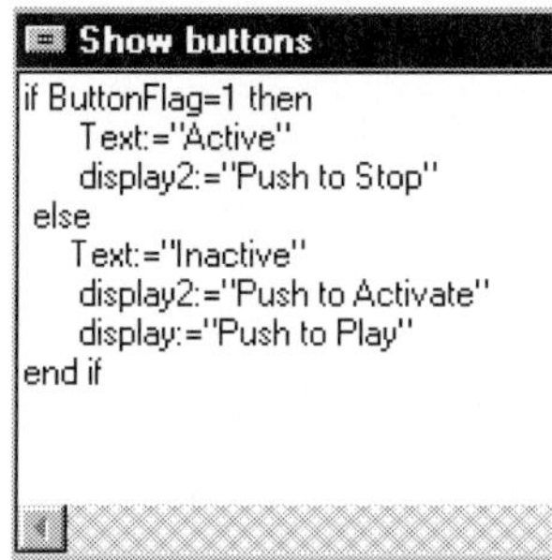

❑ Interpret the first line as: If the value of `ButtonFlag` is equal to 1, then set the value of the variable `display2` to "Push to Stop" and set `Text` to "Active". Otherwise set `display` to "Push to stop" and set `display2` to "Push to Activate". In other words, when `ButtonFlag` equals 0, meaning the movie won't play because the Play button is inactive, set the variable to "Push to Activate". Otherwise (the variable must be set to 1), set the variable to "Push to stop"

❑ Now add two variables to the display component of the Show Buttons icon. Begin by Shift double-clicking the icon.

❑ Add {`Display2`} below the first button, {`Display`} below the second.

❑ Be sure the Modify>Icon>Properties of Show Buttons are set this way:

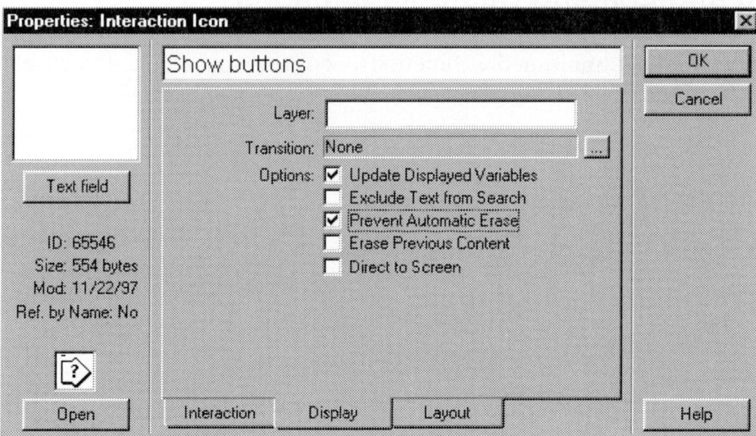

❏ Save your work as **Inactive.a4p.**

Let's look at some other uses for a calculation icon. Many of the examples cited contain references to Authorware functions. You can read more about functions within Authorware by choosing Window Functions or consulting Appendix B.

CUSTOM FUNCTIONS

Custom functions perform tasks other than the Authorware system functions and are written by programmers. Authorware comes with many such functions and are on the Authorware CD-ROM in the GOODIES\UCD folder. In fact, there are about 20 UCD folders on that CD-ROM. UCD stands for *user code document* and is an extension of a Windows component known as a *Dynamic Link Library*, or DLL for short. For users on Windows-95 or Windows 98, there are both 16 and 32-bit UCDs. The pair of UCDs will have "U16" and "U32" extensions. If you are creating a 32-bit version of your project, copy and use the .U32 version of the UCD, otherwise use the .U16 version.

Multimedia Custom Functions

Authorware's DLL for multimedia is A4WMME.U32. You may need to copy it from the Authorware CD-ROM to the folder containing your project. The 32-bit version is in Goodies\Ucd\A4WMME.

Referencing and Loading Custom Functions

A4WMME contains many multimedia functions. To see these functions, select Window>Functions. The Functions dialog box opens, which is shown in Figure 7.4.

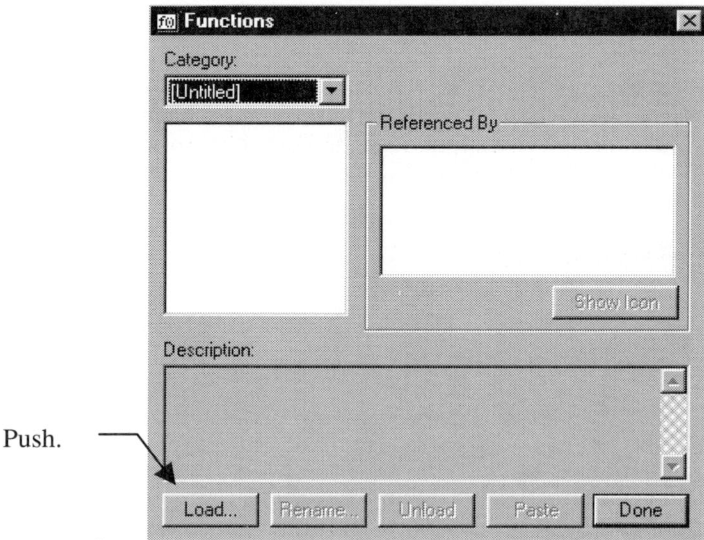

Figure 7.4. The Functions Dialog Box. Use it to open and load Authorware UCDs.

Click the Load button to open a UCD file. Choose A4WMME as the UCD containing the function you want to load. When the Custom Functions dialog box opens, shown in Figure 7.5, you can scroll through the list of available functions.

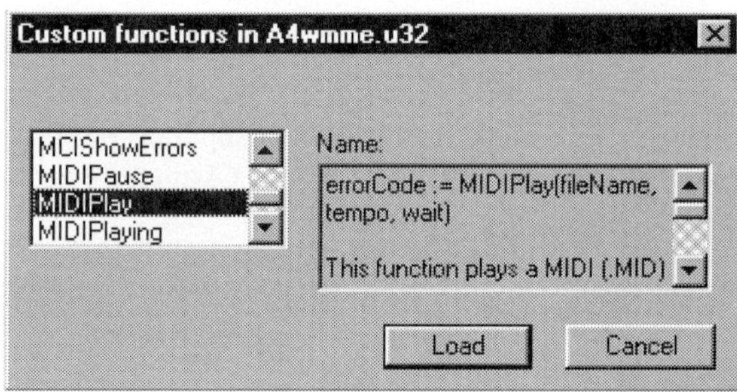

Figure 7.5. The Custom Functions Dialog Box. Use it to select the new function to be added to your piece.

Push Load when you find the function you want to use.

CONTROLLING MIDI FILES

While Authorware doesn't directly support MIDI (Musical Instrument Digital Interface), you can use a series of functions in calculation icons to control the playing of a MIDI file. Your CD-ROM contains two MIDI files in the Chapter7\MIDI folder on the CD-ROM.

Playing a Complete MIDI File

To play a MIDI file named MUSIC.MID, located in the C:\MULTIMED\MIDI directory, from start to finish, use this calculation icon entry:

```
result:= MIDIPlay ("C:\\MULTIMED\\MIDI\\MUSIC.MID",tempo,
wait)
```

Result is a variable name. If, after executing the statement, the value of *result* is anything but zero, the file didn't play correctly. In effect, *result* is a numeric variable that contains an error code.

Tempo is the playback tempo expressed as a percentage, so 100 would be normal.

Wait defines the timing of the MIDI file. If you set the value of wait to TRUE, Authorware plays the music until it's finished (Wait Until Done) before jumping to the next icon. A value of FALSE in effect sets the play timing to concurrent. Thus our complete example above might be:

```
result:=MIDIPlay ("C:\\MULTIMED\\MIDI\\MUSIC.MID", 100,
FALSE)
```

Be sure to use the double-back slash ("\\") to separate path components. As an example, the calculation below (part of **Midi.a4p** in the Chapter7 folder on the CD-ROM) will play a **Music.MID** file off a local hard drive.

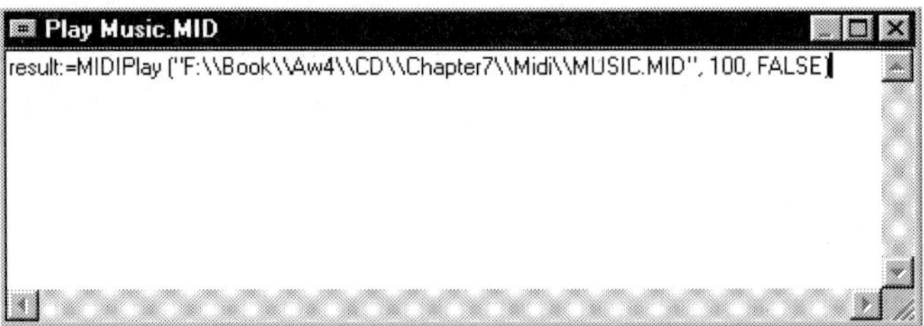

Prior to entering the statement, we loaded the MIDIPlay function from the A4WMME UCD.

Playing a Portion of a MIDI File

You can play a portion of a MIDI file from a given starting point for a given number of seconds by using this syntax inside a calculation icon:

```
result:= MIDIPlaySegment (FileName, tempo, FromSeconds, For-
Seconds, wait)
```

Stopping a MIDI file

To stop a MIDI file while it's playing, use this entry:

```
result:=MIDIStop()
```

Pausing a MIDI File

You can pause a MIDI file as it's playing by using this line inside a calculation icon:

```
result:=MIDIPause()
```

Resuming a Paused MIDI File

Resuming a paused MIDI is just as easy. Enter this into a calculation icon:

```
result:=MIDIResume
```

Testing to Determine if a MIDI File is Playing

To test if a MIDI sequence is currently playing, use this in a calculation icon:

```
result:=MIDIPlaying
```

If the value of result is TRUE, then a file is presently playing.

CONTROLLING DIGITIZED SOUND

To control digital sounds, substitute the phrase Wave for MIDI and omit all references to tempo in the expression entered inside the calculation icon. Playing, stopping, checking for an active wave file and so on are all accomplished using almost identical expressions to those we saw with MIDI.

For example, to play a .WAV file named APPLAUSE.WAV in the C:\SOUNDS of your hard drive, you would use this expression inside a calculation icon:

```
result:= WavePlay ("C:\\SOUNDS\APPLAUSE.WAV,FALSE)
```

As with MIDI, you would have to also load the function before using it.

CONTROLLING CD AUDIO

You can play selected tracks, portions of tracks, stop or pause then resume playing a CD, check to see if any CD audio sequence is playing, determine the current position of the CD audio sequence or eject a CD, all using a calculation icon.

Playing a Track from Start to End

Use this syntax:

```
Variable1:=CDPlay(track,wait)
```

Where track is the desired track number and wait defined as above.

Playing a Segment of a Track

To play a track from a starting point for a given number of seconds, use this:

```
Variable1:=CDPlaySegment (track, startseconds, for-
seconds,wait)
```

Stopping, Pausing and Resuming Play

To stop, pause resume or check to see if CD Audio is playing, simply substitute CD for MIDI as above.

Ejecting an Audio CD

To eject a CD, enter this line inside a calculation icon:

```
Variable1:= CDEject()
```

Determining the Current CD Position

If you want to know the track:minute:second:frame and store the result in a string variable, use this syntax inside a calculation icon:

```
Stringvar:=CDCurrentPosition()
```

GENERATING RANDOM NUMBERS

A random number is one whose value cannot be predicted in advance. For example, you might want to have three paths to take, but let the computer choose which path. To do this, you would generate a number between one and three. Or you might want to play a sound between 5 and 10 times. In that case, you'd place the function we are going to examine in the Play sound _____ Times text box within the Sound Options dialog box.

To generate a random number between lower and upper bounds in specified units, use:

```
NumberVariable:=random(lower, upper, units)
```

For example, to generate an integer between 1 and 3, enter:

```
Variable2:=Random(1,3,1)
```

The **Random.a4p** file in your Chapter7 folder generates five such numbers by executing a loop five times. A *loop* is a series of statements that are repeatedly executed under control of a variable or expression.

LOOPING AND THE REPEAT STATEMENT

Open the Random project at this time. Now open the Generate 5 random numbers calculation icon:

```
▣ Generate 5 random numbers
repeat with C1:= 1 to 5
V1:=Random(1,3,1)
ArraySet(C1,V1)
end repeat
```

The loop is controlled by the repeat statement, which says to start with the variable C1 set to 1, execute all statements up to end, repeat, and then increment C1 by 1. Continue to do this until C1 equals 6 (that is, do it as long as C1 is between 1 and 5).

ARRAYS AND THE ARRAYSET AND ARRAYGET STATEMENTS

The second line in the Generate 5 random numbers icon generates the random number and the third line stores it in an *array*.

An array is like a series of buckets, each having a unique number. The statement says to store the value of V1 in the bucket having the number corresponding to the current value of C1. The first time through the loop, C1 equals 1, so the initial random number is stored in bucket one. Then C1 is set to 2 and the second random number is stored in bucket 2, and so on.

Close the icon and open Show the numbers. It's a display icon, with five statements using syntax like this:

```
The first value is: {ArrayGet(1)}
```

We varied the message and also the value inside the parentheses so all five values were displayed. These statements say to display a message then the value in the array (bucket) at the position specified.

MATHEMATICAL CALCULATIONS

Like most programming languages, Authorware has many functions to perform mathematical calculations, such as rounding numbers, determining the sign of a number, extracting the remainder resulting from a division operation, calculating square roots and many more.

Determining the Integer Portion of a Number

To extract the integer portion of a number (the digits to the left of the decimal point), use:

```
NumberVar:=INT(Number)
```

Rounding Numbers

To round a number, use:

```
NumberVar:=Round( OriginalNumber, decimals)
```

where *decimals* is optional but, if present, specifies the number of decimal places you require. To round to an integer you might enter:

```
Score:=Round ((Total score/Number of Questions),0)
```

Other Mathematical Functions

Using the functions ABS, EXP LN or LOG10, MOD, and SQRT you can determine the absolute value, the value of *e* raised to a number, the natural or log base 10 of a number, the remainder of a number when divided by another, or the square root of a number. Refer to the *Authorware Reference* manual for specifics, or try the functions: They are coded in a manner very similar to that which we have been using. Appendix B also describes the mathematical functions for you.

DRAWING OBJECTS

You can use a calculation icon to automatically draw boxes, circles, and lines. To see how to do this, use the Authorware menu selection Window>Functions and choose the graphical category. The functions corresponding to the previous actions are: Box, Circle, and Line respectively. When you view the functions, you will see references to pensize.

The value of pensize determines whether the object has a frame. A value of 0 turns the frame off, while 1 turns it on. There are functions to draw graphics objects automatically or permit the user to do so.

Drawing a Box

To draw a box, use `Box(pensize, x1, y1, x2, y2)`. This draws a box from X1,Y1 to X2, Y2. The default frame is black, and the fill white. To change them, use `SetFrame` and `SetFill` functions.

To permit the user to draw a box, use

```
DrawBox(pensize, x1, y1, x2, y2)
```

To use this in a project:

- Create an interaction with a single hot spot covering the area where the user can draw the square.
- Attach a calculation icon with the appropriate X1, Y1, X2, and Y2 values. These establish limits for the boundaries of the box.

If you want to see a complete example, look at Box in the Chapter7 folder. Run the project and click and drag anywhere below the message - a box is drawn.

Drawing a Circle

To draw a circle use:

```
Circle (pensize, x1,y1,x2,y2)
```

This draws a circle in the boundary specified by x1,y2 to x2, y2. Substitute `Draw-Circle` for `Circle` to permit users to draw circles.

Drawing a Line

To draw a line from x1, y1 to X2, y2 use:

```
Line (pensize, x1,y1,x2,y2)
```

Substitute `DrawLine` for `Line` to permit users to draw lines.

OTHER GRAPHICS FUNCTIONS

Using Authorware functions, you can also perform these activities:

- Changing an object's color.
- Set the fill color.
- Change the mode (Recall matted, transparent and so on?).
- Set the line style to no arrows or start, end or both arrows.

Setting a Color

Many of the graphics-related functions enable us to alter the color of an object—its frame or fill color. Authorware uses the RGB color model where a pixel's color is determined by means of a triplet of values between 0 and 255: One each for red, green, and blue. To set a color, use:

```
RGB(r,g,b)
```

Setting a Fill Color

To change the fill color of an object, use:

```
SetFill(state,RGB(r,g,b))
```

If its state is set to True, the object will be filled with the color specified by the r,g,and b values. If it's set to false, no fill occurs.

Setting an Object's Mode

To set the mode of an object, use:

```
SetMode(mode)
```

Where the value of mode is selected from Table 7.1.

Table 7.1. Mode Values and Their Effects.

Mode	Result
0	Matted
1	Transparent
2	Inverse
3	Erase
4	Opaque

You should use this function prior to a draw command.

CONTROLLING THE PRESENTATION WINDOW

Using Authorware functions within a calculation icon you can change the cursor shape, turn the cursor viewing on or off or choose to display or not display the menu bar. The functions to do these are: SetCursor, ShowCursor and ShowMenuBar respectively.

Changing the Cursor's Shape

Use `SetCursor (`*type*`)`, where *type* is set according to Table 7.2

Table 7.2 SetCursor Parametric Values and Their Effects.

Type	Resulting Cursor
0	Arrow
1	I-beam
2	Cross
3	Plus sign
4	Blank
5	Hourglass
6	Hand

Toggling the Cursor On and Off

Use `ShowCursor (OFF)` to hide the cursor, `ShowCursor (ON)` to show it.

Toggling the Menu Bar On and Off

Use `ShowMenuBar(OFF)` to temporarily hide the menu bar, `ShowMenuBar(ON)` to show it.

SYSTEM CONTROLS

The most common calculation icon functions that fall into this category are ones to print the current screen and quit Authorware.

Printing the Current Screen

To print the current screen use the following inside a calculation icon:

```
PrintScreen()
```

Exiting Authorware

There are several ways to exit your title. In addition, the results differ between the Windows and Macintosh versions.

Both use the general syntax: Quit (*option*) or QuitRestart (*option*). Quit exits the title, while QuitRestart works like Quit, except it permits the title to pick up where it left off.

To define a Quit button you might create a perpetual button that is linked to a calculation icon containing quit, or position it as the last icon on the flowline.

Values of *option* and its effects are contained in Table 7.3.

Table 7.3 Quit Options

Option	Effect
0	The default value. Authorware exits to the Program Manager (Windows 3.x) or the Desktop for Windows 95 or NT. On Macintoshes, control returns to the Finder. If you jumped to this file from another, control returns to the initial file.
1	On Windows computers, Authorware returns control to the Program Manager (Windows 3.x) or the Desktop (Windows 95 or NT). On the Macintosh platform, the Finder.
2	On Windows 3.X platforms, Authorware exits and the computer exits to DOS. On Windows 95 or NT platforms, Windows restarts. On Macintosh computers this restarts the computer
3	On Windows 95 or NT, shuts down Windows. For Windows 3.x, same as Quit(1). On Macintosh computers, shuts down the computer.

JUMPING BETWEEN AUTHORWARE PROJECTS AND ICONS

You can use the Jump functions to exit one Authorware project, and begin another. When that one ends, control can be returned to the first project, or to the operating system. Use the `GoTo` function to transfer control to an icon within an Authorware project. Using `GoTo` is another way to alter the linear flow we are accustomed to.

The Jump Functions

When building a large Authorware project, you should partition the project into several smaller ones, with each smaller project performing a set of related tasks. For example, you might be creating a project related to Disney World. In this case, you could have subprojects for each "land": Frontier Land, Fantasy Land, and so on. To connect the pieces you would use either `JumpFile` or `JumpFileReturn`. The difference is in what happens when the project finishes. If you use the `JumpFileReturn` version, control returns when the sub-project exits.

The formats are:

```
JumpFile("filename")
JumpFileReturn("filename")
```

If the subproject isn't in the same folder as the initial project, you can attach a folder name:

```
JumpFile("filename","folder")
```

Finally, you can pass variables to the subproject by including them in the Jump command:

```
JumpFile("filename",variable1, variable2,…,"folder")
```

The GoTo Function

Use the `GoTo` function to jump from one icon to another. You might use it within a menu interaction to transfer control to a map icon based on the menu selection. Its syntax is:

```
GoTo(IconID@"IconTitle")
```

Where *IconTitle* is the name of an icon on your flowline.

Other Calculations

We have only scratched the surface of calculation icons. Using Authorware variables and functions within calculation icons, you can:

- Manage files.
- Tabulate then report user performance.
- Perform text manipulation
- Check memory or disk space availability.
- Extract information about icons.
- Check mouse and keyboard status.
- Check what kind of computer is being used.
- Perform mathematical operations using logical and mathematical operators.
- Modify graphic layer values.
- Determine an object's location.

We suggest using the Authorware Window>Functions and Window>Variables to learn more.

DECISION ICONS

Decision icons establish structures called *paths*. When a decision icon is encountered, Authorware takes one of the branches to the right of the decision icon. A branch or path is an attached icon. You can assign as many paths as you want. Authorware can branch to the paths sequentially, randomly, randomly to only untraveled paths, or based on a calculation.

The Decision Icon Dialog Box

Figure 7.6 shows the Decision Icon Properties dialog box that opens when you double-click on a decision icon.

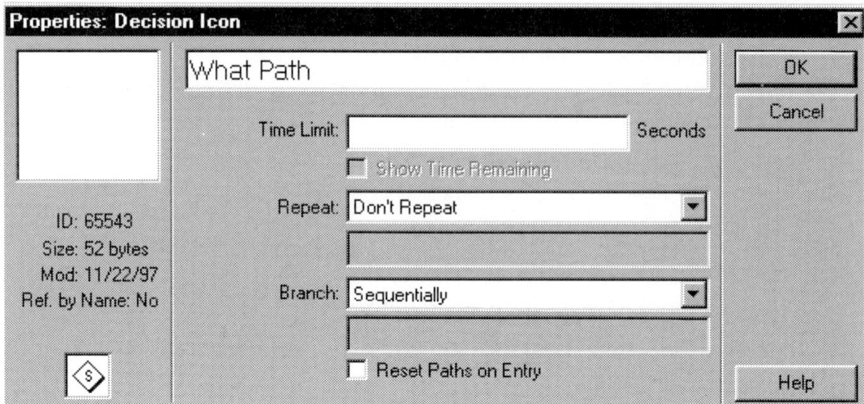

Figure 7.6. The Decision Icon Dialog Box.

There are three main sections in the Decision Icon Properties box: Branch, Repeat, and Timing.

Branch Options

There are four options to choose among: Sequentially, Randomly to Any Path, Randomly to Unused Path, and To Calculated path. We begin with the sequential option.

Sequential Branching If this option is chosen, Authorware will take the first path the first time through the icon, then the second path, and so on. This might be useful if you are presenting material in a sequential manner, with each path representing a map icon, or giving a sequential quiz or test.

Random Branching to Any Path Choose this option to have Authorware randomly pick the path to follow. This might be used to produce special graphics effects: show one of several images of a sky, for example.

Branching Randomly to Unused Paths If chosen, Authorware will again use a random number to select the path. However, no path will be revisited until all have been chosen.

Branching Based on a Calculation Select To Calculated Path and provide the expression or variable to base the branching on in order to specify which path to take. If there are four paths, the variable/expression must evaluate to 1-4.

There is a field named Reset Paths on Entry, which resets the decision icon. Used with Sequential and To Calculated Path branching, this option will delete information once the decision icon exits. This way, when control returns to the decision icon, it is as if it's the first time.

Repeat Options

These five options specify how many times Authorware should re-enter the decision icon prior to exiting.

Fixed Number of Times Select this option to explicitly set the number of iterations. This can be a constant, a variable, or an expression.

Until All Paths Used This option causes Authorware to revisit the decision icon repeatedly until all possible paths have been traveled. You might use this to provide a test or quiz, and you want the user to see all the questions.

Until Click/Keypress When this option is chosen, Authorware will continue down attached paths until the user clicks the mouse or presses a key. One possible use for this option would be for animations that you want to continue until the user invokes a stop-action.

Until True We've seen this option before: It means continue down the attached paths until the expression evaluates to True.

Don't Repeat This means to make a single visit to the decision icon. Once a path is chosen, control will pass through that path and then exit to the main flowline.

Time Limit

Use the Time Limit field to specify a maximum duration for the icon. If you check the Show Time Remaining option, a countdown clock will display.

The Attached Icon Options Dialog Box

When you attach an icon to a decision icon, the flowline resembles that of an interaction. This is shown in Figure 7.7.

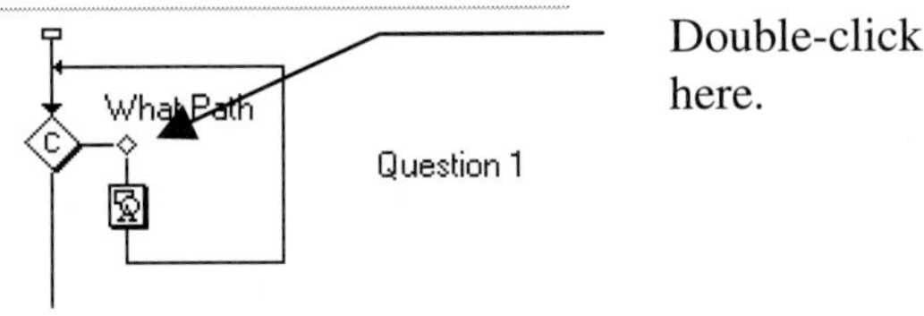

Figure 7.7. A Decision Icon with a Display Icon Added as a Path.

Double-click the symbol above the attached icon to reveal the dialog box shown in Figure 7.8.

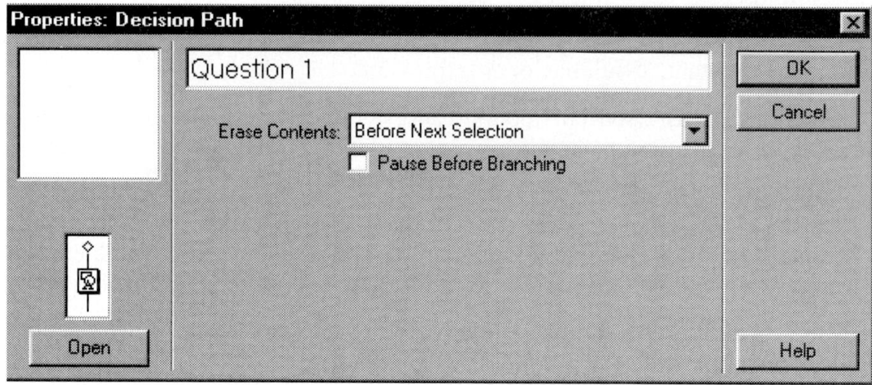

Figure 7.8 The Attached Decision Icon Properties Dialog Box. To view it, double-click any attached icon.

Erase Contents

This drop-down box has three options that specify how to erase the contents of the attached icon.

Before Next Selection This option will erase the contents of the attached icon just before displaying the content of the icon visited next. This is useful for showing sequential materials: Attach display icons, choose Branch Sequentially, and then specify Erase Before Next Selection.

Upon Exit This option will force Authorware to erase the displayed content only when the decision icon is exited.

Don't Erase If this option is chosen, the displayed content won't be erased. You will need to add an erase icon if you want to remove it.

Pause Before Branching

If this option is checked, Authorware will show the default Wait/Continue button as the icon is exited.

Let's now use our knowledge of decision icons to build a few examples. We're first going to create a decision icon that plays one of two movies based on a random number.

Using Decision Icons to Randomly Play Digital Movies

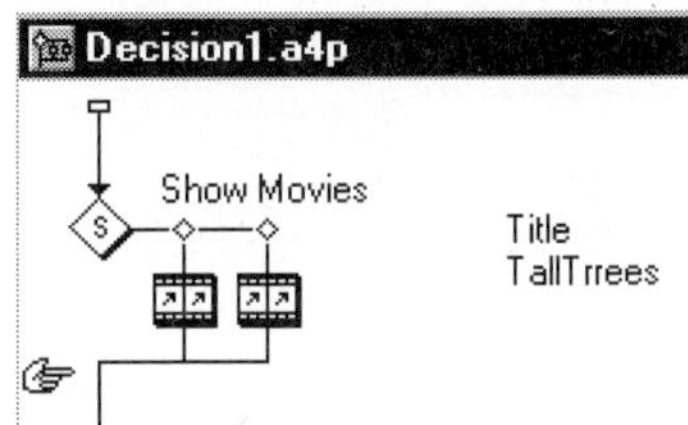 **Sample File** To see the piece you're about to build, open and run the **Decision1.a4p** file in the Chapter7 folder on the CD-ROM. Watch for two digital movie to play. They are chosen randomly and play twice to completion. Let's see how to build this piece.

☞ Your Turn

❑ Start a new project.

❑ Add a decision icon and two movie icons. Name them as in the following figure.

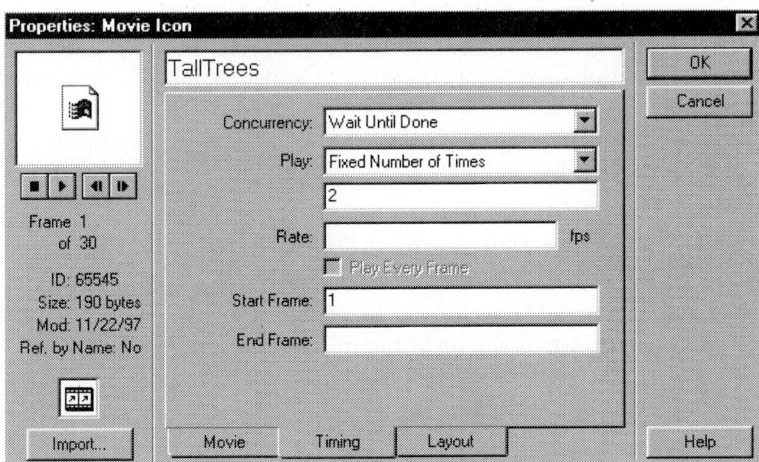

❑ Double-click the first movie icon and import the **Title.MOV** QuickTime movie from the Chapter7 folder.

❑ Do the same for the second, but import **TallTrees.mov**.

❑ Because the movies play quickly, set them to repeat two times. Also set their mode to Wait Until Done. The Movie Properties Timing dialog box for Tall-Trees is shown below.

❑ Now open the Show a movie decision icon.

❏ Select the To Calculated Path option and enter this into text box: random(1,2,1). Refer to the Random Number Generation section earlier in this chapter for details on the function.

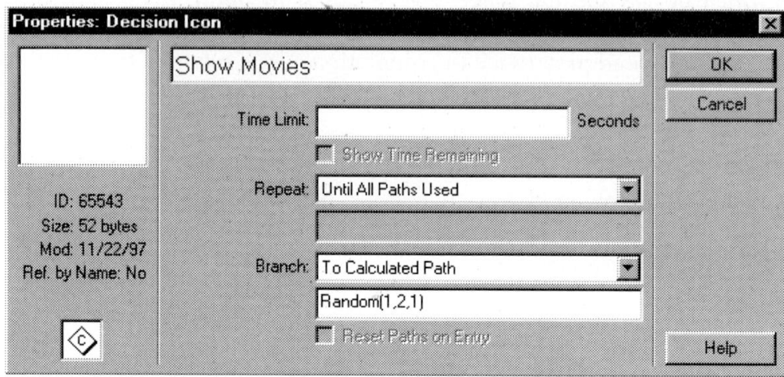

❏ Check the Repeat Until All Paths Used option.

❏ Import the **Tmplate1.BMP** from the Templates folder on the CD-ROM into a display icon named Show Template, at the beginning of the flowline.

❏ Run your project and position the movies so they play inside the panel. Place TallTrees on top of one of the smaller openings, and place Title in the center. You can move a movie as it's playing, or use the Control Panel to pause the title, then move the objects.

❏ Add an erase icon and choose to erase the panel. Name the icon - panel.

❏ Run your project until both movies have played.

❏ Save your work as **Decision1.a4p**. Your movies should randomly play until both have been shown. This is because we selected the To Calculated Path option. Notice the decision icon has a "C" inside it to denote which branching option we chose. When finished, close the decision map icon.

The next example shows how to create a sequential quiz.

Using Decision Icons for Sequential Branching and Quizzes

One useful purpose for sequential branching is in the construction of tests or quizzes. The general structure of such a module is shown in Figure 7.9.

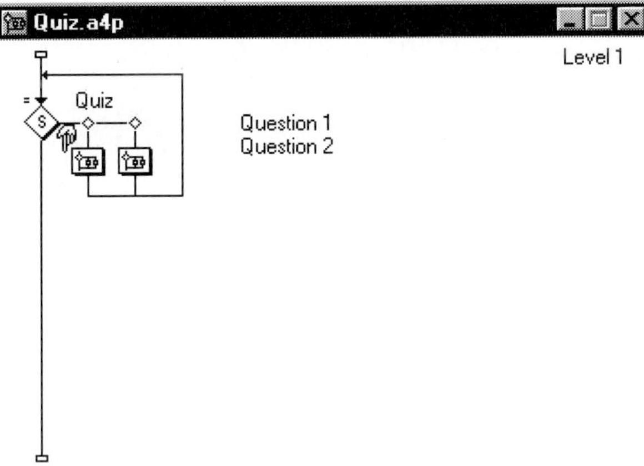

Figure 7.9. A Typical Quiz Flowline.

Sample File To see such the actual structure, open the **Quiz.a4p** file in the Chapter7 folder. Run the project. It presents two sequential questions. The answer to the first question is bus, and to the second, clock.

Question 1 is a map icon that contains a text entry interaction icon with the following content:

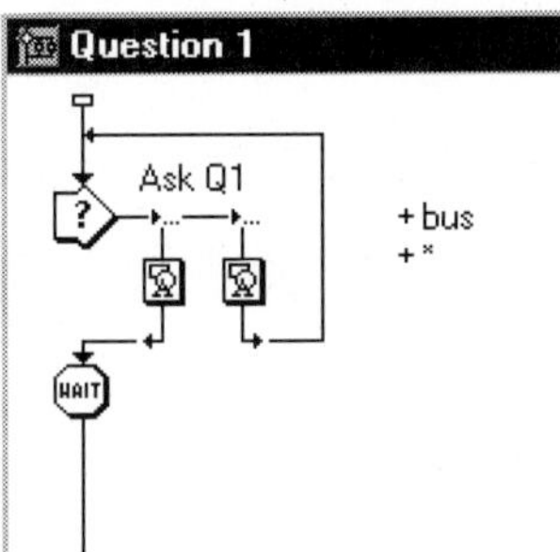

Ask Q1 contains the first question, the first display icon is attached to a text entry response that looks for the correct response (bus), while the second text entry response traps all other responses. The other map icon, Question 2, is similar (the answer there is clock).

Tracking the Number of Questions Answered

Suppose you want to track how many questions the user has seen at any point in time. One way to do this is to use a calculation that simply adds one to a variable, called a *counter*, every time the decision icon is visited. This calculation isn't entered into a separate calculation icon. Instead it's attached to the decision icon. In our example, the calculation attached to the Quiz decision icon might be like Figure 7.10.

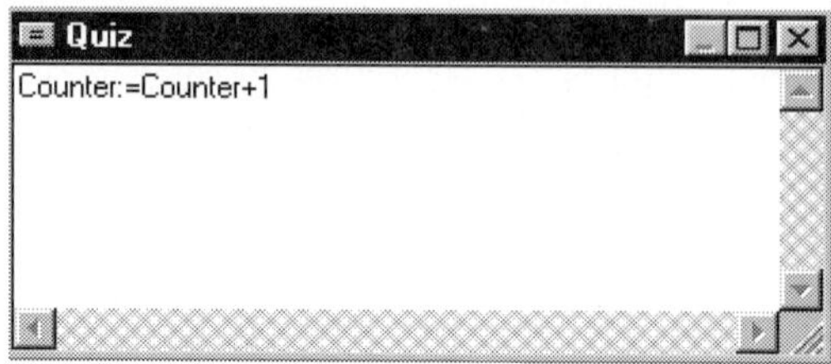

Figure 7.10. A Counter. Use it to increment a variable by one with each navigation.

You can see this if you click the Quiz decision icon, then choose <u>M</u>od-ify><u>I</u>con><u>C</u>alculations (Ctrl+=). This statement is interpreted as meaning add one to the prior value of `Counter` each time Authorware passes through the Quiz icon. Because counter is a new variable, a dialog box will open asking what value to assign as counter's initial value. Enter 0 (zero).

Next, assume we want to set the repeat option so all questions are asked or the user gets 50 percent of the questions wrong. Here's how to do it.

Open the Quiz decision icon (Double-click it) and click the Repeat Until True radio button. Then enter this into the text box:

```
Counter=2|PercentWrong>50
```

The vertical bar means "or". Figure 7.11 shows the completed dialog box.

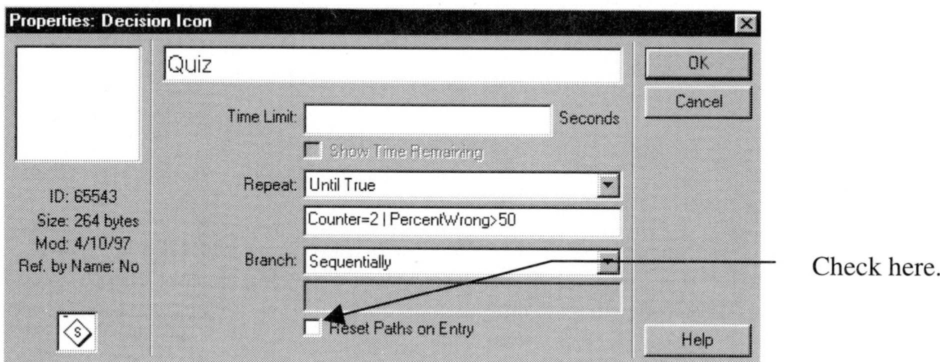

Check here.

Figure 7.11. The Completed Dialog Box. It sets up an interaction where all questions are asked, or the user gets 50 percent wrong.

Finally, we need to tell Authorware what to do if control ever returns to this icon. Recall that's the purpose of the Reset Path on Entry option. If selected, this causes Authorware to start all over again with the first path. If not selected, Authorware remembers where the user left off and continues to the next path on the right if control returns to this decision icon. Normally you would check the option.

We conclude by returning to our digital video piece.

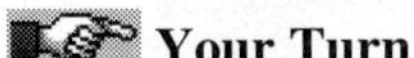 **Sample File** You can open **DigVid7.a4p** and run the piece. Push the start button and a pretest begins. It's a target area. The user is to drag the "1" to the first step, 2 to the second and so on. The correct answer for "1" is to write the script. Any other response moves the "1" back to its starting location. Numbers "2" and "3" are under construction (for you to finish). Next we have a true false question followed by a text entry question.

☞ Your Turn

❏ Open **DigVid5.a4p**.

❏ You will do much of the work, once we show you how.

❏ Start by adding the icons to the flowline.

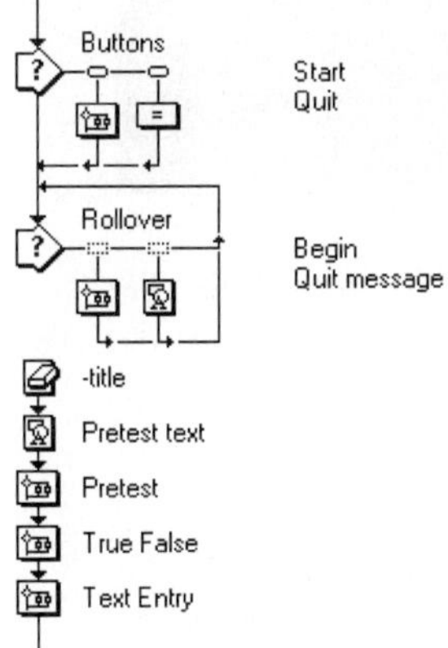

❏ Actually, the first task is to make the Start button jump to the -title icon, where we erase the Digital Video text. To do so, select the current Start response icon, which is a calculation icon containing only a comment.

❏ Strike Ctrl+G, which converts the selected icon()s into a map icon.

❏ Open the new Start map and add a new calculation icon that contains the text in the following figure.

❏ As we saw in this chapter, the statement means Authorware is to pass control to the icon with the name "'title", exactly what we want to do.

❏ Close the calculation dialog box.

❏ The - Title erase icon erases the Digital Video title.

❏ Next comes the first pretest icon—It's a display icon named Pretest Text.

❏ Open the Pretest Text display icon and add the word PreTest in the panel at the top. Enter directions in white text as we did below.

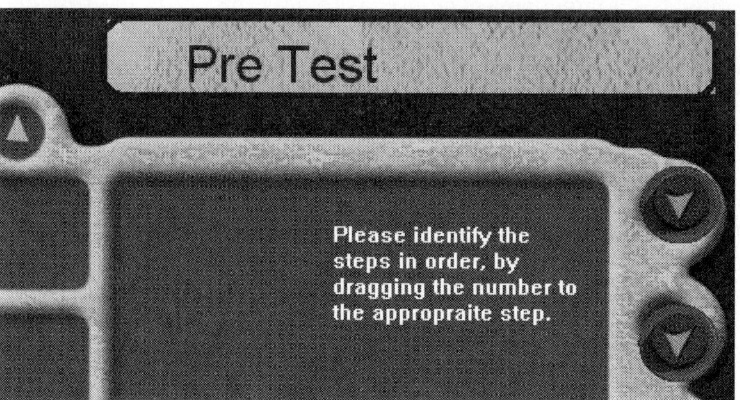

❏ Open the Pretest map icon, and add icons as in the following figure.

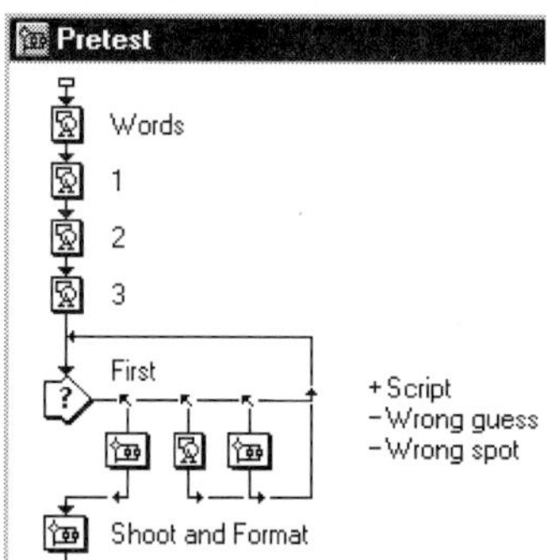

❏ Open the Words icon and enter the following. Leave a blank line between each.
Decompress
Format
Write the Script
Capture
Compress
Shoot the Video

❏ Make the text yellow. These words represent the drop-zone for each of the numbers. For example, the user should drag the "1" to the Write the Script" line. We will check for a couple of wrong answers as well (shoot the video among others). The other two numbers (we're only going to match three values) we leave up to you.

❏ The "1", "2" and "3" display icons merely add the corresponding number into one of the three blocks on the left. The block containing "1" is shown below.

❏ Add an interaction icon and name it First.

❏ Attach a display and two map icons. One map will be used for the correct target, the display used to show text when a wrong answer, but an anticipated one, is given, and the other map for a catchall.. All three should be target areas and named Script (the correct answer), Wrong guess and Wrong spot (a catchall). This is shown in the figure below.

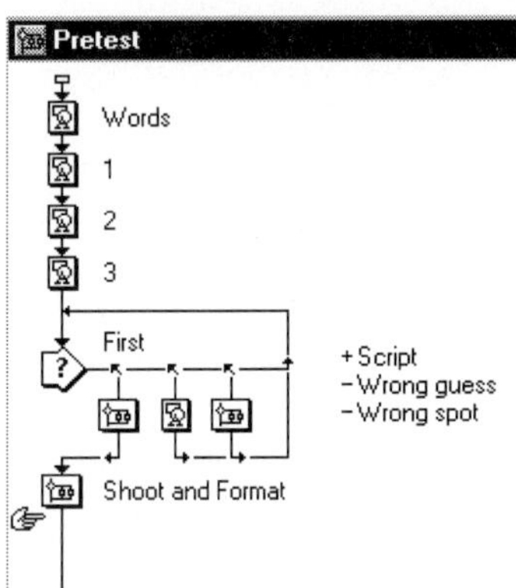

❏ Open the Script response type icon and click on the "1" as the target object. Move the "1" to the word Script, then size the target box so it completely covers the word. Specify the On Drop option as Leave at Destination (because this is the correct response). Use the figure below as a guide.

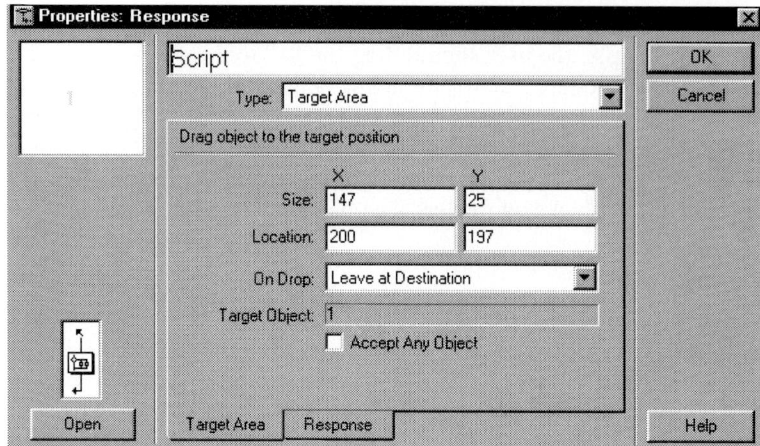

❑ Because Script is the correct response, set its branching to Exit the Interaction, and designate it as being the correct response. Open the map and add icons as in the following figure.

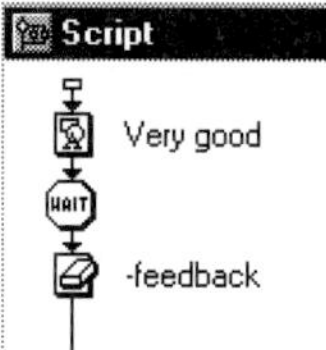

❑ The Very Good display icon provides feedback, saying in black text, placed near the bottom of the template "That's right! You must first develop a script".

❑ The Wait icon passes for 3 seconds and the -feedback icon erases the positive feedback.

❑ The Wrong guess response tracks the possible response "Capture" That's a wrong response. The user should be sent back to try again, and a suitable message should be displayed.

❑ Finally, the Wrong spot is a catchall. We leave the details of these last two icons to you. But be sure to use the Put Back on Drop option for both wrong answers, and designate them as Wrong Responses.

❑ The Shoot and Format map is "under construction" as you can see from the figure below. Just add a suitable message to each display icon, and erase it after 2-3 seconds.

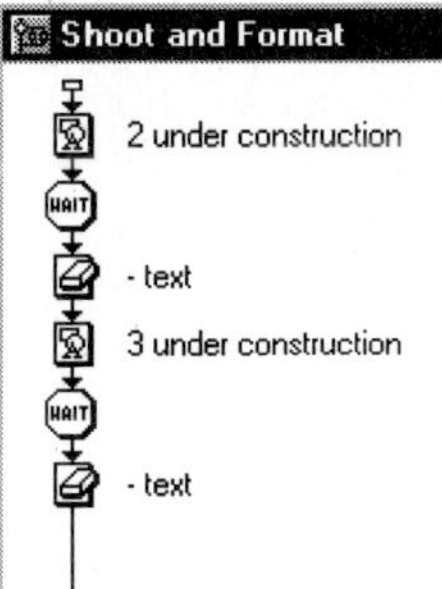

❑ Next comes a True/False test. Open the map and add the following icons to its flowline.

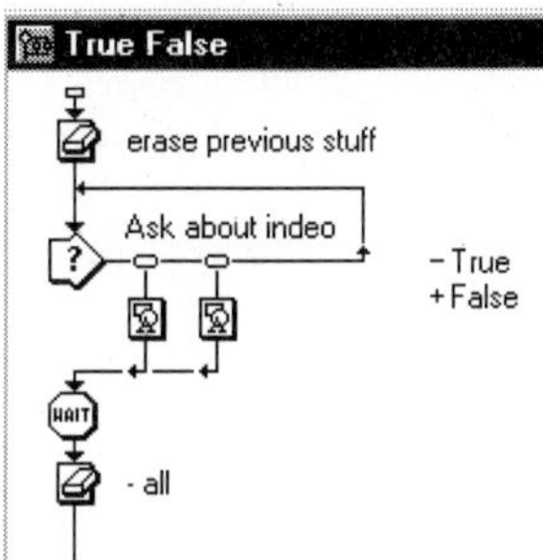

❑ The Ask about indeo interaction uses button responses. We chose Windows 95 radio buttons and placed each button inside one of the circles on the left side, as shown by the figure below.

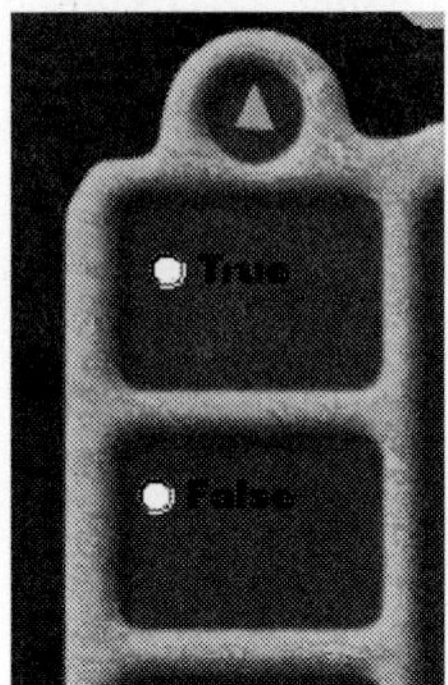

❑ The text inside the main window asks "Indeo is a Microsoft codec T/F?" (The answer is false, it's made by Intel.) This question is placed in the interaction icon.

❑ Finally, set up a text entry response that asks the question "Apples digital format is known as:" (The answer is QuickTime). The response should check for QuickTime, ignore capitalization, and accept MOV. The flowline should look this way:

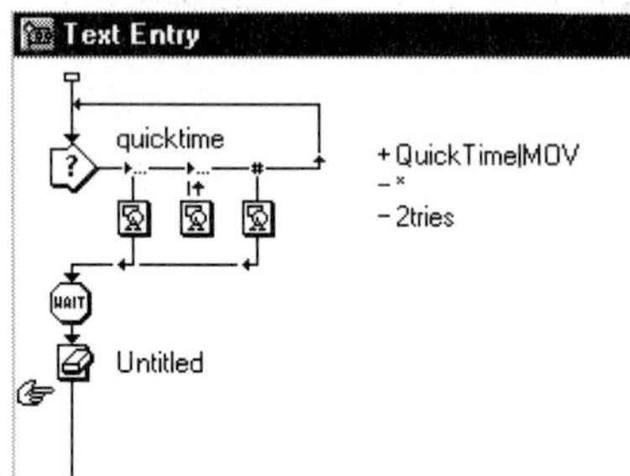

❑ The correct response exits the interaction, while the catchall uses Continue branching. The third response icon is a Tries Limit because we don't want the user to be forever stuck, unable to proceed until he or she gets the correct answer. We set the maximum tries to 2.

❑ Save your work as **DigVid7.a4p**.

SUMMARY

Calculation icons can be used by themselves or attached to other icons. They contain expressions, variables, or functions. Their uses include altering the appearance of the presentation window, performing file management tasks, and making buttons and other objects inactive, generating random numbers and many other tasks.

Branching or decision icons are used to specify which paths or how many paths to follow. Especially useful for quizzes, branching icons can be used to ensure all paths are taken in order or randomly. If the random option is chosen, you can guarantee no path is taken twice before all paths have been taken.

Study Exercises

7.1. Create a new project called C7Q1. It should use a decision icon to display a sky with stars that appear to twinkle. Attach two or more decision icons to the decision icon, each with a black background and a series of white dots representing the stars. Most of the dots will be common, but a few will change. Use a random number generator to choose the paths

7.2. Create a new project called C7Q2. It should show the offint graphic found in the Chapter7\Images folder. There are to be two hot spots: One for the filing cabinet and one for the computer. When either is clicked, jump to C7Q2A and C7Q2B respectively. Those subprojects describe the object just clicked by popping up dialog boxes found in one of your libraries. When the dialog box closes, return to the offint graphic.

7.3. Create a project called C7Q3 that presents a five-question interaction where two or more of the answers are correct. For example; "Click in the box next to the names of the Three Stooges" or "Press the key associated with each of the Civil War generals in the following list".

7.4. Finish the under construction parts of **DigVid7.a4p**.

Using Framework and Navigate Icons

*T*he last chapter examined how to make Authorware do automatic branching. This chapter examines the second way to permit users to select paths through your title. This second method requires the use of two icons: framework and Navigation. The framework icon permits the user to jump to a topic, then another, then another, yet be able to see what "pages" were visited, and revisit any of them. In addition, the user has the option of jumping to a topic, then returning to the page that was active prior to the jump. A page is anything directly associated with a framework. For example, you cannot jump to a display icon that's part of a map. That display icon must be associated with a framework icon.

At the conclusion of the chapter, you will be able to:

- Define the components of a framework.
- Use frameworks as non-linear branching tools.
- Use navigation icons to jump to framework pages.

- Create interactive pieces.
- Use nested frameworks.

THE FRAMEWORK ICON 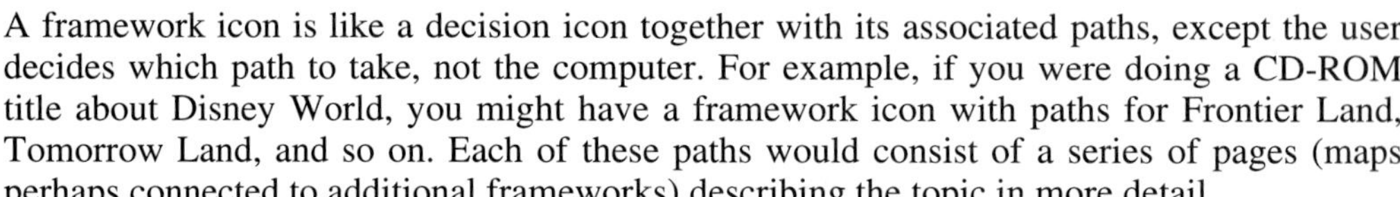

A framework icon is like a decision icon together with its associated paths, except the user decides which path to take, not the computer. For example, if you were doing a CD-ROM title about Disney World, you might have a framework icon with paths for Frontier Land, Tomorrow Land, and so on. Each of these paths would consist of a series of pages (maps perhaps connected to additional frameworks) describing the topic in more detail.

When you drag a framework icon to the flowline, you create three components:

- The framework itself.
- A series of default navigation controls.
- The icons, called *pages*, you attach to the framework.

A page doesn't have to be a single screen of text or graphics. A page can be a digital movie, a sound, or a map icon with its possible myriad of options. Let's look at the anatomy of a framework icon.

The Anatomy of a Framework Icon

If you double-click a framework icon, you'll see what's in Figure 8.1.

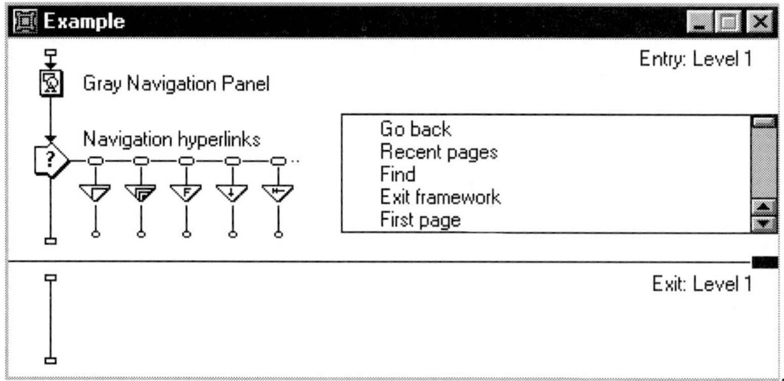

Figure 8.1. The Framework Icon.

The Gray Navigation Panel is a background upon which eight default buttons are placed. Figure 8.2 shows the content of that display icon.

Figure 8.2. The Gray Navigation Panel Contents. It forms the background for the eight default buttons making up a framework.

You can delete, modify, or add to the eight default buttons. Later, you will see these buttons provide the ability to:

- Go forward a page.
- Go to the first page.
- Go to the last page.
- Navigate backwards a page.
- Jump to any page.
- Find text or keywords.
- View a history of pages already visited.
- Exit the framework.

Each button is attached to a navigate icon, which provides the button's functionality. The buttons are within an ***entry panel***. Any icon placed here will be executed when control passes to the framework. At the bottom of the window in Figure 8.1 you can see the ***exit panel***. As you might expect, icons placed here are executed when the user exits the framework.

The Entry and Exit Panels

When control passes to a page within a framework, any content in the entry panel is executed. The default content displays eight buttons on top of a gray panel.

When we exit the framework, content within icons in the Exit panel is executed. As you can see from Figure 8.1, the default exit panel contains no icons.

The Default Navigation Buttons

The new icon type is the navigate icon ▽. Each of the eight default buttons is attached to a navigate icon. Much like the GoTo function we discussed in Chapter 7, the navigate icon is used to jump from one page to another, within the current framework, or to any page attached to other frameworks. Default navigate icons can be deleted or edited, and you can even add your own icons.

Use the scroll bars and take a look at the eight default navigate icons in the entry panel that are shown on every page of the framework.

The Eight Default Navigation Buttons

When a default framework is encountered, the eight standard buttons shown in Figure 8.3 are displayed in the Presentation Window.

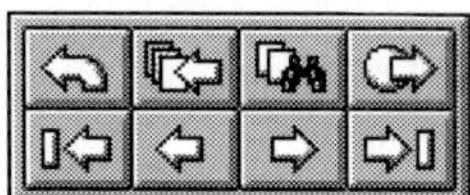

Figure 8.3. The Eight Default Buttons Associated With A Framework Icon.

You can delete or alter any of the default controls. You can even add sound icons, movie icons or display icons so that sounds or images appear on every page of the framework. Remember: Any icons that appear in the entry panel will be in effect while that framework is active. Let's examine each of the buttons.

First Page This button will cause a jump to the icon farthest to the left of the framework icon.

Previous Page This button passes control to the page on the immediate left of the current one. Note: To the left of the first icon is the last one.

Next Page This button passes control to the page on the immediate right of current icon. Note: The next icon to the right of the last one is the first one.

Last Page Pushing this button jumps you to the icon farthest to the right of the framework icon.

Go Back (last page viewed) This button jumps the user to the page viewed just prior to the current one. It is not concerned at all with the ordering of the icons attached to the framework (called the *physical order*). Rather, it tracks the pages viewed in order by the user (called the *logical order*). When the button is pushed, the previously viewed page is redisplayed as control is transferred to that page.

View Recent Pages Use this button to display a "bread crumbs" trail of pages recently visited. When the list is displayed, clicking on any page contained in the list will make Authorware jump to that page.

Selecting Navigation Setup from the File menu can customize the recent pages dialog box. The Recent Pages options are to the right of the Navigation Setup dialog box. You can change its title and set the number of pages that are kept in the list. You can also force Authorware to close the dialog box once a page is selected from the list.

Find 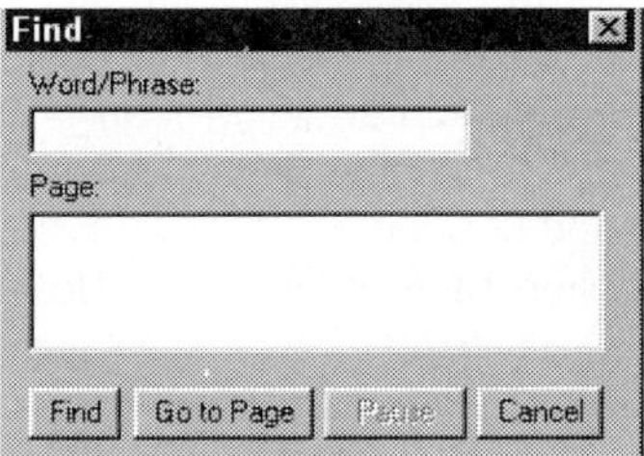 Pushing the Find button opens the Find dialog box, which is shown in the figure below.

The Find dialog box prompts the user to enter a word. Authorware then searches for that word and displays a list of pages where it can be found. By selecting a page from the list, then pushing the Go to Page button, the user will jump to the page containing the search word.

Exit Framework The Exit framework button will exit the current framework. Authorware then executes any icons in the exit pane. Control is finally passed to the next icon on the flowline below the framework.

The Button Options Dialog Box

Each navigate icon is attached to a button. If you double-click the button response type, the by now familiar Button Properties Dialog box, reproduced for you in Figure 8.4, opens.

Notice the button is perpetual so it remains active throughout the framework. Perpetual objects are erased when the framework exits. Like all buttons, this one can be edited by clicking on its current representation.

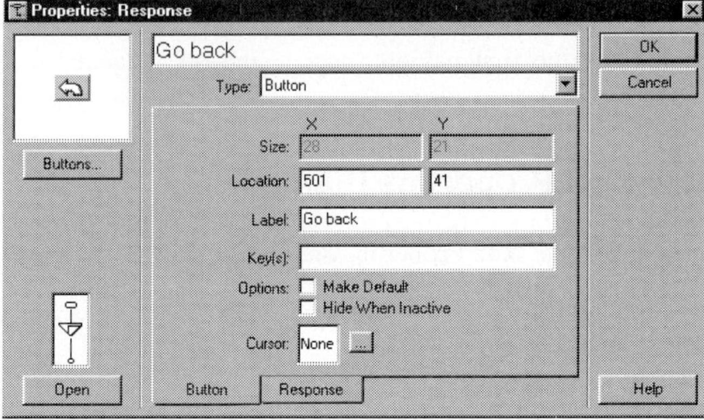

Figure 8.4. The Default Button Properties Dialog Box Associated With each of the Eight Standard Framework Buttons.

THE NAVIGATE ICON

A navigate icon enables us to jump to another icon, as long as that destination icon is attached to a framework. Recall any such attached icon is called a page and can be a map, a display, or one of several other icon-types. When a navigate icon is encountered, Authorware transfers control to the page defined as the destination of that icon. There is no default destination, as it is unlinked when first added to the flowline. It's up to you to specify the destination icon's name.

Recall the interaction icon. There are eleven interaction types — buttons, text entry, keypress and so on. Each type has an associated symbol that appears next to the Interaction icon. The response icon is attached to this response type. As you will see, navigate icons are similar: There are several types and each has an associated symbol on the flowline.

Let's begin our exploration of navigate icons by looking at the eight default navigate icons that are attached to framework icons. We should point out, however, that a navigate icon can be used almost anywhere.

Your Turn
❏ Start a new project and add a framework icon to it.
❏ Double-click the framework icon.

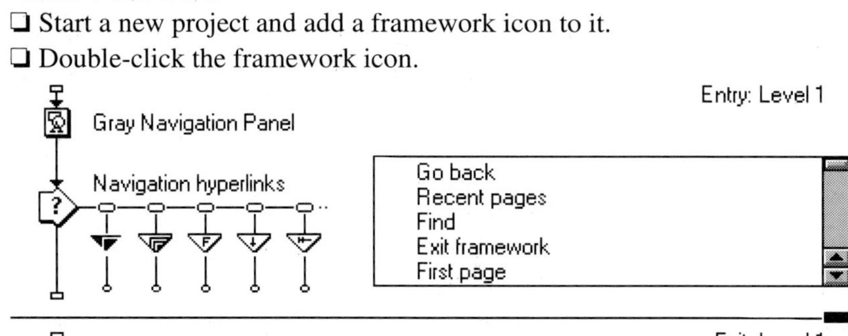

❏ Double-click the first navigate icon – the one attached to the first button response.

The Navigate Icon Properties Dialog Box

You should see this Navigate Icon Properties dialog box shown in Figure 8.5.

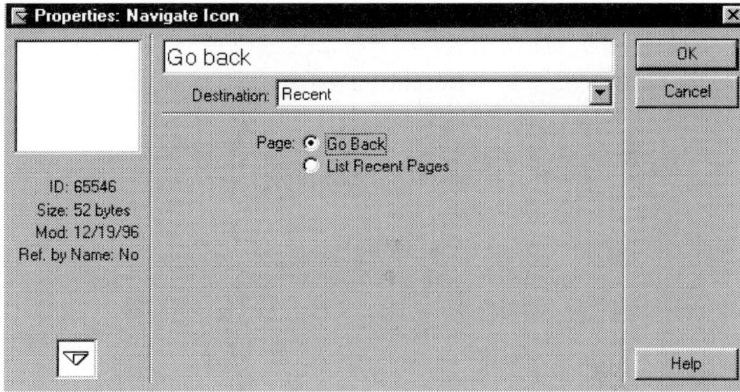

Figure 8.5. The Navigate Icon Properties Dialog Box.

The Navigate icon properties dialog box has two common sections: Destination and Page.

Destination Types

The Destination drop-down list is used to choose the type of destination. Let's look at the five destination-types in detail.

Recent

Use the Recent Destination option to set up links to pages the user has previously visited. Note the portion of the dialog box then lists two Page choices: Go Back and List Recent Pages. Figure 8.6 shows the dialog box associated with the Recent Destination option.

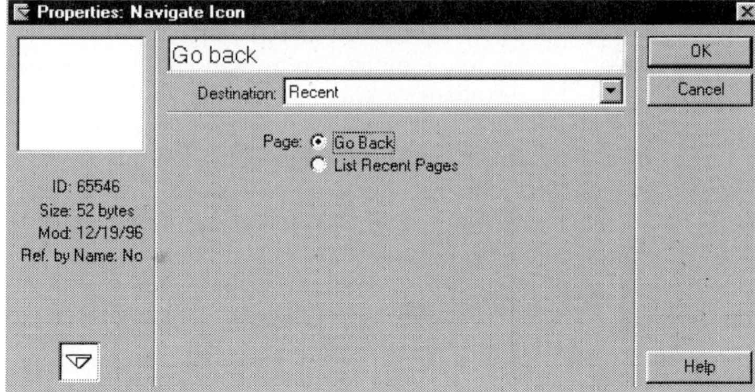

Figure 8.6. The Recent Destination Dialog Box.

Go Back If Go Back is selected, the user will be sent to the page the user viewed just prior to the current one.

List Recent Pages Use List Recent Pages to produce a "bread crumb" trail, so users can backtrack to all locations previously visited.

Nearby

When Nearby is selected, the user can only navigate among pages of the currently active framework. No jumps to pages outside the framework are permitted. As you can see from Figure 8.7, there are five page options: Previous, Next, First, Last, and Exit Framework/ Return.

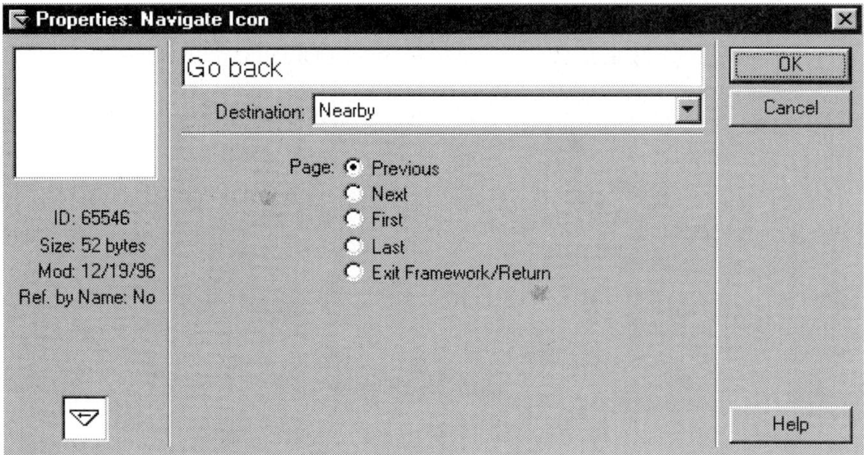

Figure 8.7. The Dialog Box for Nearby Destination.

The first four options should be obvious, they navigate to the prior, next, first or last page. The Exit Framework/Return option is a bit more complicated.

Use Exit Framework option like the one you did the Exit Interaction option in Chapters 5 through 7. A framework establishes a kind of closed environment, where the only way out is to push a button that exits the framework. Maybe the framework provides information about rollercoasters in a theme park. To see about restaurants, that framework must be exited, and a new one entered.

A Return is used when one framework is called from another. The calling framework might reference a help page in a Help framework. When the help is presented, you want to return from the called (help) framework and return to where you were. We'll see examples of these as we go along.

Anywhere

The Anywhere choice under Destination permits linking to any page within the file, provided that page is attached to a framework icon. Figure 8.8 shows the associated dialog box.

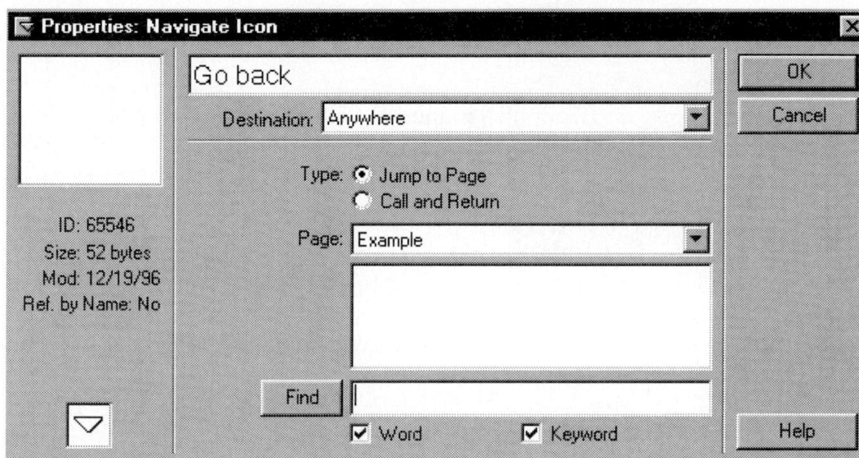

Figure 8.8. The Navigate Properties Dialog Box For Anywhere Destinations.

Using this destination, you can transfer control to any page attached to any framework in any piece. You have the option of returning from that framework or making a one-way trip.

Here's a simple example. Figure 8.9 shows a dummy flowline with two frameworks, each having two pages.

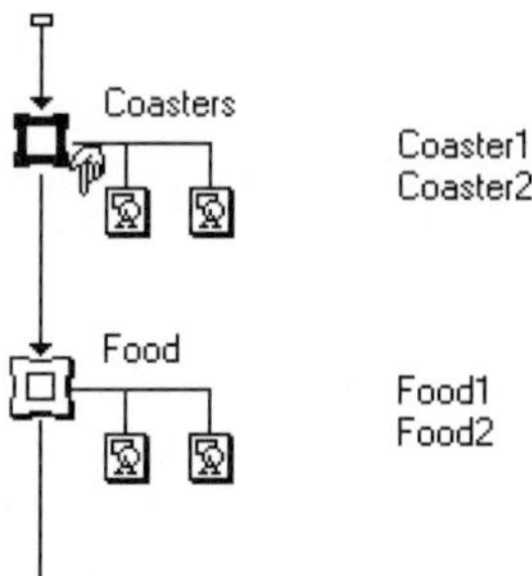

Figure 8.9. A Flowline with Two Frameworks, and each Framework having Two Pages.

When the navigate icon for Go Back is opened, and Anywhere chosen as the Destination option, you'll see Figure 8.10.

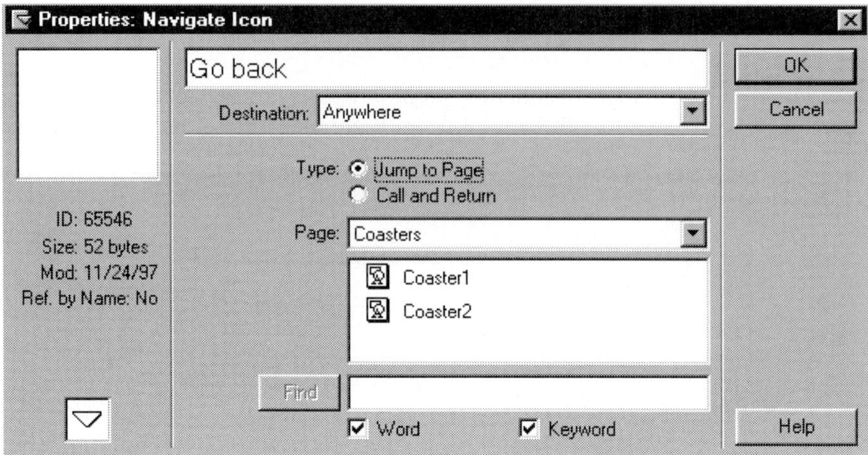

Figure 8.10. An Anywhere Destination with Two Frameworks Containing Pages to Select Between.

When the button is pushed, you are specifying to which page to transfer. In our example, there are two frameworks to choose between. The current framework is Coasters, so it's listed in the Page drop-down. Coaster has two pages, Coaster1 and Coaster2, which display below the framework's name in Figure 8.10. If you choose Coaster2, when the button being defined is pushed, control will be transferred to that page.

To select a page in the other framework, Food, select it from the drop-down, and then choose a page within that framework.

Instead of using the drop downs, you can enter a word or phrase in the Find field then push the Find button to search for pages containing the word. The third option uses *keywords*, something we haven't seen yet.

Assume you have a file with many video clips. You could assign a keyword "Video", then tell Authorware every page that had a video object on it. This would permit easy access to all pages containing digital video. If Keyword is checked, Authorware will also search for keywords.

Calculate

With a calculate destination, the link to go to isn't determined until the title runs. Each icon has a unique number associated with it called the icon ID. You can see this ID by selecting an icon, then choosing the Modify>Icon>Properties menu item.

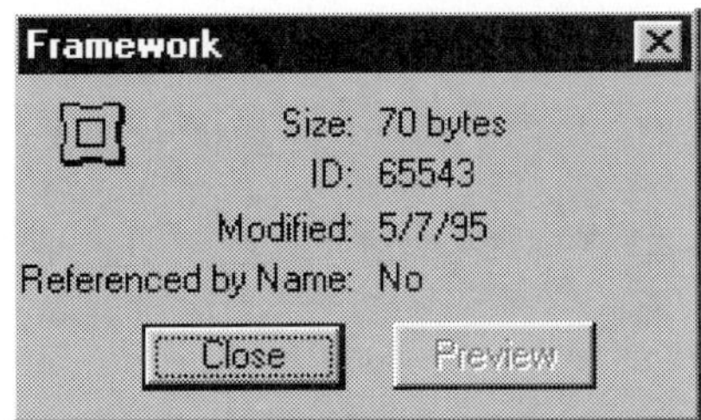

Figure 8.11 shows the Navigate Icon Properties dialog box associated with a calculate destination.

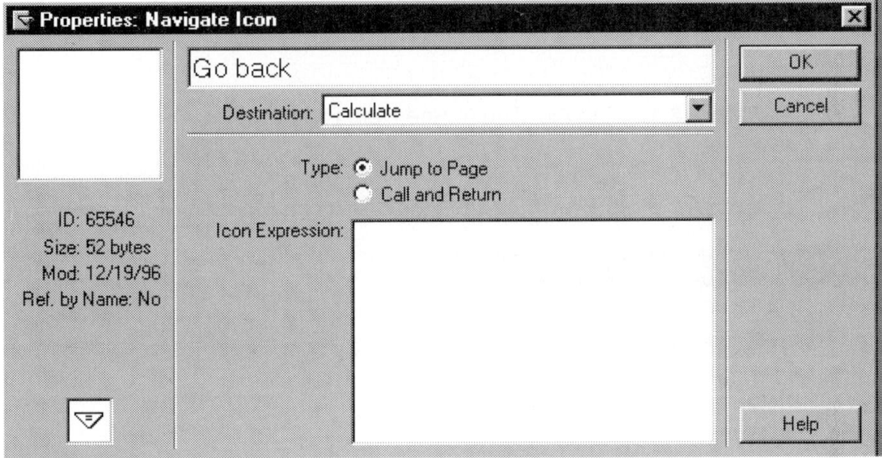

Figure 8.11. The Navigate Icon Properties Dialog Box For Calculate Destinations.

In the Icon Expression area, you enter the expression that evaluates to a valid IconID or page name. An example should help you understand this concept.

Sample File You can use a calculate destination to create context sensitive help. To see this, open the **Help.a4p** file in the Chapter8 folder on the CD-ROM.

Run the project and push the Next button. Note that you are on a page that would show content about a mythical area called fantasyland. Push the help button to see help about that land.

Now push the Previous button. Now you're seeing content about Frontier Land. Push the Help button again. Now the help pertains to Frontier Land. We have one button that routes us to different destinations, depending on the page we were on. Let's see how this was done.

The flowline is shown in Figure 8.12.

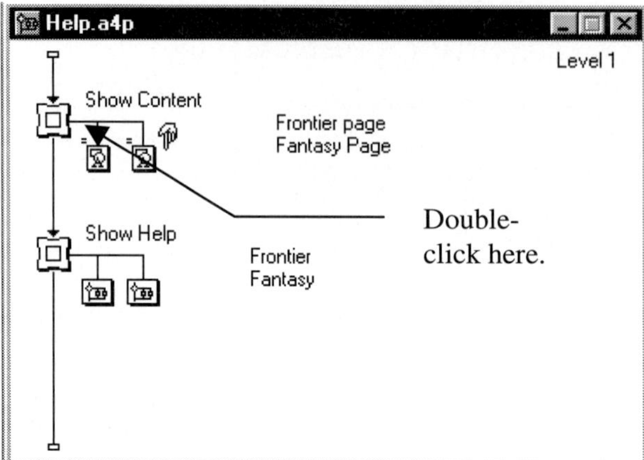

Figure 8.12. The Flowline for the Help Project in the Chapter8 Folder.

Open the Show Content framework. There are three navigate icons attached to button responses: one each for Next, Previous, and Help. You can see them in Figure 8.13.

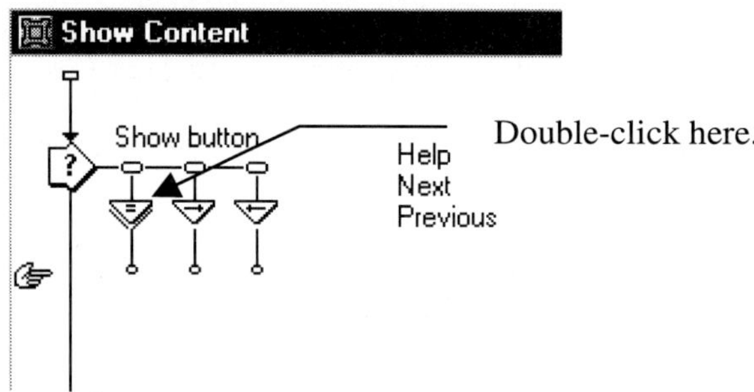

Figure 8.13. The Navigate Icons Associated with the Show Content Framework. To see them, double-click the framework icon on the main flowline.

The Next navigate icon uses the Nearby Next setting, the Previous navigate button uses Nearby Previous. The Help button is attached to the calculate navigate icon. Open the navigate icon and you'll see how we specify the expression that evaluates to a valid page name. The resulting dialog box is shown as Figure 8.14.

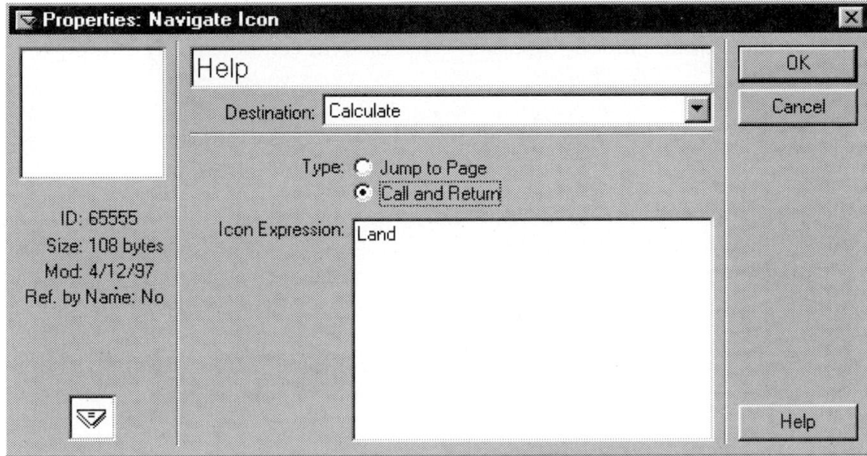

Figure 8.14. The Icon Expression Used To Specify a Valid Page Name for the Help Project from Figure 8.12.

The Icon Expression has the value "Land". It says to jump (and return when done) to the icon whose value matches the current value of Land. We need to set the variable to a valid page name so Authorware can display the suitable help found on that page This is done by the attached calculation you can see on each page of the Show Content icon.

If you select the Frontier Page, then choose Modify>Icon>Calculation (Ctrl+=) you'll see what we reproduced as Figure 8.15.

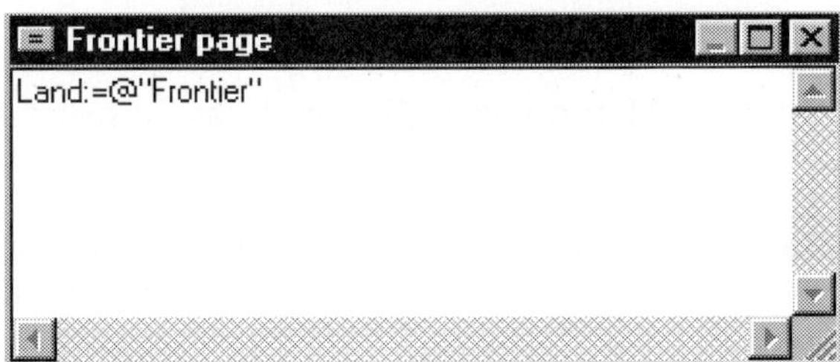

Figure 8.15. The Calculation Attached to the Frontier Page Icon. It sets the value of "Land" to the page to which we want to jump when the help button is pushed.

Notice that we set the value of Land to @"Frontier". This means "Go to the page named Frontier". That page contains the help for Frontier Land. If you open the calculation attached to Fantasy Page you'll see we set Land to @"Fantasy". Thus if the user is on this page, Land will be set to the help page for that page.

As you can see, calculation destinations, while a bit complex to set up, offer powerful abilities for the Authorware author. The next type, Search, can be equally complex, but just as useful.

Search

The search option presents the user with a dialog box, into which they enter a word. Authorware will then find all pages that contain that word. The page name plus the word in context are shown as a list. The user can then select the page from the list, and Authorware will jump to that page.

Sample File Open the **Search.a4p** project in the Chapter8 folder. Run it and push the small button you see. Enter the word "codec". You should see Figure 8.16.

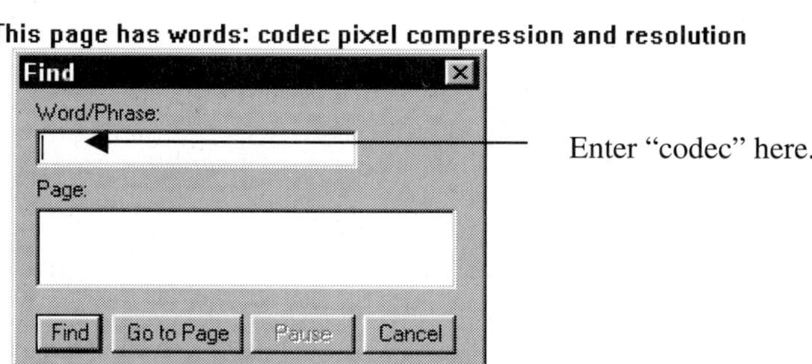

Figure 8.16. The Presentation Widow For The Search Project After Pushing The Find Button.

Notice the dialog box shows all pages containing the word you entered, and the word is shown in context. If you select the desired page (only two contain the word "codec"), then push Find, you'll go to that page. Figure 8.17 shows the Presentation window after entering the word codec.

This page has words: codec pixel compression and resolution

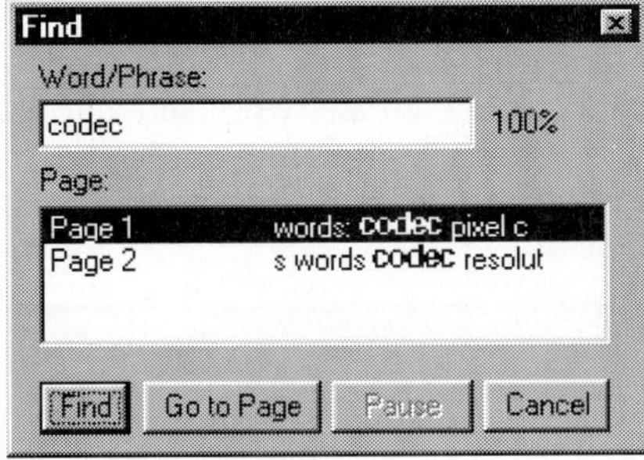

Figure 8.17. The Presentation Window after Entering a Word to Find. The word was codec.

To see how this was done, open the Search Framework, then double-click on the Find Navigate icon. You should see the dialog box in Figure 8.18.

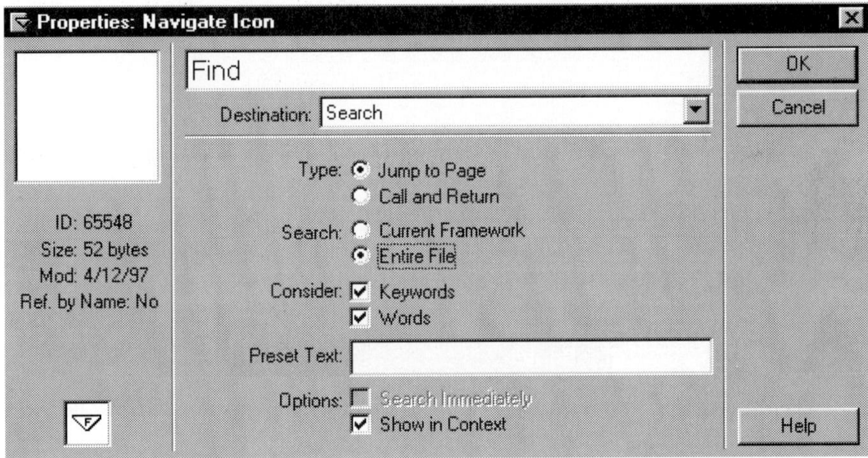

Figure 8.18. The Navigate Dialog Box For Find Destinations. This particular dialog box is associated with the Find button in the **Search.a4p** project.

You can jump to the destination page and stay there, or make a round-trip (Call and Return). The scope of the search can be the entire file or just the current framework. If the former option is selected, the searching will span the entire project. Choosing the latter means Authorware will limit its search to just the current framework.

Another option specifies whether to search words, keywords, or both. Use of the Preset option is a bit more complicated.

The purpose of the Pre-Set field is to eliminate the need to have the user key in the word to be searched. Instead, you would like the user to click on a word, then search for that word.

Sample File Open the **ClickSrc.a4p** project. It is almost identical to **Search.a4p**; the project we just finished looking at. The difference is: click on any word and all pages having that word will appear in the Find dialog box. For example, click the word "codec." As you can see from the open dialog box, shown in Figure 8.19, there are two pages containing that word.

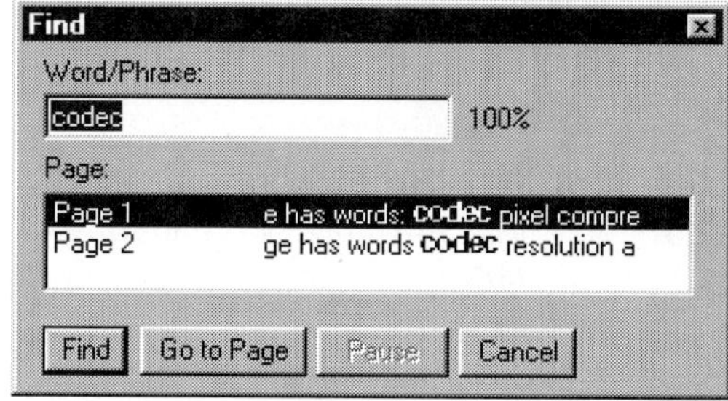

Figure 8.19. The Result of Using a Find Navigate Utilizing the Preset field.

To create this piece we used the following steps:

- Changed the response type to a hot spot.

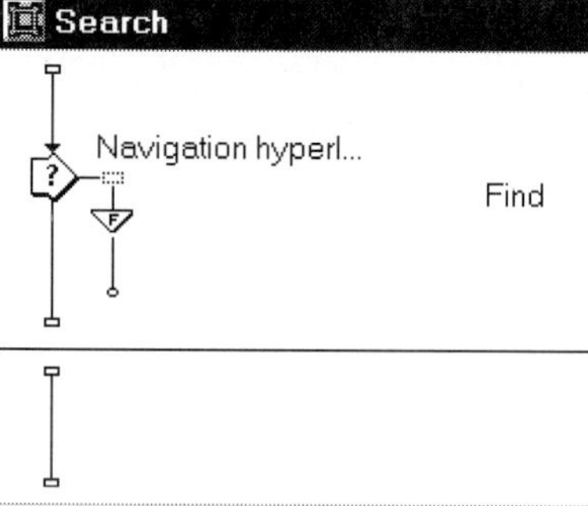

- Sized the hot spot so it covered the entire page:

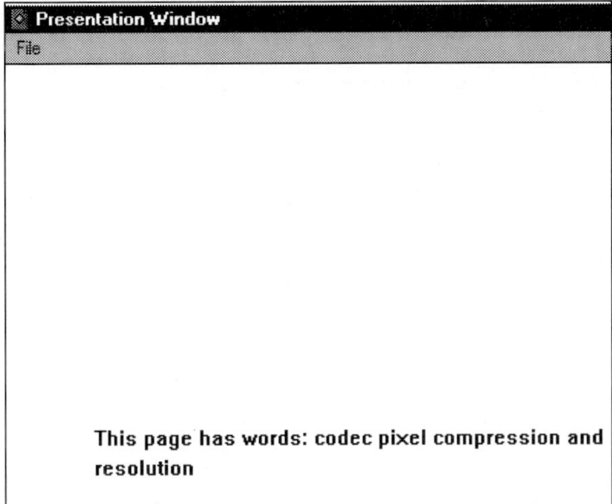

- Entered `WordClicked` as the Pre-Set value, as shown in Figure 8.20.

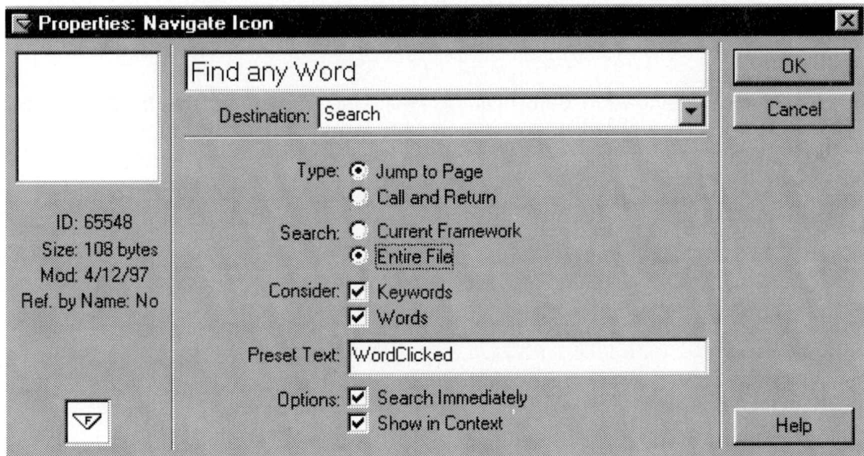

Figure 8.20. Using the Preset Field to Enable users to Click on a Word and Receive a Message.

- Checked the Search Immediately and Show in Context check boxes.

This process works because when a word within the hot spot is clicked, Authorware puts that word into the `WordClicked` variable. Authorware then executes the content of the attached icon, the navigate find icon.

Skipping Words You can tell Authorware which words to ignore when performing the search. This requires that you create a file of words to be skipped (use any word processor but be sure to save the file in ASCII format, each word on a separate line).

Once the file is created, open the <u>M</u>odify><u>F</u>ile><u>N</u>avigation Setup dialog box shown in Figure 8.21.

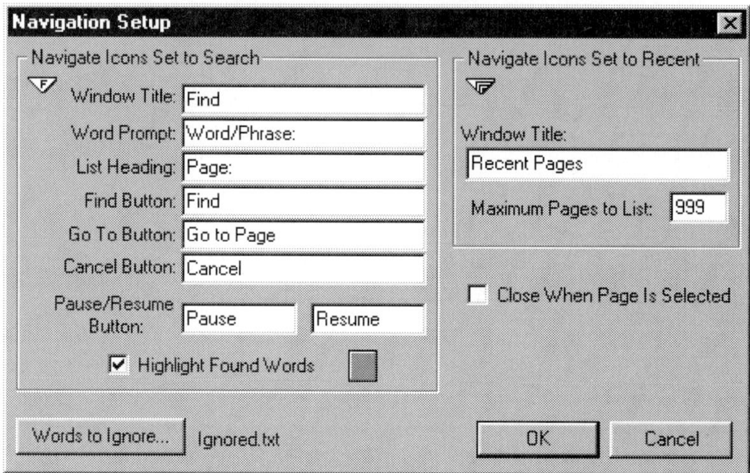

Figure 8.21. The Navigation Setup Dialog Box. Use it to customize framework settings, including specification of words to ignore while searching.

Click the Words to Ignore button in the lower left corner, and then import your file. The other choices let you:

- Specify new headings for the Find dialog box.
- Specify your own prompt when Authorware requests a word for which to search.
- Enter your own heading for the dialog box that presents the list of pages.
- Specify a button label for the button that initiates the search.
- Enter a new label for the button that when pushed displays the selected page.
- Specify a new caption for the Cancel button.
- Enter new captions for the Pause and Resume buttons.

Another option enables you to highlight found words. If this box is checked, Authorware will highlight the found words. The color swatch next to the checkbox is to let you choose the color of the highlight. Finally, check the Close When Page Is Selected option if you want to automatically close the Find dialog box, once a found page is visited.

Let's return now to two options present with many of the Destination types: Jump to Page and Call and Return.

Jump to Page

Use this option to create a one way trip. Control will pass to the destination page and remain there. Most of the time this is what we want. For navigation within a framework, this is the only option.

Call and Return

If you click the Call and Return option, a "round-trip" execution will result: Control will be passed to the designated page, then control will return to the icon that called it. This option is available for the Anywhere, Calculate, and Search destination types. Note that these three types can cause a jump to any page associated with any icon. Round-trip navigation can only be used when you are setting up navigation between frameworks, or from a navigate icon on a flowline to a page in a framework.

SIMPLE FRAMEWORKS

Now let's see how all this works by creating our first framework. This example will be a practice one that uses navigation icons plus frameworks.

Sample File You can preview what we'll be doing by running the **Framewrk.a4p** project in the Chapter8 folder on your CD-ROM. If you run that project you will see four buttons. Push the one labeled Topic 1. You will then see the display in Figure 8.22.

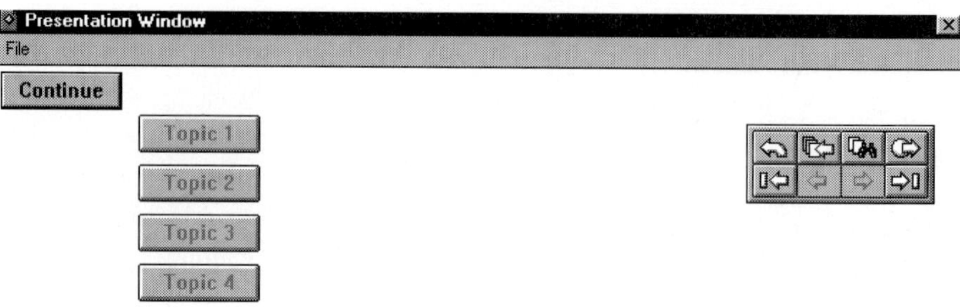

Figure 8.22. The Presentation Window from the **Framewrk.a4p** Piece. It shows the eight default framework navigation buttons.

Push the Continue button to return to the screen with the four buttons. Next push the Topic 3 button, followed by Continue. Now push Topic 2's button. We've visited three pages: Topic 1, Topic 3, then Topic 2. Let's see how this project was constructed.

Your Turn

❑ Start a new piece.

❑ Drag a framework icon to the flowline, save it as **Framewrk.a4p**.

❑ Add four maps to its right. Call them Topic 1, Topic 2, and so on.

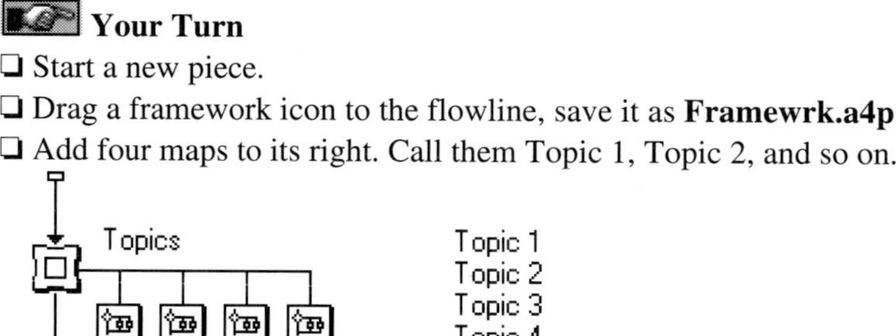

❑ Next, open each map, and add a display and a wait icon.

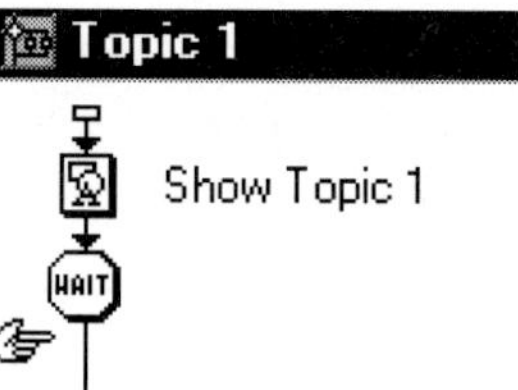

❑ Inside each Presentation window add a line like "This is topic one", "This is topic two" and so on.

❑ For example, the Presentation window for Show Topic 1 looks this way:

This is topic 1

❏ Do this for all four Topic maps.

❏ All done? OK, next we'll add four buttons through an interaction. Each of the responses will be a navigate icon. The navigate icon is discussed later in detail. At this time, we merely want to show the power of frameworks.

❏ The buttons, when clicked, will transport the user to the appropriate topic map. After viewing the content, control will return to the interaction with its four buttons.

❏ Drag an interaction icon to the beginning of the flowline.

❏ Drag four navigation icons to the right of the interaction, and select button as their interaction type. Name them Topic 1, Topic 2, Topic 3, and Topic 4.

❏ Name the interaction Show Buttons.

❏ Double-click the first navigation icon, to view the Navigate Properties dialog box, shown below.

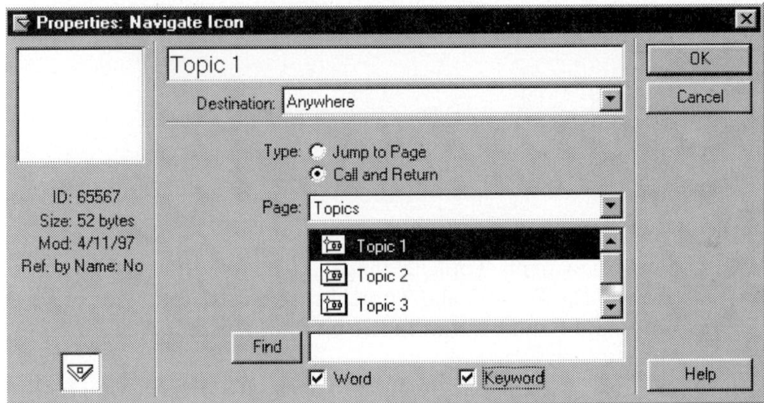

❏ Choose the Anywhere option, as we did above, and then check the Call and Return button. Choose Topic 1 as the page to which to jump. This means that when the button is pushed, control passes to the page named Topic 1 in the Topics framework. When that page exits, control should return to our screen with the buttons on it.

❏ To complete the piece, we must add a Return navigation to each Topic page.

❏ Open the Topic 1 map.

❏ Add a navigation icon to its end and choose the Nearby Destination option and Exit Framework/Return as the type. The flowline for Topic 1 should look like the figure below.

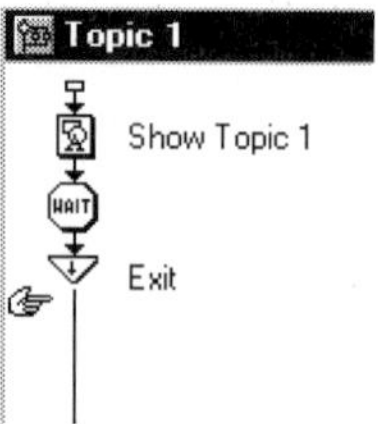

❏ The Navigate Properties for the Exit icon should be set like those in the figure below.

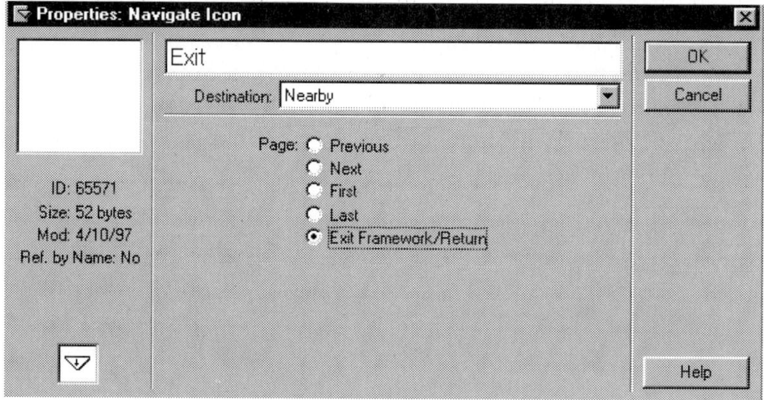

❏ Repeat for the other three pages. To facilitate this, copy the Exit Navigate icon to the Clipboard, then open Topic 2 map and then Edit Paste to the end of the flowline., Repeat for Topic 3 and Topic 4 map icons. Test your piece. If you had trouble, refer to the **Framewrk.a4p** file on your CD-ROM.

We just illustrated that a framework icon has pages attached, to which we can jump. This jump is implemented through navigate icons. Attach navigate icons to Interactions, such as button interactions.

The next section examines the eight default buttons that are set up when you define a framework icon. Since we don't have need for the four Topic buttons any more, we'll be using the Start flag to skip over that part of our project.

Exploring the Default Navigation Buttons

We will now explore the framework we created. We begin by using the Next and Previous.

Exploring the Next and Previous Buttons

Let's look at an example that uses next and previous navigation.

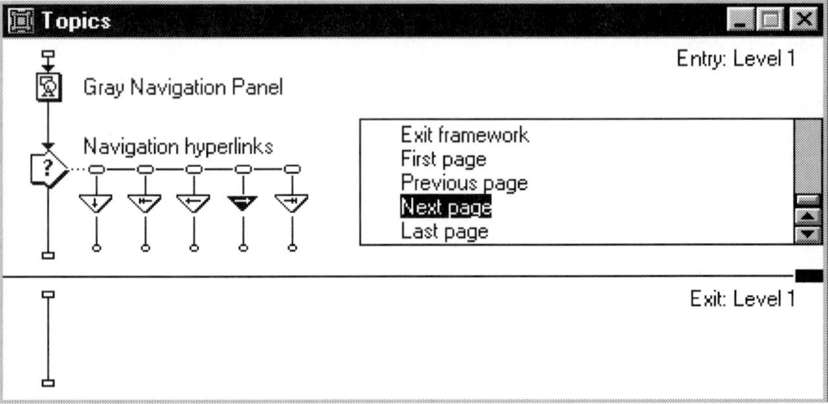 **Your Turn**

❑ Set the Start flag to just before your Topics framework icon, and then Run from the Flag. (Or open and run Chapter8**Framewrk.a4p**).
❑ Push the Next button.
❑ Push the Next button again to move to the Topic 2 page.
❑ Click the Previous button. Now you're now back to Topic 1.

Here's a question. What will happen if you again push the Previous button? Will we see an error message saying there is no previous page? Or will the previous button be dimmed, indicating it's now inactive? Or will control pass to the Topic 4 map, the last attached icon?

The correct answer is control passes to the Topic 4 page because Previous means, "move to the page to the left of the current one. "

Preventing Page-wrap

As noted above, if the current icon is the first one and the Previous button is pushed, Authorware would jump to the last icon. A similar set of actions can be constructed around the Next button and the last icon. To prevent this wrapping effect, you must use some more Authorware variables.

- Open the framework window and you will see the two panels.

- Double-click the button response symbol for Next page in the Entry panel, as shown in the following figure:

- Click the Response tab and in the Active If field enter: `CurrentPageNum<>PageCount`, as shown in the following figure:

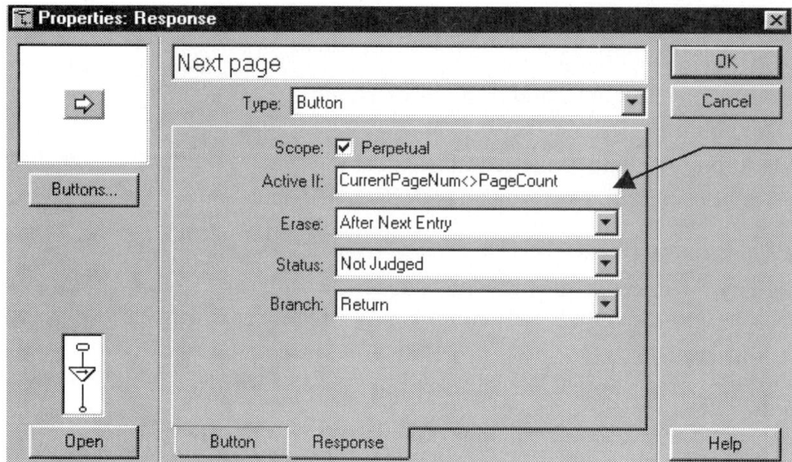

Button is
active only
when the
current page
number isn't
equal to the
total number
of pages.

- Each page is assigned a number (CurrentPageNum). As long as the current page number isn't equal to the highest page number (PageCount), the button is active. Otherwise Authorware should dim the button.

- Next, define when the Previous page button should be active. Open the response for the Previous page button and enter this text: CurrentPageNum>1.

Run your project and watch the Next and Previous buttons dim when you're at one of the end points.

Exploring the Recent Pages Button

We will next examine the recent pages, or history button. Authorware can track the pages a user has visited. This button displays them so the user can select one to revisit.

Your Turn
❑ Set the start flag to just before the Topics framework.
❑ Run from flag.
❑ Push the Next button 3 times, then the Previous button.
❑ Push the Recent Pages button. You should see this dialog box:

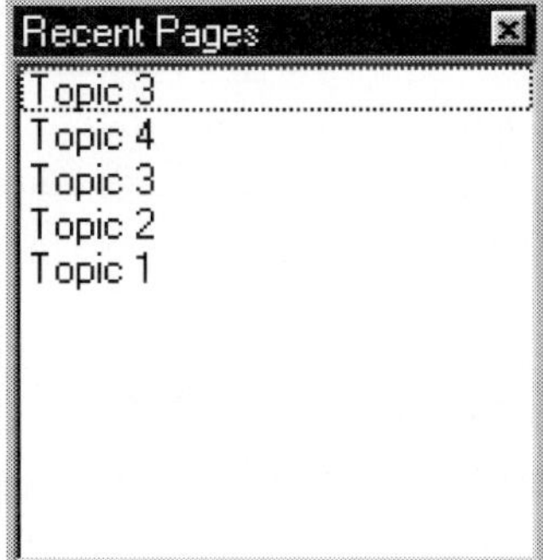

❏ Authorware keeps track of the pages you have visited within the framework. When this button is pushed, 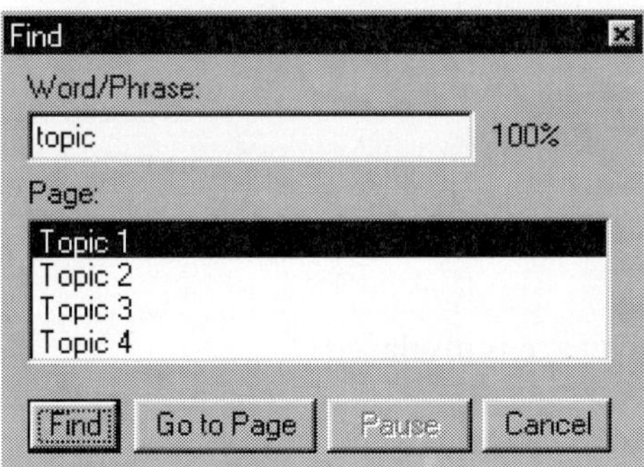 those page names are displayed with the most recent page listed first. Recall the title of the dialog box, and the number of entries in the list can be changed.

❏ Double-click a page in the list and you will go to that page.

❏ Close the Recent Pages dialog box. Recall this can also be done automatically when a page is selected.

❏ Click the Last page button. ⇥ You're now at the Topic 4 page, the last icon attached to the framework.

Exploring the Find Button

❏ Click the Find button and enter the word "topic".

❏ Either push the Enter key or push the Find button. Note all pages have reference to the word "topic".

❏ Select any page from the list and then click the Go to Page button, you should be at a page containing the word topic, and the search word, *topic*, is highlighted.

APPLYING TRANSITION EFFECTS

You can apply a transition to each page, or to individual pages within a framework. To apply a global transition to every page:

- Select the framework.
- Choose <u>M</u>odify><u>I</u>con><u>T</u>ransition (Ctrl+T).
- Select the desired transition from the Page Transition dialog box shown in Figure 8.23.

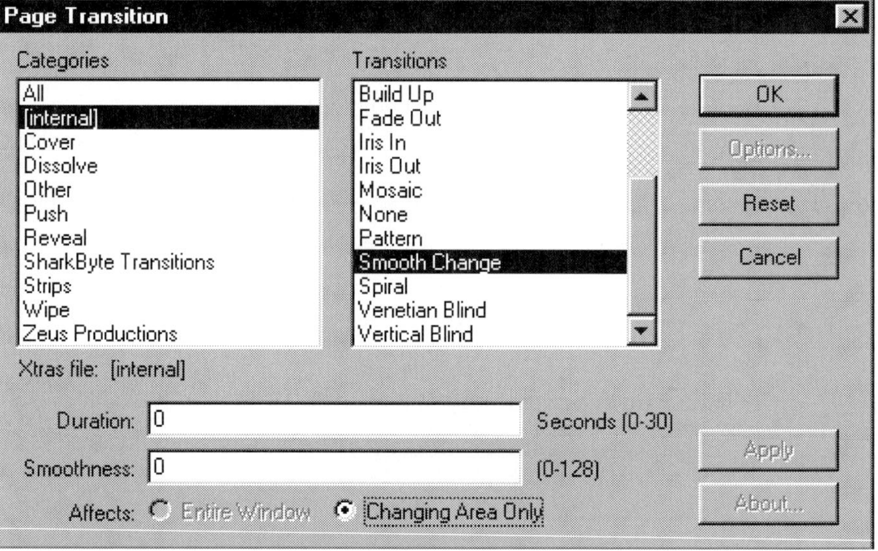

Figure 8.23. The Page Transition Dialog Box. It applies the same transition to every page within a framework.

Let's add some special effects, as each page is displayed.

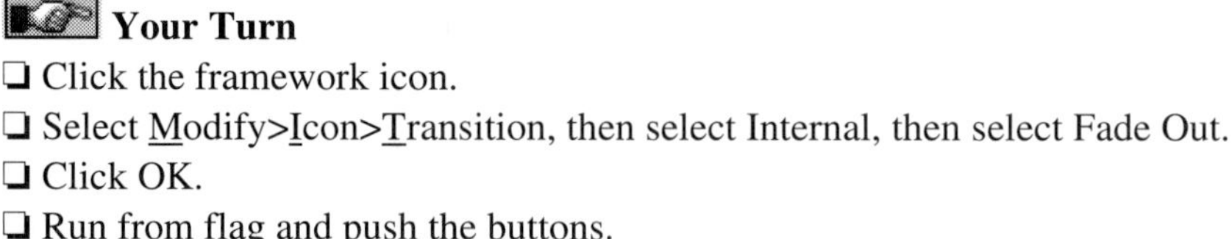 **Your Turn**

❑ Click the framework icon.

❑ Select <u>M</u>odify><u>I</u>con><u>T</u>ransition, then select Internal, then select Fade Out.

❑ Click OK.

❑ Run from flag and push the buttons.

❑ Try other effects, such as Build to Right, which wipes the screens from left to right.

❑ The effect you choose determines which transition to use as each subsequent page is displayed. This effect is global; applying to all pages attached to the framework. You can override the effect for any given page by means of the Modify>Icon>Transition for that icon alone.

❑ Jump to the Display window (Ctrl+1) then select the Topic 1 icon.

❑ Open it and select the Show Topic 1 display icon.

❑ Enter Ctrl+T.

❑ Select Spiral from the Effects drop-down list.

❑ Run from flag and move among the pages, paying particular attention when you move to the Topic 1 page.

❑ Save your work as **Framewrk.a4p**.

Creating a Find Piece Using Hot Spots

This example will build the **ClickSrc.a4p** piece we looked at earlier.

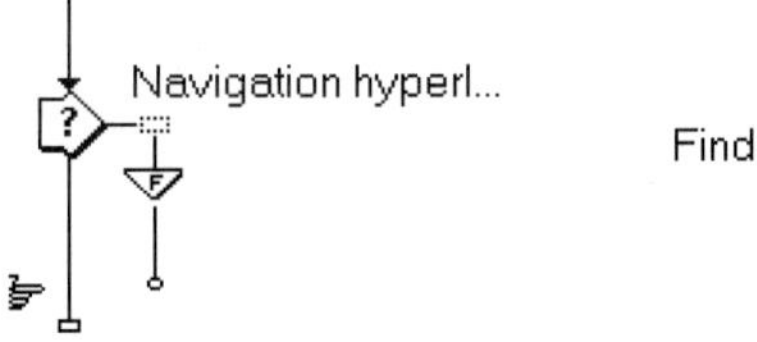 **Your Turn**

❑ Start a new project.

❑ Add a framework icon and name it Search.

❑ Add three display icons and name them Page 1, Page 2, and Page 3.

❑ Open the framework icon by double-clicking it.

❑ Delete all but the Find navigate icon.

❑ Associate a hot spot with the Find icon in the entry pane. Do this by changing the type from button to hot spot.

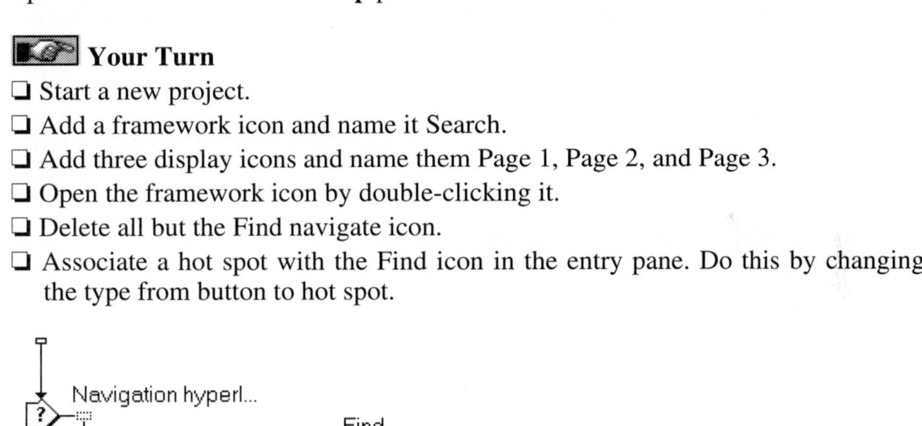

❑ Call it Find Any Word. Recall anything we do in an entry panel applies to the entire framework. This means every page will have a hot spot.

❑ Size the hot spot so it covers the complete page where text will appear.

❑ Open the Navigate Properties dialog box for the new Find Any Word navigate icon.

❑ Set the options like this:

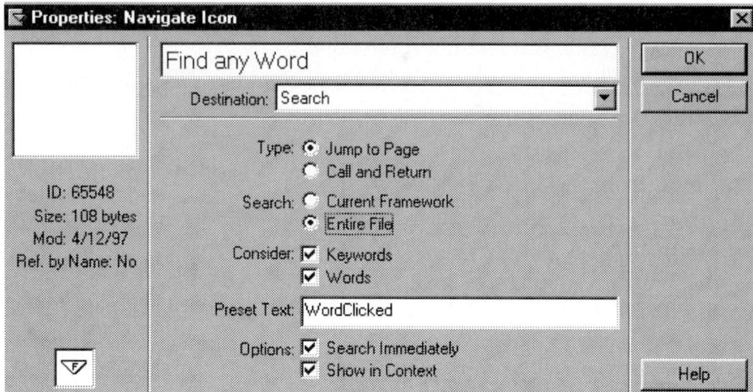

❑ Be sure to enter `WordClicked` in the Pre-Set Text field.
❑ Check the Search Immediately box, which makes Authorware begin the search without having the user push the Find button.
❑ Close the dialog box and run your piece.
❑ Select the word "Resolution."
❑ All pages containing Resolution will be listed in the Find dialog box, as shown in figure below.

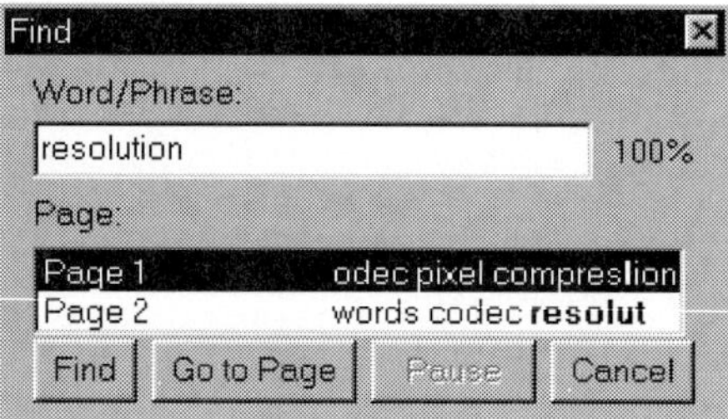

❑ Save your work as **ClickSrc.a4p**.

ADDING FUNCTIONALITY

At the beginning of the chapter, we saw a simple example where we attached buttons to a screen that jumped to various pages within a framework. Let's expand that example and nest frameworks — that is, place frameworks inside other frameworks.

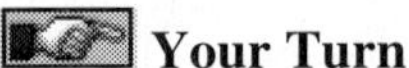 **Sample File** The complete example can be found in the **Shopping.a4p** file in the Chapter8 folder.

Open and run it. Push the Food button. You should see some new buttons. Push Pizza to view its picture. Push Fruit. Return to the main screen and navigate down the Cars path. You are going to re-create this in the next section.

We are going to show a series of buttons that allow the user to choose a major shopping group: Food, Furniture, or Cars. When one of the major topic buttons is pushed, another series of buttons will appear permitting access to subtopics within the main one. For example, when Food is selected, the user will see three new buttons: one each for Pizza, Fruit, and a Return button. Pushing either of the first two buttons will result in a graphic being displayed.

Your Turn

❑ Start a new project.
❑ Open the Backgrounds library drag the Mottled2 image to the flowline.
❑ Add a map icon and name it Shopping.
❑ Open Shopping.
❑ Add an interaction with three buttons connected to the navigate icons. Name the Interaction Show Categories. Name the three navigate icons Food, Furniture, and Cars, respectively. Each navigate icon should be Destination Anywhere types. We'll specify the locations later.
❑ Your flowline should look like this:

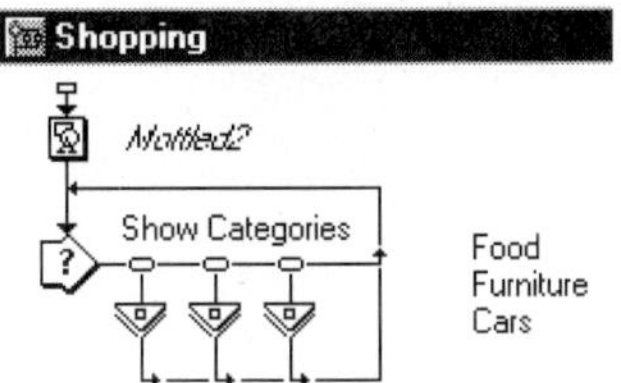

❑ Double-click the Show Categories Interaction icon and enter "Select a category" in its Presentation window. Your display should look this way:

❑ You've now finished presenting the main topics.
❑ The responses Food, Furniture, and Cars should all be buttons. Set the Food Button Response Properties like this:

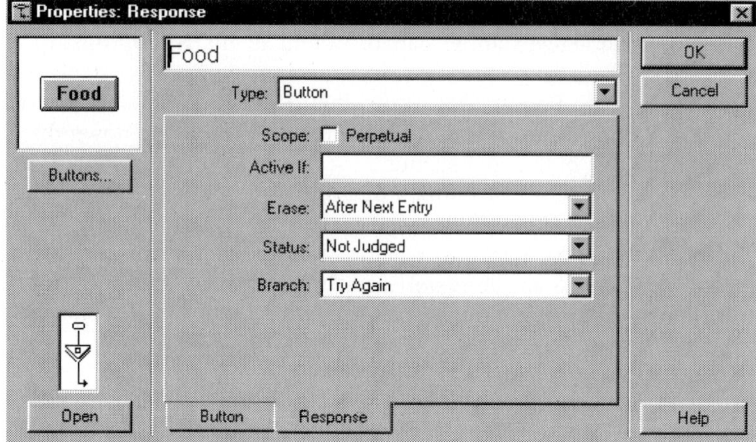

❏ When the user is finished exploring a category, we want them to return to the main screen (Show Categories). All of this is accomplished by the three navigate icons attached to Show Categories. Each will perform a Call and Return jump to a page within a framework called Show sub buttons. There the additional buttons will be displayed. The buttons inside Show sub buttons will in turn do a jump and return to a page that shows the actual graphic. We have to construct those content pages next so we can specify their names in the navigate icons within Show sub buttons.

❏ Add a framework called Items.

❏ Attach four maps: Pizza, Sofa, Fruit, and Mazda.

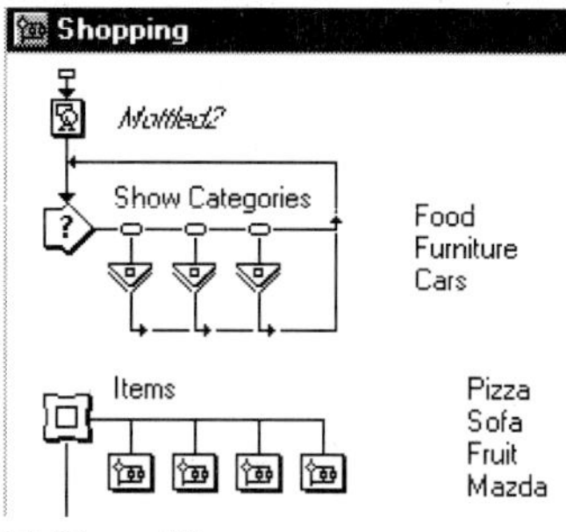

❏ Open Pizza.

❏ Add a display, a wait, and an Exit/Return navigate icon:

❏ Open the Show Pizza display and import the Pizza bitmap from the Chapter8\Images folder.

❏ Add the words "Our Pizza delivers", in red text.

❏ Add "Sofa" next. Import the Sofa image, and move and resize so it's about the same size as Pizza. Add the red text: "Comes with our Patented Pizza-Guard!"

❏ Do the same for Fruit, but import the Fruit image. Add "Goes Great with Pizza" in white text along the top.

❏ Finally, add the Mazda image. The red text at the top should say: "Pizza won't stain these seats!"

❏ Save your work as **Shopping.a4p**.

❏ Now we're ready to ad the Show sub buttons framework.

❏ Add a framework and name it Show sub buttons.

❏ Attach three maps, named Furniture, Food, and Cars, as shown in the figure below.

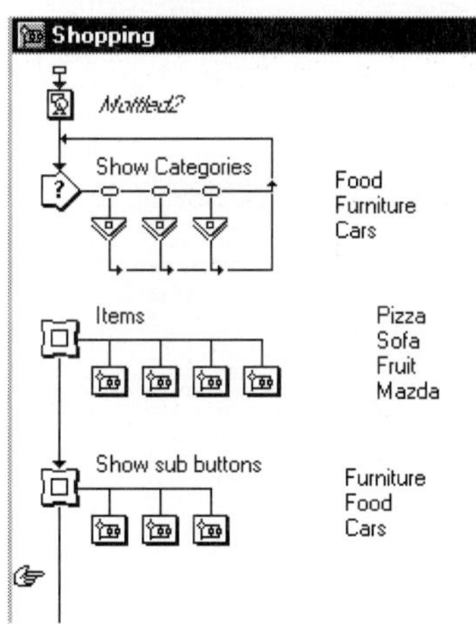

❏ Open the Furniture map.

❏ Add an interaction with two buttons: a destination anywhere - Call and Return named Sofa, and an Exit/Return button named Exit.

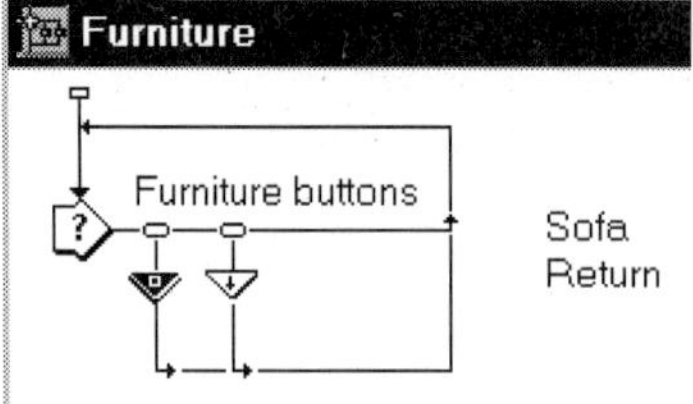

❏ The Sofa Navigate properties should look this way:

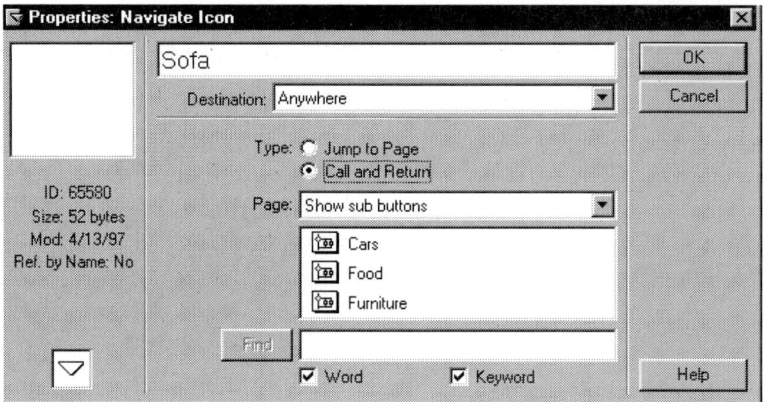

❏ Set up the Exit button's Navigate properties this way:

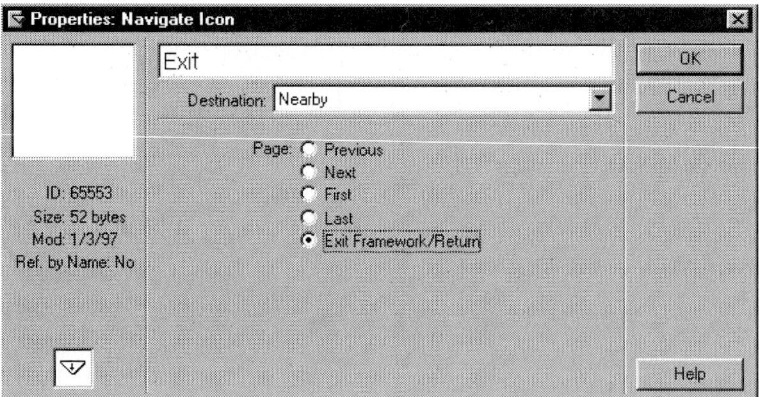

❏ Repeat this process for the Food and Cars maps.

❏ The Food map should look like this:

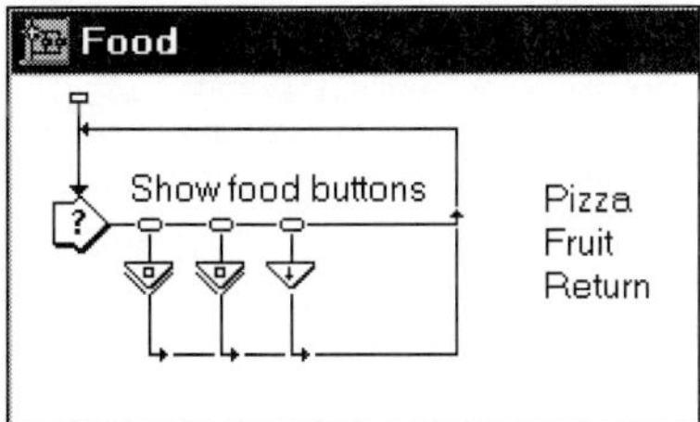

❏ The Cars map should look like this:

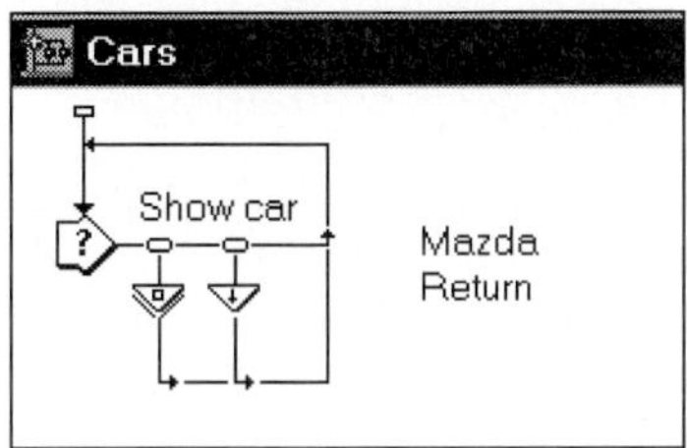

❏ For both Food and Cars, the navigate icons should be set up as destination Any-where, Jump and Return, and should specify a page to jump to that's part of the Items framework. If you get confused, look at our solution.

❏ Next, we have to go back to the Show Categories icon and specify destinations for the navigate icons.

❏ Open the Navigate Properties dialog box for Food and use these values:

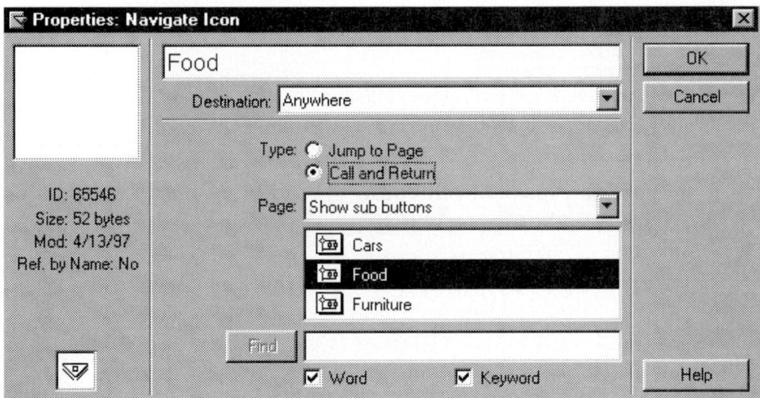

❏ Set up each of the other Show Categories buttons as just described.
❏ Save your work (**as Shopping.a4p**).

We are going to return to the continuing case at this time. If you want to preview the piece, open the **DigVid8.a4p** file in the Chapter8 folder on the CD-ROM.

The new materials include a series of hot spots that can be used to bring up informa-tion about three topics. When a hot spot is clicked, buttons appear that when pushed display the new information. Let's see how this was built.

Your Turn

❏ Open **DigVid7.a4p**.

❏ Group the testing icons into a single map, named testing.

❏ So that you don't have to keep running the piece from the beginning, copy the Background icon and rename it Background again.

❏ Place the start flag before the new icon.

❏ Add a display, name it Add text, and add this title at the top in blue 17- point text: "Choose a topic"

❏ Use the same display to add three words, one in each of the three small rectangles along the left side. The words (topics) are Capture, Format, and Compress.

❏ Add an interaction named Topics.

❏ Add three hot spot navigate icons named Capture, Format, and Compress. Make the hot spots perpetual, and they should cover the respective rectangles where you just added the text. Add a button response named Next and import the Nextup and Nextdn bitmaps. Place the button over the small opening in the lower left corner of the template.

❏ The additions, thus far, to the **DigVid7.a4p** flowline should look like the following figure.

❏ The left side of the Presentation widow should resemble the next figure, except there should be three hot spots, not two as in the figure.

❏ As you might have guessed from our framework discussion, the hot spots attached to the navigate icons will branch (and return) to pages of frameworks that discuss the associated topics. Next, build the framework.

❏ Add a Framework, name it Topic Framework Level 1, and add three pages: Capture1, Format1, and Compress1.

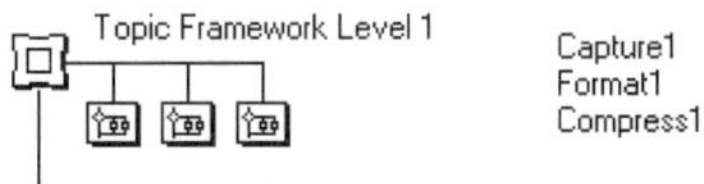

❏ We now have destination pages for our Hot spots. The Capture hot spot should jump (by way of a navigate icon) to Capture1, using a Call and Return. Similarly the other two hot spot navigate icons should call and return to Format1 and Compress1 respectively. The figure below shows the properties for the Capture navigate icon in the Topics interaction.

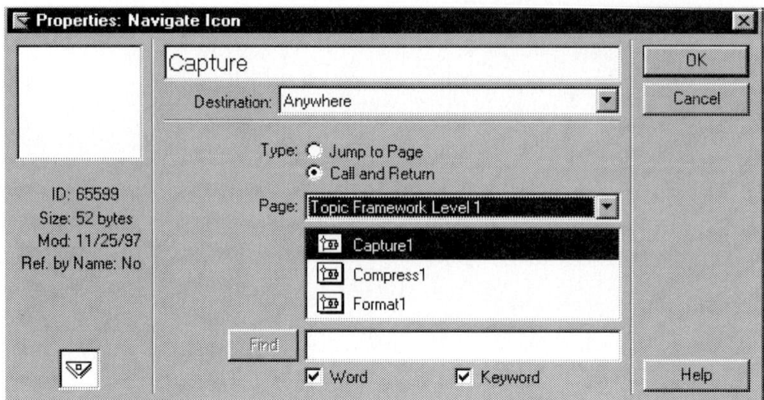

❏ This means Authorware is to jump (the return) to the map page named Capture1, whenever the hot spot is clicked. Capture1 is a page within the Topic Framework Level 1 framework.

❏ Now open the map for Capture1.

❏ Add the following icons:

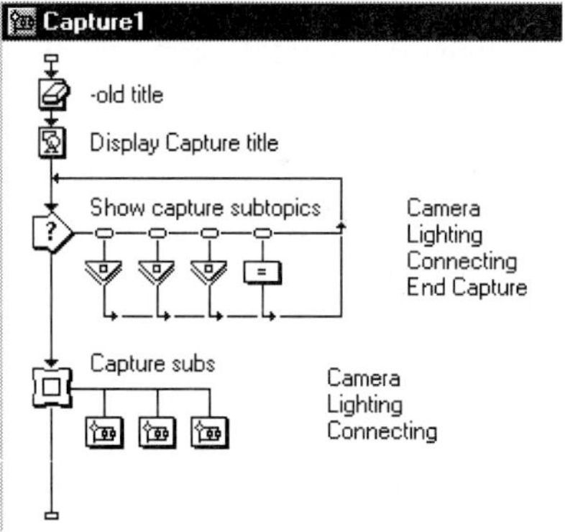

❏ The "- old title" deletes the "Select a topic" text, while "Display Capture title" displays the words "Capturing Video" in 17-point blue text at the top of the template.

❏ The Show capture subtopics interaction creates four buttons (we used the **Generic.GIF** graphic for the first three and the Standard Windows button for the End Capture button). Each of the generic button graphics is positioned in one of the three squares along the left side. The Next button should still be near the lower left of the figure. The End Capture button, we placed along the bottom. The Presentation window should look like the figure that follows.

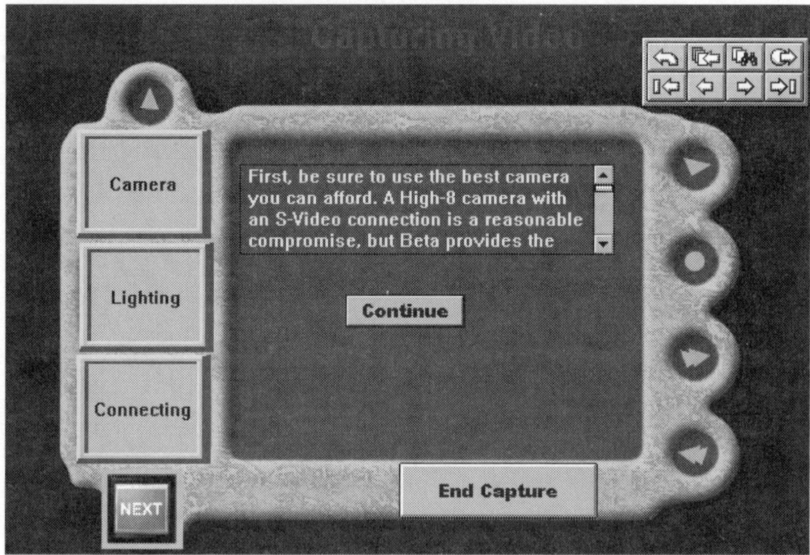

❑ The Camera, Lighting, and Connecting button properties should be set like the following figure.

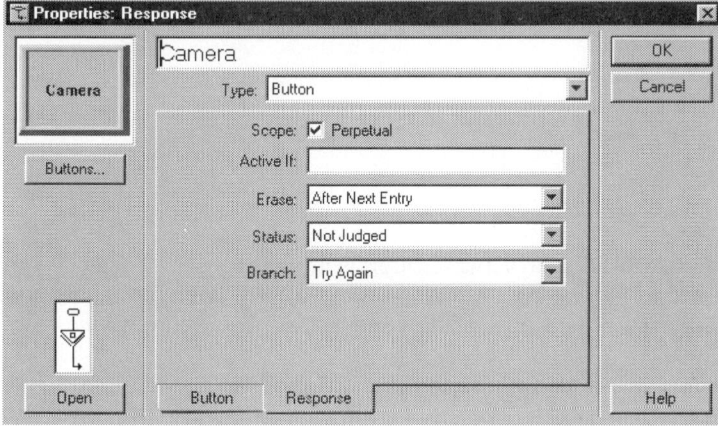

❑ The Camera navigate properties are set like the following figure.

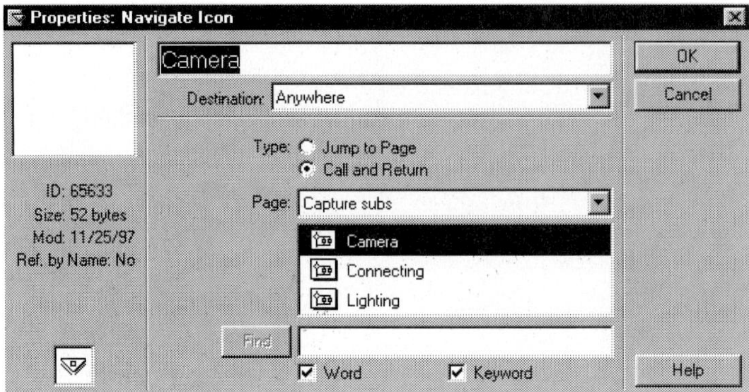

❏ This means when someone clicks on the Camera button, jump to the page called Camera within the Capture subs framework.

❏ Next, we'll work with the Capture subs framework. This will contain the pages to which we will jump when a user clicks a button on the Capture screen. The (sub) topics are camera, lighting and connecting.

❏ The three attached maps you added previously are: Camera, Lighting and Connecting.

❏ Open the Camera map and add the following icons.

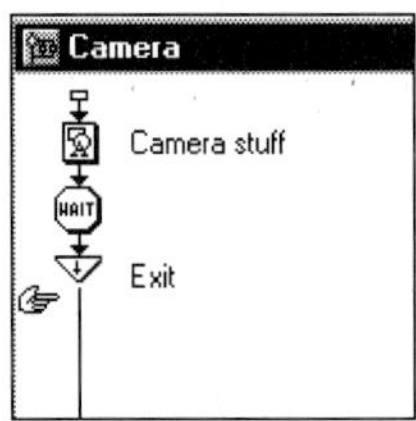

❏ The Camera Stuff displays this scrolling yellow text:

"First, be sure to use the best camera you can afford. A High-8 camera with an S-Video connection is a reasonable compromise, but Beta provides the best images.

Be sure to use the S-Video connector, if at all possible."

❏ The Exit navigate icon is a Nearby Destination with an Exit Framework option.

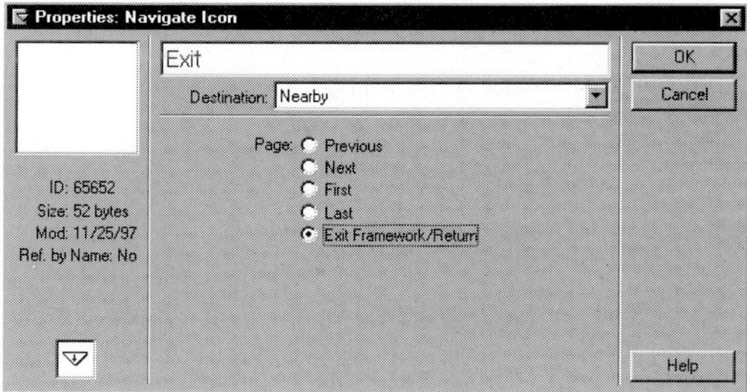

❏ The Lighting and Connecting Maps are set up similarly, but with different content. Feel free to make up your own.

❏ The Format1 and Compress1 maps display under construction messages, then wait for a keypress. The Format1 map is shown in the figure below.

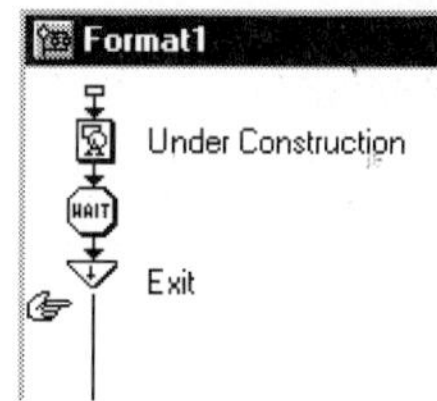

❏ The final point we wish to make is that the Exit navigate icon uses Nearby destination with an Exit/Return option.

❏ Save your work as **DigVid8.a4p**.

This concludes our first look at the framework and navigate icons. The next chapter builds on this knowledge as we look at these powerful objects in more detail.

SUMMARY

Authorware's framework icon creates a set of eight default buttons that enable one to navigate among icons attached to the framework, called pages. There are buttons for First, Last, Next, Previous, Go Back, View Recent Pages and Find. These buttons can be deleted, converted to hot spots, or added to.

Navigate buttons can also be added almost anywhere in a title. They enable the user to jump to a designated page or call that page and return. Frameworks have navigate icons as "responses" to the default buttons.

Study Exercises

8.1 Finish the example from the food example in this chapter.

8.2 Create a new project named C8Q2. It should display four buttons labeled Topic 1, Topic 2, and so on. When Topic 2 is pushed, for example, it should show four more buttons, named Topic 2.1, Topic 2.2, Topic 2.3, plus a Return button. When Topic 2.1 is pushed it should show three buttons: Topic 2.1.1, Topic 2.2.2, and Return. When Topic 2.1.1 is pushed it should display the words "This would be the content for topic 2.1.1." Each of the other buttons should function similarly.

8.3 Create a new piece named C8Q3. It should be a combination of navigate and framework icons that present four main topics: Text, Graphics, Sound and Video. These might be buttons or hot spots. When clicked, the four main topics present additional topics about that subject. For Text, show additional interactions indicating that the user can get information on Fonts, Points, and Layout. For Sound, the additional information is to be labeled Digital and MIDI. For video, use Lighting, Editing, Codecs. Finally, for Graphics, add buttons or hot spots for Storage, Representation, and Models. On all the pages, simply display a few words — you are merely creating placeholders for future content. Be sure to provide for Return buttons as we did in this chapter.

8.4 Modify exercise 8.3 to add the ability to find words by clicking on them.

8.5. Make the background template in DigVid8 nonmovable.

8.6. Finish the DigVid8.a4p example, fleshing out the under construction areas. Add submaterial to the Camera topic. Refer to 35mm, digital cameras and camcorders

Advanced Navigation

*T*he last chapter introduced you to the framework and navigate icons. While the navigate icon can be used anywhere, we usually find it used in conjunction with a framework icon. This chapter looks at some uses for both: glossaries and hypertext, hyperlinking, and finding pages containing pages containing key words. . The last section examines how to use frameworks to create complex, multi-layered titles.

At the conclusion of the chapter, you will be able to:

- Define a hot text style.

- Add hot text to your title.

- Define and use keywords as a means for users to find information of interest to them.

CREATING HYPERTEXT

Hypertext, or ***hot-text*** is the displaying of additional text when a user clicks on a word that is usually highlighted. For example, you're reading about NASA and you see the word Challenger highlighted. By clicking on that word, additional information about the ill-fated flight is displayed. When media other than text are displayed, we call it ***hypermedia***. In this section we will build a glossary containing definitions of words. When a word is clicked, its definition will be displayed.

To create hypertext in Authorware, we'll need a navigate icon and a text style. The steps are:

1. Define the hot-text style.
2. Apply the style to the desired text.
3. Associate a destination page with the text.

Let's explore this in more detail.

Define the Hot-text Style

To define a new style:

1. Choose Text>Define Styles (Ctrl+Shift+Y).
2. The Define Styles dialog box shown in Figure 9.1 opens.

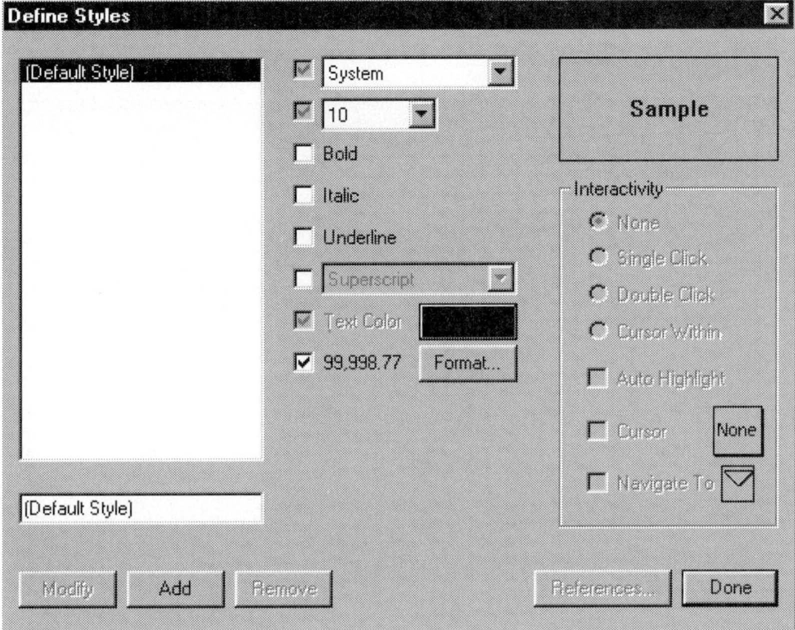

Figure 9.1. The Define Styles Dialog Box. Use it to create hot text.

3. Create a new style by pushing the Add button, then choosing the desired attributes of the style.

4. In the Interactivity section, choose the trigger action (single click, double-click, and so on).

5. Decide whether to have the text highlighted when it's triggered.

6. Decide whether to alter the cursor's shape when over a hot word.

7. Close the dialog box.

Let's define a hot-text style that we can later apply.

 **Sample File** If you want to preview what we're about to do, open **the Hottext.a4p** file in the Chapter9 folder on the CD-ROM. Run the project, push the Food button, then choose to shop for Pizza. When you see the phrase "Our Pizza Delivers", move the mouse over the word "Pizza" and click. A dialog box explaining pizza appears. Let's see how to build this piece.

First, we must define the hot-text style.

Your Turn

❏ Open the **Shopping.a4p** file in the Chapter9 folder on the CD-ROM. (This was one of the projects we created in Chapter 8).

❑ Choose <u>T</u>ext> <u>D</u>efine Styles.
❑ The Define Styles dialog box, shown in Figure 9.2, opens.

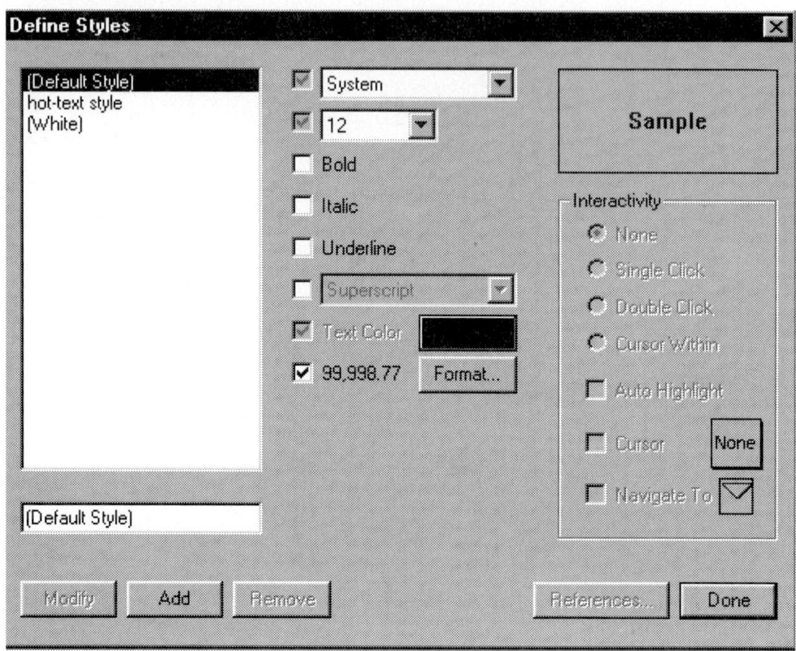

Figure 9.2. The Define Styles Dialog Box. Use it to define a new style, which can then be used for creating hypertext and hypermedia.

❑ Click the Add button.
❑ In the field near the lower left corner, enter "hot-text Style."
❑ Decide what properties you want the hot-text to have. For example, you might choose Arial, 12-point, bold, green.
❑ Push the Modify button.
❑ Under the Interactivity section, select "Single click". This means that when a hot-word is clicked, the navigation will occur.
❑ If you want the word to be displayed in inverse colors, once activated, select the "Auto Highlight" radio button.
❑ Choose the Cursor option by checking the box.
❑ Select a cursor to indicate the text is hot (use the hand cursor).
❑ Do not select the Navigate to option, as this will cause every word we apply this to to jump to the same page. We want a separate page for each hot word.
❑ Push the Done button to close the dialog box.
❑ Save your work as **Hottext.a4p**.

Define the Jump-to Framework Pages

When you apply the style you just defined to text within a page, you will need to specify the page to jump to when the hot text is selected. This means you need to define the pages before you apply the style. In other words, set up a framework with multiple pages, one for each word to be defined by means of the glossary. Then apply the style to words on one or more pages.

Your Turn

❑ Drag a map icon to the end of the main flowline and name it Glossary.

❑ Open the map and drag a framework icon to it. Name it Definitions.

❑ Attach three display icons to the framework. Name them Delivers, Pizza, and Stains.

❑ Open each display icon and import the **Information.gif** file from the Images\Misc folder on the CD-ROM. Mat the images (use the Modes Inspector).

❑ Your Glossary flowline should look like the figure that follows.

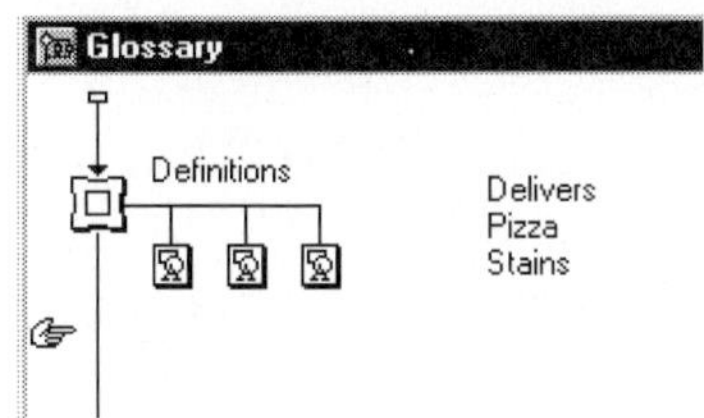

❑ Open the Delivers icon and add the text fyou see in the figure below. Note the margin settings are within the boundaries of the dialog box.

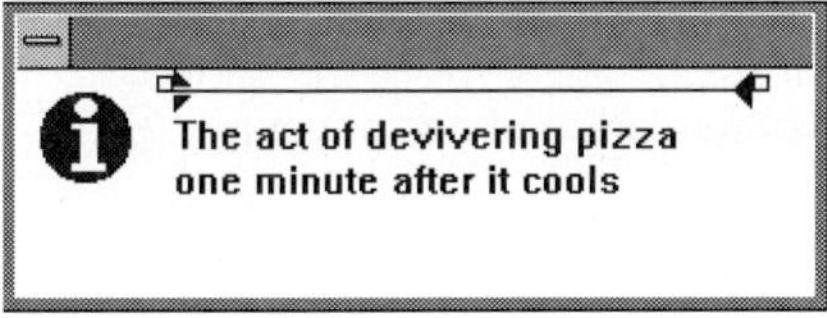

❑ Your Pizza dialog box might look like the figure that follows.

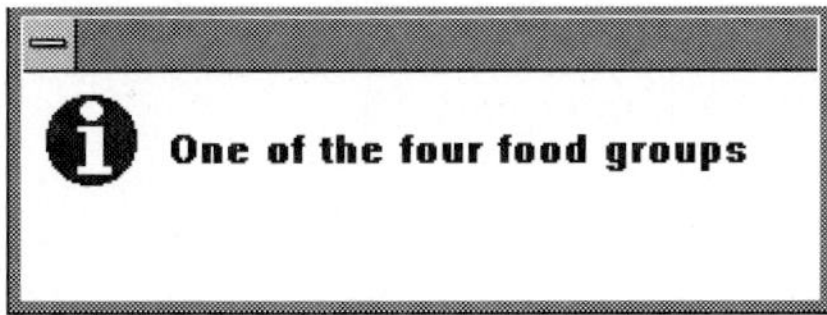

❑ Add this text to your Stains dialog box:

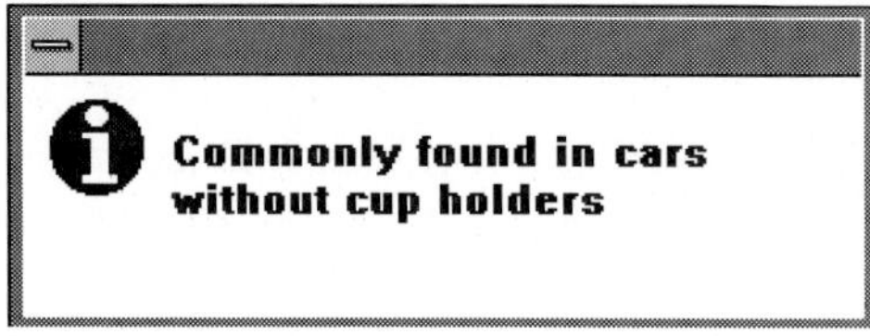

❏ Close the Glossary map.
❏ Save your work.

Now we need to apply the hot-text style to the words in our Shopping map. We need to apply the style to every occurrence of the words pizza, stains and delivers. First, let's cover the basic steps on how this is done, then we'll apply those steps.

Apply the Hot-text Style

The next step is to apply the style to the appropriate text. The basic steps for applying a style are:

1. Open the icons containing the text to be made interactive (hot).
2. Use the text tool in the toolbox to select the text.
3. Choose Text>Apply Styles.
4. Select the style you defined previously ("hot-text style").
5. Select the Call and Return option within the Navigate Icon Properties dialog box.
6. Choose the page to which to jump.
7. Close the dialog box.

Let's return to our Shopping map/ Items framework and add some hot text.

Your Turn
❏ Open the Pizza page in the Items framework.
❏ Open the Show Pizza display icon.
❏ Select the word "Pizza" in the phrase "Our Pizza Delivers!"
❏ Choose Text>Apply Styles (Ctrl+Alt+Y).
❏ You will then see the Styles palette, shown in Figure 9.3

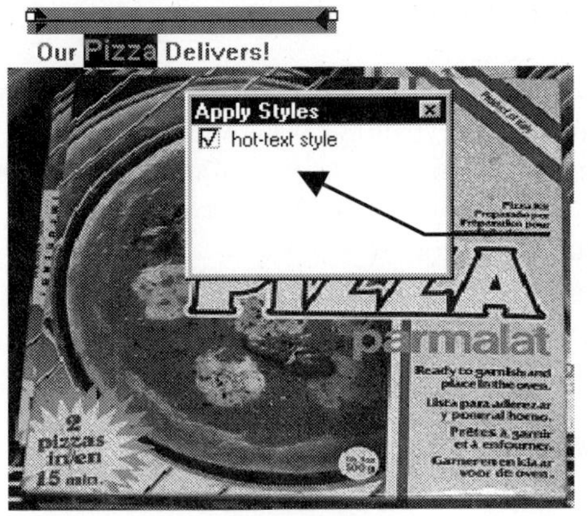

We defined this one earlier.

Figure 9.3. The Apply Styles Palette. It appears when you choose Text> Apply Styles from the menu bar.

❑ Choose the style you created and the Navigate Icon Properties dialog box will open, as shown in the figure below.

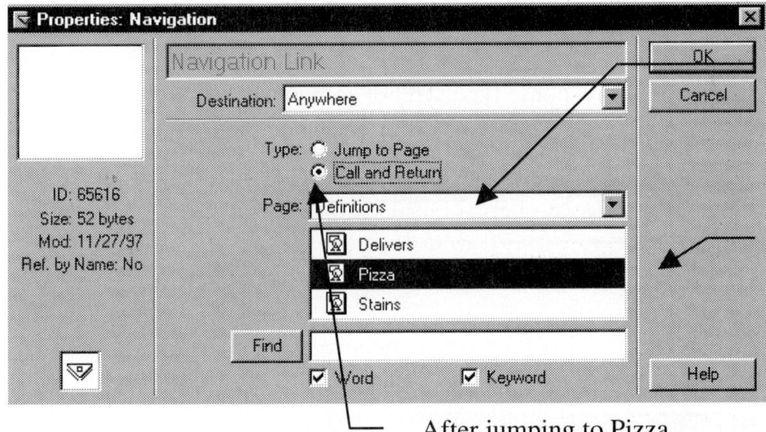

Select the framework containing the page to which to jump.

Choose the page to which to jump.

After jumping to Pizza, return to original location.

❑ Choose the Pizza page within the Definitions framework.
❑ Select the Call and Return option.
❑ Push OK.
❑ Do the same for all other occurrences of the word "pizza" in Pizza, Delivers and Stains. Now let's test our work.
❑ Run your project.
❑ Look at the Pizza page.

❏ Move the cursor over the word "Pizza" and it changes to a hand.

❏ Click on the word Pizza.

❏ Your dialog box comes up, but it won't go away! Here's one solution: Add a button that appears after the dialog box displays. The button will exit the framework (Definitions) and return to the original screen. Some of the work will be done inside the Definitions framework so we need to open it now.

❏ Double-click on the Definitions framework icon.

❏ Delete the Gray Navigation Panel icon since we're going to use our own button.

❏ Delete all the navigate icons except Go Back. Change its name to Return.

❏ Your framework should now look this way:

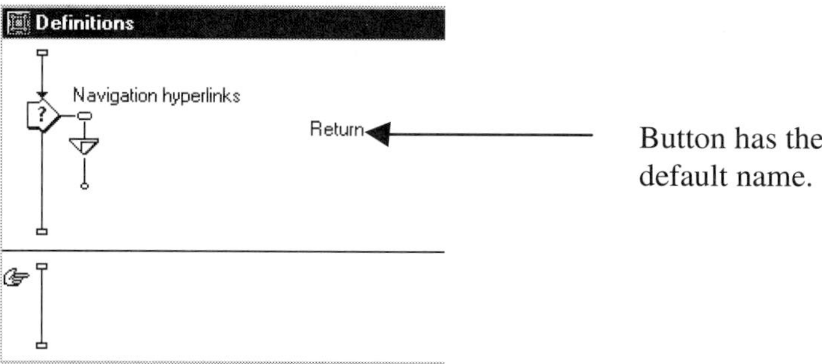

Button has the
default name.

❏ We will create a button, which when clicked, returns to the calling page.

❏ Double-click the response type symbol associated with Return.

❏ Choose a Windows 95 button-style, as shown in the figure below.

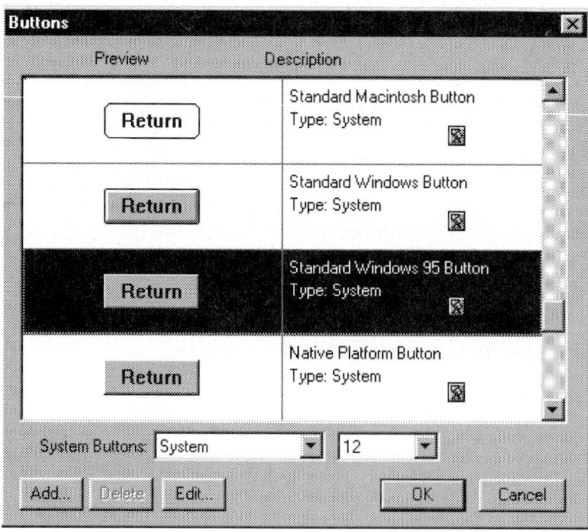

❏ Set the button response properties as in the figure that follows.

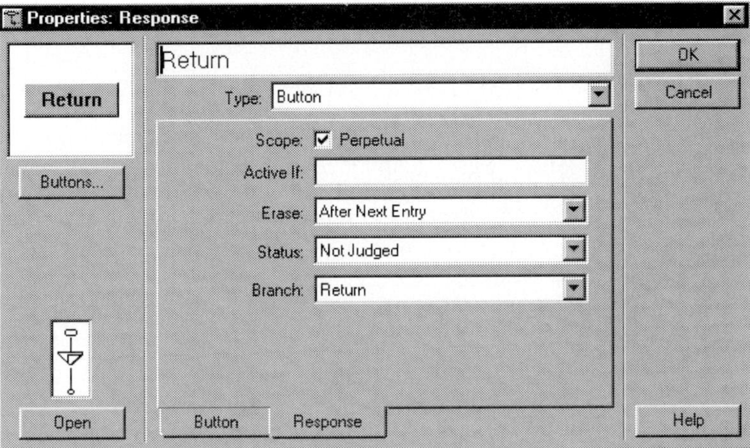

❏ Push the OK button to close the dialog box.
❏ Position the button near the lower right corner (recall this can be done at any time by pausing the title—use the pause button in the Control Panel—while the title is running).
❏ Double-click the navigate icon, and set its properties as in the figure that follows.

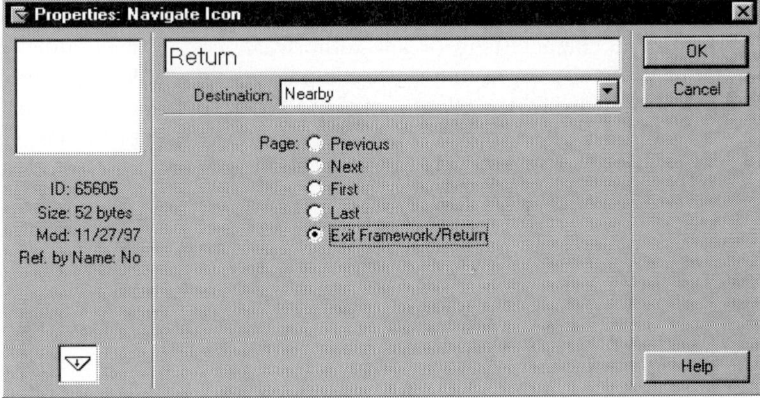

❏ Push the OK button.
❏ Run your project and click on the word "pizza". After the dialog box is displayed, push the return button and the box will be erased and control returned to your screen.
❏ Finish up by applying the hot-text style to every occurrence of the words "Stain" and "Delivers."

❏ Save your work.

Indicating a Link

Before leaving this topic, go back and look at the Items framework. Open Pizza. Notice the small triangle attached to the Show Pizza display icon. It indicates a link can be found within that icon. See Figure 9.4 for an example.

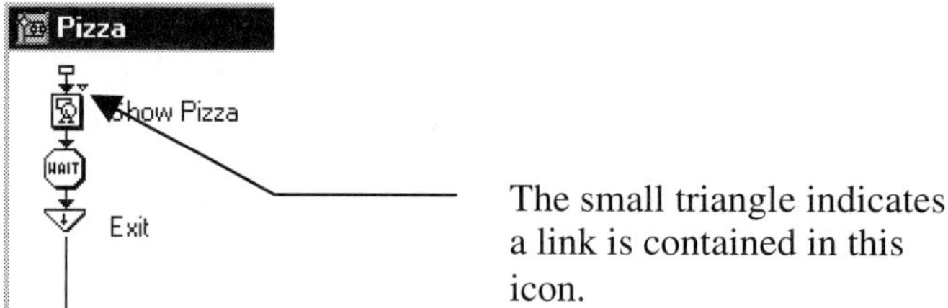

Figure 9.4. Indicating a Link.

KEYWORDS

A *keyword* describes some characteristic of an Authorware icon. For example, if several icons contained digital video clips, you might use the phrase " digital-video" as a keyword. You would then tell Authorware which pages contained such clips and provide the user the ability to search for that phrase. Authorware would then present the list of icons where digital video clips could be found and accessed. Whereas the Find/Search navigate icon is used to locate text, keywords provide the ability to search for any medium.

Creating Keywords

The process for assigning keywords to an icon is:

1. Select the icon.
2. Choose <u>M</u>odify><u>I</u>con><u>K</u>eywords.
3. The Keywords dialog box shown in Figure 9.5 opens.

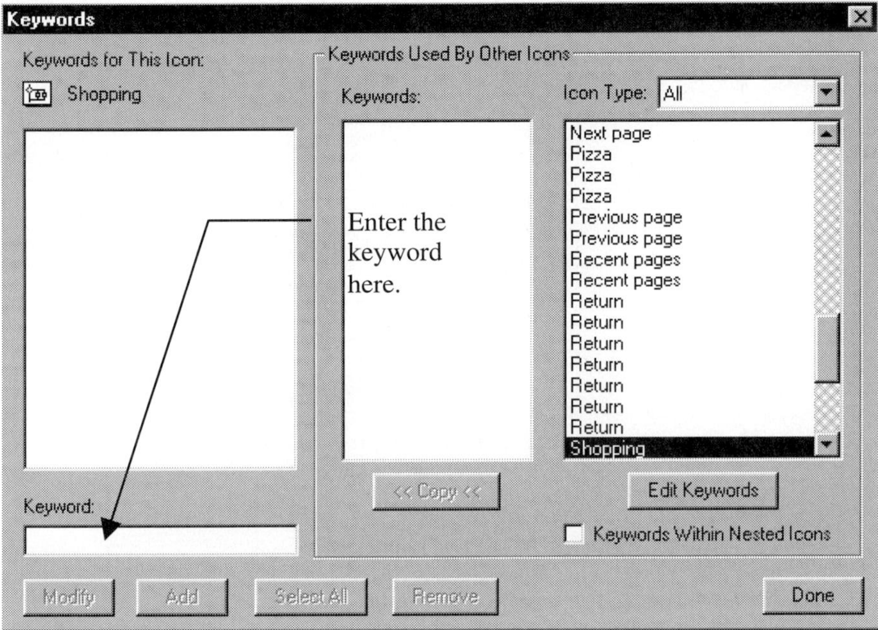

Figure 9.5. The Keywords Dialog Box. Use it to define the keyword(s) associated with an icon.

4. Enter the keyword in the field near the lower left corner of the Keyword dialog box.

5. A keyword cannot be a phrase: no spaces are permitted.

6. Push the Add button to add the word to the list.

The Keywords dialog box can be used to edit, delete or copy keywords from other icons. Once the keyword has been added, use a Find/Search navigate icon to locate it.

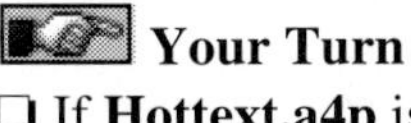 **Your Turn**

❑ If **Hottext.a4p** isn't open, do so now.

❑ Open the Glossary map icon on the main flowline.

❑ Single-click the Stains icon to select it.

❑ Choose the menu item <u>M</u>odify><u>I</u>con><u>K</u>eywords.

❑ Enter "car" in the Keyword field near the lower left corner.

❑ Push the Add button.

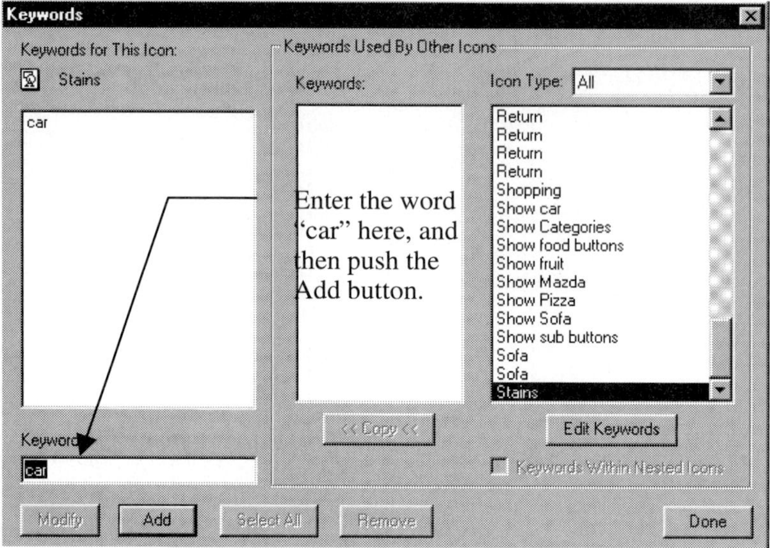

❑ Close the Keyword dialog box by pushing the Done button.

❑ Drag a navigate icon to the main flowline. Don't bother naming it because Authorware will call it Find when we're finished defining it.

❑ Double-click the navigate icon and choose the Search destination-type from the Navigate Icon Properties dialog box shown in the figure below.

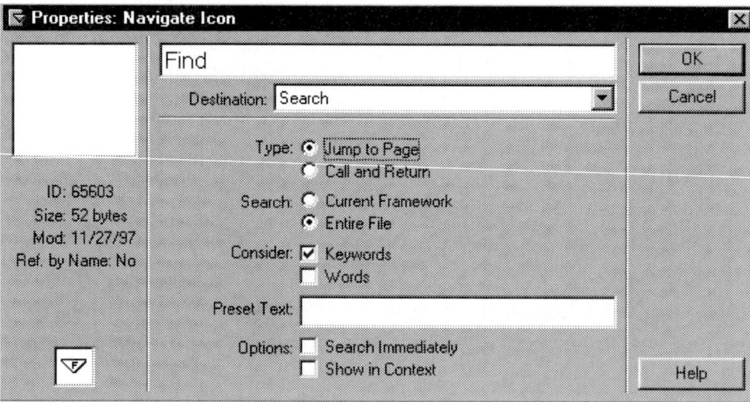

❑ Check only the Keywords box.

❑ Select Search Entire file.

❑ Drag the start icon to just before your Find navigate icon.

❑ Run from flag.

❑ Enter "car" as the keyword.

❏ The Stains icon should be highlighted.

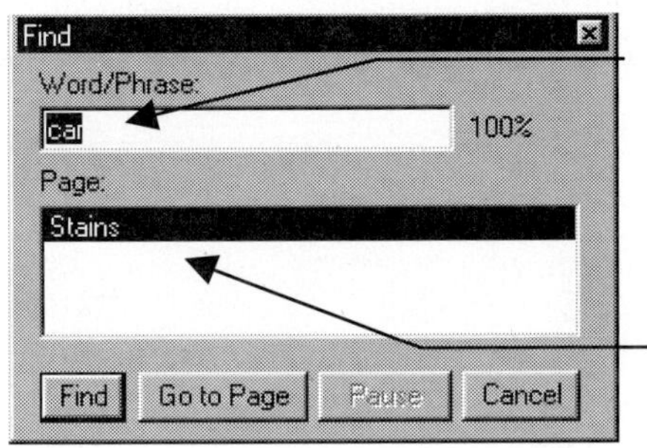

Search argument
is entered here.

The names of pages con-
taining the search argu-
ment will display here.

❏ Save your work.

Notice that the keyword was associated with an icon that was a page attached to a framework. This is a requirement.

Keywords provide the author a means for users to search on items other than text. The ability to filter and search is an essential benefit of interactive multimedia and should be included wherever appropriate.

SUMMARY

Framework and navigate icons provide the power to provide search mechanisms, informa- tion filtration based on keywords, and hypertext and hyperlinking. These abilities are what set interactive multimedia apart from traditional linear learning experiences.

Hypertext is the ability to link a word or phrase to other text, while hyperlinking in- creases the linking destination to include media other than text: sound, video clips, map icons containing several media, and so on. When a title includes such media, it is helpful if you assign keywords that provide keyword descriptions that can be used to filter the pages to just those of interest to the user.

Study Exercises

9.1 Create a new piece named C9Q1. It should do the following:

Present 5 pages, one each for these multimedia types: text, sound, graphics, video, and animation.

Each page should describe the type of multimedia as a verbal definition.

Include at least one hyperlink on each page.

Provide the ability to search on keywords.

9.2 Create a new piece named C9Q2. Find at least ten images from the Internet, or clip-art on your computer. The clip art should be from three categories. Put each piece of clip art on a separate "page" Assign one of three keywords to each icon — the keyword being the category to which the corresponding image belongs. Let the user search on any of the three keywords and your piece should display the associated images.

Multimedia

Authorware supports most of the popular multimedia types: digital sound, digital video, animation, and video overlay. These media can be started, paused, resumed, or stopped under program control. This chapter looks at the theory behind each medium and how to control each of them.

At the conclusion of the chapter, you will be able to:

- Define the two types of sounds, and when each should be used.
- Describe how sound is digitized.
- State the recording parameters for Pulse Code Modulation and the impact each has on sound quality.
- State the popular digital sound formats, and identify which are supported by Authorware.
- Use the sound icon to include sound into your titles.

- List and describe the components required for digital movies.
- Define codec.
- List the two most popular codecs.
- State the digital movie storage formats used by Macintosh and Windows computers.
- Use Authorware variables to control digital movie playing.

We begin with sound and its two types: wave and MIDI.

SOUND

Sound consists of continuous waves, called *analog signals*, which must be converted into a digital binary stream so it can be stored and played back on a computer. There are two categories of such sound: wave, or digital sound, and MIDI (Musical Instrument Digital Interface).

Wave Files

Wave files can contain any sound: voice, music or sound effects. The analog sound is converted to a digital stream by means of an *analog to digital convert*er (ADC). Analog signals have two properties that are useful for us: amplitude and frequency. The amplitude is the height of the wave, while frequency is the number of times the signal, or wave, repeats itself in a second. Frequency is measured in *Hertz (Hz).*

Humans can create sounds up to about 10,000 Hz (10kHz), the telephone transmits sounds to 4 kHz, effectively clipping all frequencies above 4,000 Hertz, while a good music system can create sounds ranging from 20 to 20,000 Hertz.

Sample Rate

The sound is *sampled* many times per second. Each sample is converted into a number, usually a binary number consisting of all 1's and 0's, and the complete process is called *pulse code modulation* (PCM). Each sample measures the amplitude of the sound at a point in time. The sample rate is also measured in Hertz. A common question is how often should we sample? The answer is "twice the highest frequency of the sound." This means for telephone clarity, sample at about an 8 kHz rate; for voice, about 20 kHz, and for music, at 40 kHz (or higher — 44 kHz is often used).

Sample Size

Each time the amplitude is determined, it is translated into a value. If we decide 256 different amplitudes are sufficient, we can store each value in a single byte, which is sometimes called an *8-bit sample*. A much richer sound results when the sample size is 16 bits.

File Size Considerations Consider the consequences of different values for the sample rate and size. Assume we want one minute of two channel (stereo) music-quality sound. This would require 2 bytes per sample * 44,000 samples per second * 60 seconds per minute * 2 channels = 10,560,000 bytes!

Try using 8-bit 22 kHz monophonic for most sounds. Like all rules of thumb, however, try it and make any adjustments you deem necessary. In fact, many prefer 16-bit 11 kHz for sounds.

Sound Formats

On a Windows computer, the resulting file is stored in a format known as a wave, or .WAV. You may also see another format, called .PCM. On a Macintosh, the standard format is AIFF, or .AIF. (Audio Interchange File Format). Both Macintosh and Windows formats are similar, differing mainly in some heading information found at the beginning of the files.

An Introduction to MIDI

MIDI, Musical Instrument Digital Interface, is a standard format for storing and playing music. There are several standards, which can cause playback problems. The primary benefit of MIDI is the greatly reduced storage requirement. Authorware cannot directly play MIDI files, which usually have a .MID file extension. The Windows version can call the *media control interface* (MCI) via a calculation icon to issue a standard Windows call. This was introduced in chapter 7. Additionally, there are Xtras which, if installed with Authorware, can also be used to play MIDI files.

THE SOUND ICON

Use the sound icon to add digital sound to your Authorware piece. On Windows machines, you can use .WAV, .PCM, and .AIF files, while on Macintoshes, you can use the same file-types, plus SoundEdit sounds.

You cannot directly use MIDI files with Authorware. Files with MID extensions can be played by making calls to the operating system. Windows refers to the operating system calls as the MCI (media control interface). Recall you can always digitize MIDI files, so if you don't want to learn the MCI syntax, you can resort to this method. There is also an Xtra called MidXtra that you can use.

Once a sound is loaded, you can control its timing, speed, when it should start and stop and how many times it should play. However, you cannot edit the sound in Authorware. All options are set within the Sound Icon Properties dialog box shown in Figures 10.1 and 10.2.

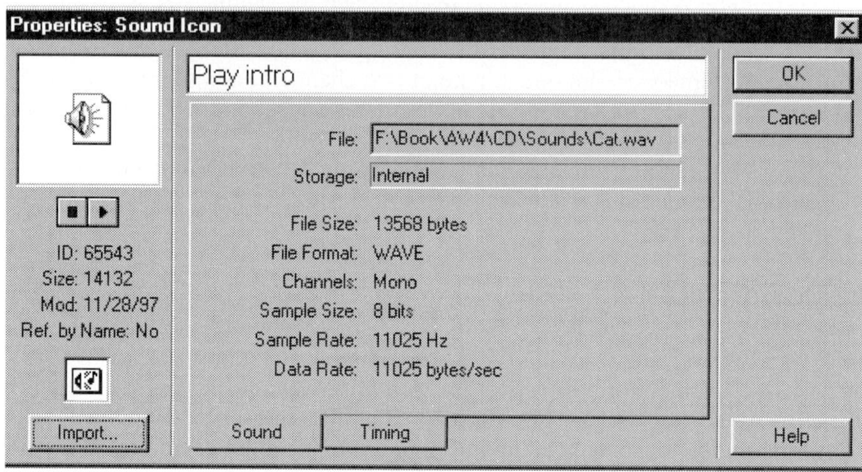

Figure 10.1. The Sound Icon Sound Properties Dialog Box. This is displayed after you select a sound file to play.

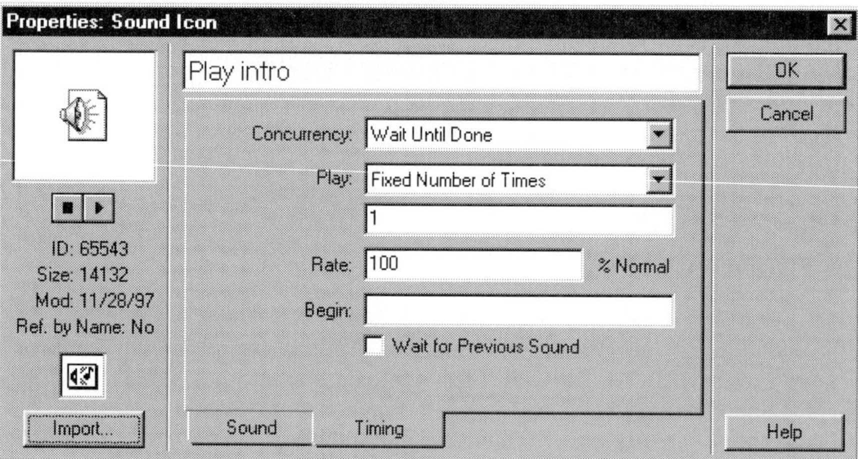

Figure 10.2. The Sound Icon Timing Properties Dialog Box.

Don't use the complete sound clip while building your project. A 30-second file at the beginning of your project will be played every time you run from that point. Not only does this reduce valuable time, but also you will find yourself hating the sound because of its repeated playing!

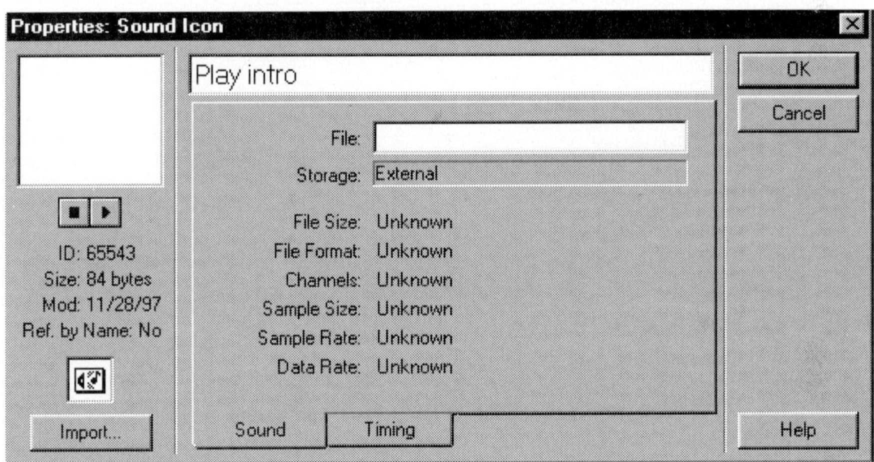

> **Your Turn**
> ❏ Open a new file.
> ❏ Drag a sound icon to the flowline.
> ❏ Double-click it.
> ❏ The first dialog box you see is Sound tab of the Sound Icon Properties dialog box, which is shown in Figure 10.3.
> ❏ Choose any sound by pushing the Import button, and then selecting a drive, a directory, and a file.

Figure 10.3. The Load Sound Dialog Box. To view this, double-click the sound icon.

The Authorware CD-ROM comes with two directories or folders containing music and sound effects. The Clpmedia\Sounds folder has 30 sounds you can associate with buttons and other interactive controls.

The Clpmedia\Sound_fx folder contains about 14 categories, each with many items. For example, the People category contains sound effects for laughing, walking, skipping, clapping, and six others.

Authorware can work with 8- or 16-bit samples and sample rates of 11 or 22 kHz.

The Sound Icon Properties Dialog Box

The Timing tab of the Sound Icon Properties dialog box we saw in Figure 10.2 and reproduced in Figure 10.4, displays once a sound is loaded.

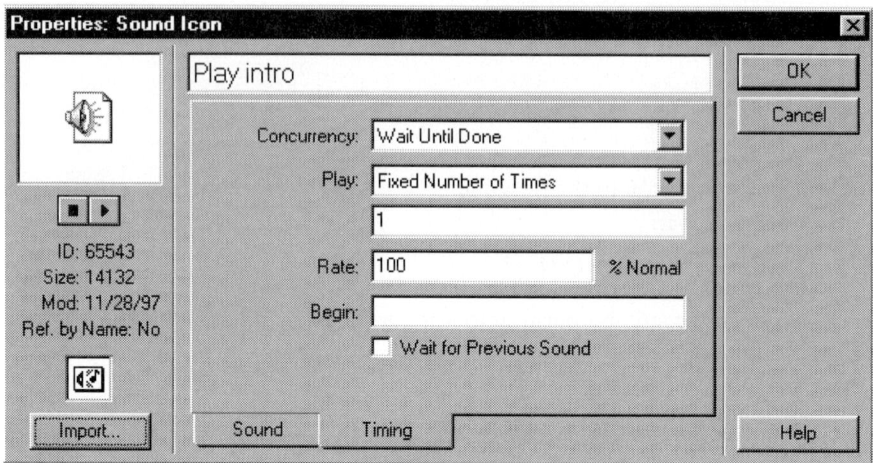

Figure 10.4. The Sound Options Dialog Box.

Concurrency Options

First, you see the familiar concurrency options in the drop-down list: Wait Until Done, Concurrent, and Perpetual. Because we've discussed these before, let's examine the options that pertain to sound, beginning with the Play field.

Play

Use this field to determine whether Authorware should play the sound a predetermined number of times, or until a condition, specified in the Begin field, is true. If you decide to play the sound a fixed number of times, enter that value in the play option field you see directly below the Play field.

Rate

Enter the desired playback speed in this field. Be careful here, because strange sounds can result from using values that significantly vary from 100! Another caution: Some sound cards cannot play back sounds at rates other than 100%.

Begin: Specifying When to Start Playing

Use the Begin text box to specify under what conditions to begin playing the sound. Authorware only plays the sound if the condition or variable entered here is true. For example, to play the sound on Fridays you would enter `DayName="Friday"` into the text box.

`DayName` is an Authorware variable. This says check the value of `DayName`. If it equals "Friday" then the statement is true and the associated sound should play.

Another example might be to play a recorded message when the user has missed a certain number of quiz questions. There is a variable called `PercentWrong`, which tracks what percentage of all judged responses was incorrect. You might use this variable and enter `PercentWrong>=30`. Now the sound plays only when the percentage wrong is 30 or higher.

Wait for Previous Sound

This option makes Authorware complete previous sounds before playing this one. As an example, you might use this to ensure the user finishes listening to a narration, even if he or she has moved to a new page.

Control Buttons

Use the Play button ▶ to listen to the sound. Once the sound is loaded and the dialog box closed, you can listen to it by clicking on its icon, using the right mouse button. To stop the sound, push the Stop button ■.

The Sound Tab

Once a sound is loaded, the Sound tab displays the information in Figure 10.5.

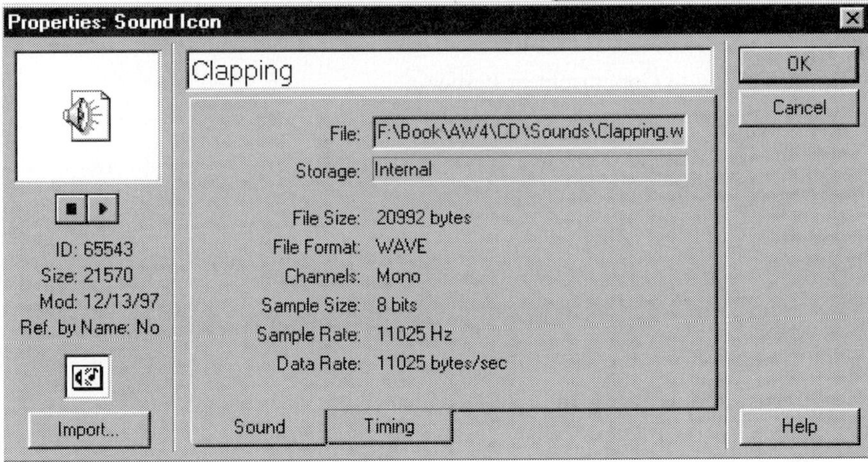

Figure 10.5. The Sound Tab.

The type and size of the file are displayed first. Next to be displayed is whether the sound is stereo or mono (one channel). The next two fields display the sample size and rate. The final field shows the playback rate in bytes per second.

You can view this information without opening the sound icon, if you right-mouse click on any sound icon.

Simultaneously Playing Multiple Digital Audio Files

A common question is: "Can I have several digital audio clips playing at once?" The answer is no. Windows can play a single WAV file at a time. If you need to play multiple sounds, use the mixer that comes with Windows and combine the two files into one digital (WAV) file. If one of the files is for music, consider using a MIDI format for it, because Windows can play a MIDI and a WAV at the same time.

Synchronizing Sound and Other Media

A common Authorware application synchronizes sound with graphics or other media. You might show an image along with an associated sound. When the sound stops, you want to display another image. One way to accomplish this is to use digital movies, such as AVI or QuickTime.

Using programs such as Adobe Premiere, you can add a voice-over or WAV file to a still image. Another method is to use Authorware's `SyncPoint` variable.

To synchronize such a piece, follow the steps below.

1. Add the sound icon to the flowline
2. Set its Timing to Concurrent or Perpetual.
3. Add a calculation icon with the content `SyncPoint(1)`.
4. Add the first display or digital movie icon.
5. Import or link the content for the icon.
6. Add a calculation to the icon (Ctrl+=).
7. Add the statement `SyncWait(n)`, where n represents seconds.
8. Continue to add digital movie or display icons with `SyncWait` statements attached.

A statement such as `SyncWait(3)`, which might be attached to a display or digital movie icon, means to wait three seconds after the timer begins to display the content of the associated icon.

Sample File Figure 10.6 shows the flowline for **Sync.a4p**, which is in the Chapter10 folder on the CD-ROM. Run the piece and watch how the images display 4, 8, and 12 seconds after the music begins. The wait button appears just as the music stops. Hers is how we built the piece.

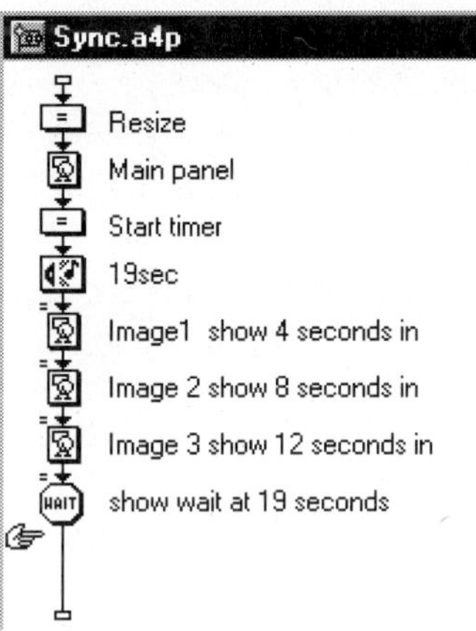

Figure 10.6. The Flowline for **Sync.a4p**.

The Resize calculation icon resizes the Presentation window by using the expression `ResizeWindow(320,240)`. The Main panel shows a background. The Start Timer calculation icon contains the statement that initializes the timer: `SyncPoint(1)`. The sound icon uses the 19secs.wav file from the Sounds folder on the CD-ROM. The Timing was set to Concurrent, so control could flow to he next icon, the first display icon.

The Image1 display icon imports a graphic named **M_Sax.bmp** from the Images\Misc folder on the CD-ROM. The attached calculation contains the statement `SyncWait(4)`. This means show the image in the display icon starting four seconds after the timer starts. The next display imports **P1.bmp** from the Chapter10\Images folder, and starts the display 8 seconds from the start of the sound file. This is because we attached the calculation `SyncWait(8)` to the icon. The last icon starts the display 12 seconds in, while the Wait button appears at the end of the sound, 19 seconds after it started.

Using MIDI

We saw examples of how to play MIDI in Chapter 7. Recall this requires use of a UCD named A4WMME, which can be found on the Authorware CD-ROM. To play MIDI:

1. Drag a calculation icon to the flowline.
2. Load the A4WMME UCD by choosing Window>Functions, and then choosing A4WMME.
3. Select the desired function from the dialog box that opens, as shown below:

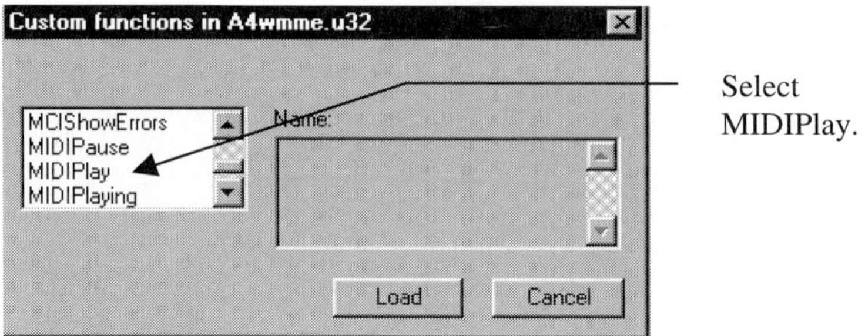

Select
MIDIPlay.

4. Push the Load button.

5. Add the MIDIPlay statement to a calculation icon. For example, to play a
   MIDI named ROW, enter:

```
A:= MIDIPlay("ROW.MID",100, FALSE)
```

Recall, a value of FALSE triggers the Concurrent timing, while TRUE triggers Wait
Until Done.

Table 10.1 summarizes the MIDI-related functions you can use in your Authorware
project.

Table 10.1 MIDI functions. They are found in the A4WMME UCD file.

MIDI Function	Purpose
MIDIPause()	Returns a zero if Authorware was able to pause the MIDI playback.
MIDIPlay(Filename,Tempo,Flag)	Returns a zero if Authorware was able to play specified file at indicated tempo. If Flag =TRUE, timing is Wait until done, otherwise Concurrent.
MIDIPlaying()	Returns zero if a MIDI is currently playing.
MIDIPlaySegment(fileName, tempo, fromSeconds, forSeconds, Flag)	Returns a zero if Authorware was able to play specified MIDI segment at specified tempo.
MIDIResume()	Returns a zero if Authorware was able to resume playing of a paused MIDI file.
MIDIStop()	Returns a zero if Authorware was able to stop a playing MIDI file.

There is a companion set of functions for controlling WAV files. You can find them as
we did above: Use the Window>Function menu and select the A4WMME UCD. Look for
WAV functions. You will find that except for the Tempo parameter, the functions are the
same as those for MIDI.

Next, let's examine digital video.

AN INTRODUCTION TO DIGITAL VIDEO

Digital video requires these components:

- Video capture hardware
- Video capture software
- Storage format
- Compression
- Decompression
- Playback

Video Capture

Capturing video requires special function interface boards. They cost from a few hundred to several thousand dollars. Typically, they do not support either sound capture or playback to video recorders, although the more expensive ones do. Separate sound and video playback boards are typically required.

To capture video you attach the composite video cable (sometimes called monitor out or video out or RCA out) from your camcorder, VCR, or television to the video-in jack on the capture card.

Some video capture cards support S-Video cables, which produce clearer results. If your video source and capture card supports S-Video, you should use it.

Once the video cables are connected, then connect the left and right audio-out cables from your video device to the left and right inputs on your sound card. If your video capture card supports audio-in, use these ports instead of those on your sound card.

Once these steps are complete, you must run some video capture software, such as Microsoft's VidCap, or Adobe Premier.

The video capture software will prompt you for some common parameters:

- Frame rate
- Image size
- Compression algorithm
- Number of colors
- Storage format

Frame Rate

Video and movie images are actually a series of still images, displayed at such a rate as to make them appear to be moving: A property called ***persistence of vision***. To show video at the same rate as the US standard (called NTSC) you need 30 frames per second (fps). The European standard (PAL) for TV is 25 fps. Film requires 24 frames per second. Any of these standards place extreme demands on the computer's ability to deliver the frames fast enough. Therefore, many developers use 15 fps as a guideline.

Image Size

A typical screen size is 640 by 480 picture elements (pixels). Higher resolutions include 800 by 600 and 1024 by 768. To store one second of video at 15 fps with 256 colors (one byte per pixel) per frame would demand:

$640 * 480 * 15 = 4,608,000$ bytes!

Because of this huge storage requirement, we typically capture in a ¼ screen window: 160 by 120 pixels.

Compression Algorithms and Codecs

Even if we reduce the size of each image and reduce the frame rate, the storage requirement is still abundant. Therefore, several mathematical algorithms have been developed to compress that data as it is stored. To play back the compressed video, the images must be decompressed. The software that does this is called a ***codec***. Common codecs include Super-Mach's Cinepak and Intel's Indeo.

Number of Colors

Showing color as accurately as the human eye sees requires that we capture about 16.7 million colors. To do this, each pixel must be represented by 3 bytes, or 24 bits. The number of bits per pixel is called the ***color depth***. If we want this kind of color reproduction the calculation we derived above for the required bytes per second of captured video must be multiplied by three, for a total of about 14MB/second!

A general rule of thumb used by multimedia developers is to always capture and store at the highest resolution. In this case, provided you have the storage necessary and a fast enough computer, capture at 30 fps, 16.7 million colors, and half or full frame. The resolution can and probably must be reduced for playback purposes: Not every user has the computer power to play back digital video at the parameters just cited.

If you decide the extra storage is justifiable, you must consider the color depth available on the prospective user's playback platform. If the computer that's playing back the video can only show 256 colors (called an 8-bit color depth) undesirable colors may result when the computer attempts to translate the 16.7 million to 256 colors. Therefore, most multimedia developers reduce color depth for playback to 256 colors.

Storage Format

The digital video must be presented in a standard format. The actual storage of the video can differ, and probably does due to the use of codecs. There are three standard formats: Microsoft's Audio Video Interleaved (AVI.), Apple's QuickTime, and MPEG (Motion Picture Experts Group). Authorware can playback any of the three formats.

The computer on which Authorware is running must also be able to playback these formats using special drivers (DLLs for Windows users). These drivers can be downloaded from Microsoft and Apple for the first two, and there are many software MPEG players available over the Internet. The next generation of digital video will use an enhanced form of MPEG called MPEG II, which promises at least full-screen, 30 fps high-quality video. IBM has a laptop capable of playing MPEG II movies. The Digital Versatile Disks (DVDs) and most satellite systems also use this compression method.

Digital Video and Authorware

We have seen several examples of using digital video with Authorware. This section reexamines the steps and restrictions for playing digital movies within Authorware.

Supported Formats

The Windows version of Authorware supports these digital video formats:

- AVI
- QuickTime for Windows
- MPEG (Certain formats only)
- In addition, Authorware can import Director movies, plus animations that use Autodesk formats FLC and FLI (sometimes pronounced "flicks" and "flies").

There are a few cross-platform issues to keep in mind. First, the Macintosh version won't play AVI movies, so these must be externally converted to QuickTime before using them on a Mac. Next, QuickTime movies must be "flattened" to play on a Windows machine. To play a Director movie on the Mac, convert it to a projector. To use a Director or QuickTime movie on a "packaged" Authorware title, be sure to add the additional "driver" files.

Loading a Digital Movie

To load a digital movie:
- Drag a movie icon to the flowline.

- Open the icon.

- Select the movie by first choosing the Movie tab located within the Movie Icon Properties dialog box that opens, and which is shown in Figure 10.7.

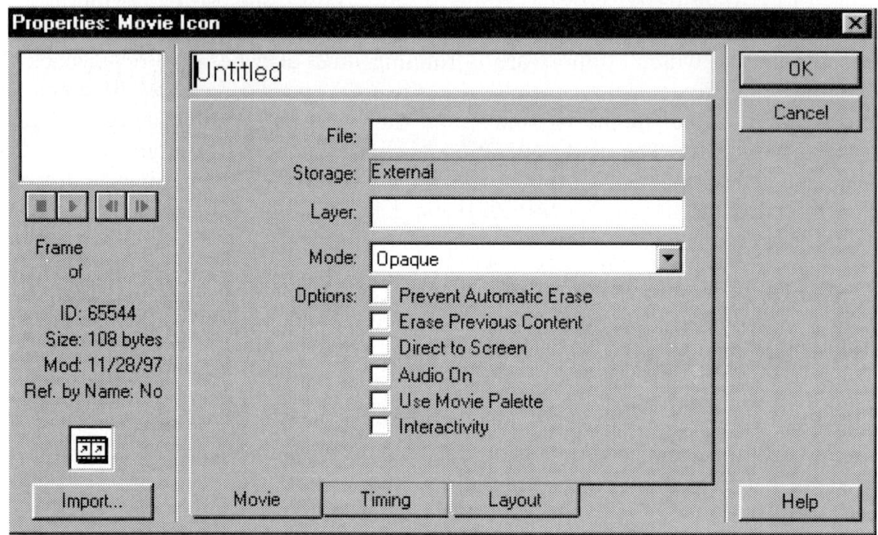

Figure 10.7. The Movie Tab of the Movie Properties Dialog Box. It opens when you double-click an empty Movie icon. Use it to select the file.

- The Import which file dialog box, shown in Figure 10.8, opens.

- Use that dialog box to select the drive, folder and movie file. If the Show Preview box is selected, you will see the first frame of the movie as a thumbnail on the right side of the dialog box.

Figure 10.8. The Import Which File Dialog Box. Use it to select the digital movie (MOV, AVI).

- Push the Import button.
- The Movie Icon Properties dialog box, which is shown in Figure 10.9, re-opens with the Movie tab being the active tab.

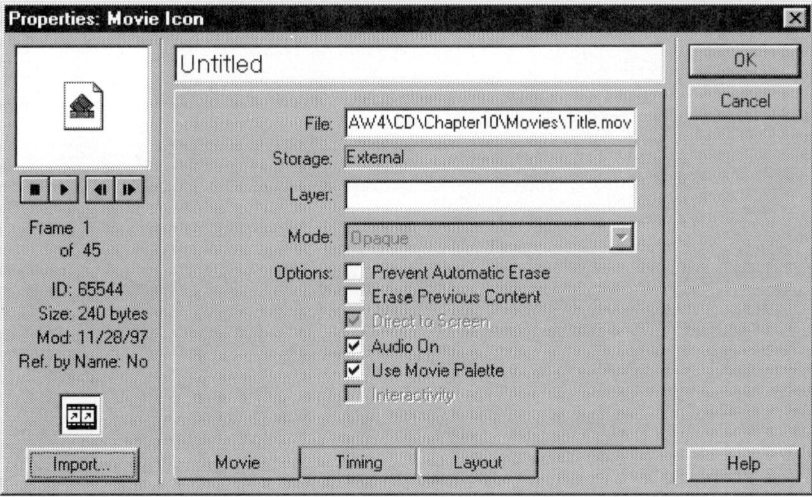

Figure 10.9. The Movie Properties Dialog Box, after a Movie is Selected.

The Movie Icon Properties Dialog Box

Let's examine the dialog box in Figure 10.9. The initial set of control buttons enable the developer to preview the movie.

Previewing the movie: The Control Buttons To see what the movie will look like, push the Play button. To advance one frame at a time, push the Step Forward button. If you need to back up a frame, push the Step Backward button. Finally, to stop the preview, push the Stop button.

Options The Prevent Automatic Erasure option prevents the movie from being erased by any means other than an erase icon. If you choose Erase Previous Content, all content still in the Presentation window will be erased before the movie begins. To make sure the movie play on top of all other content, check the Direct to Screen option. The Audio on options, if checked, will force Authorware to play the audio track, if present. If the option is dimmed, it means the movie format doesn't support sound (FLC, FLI, for example). To use the color palette of the digital movie, rather than Authorware's, check the Use Movie Palette checkbox. This isn't supported for all movie formats. Finally, if the movie is a Director movie, and you want to retain any inherent interactivity, check the Interactivity check box.

Setting Transparency: The Mode Option Provided you are using FLC/FLI or PICs movies, you have the same mode controls you do for other graphical objects. Read the appropriate section in the graphics /display chapter to review the use of opaque, matted, transparent and inverse. For PICs movies, white is the transparent color. For FLC/FLI files, it's black.

Push the Timing tab to reveal Figure 10.10.

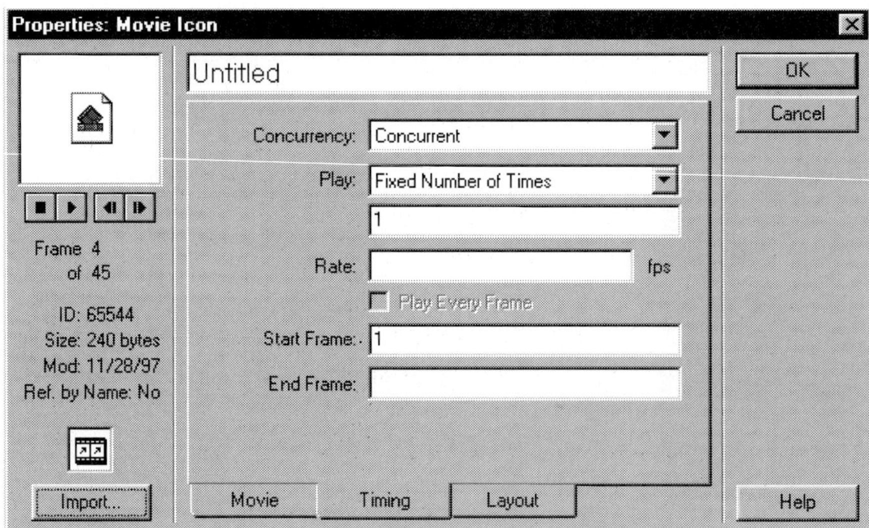

Figure 10.10. The Timing Tab for Movie Icons.

Changing the Concurrency The usual set of the Concurrency options are available: Concurrent, Play Until Done and Perpetual.

Setting the Number of Times the Movie Repeats: The Play Option Some of the options here depend on which format you've chosen. The first three: repeatedly, a fixed number of times, and while a condition is true (Until True), are always available. A useful Until True value is to enter `MouseDown` as the condition. This way, a digital movie will play until the user clicks the mouse button.

For QuickTime movies, choose Controller Play to display a controller while the movie is playing. The movie begins playing immediately. If you choose Controller Pause, the user will also see the controller, but the movie will be paused until the play button is pushed.

If a FLC/FLI or PIC file is chosen, you can then select the "Only while in Motion" option. Use the Only While in Motion option to show only the first frame of the movie. Authorware will then play the complete movie only while it's being moved within a motion icon, or being dragged by the user.

The Times per Cycle option has the same effect as Only While in Motion, but the value entered limits how many times the movie plays during each repetition. As an example, you might have a path animation (path to End) that defines the path the earth will take, and a movie of the earth that "spins" as it rotates and follows the path you defined. The Times/Cycle per second would specify how many times to play the movie of the earth spinning per time around the path.

If the file is a QuickTime movie, you can choose the Under User Control option. This permits you to create interactions that start, stop, pause, and restart digital movies.

Playing a clip: The Start and End Frame Fields Instead of playing the entire movie, if you specify the start and stop frame numbers, only the portion between those frames will play. You can even play a movie backwards by entering the lower frame number in the End Frame field.

The Current Frame field shows the current frame number of the clip that is playing.

Rate Some digital movie formats permit you to change their playback rate. Enter the desired rate or a variable whose value represents the desired rate. When the computer cannot keep up with the rate you specify, some frames will be skipped, unless you check the Play Every Frame option. In this case, Authorware does the best it can to keep up.

Play Every Frame If you choose this option, Authorware will play the frames as fast as it can. While different computers will show different results, you should generally check this option because it yields the best results.

FLCs, FLIs and PICs

If the digital movie consists of Autodesk FLCs or FLIs, or Apple's PIC formats, you can play your digital movie behind other objects. This means we might add hot spots to our movies.

Sample File Open and run the **Layers.a4p** file in the Chapter10 folder on the CD-ROM. Move the mouse over the two trees and watch the messages appear and disappear. Let's see how this was constructed.

Your Turn

❑ Start a new piece.

❑ Add a digital movie icon, and import the **TallTrees3.flc** file from the Chapter10\Movies folder on the CD-ROM.

❑ Set its layer at five.

❑ Add an interaction with two hot spots named Potted and Normal.

❑ Your flowline should look like the figure that follows.

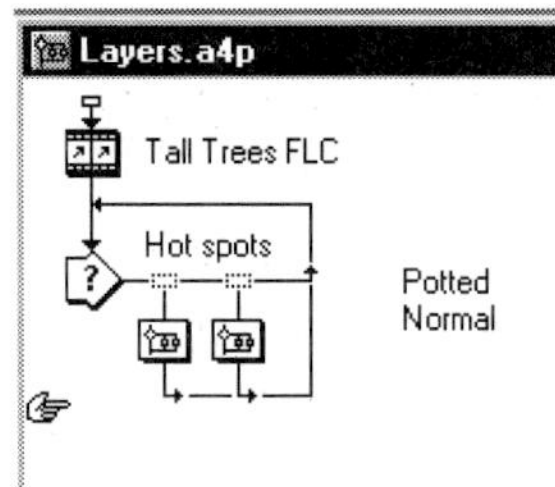

❑ Open the Potted map and add a display, also named Potted.

❑ Size the hot spot so it covers the potted plant. Set its interactivity to Cursor in Area and specify the hand cursor, as indicated by the figure below.

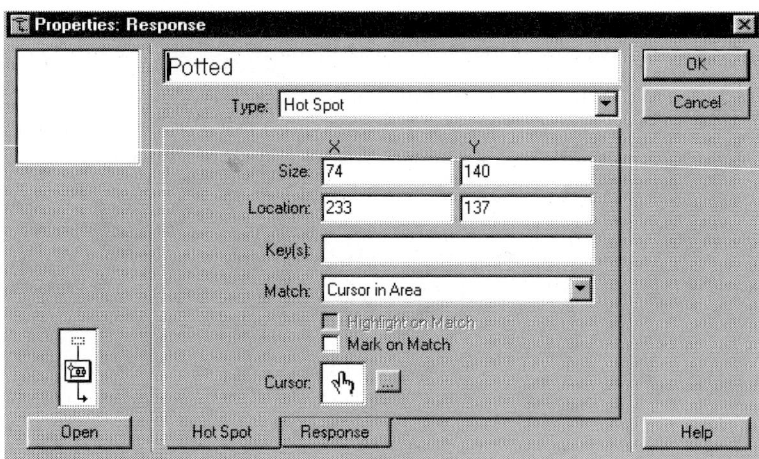

❑ Push the Response tab and set the Erase option to Before Next Entry, and Branch to Try Again.

❏ Run your piece and move the mouse over the potted plant. When the empty display icon opens, enter in yellow transparent text "My potted Plant".

❏ Do the same for the other plant. Use suitable text for when the mouse is over the other tree. If you are stumped, look at how we set up the Normal hot spot and associated map icon.

❏ Save your work as **Layers.a4p.**

Digital Movie Functions

By using functions in calculation icons, digital movie control can be made quite precise. Table 10.2 names the variables and their purpose.

Table 10.2. Digital Movie Functions

Function	Purpose
MediaPlaying	Determines if a specific digital movie is playing.
MediaPosition	Determines current frame.
Media Rate	Determines the frame rate.
MediaLength	Returns the total number of frames.

Table 10.3. Digital Movie Functions

MediaPlay	Plays a specified file.
MediaPause	Pause a movie.
GetMovieInstance	Identifies an AVI or QuickTime movie.
MediaSeek	Specifies the position

Using Variables and Functions to Start, Pause and Restart Quick Time Movies

Following are a few examples of these variables and functions. Variables we don't cover in detail here are described more fully in Authorware's help facility. This first example uses two of the functions listed above to start, pause, and then resume the playing of a Quick-Time movie.

 **Sample File** To preview what we're going to do, open the **VidCtrl.a4p** file in the Chapter10 folder on the CD-ROM. Run the piece and use the buttons to Start, Pause and Restart the video clip.

Your Turn

❏ Start a new project.

❏ Drag a map icon to the end of the main flowline and call it video control.

❑ Open the map.

❑ Add a display icon, and name it Tmplate9.bmp. Import the file having that name from the Images folder on the CD-ROM. Scale the Y dimension to 94.8%, so it just fills the Presentation window.

❑ Drag a movie icon after the Tmplate9.bmp icon.

❑ Name it Tall Trees movie.

❑ Your flowline should look this way:

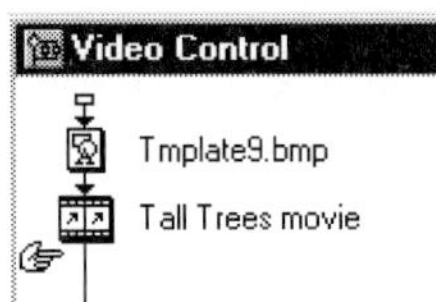

❑ Load the TallTrees2 QuickTime movie from the Chapter10\Movies folder on your CD-ROM.

❑ Set its Timing parameters like those in the figure that follows.

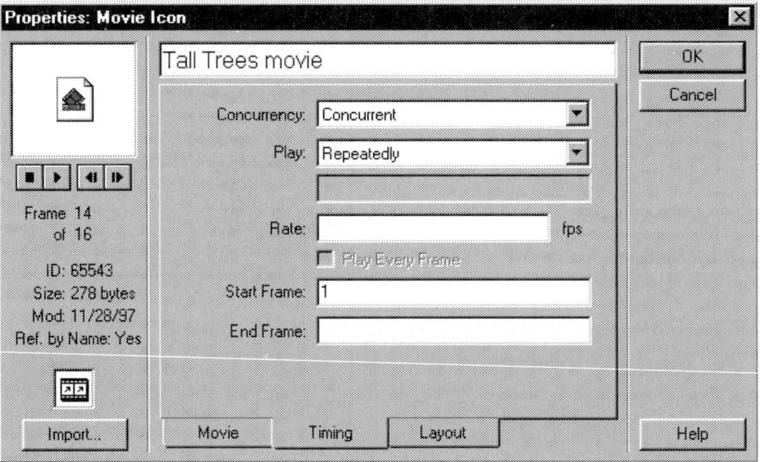

❑ Drag an interaction icon to the flowline, call it Control, and add three hot spots: Start, Pause, and Restart. Your flowline should now look like the figure below.

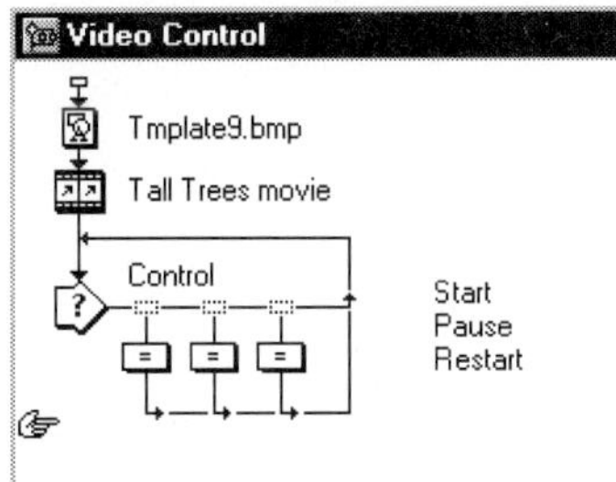

❏ Move and size the hot spots so they covers the play, stop and fast forward buttons on the template, as indicated by the figure below.

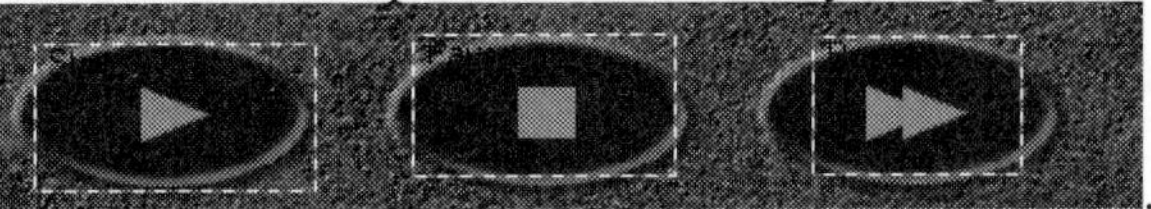

❏ In the Start calculation icon, enter this:

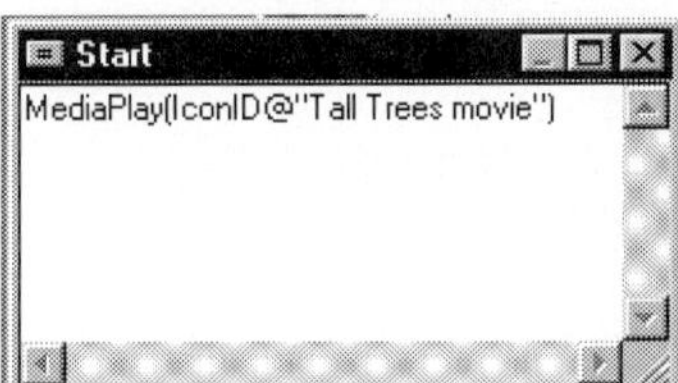

❏ Notice the *IconID*. This will be used in all three variables. The general syntax of the variable is: `MediaPlay(IconID@"icon name")`

❏ Inside the Pause calculation icon, enter the line you see in Figure 10.8.

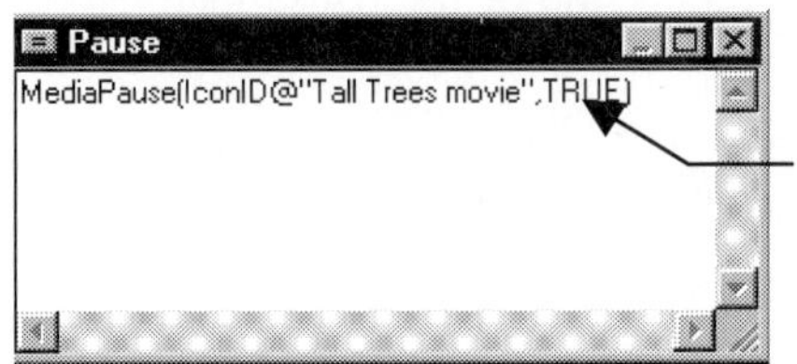

TRUE means
pause the video.

❏ The syntax is: `MediaPause (IconID@"icon name",flag)`. If the value of flag is TRUE, the video is paused. If FALSE, it's resumed.

❏ Finally, the statement inside the restart button is shown in the figure below.

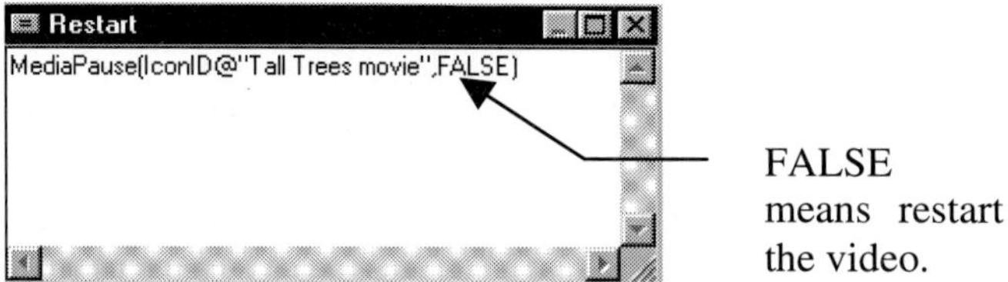

FALSE
means restart
the video.

❏ This is the same syntax that we saw for the pause calculate icon, except the value of flag is now FALSE.
❏ Run your piece. While the "movie" is playing, push your Pause button.
❏ Push the Restart button.
❏ When the clip is finished, push the start button again.
❏ Save your work as **Vidctrl.a4p.**

Other variables use formats similar to the ones we just used.

Jumping to a Particular Frame To go to the seventh frame of the movie, you'd enter this:

```
MediaSeek(IconID@"Tall Trees movie",7)
```

Determining the Current Frame Number To determine the frame where the pause stopped the clip, enter:

```
a:=MediaPosition(IconID@"Tall Trees movie")
```

You could place this in a separate calculation icon and execute it immediately after pushing the pause button, or place it on the second line of the pause icon. Notice that the letter "a" is a numeric variable.

SUMMARY

Sound and digital movies (Authorware includes animations created by other applications in this category) are important components of a multimedia title. They add interest and often improve comprehension. Using the sound and digital movie icons, such objects can be easily included in your title.

Digital sound can be 8-bit or 16-bit, and sampled at 8K, 22K, or 44KHertz rates. Always record at the highest resolution, but resample to accommodate your playback platform. Authorware can import several popular Windows sound formats and the familiar Mac AIFF sound files. MIDI files must be digitized or, on Windows versions, use the MCI calls to control the MIDI device.

Authorware's digital video icon accommodates both digitized video and externally created animations. Digital video can consume huge amounts of storage so be careful when selecting color depth and image size and frame rates. If the movie is FLC/FLI or PICs, many more options are available than if the file is AVI or QuickTime. One benefit to using QuickTime is the additional control over the movies through the use of variables.

Study Exercises

10.1 Create a new project named C10Q1. It should display a digital movie inside a panel. Provide three buttons as in the example in the chapter. Add this feature: If the movie is not playing when the stop button is pushed, a dialog box pop-up saying: "No movie Playing".

10.2 Create a new project named C10Q2 that displays buttons to play, stop, and eject a CD. It should check to see if a CD is mounted when the Play button is pushed. If a CD isn't present, display, then erase a suitable dialog box. (Hint: Look in the A4WMME UCD for CD-ROM related functions).

10.3 Modify VidCtrl so the hot spots display suitable captions as the cursor rolls over the three buttons.

Managing the Complex Title

*T*here many ways we might define a complex project: Titles used by several users, titles that permit one to stop then restart at a later time without losing one's place, titles that measure user performance, and titles that are so large we need to separate them into two or more. Once the title is complete, it must be packaged so users with or without Authorware can run it. This chapter examines ways to manage such environments.

At the conclusion of the chapter, you will be able to:

- Write to external files.
- Read from external files.
- Parse data contained in external files.
- Store user data.
- Monitor user progress.

- Use built-in quick start templates.

- Connect with, and manipulate data in, ODBC databases.

When interactive multimedia titles are used to train or educate, it is useful for the user to be able to stop the session, then restart later at the point where he or she left off. This requires that we track users by name, then save the status of the Authorware title when they exit. Let's begin by seeing how to track who is using the title.

DETERMINING THE USER'S NAME

To save a user's progress we are going to use the `UserName` variable we used in the AskID map icon that you've seen before. Recall we loaded this from a model on your CD-ROM.

 **Sample File** The model has been included in a project named **AskID.a4p**, which is in the Chaptr11 folder on your CD-ROM. Note the name is Chaptr11 and not Chapter11.

Your Turn
❑ Open Chapter1\AskID.
❑ Open the UserID map.
❑ Open the "*" calculation icon.
❑ You should see the contents of Figure 11.1.

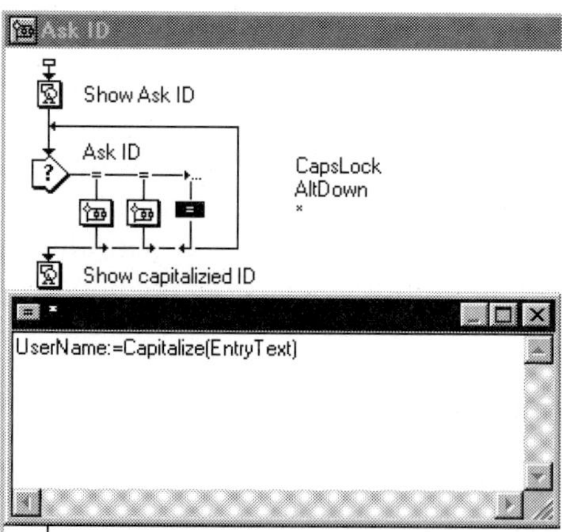

Figure 11.1. The **Askid.a4p** Flowline and The Contents of the Calculation Icon that Requests the User's Name.

We will use the user's name as part of a file we are going to create or to which to save. The `UserName` variable simply carries the user's name. You can extract the first name by using the `FirstName` function in a calculation icon, once the `UserName` variable has been assigned a value. If Authorware detects a comma in the `UserName` variable, it assumes the first name follows the comma and stores that value. It also automatically capitalizes the first letter.

To use the variable in a display, simply enclose `FirstName` inside braces, like this:

```
Welcome, {FirstName}
```

This will personalize the project by showing the user's first name. Remember, however, you must first assign `UserName` a value as `FirstName` extracts its value from this variable.

The `Capitalize` function capitalizes the first letter of each word in the string that makes up the function's argument. In this case, the first and last names will be capitalized, if the user enters both.

Now we know the user's name. Because we are going to use this variable as part of a file name, we have to be careful about the value of `UserName`. We might tell users to limit the login to just their last name, or to login with an account name, they were previously given.

Next, we need to provide the ability for the user to stop the title and resume later. The way to accomplish this is to save the current status of the program in a file. We must be able to associate the file with the user so when the title is resumed, Authorware knows exactly where *this* user left off. We do this through external files.

CREATING EXTERNAL FILES

To save user information you must transfer the data from the variables that contain the data you want to save to an external file. To save data for each user, create a separate file for each user. The function that saves the data is `WriteExtFile`. Each time `WriteExtFile` is executed, it overwrites what was there previously. To add to what was there, use `AppendExtFile`. Let's see how these functions work.

The WriteExtFile Function

The format for writing to a file is:

```
WriteExtFile ("filename",string)
```

Where *filename* is the name for the platform on which the title is running, and *string* is a variable that contains the data to be saved.

If you want to write out a series of variables, separate each with a return character. Use the variable `Return` to do this. To For example, to write out the user's name and percent correct, you might enter:

```
WriteExtFile(UserName,UserName^Return^¬
" You had "^PercentCorrect^ "% Correct"^Return)
```

The concatenation character (^) was used to combine several strings. We used the line continuation character (¬) to break the long line into several. To add the line continuation character, use Alt+Return, while keying into a calculation icon. When the contents of this file are read back into an Authorware piece, you might see:

Mary Smith
You had 90 % Correct

To properly use this function you must:

- Specify a value for filename.
- Specify the folder/path where you want to save the data.
- Provide a value for the string variable.
- Execute the function.
- Check for error codes.

Specify a Valid Filename

How can we create a naming convention that stores user data in a file that we can later associate with that user? One way would be to ask the user to login, save the user's name and use it as the filename. We will adopt this methodology but must caution you about file naming conventions: Do not use commas, a potential problem for the method we used earlier to determine a user's name.

What we'll do is use `UserName` as the filename. Recall this variable stores the name of the current user.

To save the user's name, we could enter this inside a calculation icon:

```
WriteExtFile(UserName,UserName)
```

Suppose the user's name was JONES. This would create a file called JONES and save a single value in it: JONES. The file is a pure ASCII file, readable by any word processor.

To specify an extension to the file name, use the caret "^" after the file name. For example, to write to a .TXT file, use:

```
WriteExtFile(UserName^."TXT",UserName)
```

Specifying a Folder or Directory

Authorware maintains a variable, `FileLocation`, whose value represents the default folder for storing files. Actually, it's the name of the folder where the current file was found.

On Windows computers, when Authorware is installed on drive C: a typical value for `FileLocation` might be:

"C:\TEMP"

If you use the <u>W</u>indow><u>V</u>ariables menu choice you can see the default value for `FileLocation`. Figure 11.2 shows the Variables dialog box.

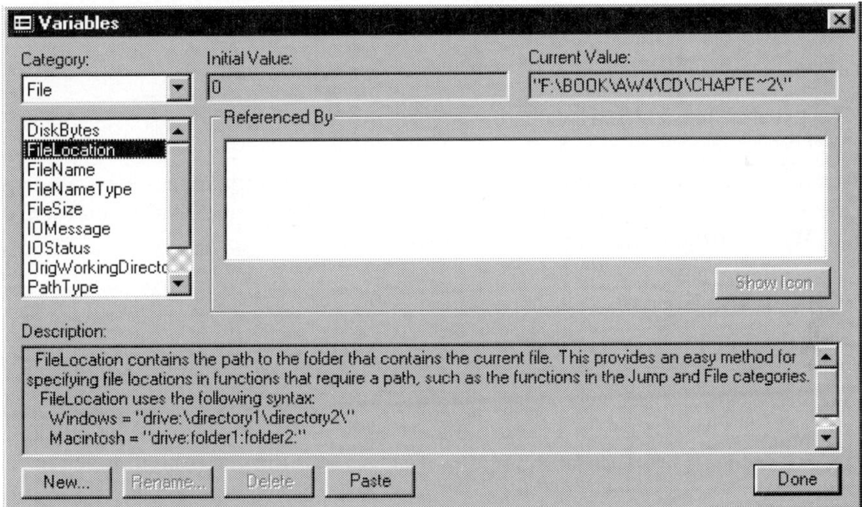

Figure 11.2. The Variables Dialog Box. Use it to determine the current value of `File-Location`.

To use this in a calculation icon, you might enter:

```
WriteExtFile (FileLocation^UserName,UserName)
```

or

```
WriteExtFile(FileLocation^"Myfile.txt",UserName)
```

There is another folder you can use: the ***user records folder***. On Windows computers, Authorware uses the A4w_data folder. The complete (default) value for the user records folder on Windows systems where Authorware is installed on drive C: is:

"C:\WINDOWS\A4w_data"

The variable that contains the user records directory is `RecordsLocation`. To use this folder instead of the `FileLocation` folder, substitute `RecordsLocation` for `FileLocation` in the previous examples.

Provide a Value for the String Field

You must assign a value to the field name that appears at the end of the `WriteExtFile` function. In our examples in this section, as the user logged in, the "string" `UserName` was assigned a value. We then used that name in the function. As we saw earlier, you can use the concatenation character to combine several strings. Use the `Return` variable to separate the strings. Instead of using the `Return` variable, you can substitute the literal "\r". Finally, if the line becomes too long, use the continuation character to break it up into several shorter ones.

Execute the Function

The function cannot be embedded in expressions, instead it must be a separate line. In addition, the function cannot be used if your piece is going to run on the Internet, or over an intranet. We'll return to these matters in Chapter 12.

Check for Errors

After executing the `WriteExtFile` function, Authorware will return values for two system variables, `IOStatus`, and `IOMessage`.

If the value of `IOStatus` is zero, the `IOMessage` variable will be blank. Otherwise, `IOStatus` contains an error number, and `IOMessage` the corresponding error message.

The AppendExtFile Function

If you perform the steps we discussed earlier to write out the user's name and wanted to now add that user's score to the same file, you'd use the `AppendExtFile` function. This adds data to an existing file.

The format for appending to a file is:

```
AppendExtFile ("filename","string")
```

Where *filename* and *string* are defined as they were for the `WriteExtFile` function.

Now that we have the ability to store a user's name and score, let's see how to use them in an Authorware project.

READING AND PARSING DATA FROM FILES

Use the `ReadExtFile` function to read the contents of a file. If the file contains several variables, use the `GetLine` function to parse the data. Let's look at how this is done.

Reading External File Data: The ReadExtFile Function

To read the contents of an external file, use this syntax:

```
string:=ReadExtFile ("filename")
```

For example, to read the user's name from a **Myfile.TXT** file enter the following inside a calculation icon:

```
MYNAME:=ReadExtFile (FileLocation^"Myfile.TXT")
```

The entire content of the file are now stored in the variable. If there are several fields within the file's contents (name plus score, for example), we must *parse* it to separate the fields from each other.

Parsing File Data: The GetLine Function

All the data in an external file is read into a single variable using the syntax from above. In most cases that file contained values for several variables, not just one. To extract the individual variables from the file you first read the file's contents into a single variable as we did above. Then use the `GetLine` function to parse the data.

If you open the <u>W</u>indow menu, then <u>V</u>ariables, and you choose `GetLine,` you can see the syntax for the function:

```
String:=GetLine("string", n)
```

Where:
String is the variable that stores the complete contents of the file, which was used as the target in the ReadExtFile function
n is the relative variable number, n = 1,2,… LastVariableIndex
For example to extract the third variable from a file called MYDAT use these lines within a calculation icon:

```
MYSTRING:=ReadExtFile ("MYDAT")
Variable 3:=GetLine(MYSTRING,3)
```

Sample File Open the **Filedemo.a4p** file in the Chaptr11 folder and run the piece. Open the flowline to reveal Figure 11.3.

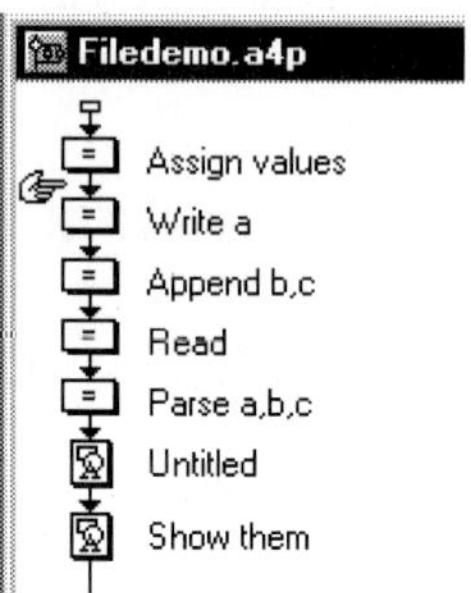

Figure 11.3 The **Filedemo.a4p** Flowline. It creates a file, then appends data to it. It has a flaw, however.

The Assign Values icon assigns the variable a the value 1, b the value 2 and c the value 3. The Write a Calculation icon executes the `WriteExtFile` function, writing out the value of a. The Append b,c icon adds (appends) b and c values to a. The Read Calculation icons opens the file, then reads from it, storing the contents in a variable, `mystring`. Finally, The Parse a,b,c icon parses the three values from the string. The display icon shows these values:

       A was 123
       B was
       C was

The problem is: The `AppendExtFile` function simply adds to the existing file. This means that 3 was added after 2, which was added after 1, so the entire file content looked like this "123". We need to add a separator, called a ***delimiter***, after each variable is written.

Sample File The **Fixdemo.a4p** project in your Chaptr11 folder contains the remedy to our problem.

To fix the problem, we added an `AppendExtFile` line like this to the Write a icon:

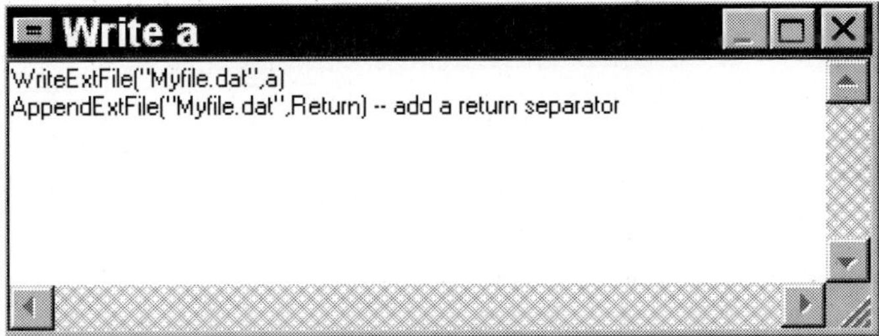

We did the same for the Append b, c icon, as shown in the figure that follows.

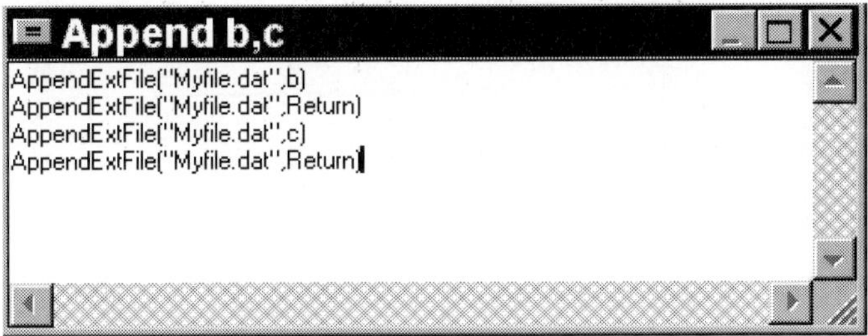

Now you have the ability to:

- Determine the user's name.
- Write multiple values to a single file.
- Read data from a file.
- Parse the data into individual variables.

SAVING USER DATA

We would like the users to be able to quit, then later resume where they left off. This requires that we store data about the present status of the title in locations that can be tied to a
given user. This is done through the user records facility.

A user records file is created when Resume is chosen in the Modify>File>Properties
dialog box. The dialog box is reproduced for you in Figure 11.4.

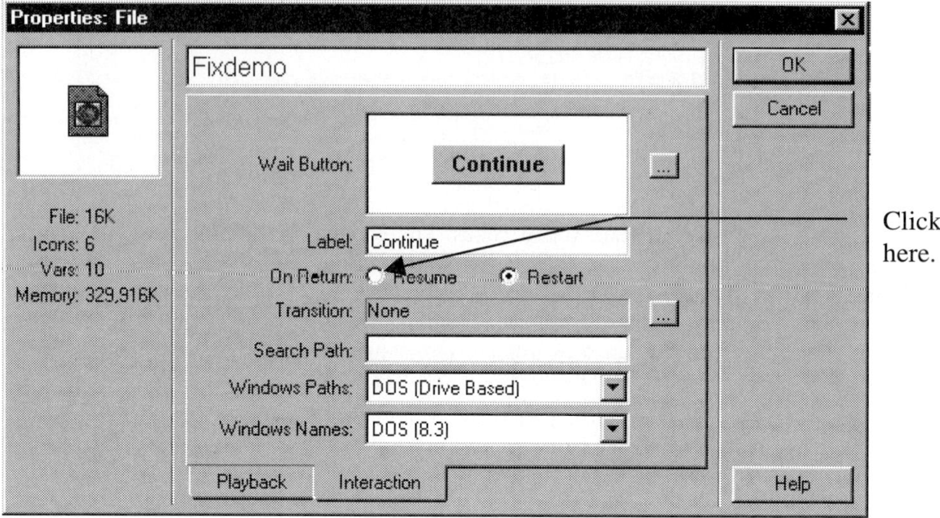

Figure 11.4. Specifying Resume/Restart Parameters.

When users exit the project, then start it up at a later time, they will find themselves at the place they were when they exited. Each project is assigned a filename containing the first eight letters of the title plus the extension .REC. On Windows platforms the file is created in A4W_DATA, which is a folder within the Windows directory. There is obviously a problem if several users run the same project because there is only one .REC file. We must be able to distinguish Barbara's .REC file from John's.

To manage several users, place each user's records file in a separate folder or directory.

CREATING NEW FOLDERS OR DIRECTORIES

The function that creates folders is:

```
CreateFolder ("FolderName")
```

Authorware creates the folder within the current records folder. As an example, use this syntax inside a calculation icon, to create a folder called JOHN in the user records folder.

```
CreateFolder(RecordsLocation ^ "JOHN")
```

The default location would be in C:\Windows\A4W_DATA

This is useful for saving user data in a folder having the same name as the file. For example, we might store John's information in John, Dawn's in Dawn, and so on.

RESUMING WHERE THE USER LEFT OFF

We need to distinguish between those cases where there is a single user, and those cases where several users might use the title and wish to resume.

In the simplest case, use `String:=ResumeFile("filename")`

When multiple users can use the title, you need to first store all the current information about the title in separate records folders. Then, after the user logs in, retrieve the file for that user, which will be inside a folder in the `RecordsLocation` folder.

The command would be:

```
String:=ResumeFile (RecordsLocation^UserName)
```

This assumes the user has logged on before and a .REC file exists in A4W_DATA\UserName. If the user is new, then you must omit the `ResumeFile` command.

MONITORING USER PROGRESS

Authorware maintains several variables that track user progress. Use the `PercentCorrect` and PercentWrong to display the percentage of all judged responses that were correct or incorrect.

To display the absolute number of correct and incorrect responses use `TotalCorrect` and `TotalWrong` in a display icon.

Use `FirstTryCorrect` and `FirstTryWrong` to display how many questions were correctly or incorrectly, respectively, answered on the first try.

Use `JudgedInteractions` to display the number of judged interactions. Finally, to see the number of responses given by users to all judged interactions, use `JudgedResponses`.

For example, at the end of the title, you might include a summary like the following:

```
Congratulations {UserName} Out of {JudgedResponses} re-
sponses to {JudgedInteractions} questions, you answered
{PercentCorrect} % correct
```

SWITCHING AMONG AUTHORWARE TITLES

There are some benefits from splitting your title up into multiple pieces. To run a title from another, use `JumpFile` or `JumpFileReturn` functions. The icon that does this is called a *router*.

A router can be a menu or a series buttons, which when pushed, jumps to another file or jumps then returns when the other title executes the Quit function.

You might set up an interaction icon with several buttons, each button tied to a calculation icon that contains the following:

```
JumpFileReturnFileName")
```

Where ("each calculation icon has a different value for "`FileName`". If the `JumpFileReturn` function is used, control will return to the interaction icon after the called title exits.

RUNNING OTHER APPLICATIONS

A related function permits you to run another application then optionally return. To do this use the following command inside a calculation icon:

```
JumpOutReturn("Application","FileToOpen)
```

Application is the name of the program to run. *FileToOpen* is an optional parameter that specifies which document to open when the application is launched.

For example, to open a Word document called CHAP11.DOC, use:

```
JumpOutReturn ("WORD",CHAP11.DOC)
```

USING TEMPLATES

Many of the functionality described in the chapter has been provided for you through a set of templates. We'll look at the educational logon template in this section. By default, it asks for a user name and identification number, followed by a password. If the user hasn't logged on before, a password confirmation is requested and a record set up for the new user. Finally, it jumps to a packaged file having a name you specify in one of the icons. Let's see how we might use the template.

Start by creating a new file. Then choose Insert>Paste Model. If the Quick Start models don't show up you need to first execute the Insert>Load Model command, and then point

Authorware to the Authorware4\Template\Education folder. Select any of the models. When the Paste Model window opens, select QS:LogOn-Edu, as indicated by Figure 11.5.

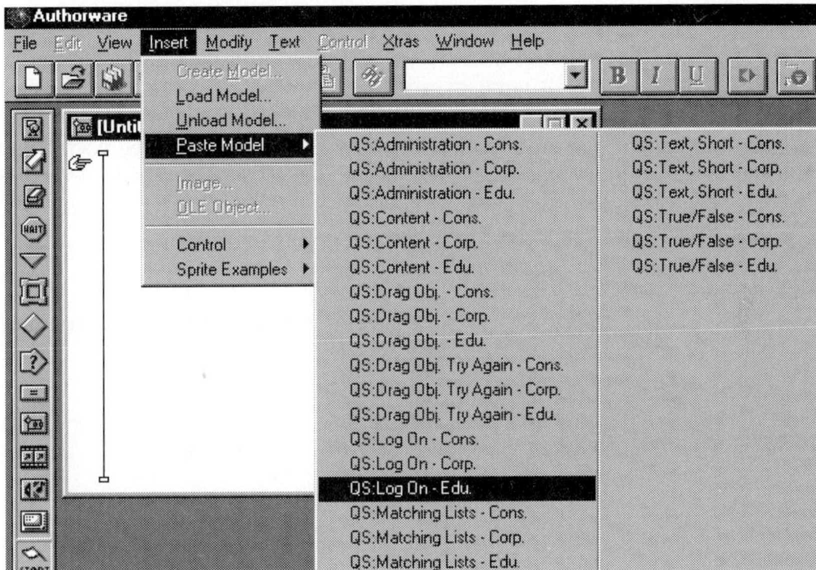

Figure 11.5. The Insert Paste Model Window. Select the LogOn model for education.

Open the Setup map icon. You will see the flowline shown in Figure 11.6.

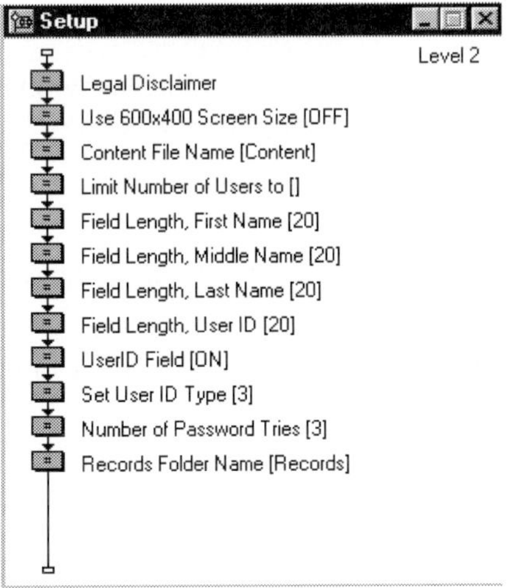

Figure 11.6. The Setup Map. Each icon contains a customizable property.

Change any parameter by opening the associated icon and editing the current content.

Use 600 x 400 Screen Size Turn this feature on if you plan to deliver the piece over the Internet. (See Chapter 12 for more details.) Enter `ResizeWindow(600, 400)` to resize the Presentation window.

Content File Name Open this calculation icon and enter the name of the packaged piece to which to jump. It is necessary that the piece you are jumping to be packaged (See Chapter 3 for a review of packaging). The packaged piece and the one you are creating through the template should be in the same folder. Otherwise, you'll have to provide the complete path to the packaged piece. For example, to jump to the **FixDemo.a4r** (the packaged version) piece we saw earlier in this chapter, change the Content File Name calculation icon to that of Figure 11.7. As you can see, we set `LO_JumpFileName` to the name of the packaged piece to which to jump.

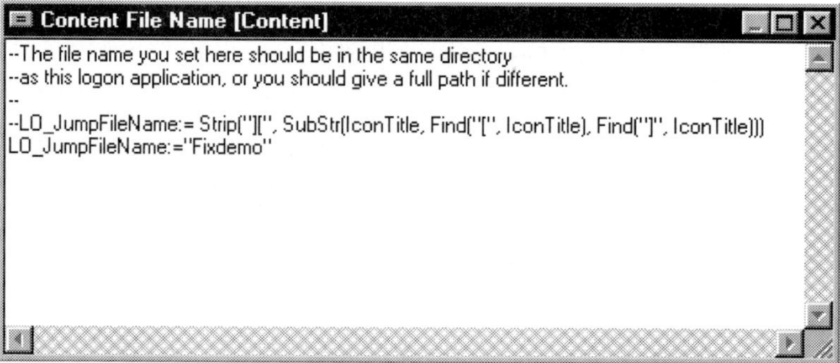

Figure 11.7. A Typical Content File Name Icon. Set LO_JumpFileName to the name of the packaged piece to which to jump.

Limit Number of Users The parameter value set within this icon limits how many users can run the piece. The default is an unlimited number.

Field Lengths Use the next four icons to establish upper limits of field lengths for first name, middle name, last name, and user ID.

Set User ID Type This icon sets the type of ID to Social Security Number (1), telephone number (2), or an employee number (3).

Number of Password Tries Use this icon to set a limit on how many incorrect password attempts to permit.

Records Folder Name This icon provides the name of the folder in which to store user records. The default is in the same folder as the piece.

 **Your Turn**

❏ Package the **Fixdemo.a4p** piece.

❑ Start a new piece and paste the logon model we just examined.

❑ Edit the Content File Name icon, so that `LO_JumpFileName` has the value "Fixdemo"

❑ Save your piece as **Student.a4p**.

❑ Run the piece, and enter your information.

❑ Control should pass to the **Fixdemo.a4p** piece.

❑ Run the **Student.a4p** piece again.

❑ This time, enter an invalid password.

❑ Quit the piece.

Other Templates

You might find QS:Content-Edu model useful as well. It is used to set up a complete educational training session, complete with objectives, quizzes, glossaries, a notepad for taking notes, and a help facility. To use this template, you'll have to create several text files containing objectives and glossary terms. Use the QS:Quiz_Edu model to create the quizzes.

DATABASE CONNECTIVITY

While you can use the built-in Authorware commands to read and write to external files, in most cases it's preferable if you communicate with organizational databases created with Database Management Systems such as Oracle, Sybase, Informix, and Microsoft Access.

To communicate with such databases, you need to use ODBC, Open Database Connectivity drivers. Each vendor has a set of ODBC drivers to enable other applications, such as Authorware, to store data, edit it, or retrieve data from the database. The common language used to manipulate data for all these databases is ***Structured Query Language*** (SQL) (pronounced SEQUEL).

To use Authorware to access an ODBC complaint database you need the ODBC UCD and the suitable driver.

The ODBC UCD

The ODBC UCD contains facilities to

- Open a new session with an ODBC database (ODBCOpen).

- Execute an SQL command (ODBCExecute).

- Close an ODBC session (ODBCClose).

The Chaptr11 folder on the CD-ROM contains an Access 97 database called Students.mdb. It contains two tables, Student, and Major. The Student column names are: SS#, StudentID, LastName, MiddleName, FirstName, andMajID. The Major table has two columns: MajID and Description. The MajID column relates the Student and Major tables. For example, a code of Student MajID value of "MM" references the Multimedia major in the Major table.

Specifying the Database Source

To access the database from within Authorware, we must first specify the data source. To do so, follow the steps that follow.

- Open the Windows 95 Control Panel.

- Double-click the 32-bit ODBC applet, which is shown in the figure below.

- The ODBC Data Source Administrator opens, as shown in Figure 11.8.

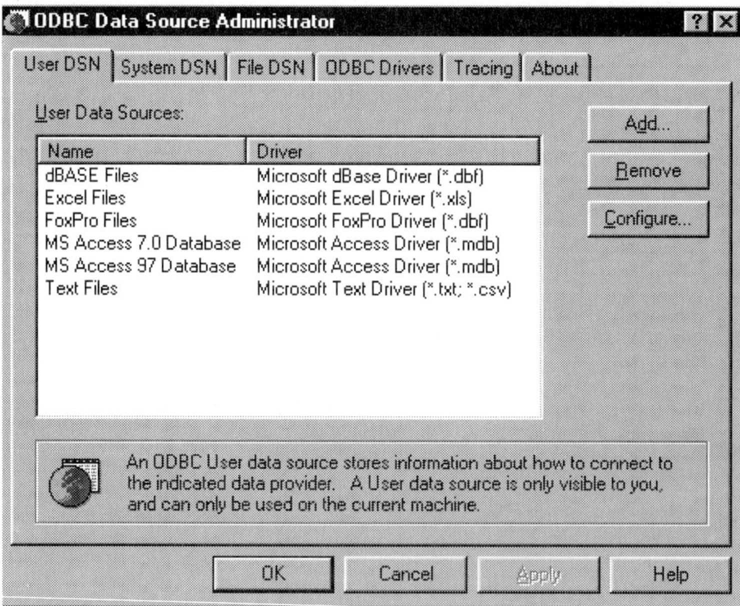

Figure 11.8. The ODBC Data Source Administrator.

- Check the list to ensure the driver-type you require is listed. We are going to use Access 97.

- Click the Add button to open the Create New Data Source dialog box. (Shown in Figure 11.9.)

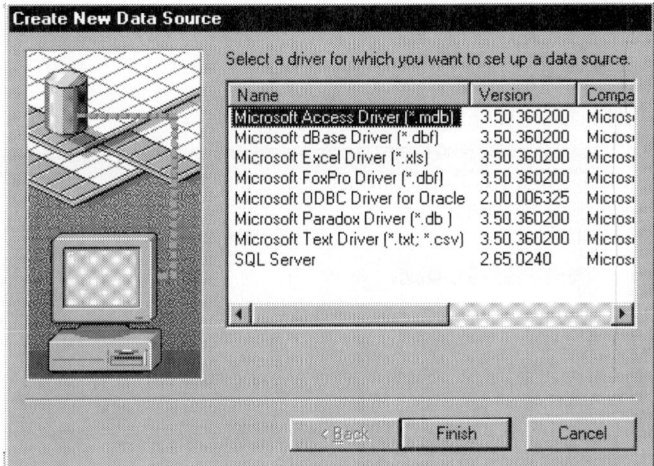

Figure 11.9. The Create New Data Source Dialog Box. Use it to specify the database type for the source.

- Select the driver, then click the Finish button to open the Setup dialog box, shown in Figure 11.10.

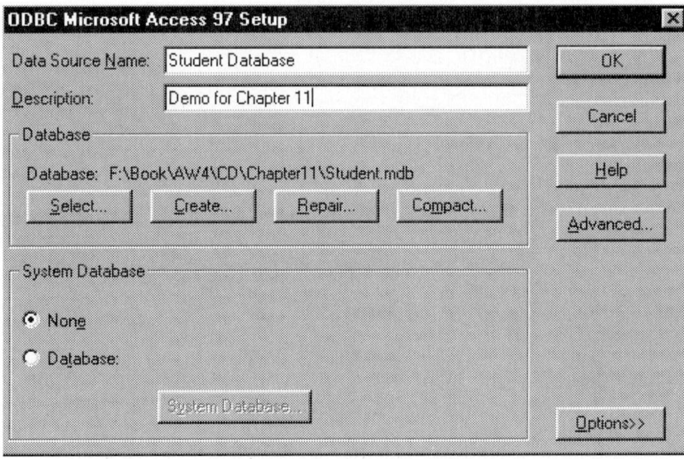

Figure 11.10. The Database Setup Dialog Box.

- Enter a name in the Data Source Name field. The name doesn't matter but you must remember it because you will reference that name when you connect to the database.
- Enter a suitable Description.
- Push the Select button.
- Specify the path to the database using the dialog box that opens (See Figure 11.11)

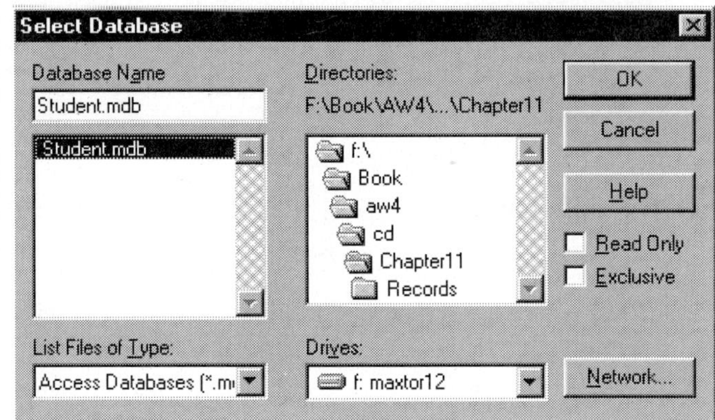

Figure 11.11. The Select Database Dialog Box. Use it to point to the database source to associate with the Data Source Name you entered previously

- Push the OK button to close the Select Database dialog box.
- Click OK to close the Setup dialog box.
- Close the Administrator dialog box.

Using the ODBC Functions

First, we have to load the ODBC functions. The ODBC functions are contained in the **Odbc.u32** file.

Loading the ODBC Functions

To load the functions, start a new piece, choose *Window>Functions*, and then specify Odbc.u32 as the file from which to load the new functions. (See Figure 11.12.)

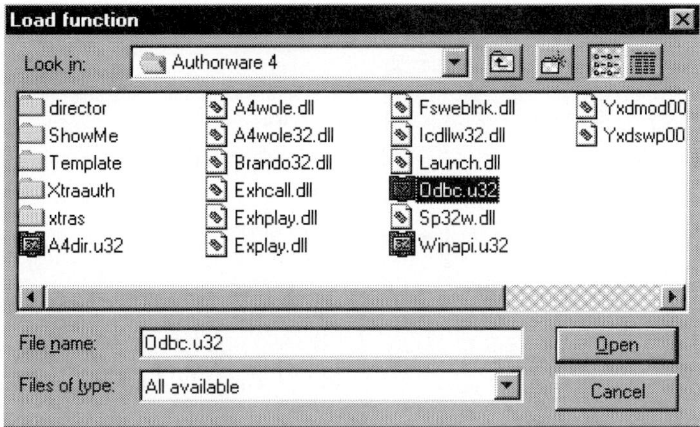

Figure 11.12. The Load Function Dialog Box. Choose the Odbc.u32 file.

Push the Open button, and when the Custom Functions dialog box opens, shown in Figure 11.13, shift-click to select all three functions.

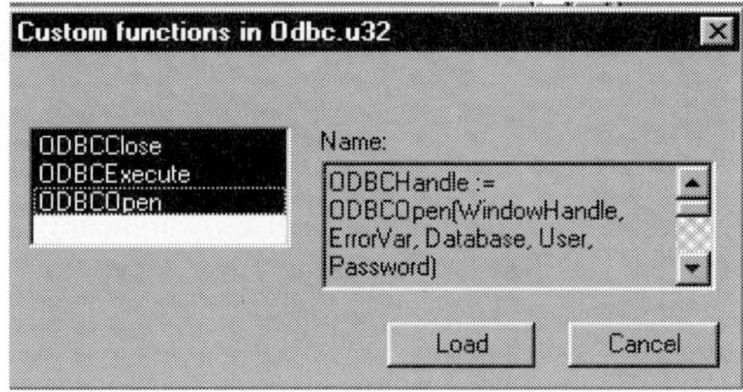

Figure 11.13. The Custom Functions Dialog Box. Shift-click on the first function and last one to select all three.

Using the ODBC Functions

First, you must connect to the database using the ODBCOpen function. If you open **Odbc.a4p** file in the Chapter 11 folder, you will see the flowline in Figure 11.14.

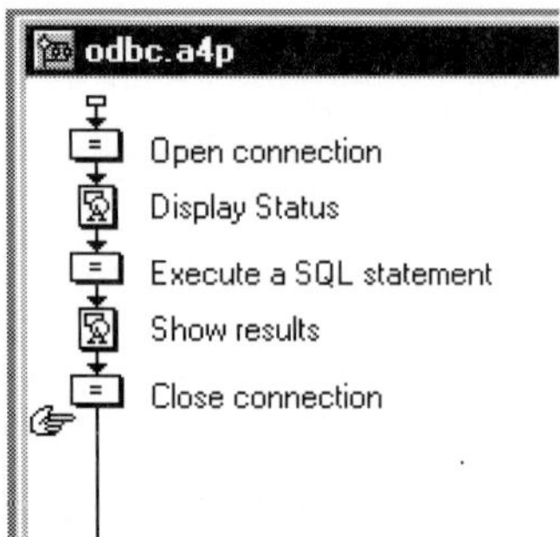

Figure 11.14. The Flowline for the Odbc.a4p Piece.

The Open connection calculation icon contains the following command:

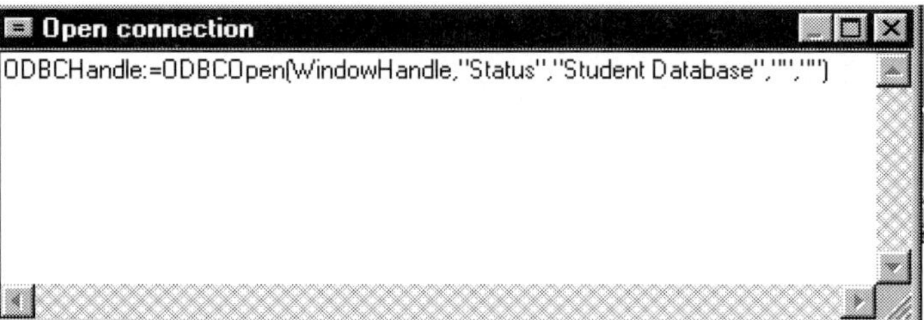

The two empty strings can be used to hold a user and password, if both were needed. User names and passwords are set up in the ODBC Administration applet. The statement returns a value in the `WindowHandle` variable. You'll need that value (you can simply refer to it by name) when you invoke the other two functions. If all is correct, you now have a session started and you're ready to access the data. If an error occurred, `Status` will contain the error message. The next icon, Display Status, displays the error message, if there was one, in the Presentation window.

To access data you'll need to use a SQL statement and the `ODBCExecute` function. We are going to retrieve all the rows in the Major table. The SQL statement to do this is:

```
Select * From Major
```

To execute this from within Authorware, use a statement like the one in Figure 11.15, which is the content of the Execute a SQL Statement icon.

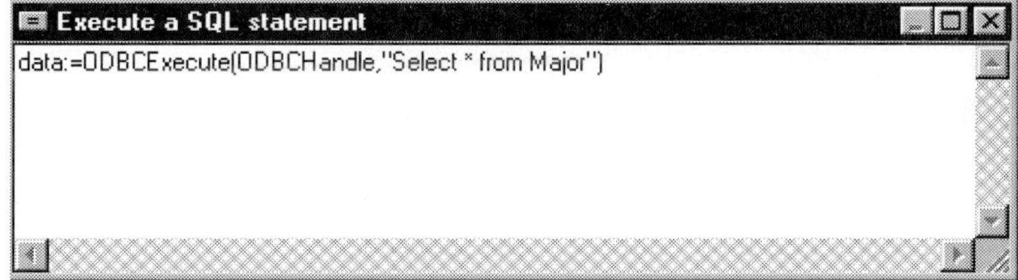

Figure 11.15. An Example of the `ODBCExecute` Function. This retrieves all the Major rows and stores them in the `data` variable.

It is preferable if you use a custom variable, and assign it the SQL command as a value, rather than "hard-coding" the string as we did in Figure 11.15.

The Show Results icon displays the value of data. Finally, the Close connection icon contains the following line:

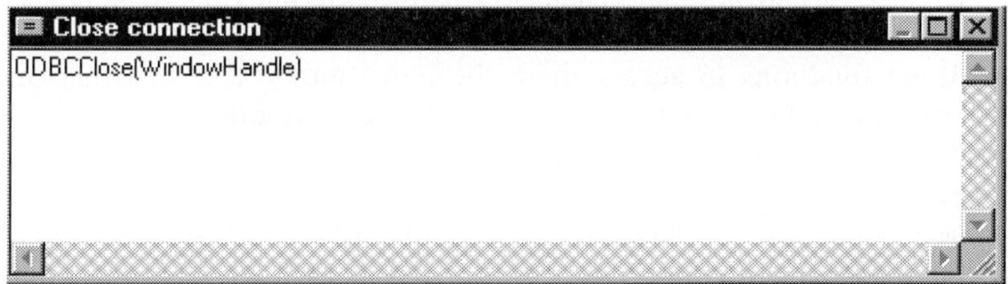

Some SQL Examples

To retrieve the students and their major description: Select * From Student,Major Where Student.MajiD=Major.MajID

To retrieve the row for the student with SS#="123-45-6789": `Select * From Student Where SS#="123-45-6789"`.

To add a new Major row: `Insert Into Major Values ("Art", "Studio Art")`.

These are only a few of the many commands available within the SQL language. The important point is you can develop a front-end interface using Authorware and reference data in organizational databases.

Distributing Pieces with Database Connectivity

When you distribute your piece, you must include the following additional components:

- The ODBC UCD. Recall this file contains the IODBC functions.
- The database that is referenced in the piece.
- The data source the piece uses (these must be set up on the playback computer as well.)

SUMMARY

Managing large titles can be made easier by using external files to hold user data, saving user progress in the records location folder, through the splitting of large titles into several, then using Jump functions to access them through routers. Use of `JumpOut` permits the running of external applications from within an Authorware title.

To display the progress of users of training titles, use variables like `PercentRight` and `PercentWrong`.

Use the Authorware templates to get a, jump-start on your piece. You can choose from over 40 models to insert into your piece. Remember to package your piece before "jumping" to it from one of the models.

The ability to connect with organizational databases expands the power of Authorware beyond that of CBT or presentations. Using the three ODBC functions in the Obdc.ucd, you can add, delete, and retrieve data from ODBC-compliant databases to and from your Authorware piece. Another use might be to create a database of quiz questions, and then use the `Random` function to retrieve questions.

For more information about ODBC and Authorware, visit the Macromedia site on the web, and look for the Authorware Developer Center.

Study Exercises

11.1 Create a new project called C11Q1. It should ask for the user's name, create a folder having the user's name, and enable that user to exit and resume where he or she left off. Make the project have four display icons on a single flowline with a perpetual quit (to Windows) button.

11.2 Create C11Q2, a project that asks the user which application to run, and, if appropriate, the name of the file to open. For example, if the user responds with MSWord and MyResume.DOC, your project should open Microsoft Word then open the MyResume.DOC file.

11.3 Create two projects: C11Q3A and C11Q3B. The first project should prompt for the user's name, then invoke the second project, which displays the name and asks for the user's address and telephone number.

11.4 Create a piece, C11Q4, which adds a new student to the Student.mdb database.

11.5. Create a new piece, C11Q5, which uses the Logon template to retrieve the corresponding row from the student database.

11.6 Create a new piece, C11Q6, which uses a random number to generate a random quiz question and three possible answers. Be sure one of the answers is correct.

Authoring for the Web

Authorware projects can be distributed on diskette, removable media, CD-ROM, or the World Wide Web. Using the WWW to distribute projects means you have to make some design tradeoffs and configure web browsers and web servers. This chapter looks at these issues as we explore the widest of all distribution systems: the Internet.

To create a project for the Internet, you must follow a few rules, then use Afterburner to prepare the project for the Internet. To view the project through an Internet browser, you have to first download and install the Shockwave plug-in. Finally; the web or intranet server must be configured to download three new *MIME* types.

At the conclusion of the chapter, you will be able to:

- Define the responsibilities of the developer, the user, and the webmaster.

- Use three new functions to jump among web pages or download files over the Internet.

- Use modified versions of `JumpFile` and `JumpFileReturn`.
- Define the two modes encountered when downloading Authorware projects.
- Install and use the Macromedia Shockwave plug-in for Netscape or Microsoft Internet Explorer.
- Utilize new File Transfer Protocol (FTP) functions for uploading and download files.
- Modify your project to account for Internet download problems.
- Use Afterburner to prepare your project for use on the Internet.
- State benefits of using the web for project distribution.
- Use Shockwave Audio to compress digital audio for the web.

WHY USE THE INTERNET OR AN INTRANET FOR DISTRIBUTION?

Common Authorware project distribution methods include diskette, hard disk, removable media, such as Iomega's Zip disks, and CD-ROM. Speed and storage capacities distinguish these media from each other. One thing is in common however, no matter which medium we choose, if we have hundreds of users and we make a change to out project, every user must be sent a new version.

Using the Internet or an organizational intranet to distribute projects alleviates this problem. However, it introduces some new ones. It's common to find long download times over modems and computers without sound cards or users with 256- or even 16-color computers.

This chapter looks at the process for preparing and deploying Authorware titles using the World Wide Web, whether over the Internet or an intranet.

The user, the developer, and the webmaster all must accommodate changes and meet new responsibilities in order for us to distribute projects this way.

USER RESPONSIBILITIES

The user of your Authorware project must have a suitable browser, download a plug-in for the browser, and decide whether to trust the site where the project resides. The plug-in that is needed is called Shockwave.

Shockwave

Authorware projects are viewed over the World Wide Web (WWW) or an organizational intranet through a browser, such as Netscape Communicator or Microsoft's Internet Explorer. However, you must first acquire an Authorware plug-in for your browser. The appropriate plug-in for Authorware is called Shockwave, which can be downloaded from Macromedia's home page at www.macromedia.com. Be sure to download the one that is right for your computer and operating system. Also, be sure to download the Authorware Shockwave plug-in, Macromedia has another Shockwave plug-in for its companion products.

Downloading Shockwave

First, you have to download Shockwave from Macromedia (www.macromedia.com). The Windows 95/ Windows NT version that was current at the time of this text had the file name Shockwave_Installer.exe. If you want to be able to run any Macromedia product on the web, choose to download "The Works". The name of this executable is Shockwave_Works_Installer.exe. Shockwave consists of two components: The Shockwave plug-in used by the browser to run an Authorware pieces, and Afterburner, the application that prepares Authorware pieces for web distribution.

Installing Shockwave

Next, double-click on the Shockwave EXE file. You will be asked if you want to install the Shockwave plug-in. If you say yes, the Install Shield will run. The first decision you must make is to specify which browser you use (see Figure 12.1).

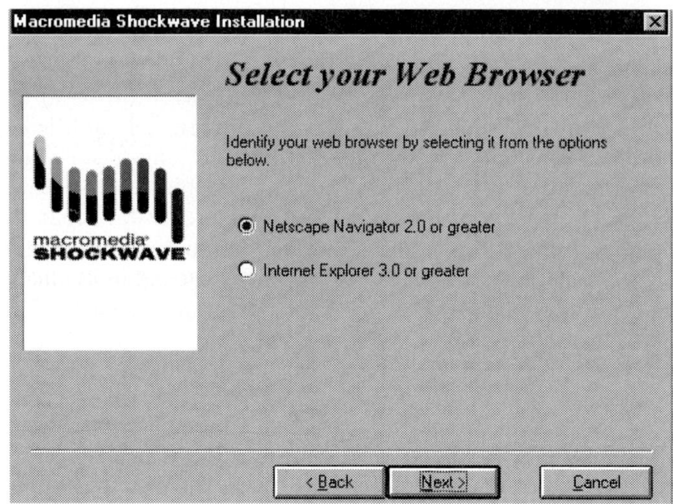

Figure 12.1. Specifying the Browser for the Shockwave Plug-in.

Choose your browser, and push the Next button. Next, you have to specify the location of the browser (See Figure 12.2). Be careful here because you might have several versions of Netscape and/or Internet Explorer. If the path that Shockwave found isn't the right one, use Browse to locate the folder that contains the executable for your browser. Netscape 4 often is stored in the \Program Files\Netscape\Program\Communicator\Programs folder.

If you're using Microsoft's Internet Explorer, you will download an Active-X control, rather than a plug-in.

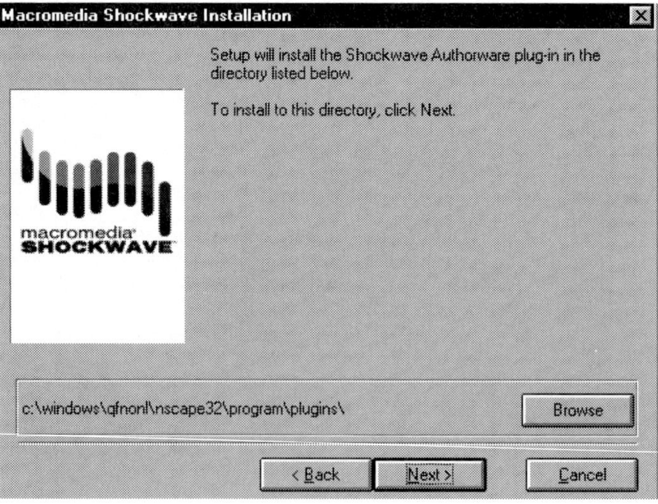

Figure 12.2. Specifying the Location of the Shockwave Plug-in.

After the plug-in is installed, be sure to reload your browser. To test your installation, visit one of the gallery pages at the Macromedia home page.

MODES

When an Authorware project runs over the Internet, it does so in one of two modes: ***trusted*** or ***untrusted***. One of the major concerns for corporations and individuals that use the Internet is security. We don't want errant or malicious programs damaging hard drives, infecting us with viruses, or threatening our security or privacy.

When you load a page with an Authorware piece in it, you're presented with a Shockwave dialog box that asks whether to trust this site.

If you choose not to trust the site, no external files will be downloaded. While this does alleviate security issues, it probably means some or all of the Authorware project won't run.

If you "trust" the site and push the Options button, the Security Options dialog box opens (see Figure 12.3).

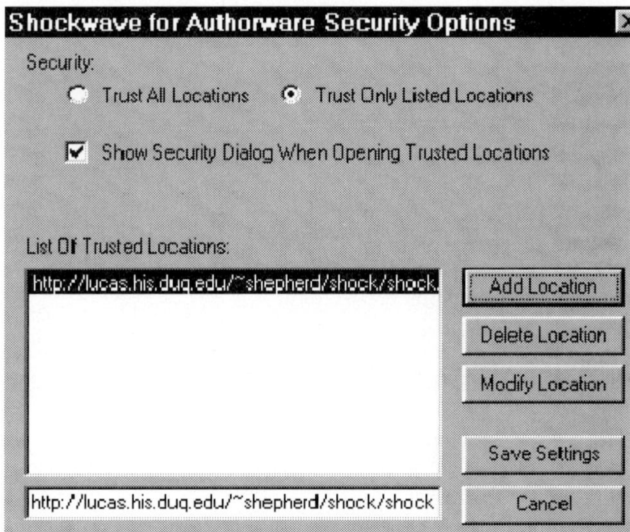

Figure 12.3. The Security Options For A Trusted Site.

If you select the Add Location button, the trust/don't trust dialog won't be displayed as long as you're downloading pages from the trusted site. Push the Save Settings button when finished.

Sites that are trusted can take full advantage of Xtras, UCDs and DLLs. Sites that aren't trusted won't download external content stored in UCDs, Xtras, and so on. In addition, a few functions, such as `DeleteFile`, `WriteFile` and others are disabled.

DEVELOPER PREPARATIONS

Before you add Authorware to your web pages, you must make some adjustments to your title. If running in untrusted mode, you need to remove the following functions: `ReadExtFile`, `WriteExtFile`, `AppendExtFile`, and `DeleteExtFile`.

Next, reduce the color depth of images to 256 or lower because most of the computers accessing the WWW use monitors and video adapters that view 256 colors at a time. To further reduce the download time for graphics, use the `ReszieWindow` function to make the Presentation window smaller.

Use GIF and JPG graphics, which are much smaller than bitmaps (BMPs). Include the new functions `NetDownLoad`, `NetPreLoad`, and `PreLoad` functions to optimize loading over the web. Finally, package the title without the runtime and choose to package libraries internally.

NEW FUNCTIONS

There are some functions that enable you to hyperlink to WWW pages download files, or cache portions of your project. Three new functions are: `GoToNetPage()`, which adds a WWW hyperlink , `NetDownload()`, which downloads the content of a page and stores it in the Authorware Shockwave plug-in directory, and `NetPreLoad()`, which caches pages while other activities are taking place.

The GoToNetPage Function

The complete format of the function is:

```
GoToNetPage(URL,targetName)
```

When the function is activated, control is passed to the URL (Uniform Resource Locators) specified. Use `targetName` as the window's title. It's optional, but if omitted, it will open a new page in the current window.

An example might be:

```
GotoNetPage("www.macromedia.com","macromedia")
```

The NetDownload Function

The complete format is:

```
NetDownLoad(URL)
```

This function downloads the file, which can be of any type, in the URL to your disk drive. When a project is converted for use on the WWW, a series of files is created, one of which is called a *map* file. One of the lines in the map file can be the location of where to load the specified file. If there is no entry, the file downloads into the Download folder within the Authorware plug-in folder

As an example, here's how to specify the function to download a text file called readme.txt from the www.myco.com site.

```
str:=NetDownLoad("http://www.myco.com/readme.txt")
```

The NetPreLoad Function

The format of the command is:

```
NetPreLoad(IconID@"IconTitle")
```

This command downloads one or more portions of a project, called *segments*, while the user is doing something else. More specifically, only the segments that make up the icon specified by `IconTitle` are downloaded. If the specified icon is an interaction, map, decision, or framework icon, all associated icons also downloaded.

Several of the Authorware functions have been enhanced to accommodate web-based titles.

FTP Functions

File Transfer Protocol is the set of rules used to communicate between two computers using a data communications protocol called TCP/IP (Transmission Control Protocol/Internet Protocol). You are using TCP/IP every time you access a web page, and more than likely when you read your e-mail. FTP is the application used to transfer files between two computers.

Authorware FTP functions are found in the FTP UCD. The file, **ftp.u32**, can be found in the Goodies folder on the Authorware CD-ROM. Load them like any UCD: Choose <u>W</u>indow> <u>F</u>unctions, select your piece's name, then push the Load button. Direct Authorware to the locations of ftp.u32, and then select all the functions listed in the Custom Functions dialog box. Table 12.1 lists and describes the FTP functions.

Table 12.1. The FTP Functions Available in the ftp.u32 UCD.

Function Name	Sample Usage	Purpose/Comments
FtpOpen	ftpID := FtpOpen( )	Allocates and initializes resources for the FTP session. It must be the first function called by your piece.
FtpClose	status := FtpClose(ftpID)	Closes the FTP current session.
FtpConnect	status := FtpConnect(ftpID, server, port, userID, password)	Establishes an FTP connection to a server using the port, userID, and password specified.
FtpDisconnect	status := FtpDisconnect(ftpID)	Ends a currently active FTP connection.
FtpRetrieve	status := FtpRetrieve(ftpID, remotePath, localPath)	Retrieves the file on the server specified by the remote path. The local path specifies the name of the file on the local file system. The file is always transferred as a binary file.
FtpAppend	status := FtpAppend(ftpID, remotePath, localPath)	This function transfers the specified file from the local system to the remote server. If the file exists at the server site, then the data is appended to that file; otherwise the file is created.
FtpDelete	status := FtpDelete(ftpID, remotePath)	This function deletes the specified file from the server.
FtpRename	status := FtpRename(ftpID, fromName, toName)	This function renames the file on the remote server 'fromName' to 'toName'
FtpList	status := FtpList(ftpID, re-motePath)	This function causes a group of files to be sent from the server.
FtpNameList	status := FtpNameList(ftpID, remotePath)	This function causes a directory listing to be sent from the server.
FtpGetWork-ingDir	status := FtpGetWorkingDir(ftpID)	This function gets the full path of the current di-rectory.
FtpChange-WorkingDir	status := FtpChangeWork-ingDir(ftpID, remotePath	This function allows the calling application to work with a different directory for file storage or retrieval .
FtpRemoveDir	status := FtpRemoveDir(ftpID, remotePath)	This command causes the directory specified by the remote path to be removed..
FtpMakeDir	status := FtpMakeDir(ftpID, remotePath)	This function causes the directory specified by the remote path to be created as a directory.
FtpStatus	status := FtpStatus(ftpID)	Returns the status of the last function.
FtpResult	string := FtpResult(ftpID)	Returns the result string of completed FTP opera-tion.

NEW FUNCTIONALITY FOR EXISTING FUNCTIONS

Recall that `JumpFile` and `JumpFileReturn` are used to execute separate Authorware titles. The former exits the current project and leaps to the second. If the latter format is used, when the second project exits, control returns to the calling project. Use these functions wisely because they make your projects easier to debug.

Using Authorware on the web gives you a new `JumpFile` feature: The ability to "jump" to a URL. For example, to jump to the URL at the myco.com site, you might use:

```
JumpFileReturn("http://myco.com/aware/piece1.aam")
```

The `ReadExtFile` function has been modified to permit the ability to download from a web site. The format is:

```
String:=ReadExtFile
(http://servername.com/MyFolder/MyFile.TXT)
```

SHOCKING YOUR PROJECT

A program called Afterburner comes with Authorware. Alternatively, you can download from the Macromedia web site. It's a utility that compresses and partitions your project so it can be included in your web page. Use Afterburner to prepare your project for deployment on the web. Before using Afterburner you must package your project, but don't include the runtime. Once packaging is done, you're ready to use Afterburner.

The processing of using Afterburner to prepare your project for web distribution is called **shocking the project.** A shocked project results in two types of files: One or more **segments** and a **map file**. For cross-platform delivery you must shock both Macintosh and Windows files.

Segments

Your packaged project is divided into one or more units called **segments**. A segment can be from 4k-488K in size. When a segment is needed but not yet downloaded, a request is sent to the web server to start the download process.

Afterburner segments your project into a series of files that have the first four letters of the map file name plus a sequential, 3-digit number. For example, a project named shock would have segment names: shoc001.aas, shoc002.aas, and so on.

The Map File

The Map file is a simple text file that can be viewed by a word processor or WordPad. It lists segments and other external files needed for the title and has an aam filename extension.

Shocking: The Steps

To shock an Authorware project:

- First, package your project without the runtime - Choose File>Package.
- Select Without runtime in the Package dialog box.
- Make any other remaining selections, then push Save File(s) and Package. The options are shown in Figure 12.4, and discussed later.

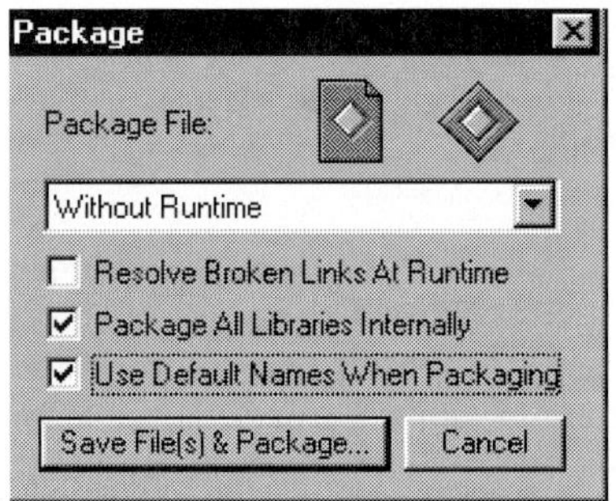

Figure 12.4. The Package Options. This dialog box is opened by selecting File Package.

- Open Afterburner for Authorware.
- Choose File>Shock. This opens the Select Packaged Source File dialog box, shown in Figure 12.5.

Figure 12.5. Selecting the Packaged File to Shock.

- Select your packaged project (we chose the Askid title).
- Push the OK button.
- Choose a destination directory and map file name. The segment and map files will be stored in the location you specify. (See Figure 12.6).

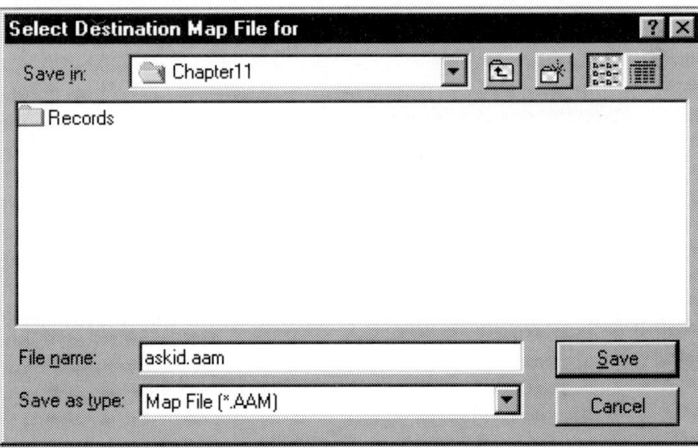

Figure 12.6. The Select Destination Dialog Box. Use it to specify where to store the map and segment files.

- Choose the segment parameters in the Segment Settings dialog box that appears (see Figure 12.7).

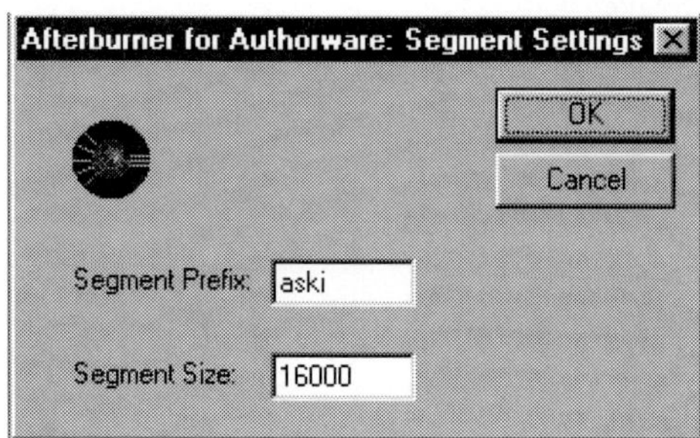

Figure 12.7. Assigning Afterburner Parameters.

- Push OK. It's recommended that you choose an empty folder to store the map and segment files because you will find it easier to upload the files to the web server.
- You will see the "Shocking File" dialog box shown in Figure 12.8.

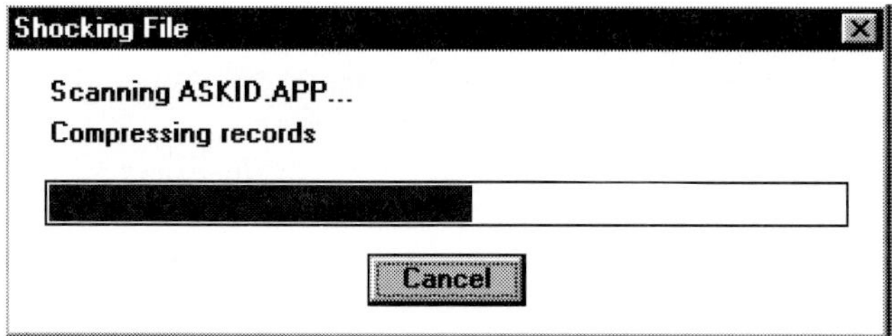

Figure 12.8. The Dialog Box That is Displayed While a File is Being Shocked.

The askid.aam for the example we have been using looks like Figure 12.9.

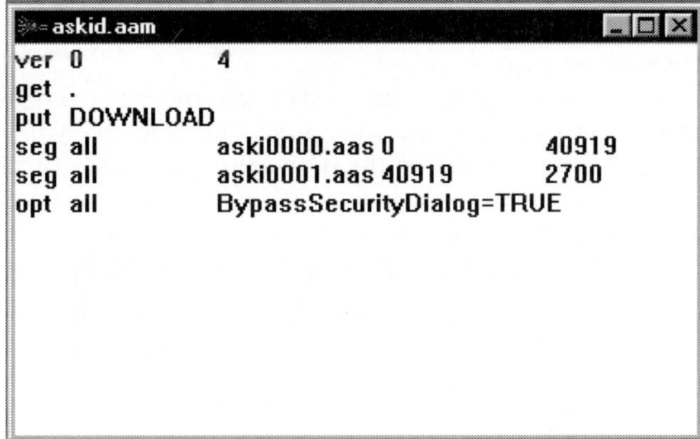

Figure 12.9. The **Askid.aam** File for the Chapter Example.

Creating a single map file for Macintosh and Windows Users

You can create a single Shocked page if you combine lines from the Macintosh and PC map files into one file.

ADD THE HTML REFERENCE

The final step is to include the shocked project into the web page using HTML — Hypertext Markup Language. To include a piece called mypage into a web page, use this format:

```
<body>
<embed src="mypage.aam" width=20 height=20 window=ontop>
```

The Authorware project can be embedded in the current page or it can be displayed on a page in a new window.

Embedding the Project in a Page

To embed the project into an existing page use `window=inPlace` instead of `onTop`. One caveat: This only works on Windows machines!

Opening a New Window

Use `window=onTop` or `onTopMinimize`. We saw the `onTop` option above. It says to leave the browser window alone and show the project in a separate window.

Use of `OnTopMinimize` causes the browser to be hidden (it's minimized) so your project can completely take over the desktop as it's shown in its own window.

Be sure to quarantine the page — warn users they must have the Shockwave plug-in to go to next page. Also, include a link to the Macromedia site so the plug-in can easily be acquired, if desired.

Libraries

When you shock a piece containing links to libraries, the libraries are also shocked. Each library that conations content linked to by your piece is shocked, and corresponding segments created. A word of warning: If your library and piece have the same first four letters in their names, one map file may overwrite the other. In this situation, specify different names for you piece and the linked libraries as you Shock the piece.

WEB SERVER RESPONSIBILITIES

The webmaster has to inform the web server software that Authorware files may be found in a page. Because such pages aren't standard Internet file types, a MIME type must be added. *MIME* stands for Multipurpose Internet Mail Extension. On Netscape web servers, MIME types are stored in the mime.types file within the config folder. The webmaster has to add the three MIME types in Table 12.2.

Table 12.2. MIME Types to be Added to the Server

MIME Type	Subtype	Extension
Application	x-authorware-map	aam
Application	x-authorware-segment	aas
Application	x-authorware-bin	aab

SHOCKWAVE AUDIO

When we discussed sound, we saw that digital audio files can get quite large. Furthermore, they do not begin playing until the entire file has been loaded. Shockwave audio (SWA) addresses both problems.

Like other sound formats, SWA files can be imported or linked externally to a sound icon. SWA files are compressed using an Authorware Xtra. When the compressed file is loaded, it is uncompressed then played.

To convert a WAV file to a SWA file, follow the steps that follow.

1. Choose <u>X</u>tras>Other Convert WAV to SWA.
2. The dialog box in Figure 12.10 opens.

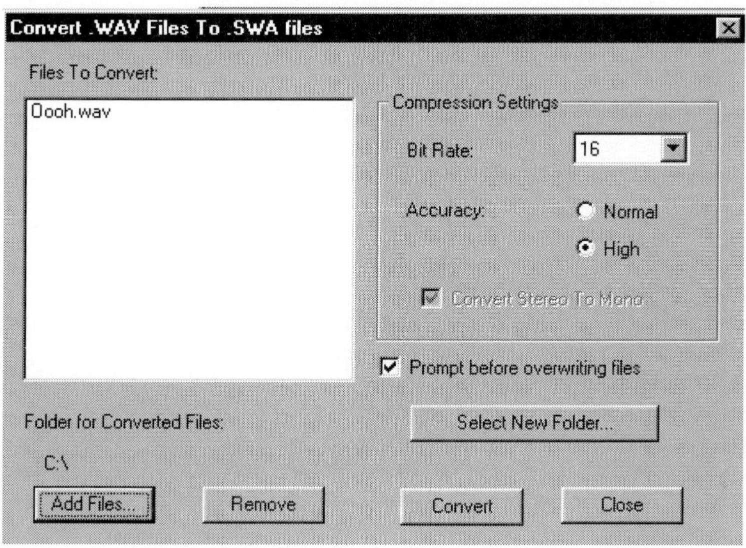

Figure 12.10. The Convert WAV to SWA Dialog Box. Click Add Files, then select a file to convert.

3. Click the Add Files button and then choose a file to convert. You can perform a multiple-select to choose several files at one time.
4. The names of the files to be converted will appear in the Files to Convert section. In Figure 12.10, we chose **Oooh.wav**.
5. Choose the appropriate sampling parameters using the Bit Rate drop-down box and the Normal or High Quality setting.
6. If the original file is stereophonic and you want to convert it to monophonic, check the Convert Stereo to Mono box.
7. Use the Select New Folder button to specify where to store the new file.
8. Click the Convert button.

SUMMARY

Distributing Authorware projects over the Web offers distinct advantages:

- Users don't have to travel to take courses, saving time and money.
- Instead of sending out a CD-ROM to each user, one copy of the project exists, simplifying maintenance.
- Central control of student progress.
- Central control of backing up student records.
- Streaming compressed audio

To distribute projects this way, new responsibilities for the developer, the user and the webmaster are required.

The developer has to take steps to provide for playback on computers with 256 colors and must allow for slow modem access. This means eliminating narrations, cutting back on digital video, and changing color palettes to 256 colors.

The project must then be added to web pages using HTML. Authorware projects can be embedded into pages or can take over the desktop.

Users have to download and install Shockwave plug-in for their browser. When the page begins downloading, a decision must be made as to whether to trust the site.

Use Shockwave audio to reduce the file size of digitized audio. An Authorware Xtra converts WAV to SWA files, which can then be embedded or linked to your project.

Finally, the web master must provide three new MIME types: aam, aas, and aab.

Study Exercises

12.1 Create a new project, named C12Q1. It should contain a button, which when pushed leaps to the Macromedia home page (www.macromedia.com).

System Variables

This appendix describes most of the system variables, but for more detail, please consult the on-line Authorware help, and the <u>W</u>indow> <u>V</u>ariables menu choice. Additional variable definitions can be found by choosing the menu option described above.

VARIABLES USED WITH DECISION ICONS

Variable	Description
AllSelected	Indicates if every icon attached to a decision icon has been selected.
PathCount	Specifies the number of icons are attached to the decision icon.
PathSelected	The relative number of the path chosen within the current decision icon.
RepCount	The number of times the current decision path has been repeated.
SelectedEver	Indicates if the current path of the current decision icon has ever been selected.
TimesExpired	Indicates if an icon is stopped because its time limit is exceeded.
TimesSelected	The number of times the current path has been chosen.

VARIABLES USED WITH FILES

Variable	Description
DiskBytes	Amount of storage available on drive containing the current file (title).
FileLocation	Path to the folder/directory containing the current title.
FileName	Name of the current file/title.
FileSize	Size in bytes of the current file.
IOMessage	Status information about current file.
OrigWorkingDirectory (Windows)	Working directory.
RecordsLocation	Directory containing user data.
SearchPath	Path used to locate external files.

VARIABLES USED WITH FRAMEWORKS

Variable	Description
CurrentPageID	Icon ID of the last page attached to a specified framework.
CurrentPageNum	The relative number of the current page.
LastSearchString	The last search string.
MatchCount	Specifies number of times the FindText function found a given word.
Navigating	Indicates whether a jump or a call is active.
NavFrom	Which page initiated the jump.
VanTo	Indicates if a destination page is the result of a jump or a call.
PageCount	Number of pages attached to the current framework.
SearchPercentComplete	What percentage of a FindText is completed

VARIABLES ASSOCIATED WITH MEDIA

Variable	Description
MediaLength	The length of the movie, sound, or video icon you specify.
MediaPlaying	Indicates whether a movie or video is currently playing.
MediaPosition	The current frame number.
MoviePlaying	Indicates if a movie is playing.
MediaRate	The rate for the movie, sound, or video icon you specify.
SoundPlaying	Indicates if a sound is playing.

VARIABLES ASSOCIATED WITH USER INPUT

Variable	Description
AltDown (Windows)	Indicates whether Alt key is pressed.
OptionDown (Mac)	Indicates whether Option key is pressed.
CapsLock	Indicates whether Caps Lock key is pressed.
ClickX/ClickY	X,Y coordinates when mouse button was last pushed.
CommandDown	Indicates whether Command key is pressed.
ControlDown	Indicates whether Control key is pressed.
CursorX/CursorY	X,Y coordinates of cursor.
DoubleClick	Indicates whether last mouse activity was a double-click.
Key/KeyNum	The key name and numeric code of last keystroke.
MouseDown	Whether the left mouse button is depressed
RightMouseDown	Whether the right mouse button is depressed.
ShiftDown	Whether Shift key is depressed.
TimeOutLimit	Time to wait for user input.
TimeOutRemaining	Returns the amount of time remaining for Authorware to wait for user activity.

VARIABLES ASSOCIATED WITH USER INPUT

Variable	Description
FirstName	The current user's first name.
Sessions	Number of times the current user has used this file.
UserName	User's complete name.

VARIABLES ASSOCIATED WITH SYSTEM INFORMATION

Variable	Description
LicenseInfo	Name, organization Authorware licensed to.
Machine	Model of machine running Authorware.
MemoryAvailable	Amount of RAM available to Authorware.
OSName/OSNumber	OS class, version.
ScreenDepth	Color depth in bytes/pixel.
SerialNumber	Serial number of Authorware.
Version	Authorware version .

VARIABLES ASSOCIATED WITH TEXT ENTRY

Variable	Description
CharCount	The number of characters the user typed.
EntryText	The last type entered.
ForceCaps	Determines whether user's response was converted to all caps.
JudgeString	Text used as a response to match an interaction.
NumCount	The number of numeric characters in the last input.
NumEntry	First number typed in response to a text interaction.
NumEntry2	Second number typed in response to a text interaction.
NumEntry3	Third number typed in response to a text interaction.
PresetEntry	Default text string.
WordCount	Number of words in last input.

VARIABLES ASSOCIATED WITH INTERACTIONS

Variable	Description
AllCorrect-Matched	Indicates whether user has matched all responses for current interaction.
BranchPath	Relative number of Exit branch for last response icon user matched.
Checked	Value is True if button is checked..
ChoiceCount	The number of response icons attached to current interaction
ChoiceNumber	The number of the last response matched by user for current interaction.
ChoicesMatched	Number of response icons matched by user for current interaction.
Correct	Title of first response identified as Correct ("+").
CorrectChoice	Relative number of first response icon marked as correct.
CorrectChoices-Matched	Number of response icons with correct status user matched in an interaction.
WrongtChoices-Matched	Number of response icons with Wrong status user matched in an interaction.
FirstTryCorrect	Number of correct responses made on first attempt in the file.
FirstTryWrong	Number of incorrect responses made on first attempt in the file.
JudgedInterac-tions	Number of judged interactions encountered by user in the file.
JudgedResponses	Number of responses given by user to judged interactions encountered by user in the file.
MatchedEver	Indicates whether user has ever matched a response icon previously.
MatchedIconTi-tle	Title of last response matched correctly.
PercentCorrect	Percentage of correctly answered judged responses.
PercentWrong	Percentage of incorrectly answered judged responses.
PreviousMatch	Indicates if specified response icon was last one matched in an interaction.
ResponseStatus	Status of first judged response the user matched in current interaction.
ResponseType	A value representing the response type of the last icon matched in an interaction.
TimesMatched	Number of times user matched current response icon in this file.
TotalCorrect	Number of correct responses to all judged interactions.
TotalWrong	Number of incorrect responses to all judged interactions.
Tries	Number of times user matched a response in an interaction.

VARIABLES RELATED TO TIME

Variable	Description
ClickSeconds	The number seconds elapsed since the user last clicked the (left) mouse button.
Date	Today's date.
Day	Numeric value of current day of the month.
DayName	Name of current day of the week.
ElapsedDays	Number of days since user last used Authorware.
FirstDate	Date and time user first used current file.
FullDate	Today's day and date.
FullTime	Current time.
Hour	Current hour in 24-hour (military) format.
Minute	Current minute of the hour.
Month	Numeric month number of the year.
MonthName	Current month's name.
Sec	Current second of the minute.
SessionHours	Time since user began this session, in hours and 1/10 of hours.
SessionTime	Time since user began this session, in hours and minutes.
StartTime	Time when user began working with current file.
SystemSeconds	Number of seconds since computer was started.
Time	Current time in hours and seconds.
TotalTime	Time user has spent in all sessions, expressed in hours and minutes.
Year	Current year.

VARIABLES ASSOCIATED WITH XTRAS

EventLastMatched	Contains the event generated by the Xtra last matched through an event response.
EventQueue	Returns a list of events sent by Xtras, but not yet processed.
GlobalTempo	Specifies the rate at which Sprite Xtras receive step events.

System Functions

Authorware provides a comprehensive set of functions that enable you to manipulate input data and dates, maintain files, perform mathematical calculations and much more. There are 15 types of functions.

This appendix defines most of the built-in functions, but not all of them. Choosing the menu option Window>Functions will display the additional function definitions.

CHARACTER DATA FUNCTIONS

Function	Description
Capitalize	Capitalize the first letter of every word.
Char	Return the character corresponding to the ASCII code.
CharCount	Returns the number of characters in the supplied string.
Code	Returns the ASCII code corresponding to the supplied character.
DeleteLine	Delete the nth line in the string.
Eval	Evaluates expressions based on user input.
Find	Locates the specified characters in a search string.
GetLine	Retrieve specific line in specified string.
GetNumber	Get nth number in specified string.
GetWord	Retrieve nth word in specified string.
InsertLine	Add nth line to specified string.
LineCount	Returns the number of lines in specified string.
LowerCase	Set all characters in specified string to lower case.
MapChars	Map characters between platforms.
NumCount	Returns number of numbers in specified string.
Reduce	Remove specified repeating characters in a string.
RepeatString	Repeat specified string n times.
Replace	Exchange one set of characters for another.
ReplaceLine	Replaces one line in a string with another.
ReplaceString	Exchange a portion of one set of characters for another.
ReplaceWord	Replaces one word with another.
Rfind	Searches a string and returns position of the match.
String	Converts data into string data.
Strip	Remove a specified set of characters from a string.
SubStr	Return characters between nth and mth bytes.
UpperCase	Make all characters in a string upper case.
WordCount	Returns the number of words in specified string.

FILE FUNCTIONS

Function	Description
AppendExtFile	Add data to existing file.
Catalog	List contents of current folder or directory.
CreateFolder	Add a new folder or directory as child of current folder.
DeleteFile	Delete specified file.
FileType	Returns the file type for specified file.
ReadExtFile	Returns a string containing contents of specified text file.
RenameFile	Changes the specified file to a new name.
WriteExtFile	Add specified string to a new file.

GRAPHICS FUNCTIONS

Function	Description
Box	Draw a box.
Circle	Draw a circle.
DrawBox	Let user draw a box.
DrawCircle	Let user draw a circle.
DrawLine	Let user draw a line.
Line	Draw a line.
Overlapping	Check if objects within given icon overlap.
RGB	Combine individual red, green, and blue values into one.
SetFill	Determine if specified object is filled.
SetFrame	Determine if frame is filled.
SetLIne	Determine if line has arrow endpoint.
SetMode	Set drawing mode.

JUMP FUNCTIONS

Function	Description
GoTo	Jump to specified icon.
JumpFile	Continue presentation by jumping to specified file.
JumpFileReturn	Same as JumpFile but return when the destination file is finished.
JumpOut	Launch specified application.
JumpOutReturn	Return to Authorware when launched application exits.
JumpPrintReturn	Launch a given application, print specified file, return to Authorware.
ResumeFile	Return to file that was active when Authorware was exited.
ResumeFileName	Returns name of active file when Authorware was last exited.
TimeOutGoTo	Jump to specified icon if no response from user within stated time limit.

LOOP FUNCTIONS

Function	Description
Exit Repeat	Exit a repeat loop.
Next repeat	Skip to end of loop structure.
Repeat While	Repeat loop until specified condition is true.
Repeat With	Repeat loop specified number of times.

MATH FUNCTIONS

Function	Description
ABS	Returns absolute value.
ACOS	Returns arc cosine.
ArraySet	Store item in nth position.
ArrayGet	Retrieve nth item from array.
ASIN	Returns arc sine.
ATAN	Returns arc tangent.
Average	Returns the average of a list of values.
COS	Returns cosine.
EXP/EXP10	Returns value of e (x) or 10x.
Fraction	Returns the fractional part of a number.
INT	Returns the integer portion of a number.
LN/LOG10	Returns natural log or log base 10.
Max	Returns the largest value in a list.
Min	Returns the smallest value in a list.
MOD	Returns remainder from dividing two values.
Number	Converts values into numbers.
Random	Returns a random number.
Round	Rounds a number to specified number of decimal places.
Sign	Determines if specified value is positive, negative or zero.
SIN	Returns Sine of a number.
SQRT	Returns the square root.
Sum	Returns the sum of the values in a list.
TAN	Returns tangent.

MEDIA FUNCTIONS

Function	Description
MediaPause	Pause current video or digital movie.
MediaPlay	Start playing specified movie.
MediaSeek	Begin playing movie at specified frame number.

MISCELLANEOUS FUNCTIONS

Function	Description
Beep	Make the system "beep".
CallIcon	Calls a method of the object associated with a sprite Xtra
CallObject	Calls a scripting Xtra handler.
CallParentObject	Calls a scripting Xtra handler parent method.
CallSprite	Calls a sprite method.
DeleteObject	Deletes occurrence of a script Xtra created by the NewObject function.
FlushEventQueue	Discards all pending events from the event queue.
FlushKeys	Remove remaining keystrokes from keyboard buffer.
GetIconProperty	Returns the value of the property of a sprite icon.
GetSpriteProperty	Returns the value of the property for a sprite.
Initialize	Reset all variables to their initial values.
NewObject	Creates a new instance of the scripting Xtra and then calls this new method of the instance with the arguments.
PressKey	Simulate user striking given key.
Test	Compare two expressions and take one of two paths based on result of comparison.
Trace	Turn tracing on.
TypeOf	Returns data type.
SyncPoint	Restarts timer for synchronization. Value of 1=start timer now. Value of 2, start timer after user matches a response or exits interaction.
SyncWait	Pauses the piece for specified number of seconds. Uses last SyncPoint a starting point.
WaitMouseUp	Pause presentation until user releases mouse button.

PLATFORM FUNCTIONS

Application	Returns value COA (Course of Action).
TestPlatform	Determines platform a piece is running on.
CloseWindow	Closes specified window created by a UCD.
GetProperty	Retrieves property value for specified object.
SetProperty	Sets the value for a property of the specified object.

PRESENTATION WINDOW FUNCTIONS

Function	Description
MoveWindow	Move Presentation Window.
ResizeWindow	Resize Presentation Window.
SetCursor	Change cursor shape.
ShowCursor	Show or hide the cursor.
ShowMenuBar	Show or hide the menu bar.
ZoomRect	Zoom from a specified point to the border of the display.

SYSTEM FUNCTIONS

Function	Description
PrintScreen	Print current screen contents.
Quit/QuitRestart	Exit current file; Restart ensures always restarting at beginning.
Restart	Start file at beginning.
SaveRecords	Save user data to disk.

TIME FUNCTIONS

(All dates are based on a base date of 01/01/1900)

Function	Description
Date	Number of days since base date, converted to short-date format.
DateToNum	Convert current date to days since base date.
Day	The number of the day of the month for specified date as number of days since base date.
DayName	Name of the day of the week for specified date as number of days since base date.
FullDate	Full-date format for specified date for number of days since base date.
Month	Month number for specified date specified as number of days since base date.
MonthName	Month name for specified date specified as number of days since base date.
Year	Year for date specified as number of days since base date.

Index

X

TAKE THE LEAD IN WEB-BASED LEARNING

macromedia
AUTHORWARE® 4 INTERACTIVE STUDIO™

Creating interactive courses for delivery over intranets and the Web is easier than ever before with the Authorware 4 Interactive Studio. It features visual authoring, streaming Shockwave™, and a full suite of integrated tools.

GR10032 (CD-ROM)
$2999⁰⁰

AUTHORWARE4
Author interactive multimedia lessons for the Web.

DIRECTOR®6
Create and synchronize animation with sounds, graphics, and text.

AUTHORWARE 4
$1999⁰⁰

BACKSTAGE™2
Build database-connected web sites for business critical applications.

XRES™3
Quickly create, edit, and composite images.

AUTHORWARE SYNERGY
$499⁹⁵
Designer's Edge translation engine for Authorware 4

SOUNDEDIT™ 16/Sound Forge XP
Produce and edit professional-quality digital audio.

PATHWARE™
Track, record, and report student or employee performance.

Only the Authorware 4 Interactive Studio offers all this and unlimited extensibility through ActiveX support. It has everything you need to take the lead in learning. Call today for more information:

800 457 1779
www.macromedia.com/learning

macromedia®

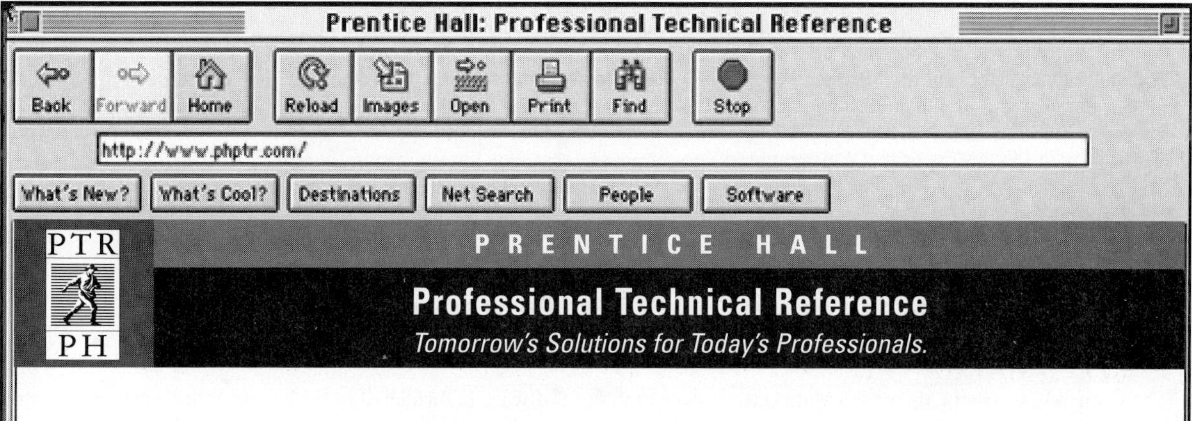

Keep Up-to-Date with
PH PTR Online!

We strive to stay on the cutting-edge of what's happening in professional computer science and engineering. Here's a bit of what you'll find when you stop by **www.phptr.com**:

Special interest areas offering our latest books, book series, software, features of the month, related links and other useful information to help you get the job done.

Deals, deals, deals! Come to our promotions section for the latest bargains offered to you exclusively from our retailers.

Need to find a bookstore? Chances are, there's a bookseller near you that carries a broad selection of PTR titles. Locate a Magnet bookstore near you at www.phptr.com.

What's New at PH PTR? We don't just publish books for the professional community, we're a part of it. Check out our convention schedule, join an author chat, get the latest reviews and press releases on topics of interest to you.

Subscribe Today! **Join PH PTR's monthly email newsletter!**

Want to be kept up-to-date on your area of interest? Choose a targeted category on our website, and we'll keep you informed of the latest PH PTR products, author events, reviews and conferences in your interest area.

Visit our mailroom to subscribe today! **http://www.phptr.com/mail_lists**

END USER LICENSE AGREEMENT

You should carefully read the following terms and conditions before breaking the seal on the disk envelope. Among other things, this Agreement licenses the enclosed software to you and contains warranty and liability disclaimers. By breaking the seal on the disk envelope, you are accepting and agreeing to the terms and conditions of this Agreement. If you do not agree to the terms of this Agreement, do not break the seal. You should promptly return the package unopened.

LICENSE

Prentice-Hall, Inc. (the "Company") provides this Software to you and licenses its use as follows:
a. use the Software on a single computer of the type identified on the package;
b. make one copy of the Software in machine-readable form solely for back-up purposes.

LIMITED WARRANTY

The Company warrants the physical diskette(s) on which the Software is furnished to be free from defects in materials and workmanship under normal use for a period of sixty (60) days from the date of purchase as evidenced by a copy of your receipt.

DISCLAIMER

THE SOFTWARE IS PROVIDED "AS IS" AND COMPANY SPECIFICALLY DISCLAIMS ALL WARRANTIES OF ANY KIND, EITHER EXPRESS OR IMPLIED, INCLUDING, BUT NOT LIMITED TO, THE IMPLIED WARRANTIES OF MERCHANTABILITY AND FITNESS FOR A PARTICULAR PURPOSE. IN NO EVENT WILL COMPANY BE LIABLE TO YOU FOR ANY DAMAGES, INCLUDING ANY LOSS OF PROFIT OR OTHER INCIDENTAL, SPECIAL OR CONSEQUENTIAL DAMAGES EVEN IF COMPANY HAS BEEN ADVISED OF THE POSSIBILITY OF SUCH DAMAGES.

SOME STATES DO NOT ALLOW THE EXCLUSION OF IMPLIED WARRANTIES OR LIMITATION OR EXCLUSION OF LIABILITY FOR INCIDENTAL OR CONSEQUENTIAL DAMAGES, SO THE ABOVE EXCLUSIONS AND/OR LIMITATIONS MAY NOT APPLY TO YOU.

LIMITATIONS OF REMEDIES

The Company's entire liability and your exclusive remedy shall be:
1. the replacement of such diskette if you return a defective diskette during the limited warranty period, or
2. if the Company is unable to deliver a replacement diskette that is free of defects in materials or workmanship, you may terminate this Agreement by returning the Software.

GENERAL

You may not sublicense, assign, or transfer the license of the Software or make or distribute copies of the Software. Any attempt otherwise to sublicense, assign, or transfer any of the rights, duties, or obligations hereunder is void.

Should you have any questions concerning this Agreement, you may contact Prentice-Hall, Inc. by writing to:

Prentice Hall
Engineering
1 Lake Street
Upper Saddle River, NJ 07458
Attention: Electrical Engineering Editor

YOU ACKNOWLEDGE THAT YOU HAVE READ THIS AGREEMENT, UNDERSTAND IT, AND AGREE TO BE BOUND BY ITS TERMS AND CONDITIONS. YOU FURTHER AGREE THAT IT IS THE COMPLETE AND EXCLUSIVE STATEMENT OF THE AGREEMENT BETWEEN US THAT SUPERSEDES ANY PROPOSAL OR PRIOR AGREEMENT, ORAL OR WRITTEN, AND ANY OTHER COMMUNICATIONS BETWEEN US RELATING TO THE SUBJECT MATTER OF THIS AGREEMENT.